HURONIA

**A History and Geography of the Huron Indians
1600-1650**

RENE GADACZ

CONRAD HEIDENREICH

HURONIA

**A History and Geography of the Huron Indians
1600-1650**

**Winner of the Sainte-Marie prize in History, 1971
Historical Sites Branch,
Ontario Ministry of Natural Resources**

McClelland and Stewart Limited

Table of Contents

VI. The Huron Subsistence Economy

List of Tables

List of Figures

List of Maps

PREFACE

Sainte-Marie among the Hurons
Midland, Ontario, Canada
September, 1973

There is little doubt that Conrad Heidenreich's work on the Huron and Huronia ranks among the best of the literature published on the subject, and surpasses much of it in its scope. It will be a standard reference in its field and constitutes a model of historical geographic investigation.

The eminent jurors for the Sainte-Marie Prize in History were unanimous in giving the first of these annual awards to Dr. Heidenreich, and were lavish in their praise. One described it as a monumental work, a masterpiece of its kind. Another said: "I was progressively more impressed with its broad scope, extensive research and scholarship". The third remarked, "Here is a book that at last presents all we need to know to-day concerning Huronia, its geography, ethnology, economics and socio-political."

All remarked on its cautious, critical approach, "inspiring of confidence".

The choice of the jurors sets high standards, indeed, for the future and is fitting evidence of the need for, and values of, such a prize.

The prize grew from the consideration over a period of years of the philosophy which should guide the development of historic resources in the Province of Ontario.

It was felt that the marking, restoration, or reconstruction of historically important places was not enough. Even making these places examples of living-period social environments was insufficient.

These historic sites had also to play broad roles in today's contemporary life. In education and cultural exchange. They had to be catalysts, encouraging the further exploration of history, its interpretation, and its application to the present. They had to evolve from their traditional development in historical isolation.

The Sainte-Marie Prize, established at and named for Sainte-Marie among the Hurons, is an example of one programme aimed to achieve some of these goals. It is offered annually and awarded for excellence in original research, and/or interpretation of 17th-Century Canadian history, or international circumstances and events directly influencing Canada's development in that hundred-year period.

In his work, Heidenreich extended the traditional limits of geography as a field of study. He has taken it in its broadest sense and made of it a discipline of historical synthesis, calling on a host of analytical disciplines of the natural and social sciences: archaeology, zoology, botany, economics, history, and anthropology. Integrating the results of these studies with the geographer's more traditional concerns, Heidenreich has created a picture of many of the ways in which a group of people interacted with each other and with their environment, and of the way in which an area was utilized and transformed into a reflection of their culture. Understanding these historical interactions and relationships, we may be better able to comprehend and guide contemporary social evolution.

John R. Sloan
Director
Historical Sites Branch
Sainte-Marie among the Hurons
Ontario Ministry of Natural Resources

ACKNOWLEDGEMENTS

The writer would like to thank Dr. R.L. Gentilcore of the Geography Department, McMaster University, for his interest and comments on this study. Also appreciated are the comments and suggestions from Dr. C.M. Johnston (History, McMaster), Dr. W.C. Noble (Archaeology, McMaster), and Dr. B.G. Trigger (Anthropology, McGill). The author is also indebted to his many colleagues at York University, especially Dr. A. Ray and Dr. W.C. Found, for their stimulating ideas and the patience with which they listened to innumerable ramblings on the history of Ontario.

Dr. J.N. Emerson of the University of Toronto and the late W.D. Bell deserve special thanks for stimulating the author's interest in Ontario pre-history and giving him the opportunity to participate in archaeological field work.

Through the courtesy of Dr. J.V. Wright the author was permitted to consult the files of the National Museum at Ottawa, and Mr. Frank Ridley kindly made his field notes available which are deposited in the Ontario Archives. The courtesies extended by Dr. J.V. Wright and Mr. Frank Ridley were greatly appreciated.

Finally, the author would like to thank the cartographic staff of the Department of Geography at York University, for the final drafting of the maps and figures; and the secretaries of the Geography Department and York typing pool for labouring over the typing of this study.

INTRODUCTION

a) *The Importance of Huronia*

Today, Huronia is best known as a tourist area encompassing most of Simcoe County, Ontario. In the early part of the 17th century, the northern part of this area was the territory of the Huron Confederacy; a group of semi-sedentary, agricultural Indians, belonging to the larger family of Iroquoian-speaking peoples. With a population estimated at 21,000, in a territory of some 340 square miles, Huronia was perhaps the most densely settled area of aboriginal Canada.

By the beginning of the 17th century, when the French arrived in the St. Lawrence Valley, the Huron were joined with the Algonquian bands of the Canadian Shield and the Petun of the Collingwood area in a military and trading alliance against the powerful Iroquois tribes located south of Lake Ontario. Together, the Huron and Algonquian groups controlled the access to the lands north of the Great Lakes and, in particular, the resources of the Canadian Shield. Realizing this, the French were obliged to commit themselves to the Huron-Algonquian alliance. Soon after initial French-Huron contact, the Huron joined the Algonquians as major suppliers of fur to the French traders in the upper St. Lawrence area. They thus became one of the most important commercial allies of French trading interests in North America.

Out of a genuine missionary zeal, and to further cement the French-Huron alliance, at first Récollet and later Jesuit missions were established among the Huron. The hope of these able and courageous men was to build a Catholic Christian community allied to the French cause in North America. With their large, semi-sedentary agricultural population, housed in villages with up to several thousand people, the Huron offered an unusual opportunity for missionary ambitions. That these ambitions were not realized can be attributed to the onslaught of European diseases, trade rivalries and the age-old rancours of inter-tribal warfare. Until the late 1630's, however, when disasters began to overtake the Huron, Huronia was a stable territorial entity, and, as such, offers the geographer a good opportunity to study a significant aspect of the aboriginal geography of Canada.

In spite of the shortcomings of the ethnohistorical and archaeological material on the Huron,[1] more is known about this group of Indians than any other group in Canada. Yet no geographer has ever attempted a study of the Huron. It is, therefore, not surprising that other early Canadian Indian groups have also been ignored by geographers. This study is therefore somewhat of a pioneer effort in a field that has traditionally been left to the archaeologist and anthropologist. It is hoped that the author can demonstrate that the geographer can also make a contribution, and thereby point the way to further research in the aboriginal geography of Canada.

b) The Purpose and Approach to the Study

One of the principal themes in historical geography is the reconstruction and interpretation of past landscapes. In keeping with this theme, the problem of this study is to reconstruct the geography of Huronia during the first half of the 17th century. In attempting such a reconstruction, some emphasis will be placed on the functional relationships that existed between the various cultural and natural phenomena in the landscape. Unlike some historical geographies, little attempt will be made to trace the origin of the geographical patterns of Huronia. Until considerably more archaeological work has been done in Huronia and adjacent areas, most attempts to explain the origins of a particular feature, let alone a complex geographical pattern, would at best be a guess. Rather than tracing the origin of the geography of Huronia, an effort will be made to reconstruct the area and explain how the Huron functioned within it. The approach to the problem of reconstructing the geography of Huronia is, therefore, ecological rather than historical.

The major difficulties underlying such a research problem are primarily attributable to a lack of adequate source material. Intensive archaeological and palaeoecological work has only recently begun in the area; much of the potentially significant work of previous years, particularly on the excavations at *Cahiagué,* has not been published. In order to overcome the lack of a wide range of comparative material it was necessary to generalize and extrapolate from particular archaeological and written information for an area and culture as a whole. While the author is keenly aware of this shortcoming, he also realizes that only decades of intensive archaeological work could provide enough material to overcome this problem. Generalizations from particular instances would not be permissible in the study of

1. A discussion of the ethnohistoric sources as well as 17th century maps relating to Huronia can be found in the preface to the bibliography, Appendix II.

16

societies that exhibited great variations in their cultural behavior. Similar to most tribal societies, the latitude of Huron group behavior was prescribed and restricted by traditional social norms. It can therefore be reasoned that, to a large extent, individual social behavior and particular archaeological remains are a fairly accurate reflection of a total way of life. Whether stated explicitly or not, practically all the ethnohistorical work that has been done on the Huron has had to proceed from this principle; and this study is no exception. In all cases the authors had to build, what they considered to be, a "reasonable situation" from a few scraps of evidence. The result has been, and always will be until more archaeological work has been done, a rough approximation of a culture group in its area of settlement, rather than a description of a group in all its complexities. Similarly, some of the features of resource exploitation are only briefly described. Here a "reasonable case" had to be built out of the interrelationships between Huron technology, social behavior, and the natural environment. Technology, social behavior and the natural environment can be fairly accurately reconstructed; the interrelationships and their end results measured in corn, fish, or meat production are not known, and must be reconstructed in terms of "a reasonable case." The unfortunate aspect of such arguments is that it is difficult to prove or disprove a particular case. Instead, each case is examined in terms of whether it is more or less reasonable.

A related problem to the one of inadequate or particularised material is the problem of change over time. No cultural group or area stays static; the Huron are a good example of a society that changed rapidly and ultimately collapsed due to outside pressures and internal weaknesses. Unfortunately the ethnohistoric sources only hint at some of the social changes that were occurring and, except for the development and intensification of French-Huron trade, are almost entirely mute on other aspects of geographical interest. The archaeological record supports the contention that trade became intensified over time, and that there may have been some changes in the construction of palisades and houses. Neither source offers any information on other aspects of geographical change. There is, for example, as yet no evidence that there was any major change in the subsistence economy, or in the size and distribution of settlements. The introduction of metal goods such as copper kettles, iron axes or iron fish-hooks does not seem to have altered the Huron's way of life, but certainly made it more efficient. Since such changes can only be guessed at, the bulk of this study will deal with a more or less stable situation prior to the disruptions of the late 1630's brought on by the ravages of European diseases; the social conflict of the 1640's precipitated by religious conversions; and the final disasters of the late 1640's at the hands of the Iroquois armies. Since the final result of these disruptive elements was the total disintegration of a way of life and the disappearance of an entire cultural group, a study of the demise of Huronia should perhaps be left to a sociologist or anthropologist rather than a geographer.

The organization of the study follows a standard pattern. The first chapter is devoted to defining Huronia and delimiting the area of active occupance. This is followed by a discussion of the physical geography of the area as it might have been during the period of the Huron occupation. Once the area is delimited and the physical environment established, some of the pertinent social determinants underlying the major geographical patterns are discussed. These are the socio-political organization of the Huron, the distribution of the tribal groups, and estimated populations. Such a discussion is considered essential as a prelude to a better understanding of Huron settlement patterns and their subsistence economy. In general, settlement is here considered to be "the facilities man built in the process of occupying an area." (Kohn, 1954:125). This definition is elaborated in the proper chapter. For the sake of clarity, a discussion of subsistence economies is treated separately. This separation is, of course, somewhat artificial, because subsistence economies result in a cultural landscape and are therefore a part of "the facilities man built in the process of occupying an area." In this case, however, clarity of organization was considered a greater virtue than geographical philosophy. Of all the chapters in the study, the one on Huron agriculture is the most hypothetical. This is, again, due to a lack of adequate data. Perhaps the only way in which these difficulties can be overcome is to launch a long-term experiment in Huron agriculture similar to the one conducted in Denmark in European Neolithic agriculture (Iversen, 1956; Steensberg, 1957). The final chapter of the study is concerned with the reconstruction of Huron trade. It was necessary here to combine a discussion of trade with that of external politics because the two, at least to the Huron, were inseparable. Pre-European and French-Huron trade are considered. The later French period, from the mid 1630's on, will be treated lightly, not only because the subject is large enough to be treated separately, necessitating a thorough discussion of European trading practices, motives and policies; but also because this was a period of rapid interrelated change.

Although this study is primarily concerned with Huronia before the period of rapid change beginning in the mid-1630's, constant reference must be made to events and situations in that period in order to gain a clearer understanding of the earlier period. In essence, therefore, the problem of this study is to reconstruct the geography of Huronia from the earliest period of direct French-Huron contact in 1609 to the mid-1630's. This is the period, when, with the onslaught of European diseases, rapid changes started to disrupt traditional Huronia, ending in the extinction of the culture and the disappearance of the area as a geographical region.

Chapter I

Huronia: The Position and Delimitation of the Occupied Area

INTRODUCTION

The main purpose of this chapter is to define Huronia, and to delimit the extent of the occupied area during the 17th century. This discussion will be prefaced by an explanation of the names "Huron" and *8endat* along with some of the geographical implications of these names.

Until the arrival of the Jesuits, Huronia was an ill-defined territory. Both Champlain and Sagard imply a well-defined area, but do not delimit its boundaries. Before Huronia is delimited by means of the Jesuit source material, it will be shown how knowledge of Huronia slowly built up from Champlain's first references to the Huron until the arrival of the Jesuits.

The actual delimitation of Huronia will be done in two ways: 1) by determining the probable location of Huron villages and Jesuit missions mentioned on the comtemporary maps and in the written descriptions; 2) by examining the distribution of archaeological sites which reportedly contain French trade material. The discussion of the location of villages and missions might seem unnecessarily detailed, and therefore somewhat tedious. This detail is necessary, not only because the subject is surrounded by a great deal of controversy, but also because much of the material introduced here will be made use of in later chapters – such as population estimates, the establishment of the trail network, and estimates of resource potential.

1. THE NAMES "HURON," "HURONIA," AND WENDAT

a) The Derivation of the Words "Huron" and "Huronia"

The name "Huron" first came into common usage sometime shortly before 1623. The first reference in Champlain to the Huron by that name was in July, 1623 (Champlain 5:100). Prior to that time, he had called them either by the name of one of their chiefs, (*i.e.,* Ochateguins after chief *Ochasteguin*), or by the name of one of the four tribal groups that made up the Huron nation (*i.e., Attigouautan*). Sagard uses the name Huron throughout his whole book, while in the *Jesuit Relations* it appears for the first time in 1625 (JR 4:171).

According to Jérôme Lalemant the word Huron was first used by some French soldiers or sailors as a nickname for a group of Indians whose haircut reminded them of the fur on the head of a wild boar (*hure*) (JR 16:231–233). Lalemant goes on to explain that at first this name was applied to all the sedentary Indian groups in New France. Later, as French contact became more and more concentrated on the Huron, the name was exclusively used for them. An alternate explanation of the name comes from Old French, meaning a "ruffian," "unkempt person," "knave," or "lout."

To all the early travellers the territory occupied by the Huron was called *Le Pays des Hurons* (The country of the Huron). A resident in Huronia would describe himself as being *aux Hurons* (among the Huron), or in *le pays des Hurons*. The name "Huronia" does not occur in any of the early sources, yet it has been in common usage since the latter part of the 19th century. When the word was first coined, is not known. The earliest reference the author has been able to find is one in Potier's *Elementa Grammaticae Huronicae* (1745), which refers to *la défunte huronie* (the deceased or defunct Huronia) (Potier 1745:30).

The name "Huronia" does not appear on any 17th or 18th-century maps. On these maps the area is usually referred to as *Contree des Hurons, Pays des Hurons,* or simply *Hurones, Hurös or Hurons*. Yet the name has a familiar ring, and to a modern writer it would be unthinkable not to use it.

b) The Meaning and Implications of the Word "Wendat" in Defining the Occupied Area of Huronia

The Huron seemed to have called themselves *8endat* (pronounced *Ouendat* or *Wendat*) (Jones 1908:419). This appellation occurs only once in the *Relations* (JR 16:227), and most probably came into common usage after the destruction of the confederacy. The Jesuits simply referred to them collectively as Huron, or, if a more specific reference was necessary, by the name of one of the tribal subdivisions of the Huron. If this reflects common Huron practice, *i.e.,* that they referred to themselves primarily by their tribal affiliations rather than a common collective name, it supports the theory that the Huron considered themselves a confederation of tribes, rather than a nation with a common national identity.

According to Jones (1908:419–420), the term *Wendat* can have three meanings. Either, "The One Language," "The One Land Apart," or "The One Island."[1] Jones made a good case for every one of these translations,

1. For translations of Huron tribal, village, and place names see Appendix I.

but the latter two seem the most likely. It would be illogical for the Huron to call themselves speakers of "The One Language," because theirs was only one of several Iroquoian dialects. As a matter of fact, there were even differences in the dialect spoken among the four Huron tribes (JR 10:11). The Huron language set the Huron apart from the Algonquian speakers, but not from the other Iroquoian groups.

Does "The One Land Apart" or "The One Island" make more sense? The meaning of these two translations is very similar; both refer to an area set apart from other land in a physical or conceptual way. Generally speaking the Huron occupied what is now northern Simcoe County, and this was indeed a land "set apart." In fact, the northern half of the County could, for all practical purposes, be considered an "island." In pre-European times it was almost entirely surrounded by water or vast swamps.[1] In the east was Lake Simcoe and Lake Couchiching. These drained into the Severn River, flowing through the great swamps that are so characteristic of the edge of the Canadian Shield. To the north-west and west lay Georgian Bay and Nottawasaga Bay. The southern approaches to Huronia were effectively blocked by the drainage basin of the Nottawasaga River, which was in effect a huge swamp stretching from Nottawasaga Bay through Flos and Vespra Townships all the way to Kempenfeldt Bay. Prior to the opening of roads and drainage operations, the northern half of Simcoe County was a fairly well-defined physiographic region which was effectively separated from the rest of the Province. It was an island of well-drained soils surrounded by water and swamp (Map 20). This held true well into the 19th century, and was the cause for somewhat different settlement histories in the northern and southern halves of the County.[2]

The theory that *Wendat* meant a "land apart" and was considered an "island" by the Huron, is re-enforced by a reference to a conversation between the Jesuits and some Huron, in which the latter refer to themselves as "inhabitants of the Island" (JR 15:21; 33:237–239). Admittedly, the entire theory is somewhat tenuous; but, considering the extent of the evidence, it is at least plausible.

2. EARLY ATTEMPTS TO DEFINE THE POSITION AND AREAL EXTENT OF HURONIA

1. The physiography of Huronia is more fully discussed in Chapter II.
2. Williams (1908:66) reports that the early settlers of the southern townships of Simcoe County had little communication with the northern townships and quite erroneous ideas what the physical conditions of the northern townships were like.

a) The Growing Awareness of Huronia

In 1603, on his return from having explored the Lachine Rapids, Champlain questioned a couple of Algonquians about the geography of the lands beyond the areas he had visited. Among other things, he was told of a "nation" of "good Iroquois" who traded with the Algonquians and who had access to a northern coppermine (Champlain 1:164). It is not clear exactly who these "good Iroquois" were; but, from what is known about intertribal relations at that time, there seems little doubt that Champlain was being told about the Huron.

Between 1604 and 1607 Champlain explored the eastern seaboard of Canada and the north eastern United States. In 1608 he returned to the St. Lawrence Valley and built his "habitation" at Quebec. By June, 1609, he was ready again to explore the country of the Iroquois south of the St. Lawrence. On St. Eloi island he met his Algonquian allies, who were accompanied by a group whom Champlain called *Ochateguins* after their chief *Ochasteguin*. These people had never seen the French before, but were allies of the Algonquians, and were well-acquainted with the Iroquois country. The reason why the *Ochateguins* had come to the St. Lawrence was to participate in a joint French-Algonquian raid on the Iroquois and to cement a military alliance with the French. In turn, they promised Champlain to help him explore the area adjoining the St. Lawrence (Champlain 2:110,119). The *Ochateguins,* Champlain informs his readers, were the "good Iroquois" (Champlain 2:109).

In 1610 the *Ochateguins* returned to the St. Lawrence to participate in another raid, but did not arrive in time. Disappointed, they returned to their country, but left a youth with Champlain to learn French (Champlain 2:142).[1]

The next meeting between Champlain and the group of Indians under *Ochasteguin* was in June of 1611. He now calls them *Charioquois* and renews his pledge to help them and visit their country (Champlain 2:186, 195–196).[2] He learns that the country of the *Charioquois* is some 150 leagues from the Lachine Rapids and decides to send a French youth named Brulé with the *Charioquois* to learn their language (Champlain 2:204).[3] [4]

1. In relating these events in the 1632 edition of his *Voyages,* Champlain identifies the *Ochateguins* as Huron (Champlain 4:119).
2. In the 1632 edition he substitutes "Hurons" for *Charioquois* (Champlain 4:-136).
3. In the 1632 edition he calls the *Charioquois* Huron and places them 180 leagues from Lachine.
4. The league is generally taken as about three miles, or the distance a strong man could walk in an hour.

The year 1612 was spent in France helping to reorganize de Mont's trading company. In 1613 Champlain returned to New France and at once set out to explore a passage to the Northern Sea. On May 29th he departed up the Ottawa with only one Indian guide. At the juncture of the Ottawa and the St. Lawrence he explains that the latter flows due west to the country of the *Ochateguins* some 150 to 200 leagues away (Champlain 2:260; 4:158). On reaching Morrisson Island on the Ottawa, Champlain learns that the northern salt sea was much farther away than he had been led to believe. One Indian claimed it was some 35 to 40 days' journey north of the country of the *Ochateguins* (Champlain 2:293).

In 1612 and 1613 Champlain published two maps of eastern Canada. The 1612 map (Map 1) is fairly accurate up to the Lachine Rapids (*grant sault*). The western portions of the map seem to be constructed from hearsay. The *Chariocay (Charioquois)* are placed due west of Lachine and north of what seems to be Lake Ontario. On the 1613 map (Map 2) the Ottawa is depicted, but the geography of the areas east of Lachine is poor. The *Charioquois (Charioquet,* on map) are placed west of Lachine and south of the Ottawa, while the *Hochataigains (Ochateguins?)* occupy a position near the north eastern end of Lac St. Louis (Lake Ontario). It is curious that Champlain should make such a distinction between the *Ochateguins* and the *Charioquois,* because they seem to represent the same group of Huron. None of these names appear in any later ethnohistoric sources or maps. In all likelihood, for want of a better name, Champlain simply called the Huron after the chief who happened to be leading them at a particular time.

In summary, then, before 1615, the year he visited Huronia, Champlain knew that a fairly numerous agricultural people lived about 150 to 200 leagues west of the Lachine Rapids. These people were called the "good Iroquois" by their northern neighbors, the Algonquians, to distinguish them from the Iroquois south of the St. Lawrence with whom both groups were at war. Champlain also knew that a large lake, Lac St. Louis (Ontario), separated the two Iroquois groups, and that to get to the "good Iroquois" one could not take the shorter St. Lawrence – Lac St. Louis route, but had to pass up the Ottawa and later south again; the southern Iroquois made the shorter route too hazardous.

24

b) *The Position and Extent of Huronia According to Champlain's Visit in 1615-1616*

After spending the year 1614 in France, Champlain returned to Quebec. This time he was determined to get to the country of the "good Iroquois." He departed from Quebec on July fourth, 1615, having been preceded by Father Joseph Le Caron, a Récollet priest, a few days earlier. After paddling up the Ottawa, Champlain cut across to Georgian Bay *via* the Lake Nipissing-French River route, and then south until he landed on the northern tip of the Penetanguishene Peninsula on August first.

During this visit Champlain calls Huronia the "country of the *Attignao-uantan*" (Champlain 3:46). Later sources explain that *Attignaouantan* were only one of the five major tribes that constitute the Huron confederacy, but Champlain made no such distinction. In his description of Huronia, Champlain mentions that it is "shaped like Brittany and similarly situated, being almost surrounded and enclosed by the Freshwater Sea" (Champlain 3:122). In length, it stretched some 20 to 30 leagues and in width 10 (Champlain 3:50). The western limit of Huronia was the northern tip of the Penetang Peninsula and the eastern limit presumably Lake Couchiching. He makes no mention of a southern boundary or of any habitations east of Lake Couchiching or Lake Simcoe. As a matter of fact, while travelling through the Kawartha Lakes on his journey to the Onondaga he writes that the area was abandoned sometime earlier, due to enemy pressure (Champlain 3:59). In a rather cryptic passage Champlain mentions that the Onondaga once forced the Huron to move some 40 to 50 leagues (Champlain 3:125). Although he does not state from where this movement took place, it could have been the Kawartha area, which is close to the Onondaga frontier. This passage will be re-examined in Chapter III.

Beyond stating that the country of the *Attignaouantan* lay in latitude 44°30′, Champlain says little else that can be used to give the area a sharper definition. His estimate of 20 to 30 leagues for the length of Huronia and 10 leagues for its width are almost certainly over-estimations. The distance from Lake Couchiching to the northern tip of the Penetang Peninsula is only 38 miles, or roughly 12 leagues. As will be seen later, Gabriel Sagard and the Jesuits use the same dimensions of Huronia as Champlain, but define their limits more accurately in terms of fixed landmarks. Champlain's calculation of latitude was much more accurate. In fact he was only about 10′ out, Huronia being in latitude 44°40′.

Before his death in 1635, Champlain drew two more small-scale maps. The first of these was engraved in 1616, but was never completed (Map

3). The incomplete plate of this map was later discovered by P. du Val (Geographe du Roy), who embellished it with place names and published it in 1653 (Map 5). Both maps incorporate Champlain's discoveries in 1615 and 1616, including the Ottawa River-Lake Nipissing-Georgian Bay route, Lake Simcoe, the Penetang Peninsula, the Kawartha Lakes chain, and Lake Ontario. Du Val's version has the name "Hurons" written in the general area of south-central Ontario. There is no mention of any Huron tribe on Champlain's incomplete copy.

Champlain's last map was published in 1632, and is a fitting summary of the work of this great man (Map 4). Huronia is shown as a peninsula lying between what is now Lake Simcoe, the Severn River, Georgian Bay, Nottawasaga Bay, and what seems to be the Nottawasaga River in the south. The figure 86, written in the middle of this area, means:

> Country of the Hurons, thus named by the French, where there are numerous people and 17 villages enclosed each by three palisades of wood, with galleries all round in the form of a parapet for defense against their enemies. This country lies in latitude 44 and one half degrees; it is very good, and its lands are cultivated by the Indians. (Champlain 6:244).

c) The Position and Extent of Huronia According to Sagard's Visit in 1623-1624

Sagard was a Récollet lay brother who came to Huronia in June 1623 and stayed until the autumn of 1624. During his visit he lived at the villages of *Tequeunonquiaye*[1] and *Quieunonascaran,* both situated in the western part of Huronia (Map 17).

Much of what Sagard wrote about the geographical position of Huronia seems to have been copied from Champlain's 1619 edition of the *Voyages;* which shows at least that Sagard did not disagree with Champlain. His most important contribution to defining the extent of Huronia was in naming *Tequeunonquiaye* as the last village on the south-western frontier (Sagard 1939:74). The Jesuit sources, to be discussed later, suggest that this village lay somewhere north of Spratt Point on Nottawasaga Bay. Unfortunately, Sagard relates nothing of the eastern areas of the occupied territory. Unlike Champlain, he does however recognize that Huronia had territorial subdivisions, for he relates that:

1. *Tequeunonquiaye* was also called *Quieuindahian* and during the Jesuit period, *Ossossane.* The French called it La Rochelle, Rupella and La Conception.

There are several districts or provinces in the country of the Hurons, with different names, just like the different provinces of France. The one under the rule of the great chief Atironta is called Henarhonon, that of Entauaque is called Atigagnongueha, and the Bear tribe, amongst whom we were living under the great chief Auoindaon, is called Atingyahointan. . . . (Sagard 1939:91)

Linguistically, the *Atingyahointan* (Bear tribe) can be identified with the *Attignaouantan* of Champlain. The Jesuit sources identify the *Henarhonon* with the *Arendaronnon* or Rock tribe, and the *Atigagnongueha* as the *Attingneenongnahac* (Map 17). All these tribal names have various spellings but identifications can usually be made. Beyond stating that the Bear tribe occupied the western part of Huronia, Sagard makes no attempt to locate any of these groups precisely.

d) *The Position and Extent of Huronia According to the Jesuits, 1634-1650*

In 1639, Jérôme Lalemant attempted to define Huronia in terms of its areal extent. He wrote that:

By the term "country of the Hurons" must be understood, properly speaking, a certain small portion of land in North America, which is no longer than 20 or 25 leagues from East to West, – its width from North to South in many places being very slight, and nowhere exceeding seven or eight leagues. (JR 16:225).

In 1652, while reminiscing about the people that were once the Huron, an anonymous Jesuit made Huronia "a stretch of territory of only seventeen or eighteen leagues" (JR 40:223). De Quen's Relation of 1655 concurs, giving a length of about 17 leagues (JR 42:221).

All the Jesuit writers, with the exception of Jérôme Lalemant, agreed that Huronia lay somewhere near latitude 44°30'; Lalemant places the country a full degree further north (JR 16:225). It is in the Jesuit Relations that we find the first attempts to establish the longitude of Huronia. Standard methods for estimating longitude had not been established yet, but it is interesting how close some of the estimates were. Longitude was measured in hours or leagues; one hour being 15° and one degree being 17.5 leagues (Champlain 6:287). Jérôme Lalemant estimated that Huronia was 1,300 leagues west of France or just over 74° (JR 16:227). A second estimate he made was 200 leagues from Quebec, or 12°. The actual figures are about 80° from France and 9° from Quebec. Paul Ragueneau estimated one half hour from Quebec, or 7°30' (JR 33:61). The closest was Francesco Bressani, who placed Huronia six hours west of Rome (90°) and three-quarters of an hour west of Quebec (11°15') (JR 38:235), the actual figures being 92°30' west of Rome and 9° west of Quebec. The fact that the Jesuits came so close in their estimates is a great tribute to their training and interests.

The frontier of Huronia was defined by the priests in terms of three villages, *Ossossane* (Sagard 1939:74), St. Jospeh II (JR 39:239), and St. Jean Baptiste or *Contrarea* (JR 23:105; 33:81) (Map 17). To these might be added St. Michel, which at least by implication was on the southern frontier, because there is no mention of any villages further south. The precise location of these villages will be discussed in the next section of this Chapter.

Internally, the Jesuits divided Huronia into four tribal areas (JR 16:-227); the *Attignaouantan* (Bear Tribe), *Attingneenongnahac* (Barking Dogs), *Arendaronnon* (Rock Tribe), and the *Tahontaenrat* (White Ears or Deer tribe)[1]. Later a fifth tribe was mentioned, the *Ataronchronon* (Tribe-Beyond-the-Silted-Lake), near Ste. Marie I. The location of these tribal areas will be discussed in Chapter III.

3. THE LOCATION OF HURON VILLAGES AND THE DELIMITATION OF HURONIA

a) Introduction

The precise extent of Huronia can best be determined by establishing the location of Huron villages and Jesuit Missions. From the written source material and maps a tolerably accurate reconstruction of the occupied area of Huronia can be made.

In the last century a multitude of writers attempted to reconstruct Huronia. Among these Shea (1855) and Parkman (1867) are probably the best known[2]. However, detailed work did not begin until the turn of this century, with the extensive archaeological reconnaissance work of A. F. Hunter (1899-1906), and the superb historical detective work of Rev. A. E. Jones (1908). Both Jones and Hunter assisted in the preparation of the Thwaites edition of the *Jesuit Relations*; however, both writers changed their minds on many points after the *Relations* were published.

Of all the works on Huronia, Jones's *Old Huronia* deserves special mention. It is an exhaustive search of all the pertinent literature, including extensive linguistic work on Huron place names. Little criticism can be levelled at Jones. At times he misread some evidence or was too literal in

1. For translations of tribal names, see Appendix I.
2. See also Martin (1848); Harris (1893); de Rochemonteix (1895).

interpreting the distances quoted in the Journals. Perhaps his greatest fault was in measuring all distances in a straight line, ignoring physical obstacles and natural routes of travel. Jones, however, was writing before the advent of topographic maps and before the discovery of three of the four large-scale Jesuit maps of Huronia. In this light, his work stands as one of the monuments of Canadian historical-archaeological research.

One of the consequences of Jones's massive study was that few writers after him re-investigated the problem of reconstructing the spatial distribution of Huron villages, or made any attempt to relocate the lost Jesuit maps. Most of these recent studies are papers attempting to relocate a single village or mission. Among these, Ridley's (1947) and Kidd's (1953) studies of *Ossossane* are noteworthy examples. Others are McIlwraith's (1947) work on *Cahiagué*, Heidenreich's study of *Carhagouha* (1968), and Jury's (1955) work on St. Louis. Less successful attempts are Jury and Fox's study of St. Ignace II (1947), and E. M. Jury's *Toanché* (1967). Three broader studies can be mentioned, but these add little that is new. Of these, Shaw's (1942) paper is a rehashing of Jones's discussion on Sagard's estimates; E. M. Jury's (1963) article is a popularized version of Jones; and Kidd's (1949 b) paper a discussion on the methodology used in attempting an identification of Jesuit Missions.

Since Jones's work, only one attempt has been made to present a reconstruction of Huronia in the light of a re-examination of the primary sources with the aid of some of the Jesuit maps (Heidenreich, 1966).

b) Problems Encountered With the Source Material

In reconstructing the early geography of Huronia one encounters a host of problems which need some explanation.

Since the authors of the *Jesuit Relations* and the authors of various other primary sources were mainly concerned with the progress of the Church in Huronia, any geographical information that slipped into their writings did so only incidentally. Consequently, many statements regarding the location of villages are ambiguous and leave themselves open to different interpretations. Any distances given between villages were estimates, and not once do any of the authors give compass directions. If we did not have the early maps, a reconstruction of Huronia would be a hopeless task, simply because we would have no idea in what direction the villages and missions lay from each other. One of the greatest problems, and perhaps the most easily overlooked, was the Huron's custom of changing the location of their village about once every ten to twenty years. According to contemporary descriptions, this usually occurred when sources of firewood and suitable agricultural soils in the vicinity of the village were exhausted. To compound this problem, during a move a village was sometimes split into two or more villages, each one receiving a new and different name. If in some cases a mission name had not been associated with a village, we would never know what had happened to it. Thus, for example, if Sagard had not mentioned that *Tequeunonquiaye* was called La Rochelle by the French, we would not have known that it was the *Ossossane* of the Jesuit period. According to Champlain such a change of sites could be anywhere up to three leagues from the original location (Champlain 3:124).

c) Reconstruction of the Physical Geography of the Jesuit Maps

To anyone unfamiliar with northern Simcoe Country, the original Jesuit maps may seem very crude indeed. For this reason, a comparison between the *Corographie* and a modern map might be instructive (Map 16). The other three large scale maps of Huronia contain the same imperfections as the *Corographie,* and need not be discussed separately.

The most glaring defect of the Jesuit maps concerns what purports to be Kempenfeldt Bay and the north-west shore of Lake Simcoe. Kempenfeldt Bay is represented as an atrophied little inlet on a concave Lake Simcoe shoreline, instead of the nine-mile-long bay that it is, on a convex shoreline. In other words, 18 miles of land between Orr Lake and Lake Simcoe are missing. This territory was probably little known to the missionaries, because by the time that they were in Huronia there were few, if any, villages south of St. Michael, St. Joseph II and St. Jean Baptiste. Neither the *Corographie* nor Du Creux's map show the "Narrows" of Lake Couchiching. This was probably just an oversight, because this gap of water is shown on the other two maps.

Passing west along the shore of Georgian Bay from the Severn River, each bay and river are perfectly identifiable until we come to an extra bay between Penetang Bay and Thunder Bay. This feature is important, because Bressani places the mission *Ihonatiria* on its north-west corner (Map 13). To explain this bay, the following theory can be advanced. On a modern map the area represented by the bay is occupied by three little lakes,[1] lying within a long bedrock valley which opens toward the shore of Georgian Bay. This valley could not have been filled with water during Huron times; even though the water levels in the little lakes and Georgian Bay probably stood higher then. Anyone walking over the area and attempting to draw a map at the scale of the *Corographie* might have mistaken

1. **Gignac Lake, Kettle (Second) Lake, Farlane (Farlaine) Lake.**

these little lakes with the stream that connects them, lying within a large valley, for a bay emptying into Georgian Bay. The little lakes on the *Corographie* lying between this "bay" and Penetang Bay correspond very well with some large swamps, which were probably more extensive at one time. From a knowledge of the area, the foregoing seems to be the most likely explanation.

The fictitious bay on the Nottawasaga shoreline, ending at Ste. Magdalaine, is more difficult to explain away. In all likelihood, it is an unsuccessful attempt to portray one of the little creeks flowing into Nottawasaga Bay. The little lake beside Ste. Magdalaine must be Lalligan Lake.

The remaining features on the Jesuit maps need little explanation. Both the *Corographie* and the Bressani map show Cranberry and Orr Lakes. Cranberry Lake (*L. Anaouites*) had disappeared, due to a general lowering of the water table and extensive drainage operations in the 19th and 20th century. Recently the Ontario Department of Lands and Forests have made an effort to reestablish the lake. On the *Description* only Orr Lake is depicted (Map 15). For some reason, Bass Lake is left off all of the maps – pointing out again that the eastern part of Huronia was probably not as well-known and as heavily-settled as the western half. There were evidently two lakes named *Contarea;* Midland Park Lake (*Corographie*) (Map 14), and Lake Couchiching (Bressani map, Map 13). The name simply means, "the little lake."

Rev. A. E. Jones devoted a great deal of space to a translation of the place names of Huron villages and geographic features. For a list of Huron place names and an English translation by Jones and the author, see Appendix I.

d) Ihonatiria and the Northern Part of the Penetang Peninsula

Prior to 1638 most of the Jesuit missionary activity was carried out from their central residence at *Ihonatiria* (St. Joseph I). Because the village lay in the western extremity of Huronia and no subsidiary missions were in existence until the establishment of La Conception (*Ossossane*) and St. Joseph II (*Teanaustaye*), their principal missionary efforts were confined to the villages in the vicinity of *Ihonatiria*. Since none of the villages (except *Ihonatiria*) had permanent missions attached to them, they bear only Huron names; their later French appelations are unknown, and consequently the sites of a large number of missions belonging to the later period of La Conception cannot be determined.

On August 5, 1634, Father Brébeuf landed at the "port" of what used to be *Toanche* or *Teandeouiata,* a village where he and Father Noue had

31

lived in 1625 (JR 8:89). He found the shore deserted because the village had been moved in the meantime. This, he tells us later, was done because the Huron feared French revenge for the death of Brûlé, Champlain's former interpreter, who had been murdered at *Toanche*. The Indians who had transported Father Brébeuf left him on the deserted shore and resumed their journey. He hid his belongings in the woods beside a stream (Du Creux 1:184), and after wandering about for three-quarters of a league found the new *Toanche* (JR 8:93). Along the way, he saw the old village standing deserted. He was welcomed by his old friends and decided to lodge with one of the " . . . most important men of the village . . . until . . . our cabin was ready," (JR 8:93). He goes on to say that he decided to build his cabin " . . . here at *Ihonatiria* . . . " where the people knew him (JR 8:99). This is an important point. Nowhere does Brébeuf say that he moved from his friends at the new *Toanche* to *Ihonatiria*. As a matter of fact, his whole story sounds as if *Ihonatiria* was but a new name for *Toanche* or *Teandeouiata*. This is entirely possible, because the names of villages were often changed after a move. Moreover, the names of *Toanche* or *Teandeouiata* do not appear at any place in the *Relations* after the first mention of *Ihonatiria*. This would be highly unusual if these were neighbouring villages, especially when we take into consideration the fact that *Ihonatiria* along with *Oenrio* were offshoots of the old *Toanche* (JR 14:23). Thus one can assume that *Ihonatiria* and the new *Toanche* were one and the same village, or at least so close together that the same name can be used to describe both.

In a discussion with an Indian, Brébeuf tells us that *Ihonatiria* was not directly on the lake, but close enough for easy communication (JR 10:-243). In a later conversation, we find that *Ondiatanen* or Giant's Tomb Island could be seen from near the village (JR 13:229). These descriptions agree so well with the position of *Ihonatiria* on Bressani's map that there seems little doubt that this village stood somewhere near the west end of Gignac Lake, Tiny Township (Maps 13 and 17).

There is no indication on which side of *Ihonatiria* the original *Toanche* stood. Jones placed *Toanche* on Penetang Bay, but mistakenly assumed that *Toanche, Teandeouiata,* and *Ihonatiria* were all separate villages (Jones 1908:56-58). His distance between *Toanche* and *Ihonatiria* is therefore much too great. This author is inclined to place *Toanche* three-quarters of a league west of *Ihonatiria*, because *Oenrio,* the other offshoot of *Toanche,* lay to the south-west of *Ihonatiria*. This would place *Toanche* near the shore of Methodist Bay close to a recently-discovered site (the Gwynne site) belonging to the early part of the 17th century (Ridley 1966).

Oenrio was situated one league from its sister village *Ihonatiria* (JR 13:169). Judging from the *Corographie* (Map 14), this was in a southwesterly direction. As early as 1635 we hear of plans to reunite with *Ihonatiria* (JR 8:105); this was still being contemplated in 1637 and after that date we hear no more of *Oenrio*. *Ihonatiria* was abandoned by the Jesuits in 1638 and at about the same time by the Huron (JR 17:11). A different location for *Oenrio* is marked on the *Description* and Bressani's map. It is possible that this marks a new site for a relocated and combined *Oenrio* and *Ihonatiria*.

Anonatea was another village about a league from *Ihonatiria* (JR 13:-189). It seems to have been a regular stopping-place between *Ihonatiria* and La Conception (JR 13:193), and must have been near *Onnentisati*, a village on route to St. Michel and St. Joseph II to the south-east (JR 13:211; 8:139; 13:195). Neither of these villages appear on the maps. All we know about *Onnentisati* is that it lay near a *montagne* (JR 13:227) on the way to La Conception. It has therefore been placed south of *Anonatea* near La Fontaine Hill, the only "mountain" in the area.

Arontaen of the Relations has been linguistically identified by Jones as the *Taruentutunum* on Du Creux's map and the *Corographie* (Jones 1908:-53). This village was two leagues from *Ihonatiria* (JR 10:285) and one league from *Tondakea* (*Tundatra, Etondatra, Tondakhra*). *Arontaen* has been placed on lot 17, concession 18, Tiny Township, a large contact site two leagues from *Ihonatiria* (Hunter 1898:12). *Tondakea*, a league west of *Arontaen*, has been placed on a site at the far western tip of the Penetang peninsula. This position agrees with the name *Tondakea* ("where the land disappears" – Appendix I). On the *Description* (Map 15) a village by the name of *Taentoaton* occupies a position near that of *Arontaen*. Unfortunately, *Taentoaton* means precisely the same thing as *Tondakea* or *Etondatra*, *i.e.*, "where the shore or land disappears" (Appendix I). Since both *Etondatra* and *Taentoaton* appear on the same map, the mapmaker either made a mistake, or there were two villages with the same name. Since there was no standard way of spelling Huron place-names, and names could be pronounced differently according to local dialects, one could expect a multitude of spellings for a single name, but always having roughly the same meaning. One would therefore suspect that the mapmaker made a slip and recorded *Tondakea* twice. The site of Ste. Cécile, which is written above *Taentoaton*, is unknown. It is recorded in the *Relations* as being under the jurisdiction of La Conception, and therefore in the country of the Bear (JR 19:209). Because it has been placed roughly where *Arontaen* should be, it has been identified with that village.

Two villages in the northern part of the Penetang Peninsula, which are mentioned on the maps, but for which there is little or no clue in the *Relations,* are *Arent (Arente)* and *Teandatetsia.* Of these, *Arent* seems to lie about three-quarters of a league to the south-west of *Arontaen (Taruen-tutunum).* From its name we know it was near the mouth of a river. It has been placed on a large contact site, identical with the one proposed by Jones (1908:134). *Teandatetsia* does not tie in with any other known village. Literally translated it means "where there is a long village," or simply, "the long village." If such a place existed, it seems to have been upstream from *Arent.* For want of further information, it has been placed on lot 15, concession 15, Tiny Township, a site described by Hunter (1898:13).

e) The Villages of Champlain and the Récollet Period

Without having first examined the early Jesuit period, it would be difficult, if not impossible, to retrace the steps of Champlain. Champlain landed at *Otouacha* (Champlain 3:46) and from there visited *Carmaron* a league away, *Touaguainchain, Tequenonquiaye* (later called *Ossossane* or La Conception) and finally *Carhagouha* where his friend Father Le Caron was living. There is no clue in any of Champlain's writings where these villages stood. Jones shows that *Otouacha* and *Toanche* are linguistically the same, and are probably only two different spellings of the same name (Jones 1908:-59-61). Jones also demonstrates that the same is true for *Carmaron* and the *Karenhassa* on the maps (Jones 1908:58). If this is so, it agrees with Champlain that the villages are a league apart, *i.e., Toanche* or *Otouacha* on Methodist Bay and *Carmaron* or *Karenhassa* a league to the east where it is on the maps. *Touaguainchain* defies analysis, and any location for it would be a pure guess. Bressani placed *Carhagouha* on Midland Bay, a place so radically different from Jones who identified it with *Arontaen,* that this placement requires closer examination (Map 13).

Le Caron lived in *Carhagouha* from 1615 to 1616 and then returned to Quebec. In 1623 he returned to *Carhagouha* and according to Le Clercq found his old cabin still standing (Le Clercq 1881:205). Brother Sagard, who had come to Huronia with Le Caron, was sent to *Tequenonquiaye.* Later in 1623 Sagard departed from his village to join Le Caron whom he found not at *Carhagouha* but at *Quieunonascaran* some four to five leagues from *Tequenonquiaye.* Both *Carhagouha* and *Quieunonascaran* were called St. Joseph by the Récollets and on his arrival Sagard had to help build a new cabin for the Récollets (Sagard 1939:76). This sounds as if *Carhagouha* had recently been moved, changed its name to *Quieunonasca-*

34

ran, but as was customary, kept the French name (St. Joseph). During the Jesuit period *Carhagouha* was unknown but *Quieunonascaran* still existed. The move from *Carhagouha* to *Quieunonascaran* could not have been too far because Sagard had no trouble finding it. Where, then, was *Quieunonascaran?* From the *Relations* of 1637 we learn that it was two leagues from *Ihonatiria,* the direction not being given (JR 13:125). From Sagard we learn that *Quieunonascaran* lay one-half league from a bay which opened to the northern fishing grounds (Sagard 1939:191). Further proof that *Quienonascaran* lay on a bay is its name, "Here-the-Thunder-Straits-Yawn-Open" or "The-Beginning-of-the-Trolling-Grounds" (Jones 1908:189-190). The only north-facing bay two leagues from *Ihonatiria* is Penetang bay. *Quieunononascaran* has therefore been placed one-half league from the southern end of Penetang Bay and two leagues from *Ihonatiria.* This situation is just over four leagues from *Tequenonquiaye. Carhagouha* can therefore be placed on Midland Bay where it is on the Bressani map, only a short three-quarters of a league from *Quieunonascaran.*

Rev. A. E. Jones had placed *Carhagouha* in the north-western end of the Penetang Peninsula, but made several mistakes in doing so. In order to explain Jones's errors it is necessary to discuss the location of *Cahiagué.*

After leaving *Carhagouha,* Champlain wandered in a very leisurely fashion to *Cahiagué* which he tells the reader is three leagues from the "Narrows" of Lake Couchiching (Champlain 3:56) and 14 leagues from *Carhagouha* (Champlain 3:49). Champlain's 14 leagues must be a gross exaggeration, because the whole of Huronia is not 14 leagues long. Since Champlain took three days to get from *Carhagouha* to *Cahiagué* his reckoning may have been sadly out by the time he got there. Thus the estimate of three leagues from the "Narrows" to *Cahiagué* is probably more correct. An interesting point to notice is that Champlain estimated the whole length of Huronia as 20 to 30 leagues (Champlain 3:50). This would make the distance between *Carhagouha* and *Cahiagué* 50 per cent or 70 per cent the length of Huronia, or 19 to 26 miles. A village fitting Champlain's description of *Cahiagué* has been found on lot 10 concession 14, Medonte Township, exactly three leagues from the "Narrows" (McIlwraith 1947). There are no other villages of similar description anywhere within a four mile radius. This site is some 19 miles from *Carhagouha* on Midland Bay.

Jones made the mistake of taking Champlain's estimate of 14 leagues literally and compounded his error by identifying *Cahiagué* with the Jesuit mission St. Jean Baptiste.[1] Unfortunately, Jones overlooked the fact that *Cahiagué* had been moved sometime before 1623 (Sagard 1939:92); St. Jean Baptiste and *Cahiagué* therefore did not exist at the same time, and could not have been the same village. A further mistake Jones made was not to examine a slip of Champlain's when the explorer wrote *Carantouan* instead of *Carhagouha* in one of his journals (Champlain 4:240). *Carantouan* was a village among the *Andastes* and had little to do with Huronia (Champlain 3:215). This slip does not occur in the earlier edition of Champlain's works (Champlain 3:49). Jones assumed *Carantouan* was a synonym for *Carhagouha* and was linguistically related to *Arontaen*. Hence he placed *Carhagouha* on the site of *Arontaen*.

The above is a perfect illustration of how easy it is to go wrong when interpreting such scanty evidence.

f) La Conception and the Western Villages

La Conception (La Rochelle, St. Gabriel, Rupella, *Tequenonquiaye, Quieuindohian*), or to call it by its most common name, *Ossossane,* was one of the villages most friendly to the French and the chief village of the *Attignaouantan* tribe. Apparently this village was first visited by Champlain in 1615, and he called it *Tequeunonquiaye* (Champlain 3:48). In 1623 Sagard lived at *Tequeunonquiaye* and mentioned that the village was also called St. Gabriel by the Récollets, La Rochelle by the French traders and *Quieuindohian* as an alternate name by the Indians. He described the village as lying five leagues from *Troenchain* (*Toanche*) (Sagard 1939:75) and four to five leagues from *Quieunonasearan* (Sagard 1939:76). These descriptions agree extremely well with the location the village has on the *Description* and the Bressani inset, namely just north of Spratt Point on Nottawasaga Bay.

When Brébeuf returned to Huronia in 1634 he was asked to establish a Church at La Rochelle, but decided to remain at *Ihonatiria* because La Rochelle was soon to be moved (JR 8:101). In 1635 the village was moved and Brébeuf was present at the Huron "Feast-of-the-Dead." during the "feast" Brébeuf stayed in "the old village," one-quarter of a league from the burial place (JR 10:291-293). The new village was four leagues from *Ihonatiria* (JR 10:291; 13:181). In 1639 the Jesuits began building at Ste. Marie I and departed from *Ossossane.* The Huron shifted the village in 1640 (JR 21:159), the new village being three leagues from Ste. Marie I (JR 26:207), where it seems to have remained until 1649.

1. Members of the Rock tribe had told the Jesuits that they remembered Champlain (JR 20:19). Jones interpreted this as meaning that Huron from St. Jean Baptiste remembered Champlain, and therefore St. Jean Baptiste was *Cahiagué.*

36

We thus have three different locations for *Ossossane* during the Jesuit period. Since each succeeding *Ossossane* was always fairly close to the old one, each of these locations agrees very well with the position of *Ossossane* on the *Corographie* (Map 14).

In the early 1950's an ossuary was excavated on lot 14, concession 7, Tiny Township (Kidd 1953), near a site on lot 16, concession 7 which Ridley (1947) had postulated was one of the village sites of *Ossossane*. This mass burial conformed fairly well to the description of the one witnessed by Brébeuf in 1635, including the quantity and type of grave goods placed in it. Since Ridley's village site is about one-quarter of a league south-west of the ossuary, and there are no other large contact sites within the vicinity it is highly likely that the *Ossossane* of the 1620's and early 1630's stood on lot 16, concession 7 of Tiny Township. Another one of Ridley's sites, lot 15, concession 7, Tiny Township, is sufficiently further north from the previous site that it could well be the Ossossane of the late 1630's. The village of the 1640's was probably still further north along the Bay.

During the latter 1630's, the closest village to Ossossane was *Angoutenc*, about three-quarters of a league away (JR 15:23). This village was built in 1636 (JR 10:203) and lay on the trail from *Ossossane* to the villages in northern Tiny Township (JR 14:69, 73). It has been placed on lot 15, concession 9, Tiny Township (Ridley 1966-1968).

Besides the villages already discussed, there are four others, which are mentioned in the *Relations* but which cannot be given a location with any degree of certainty. These are *Andiatae, Arendaonatia, Ekhiondastsaan,* and *Iahenhouton,* all within the western part of Huronia.

Andiatae appears to have been close to *Ossossane* (JR 13:237-243) on the way to *Teanaustayae* (St. Joseph II) which lay to the south-east (JR 14:-25-29). It was also frequently mentioned in connection with *Oenrio, Arent* and *Angoutenc* (JR 13:235). The best guess therefore, is that the village lay somewhere in an easterly direction from *Ossossane.* Perhaps it was the Huron name for St. Francis Xavier.

Arendaonatia, Anonatea and *Onnentisati* were all within easy walking distance of *Ihonatiria* (JR 14:13-15, 45). *Arendaonatia* must therefore have been in the eastern half of the Penetang Peninsula; most likely east of Farlain and Second Lake.

Ekhiondastsaan was located somewhere on the trail between *Teanaustaye* and *Ossossane,* and *Andiatae* was located between *Ekhiondastsaan* and *Ossossane* (JR 14:27-29). From the dates at which the Fathers visited several villages along the trail one gets the impression that *Ekhiondastsaan* was about half-way between *Andiatae* and *Teanaustaye,* or just about where La Chaudiere should be. A more detailed location for *Ekhiondastsaan* will be examined later in this chapter.

Iahenhouton is only mentioned once. It was visited in 1637 by some of the Fathers so that they might ask the local council if the village would accept Christianity, and whether it had any objections to French-Huron marriages. During this visit we learn that *Iahenhouton* had split off from *Ossossane* sometime earlier (JR 14:15-17); consequently it is reasonable to suppose that *Iahenhouton* lay somewhere in the vicinity of *Ossossane*.

During the Jesuit period, twelve villages were under the jurisdiction of La Conception: St. F. Xavier, St. Charles, Ste. Cécile, Ste. Magdelaine, Ste. Agnes, Ste. Genevive, St. Martin, St. Antoine, Ste. Catherine, Ste. Térèse, Ste. Barbara and St. Estienne (JR 19:209). Of these, only the first four appear on any of the maps, and only St. F. Xavier and Ste. Magdelaine are mentioned in the *Relations* in anything but cursory fashion. According to the *Corographie* and the *Description,* (Maps 14 and 15), St. F. Xavier was located on the west side of the Wye River half-way between Wye and Cranberry Lakes. This location is confirmed by the *Relations,* which place it south-west of Ste. Marie I across Wye Lake and call it the closest village to Ste. Marie in that direction (JR 19:172). In 1640, St. F. Xavier was placed under the jurisdiction of Ste. Marie. On the *Corographie* Ste. Magdelaine is placed inland from a non-existent bay and beside a little lake due west of Ste. Marie I. On the *Description* it is seemingly identified with *Oenrio.* This location is too far south according to the position *Oenrio* had in the mid-1630's. It could however represent a relocated and combined *Oenrio* and *Ihonatiria.* As mentioned earlier, this non-existent "bay" could possible be one of the little creeks flowing east-west across Tiny Township into Nottawasaga Bay. The little lake near the headwaters of the creek could only be Lalligan Lake. Ste. Magdelaine has therefore been placed just west of Lalligan Lake, the location of a large contact site (Hunter 1898:33). The position of St. Charles is also somewhat ambiguous. Both the *Description* and the *Corographie* put it on the peninsula between Midland and Penetang bays. For want of a better place it has been put beside Penetang Lake, the position it occupies on the *Description.* There is absolutely no clue to where the other missions were located or what their Indian names might have been.

g) St. Joseph II and the Eastern Villages

During the Jesuit period St. Joseph II (*Teanaustaye*) was described as "the most important village of all" or "the largest and most populous village in all the country" (JR 17:11; 19:185). It was the capital of the *Atting-neenongnahac* and in 1648 was listed as having 400 families (JR 34:87). It was reported as being seven or eight leagues from *Ihonatiria* in 1635 (JR

8:139), and five or six leagues from La Conception in 1638 (JR 15:157). In June 1638, the mission of St. Joseph at *Ihonatiria* was transferred to *Teanaustaye,* and *Ihonatiria* was abandoned. After Ste. Marie I was built, it was reported that St. Joseph stood five leagues from that place (JR 26:211). St. Joseph II was one of the first villages to be destroyed by the Iroquois. This took place on July 4, 1648, and there Father Daniel met his death. From the description of the attack we learn that the village stood on the southern frontier of Huronia and was heavily fortified by natural and man-made defences (JR 39:239).

On the *Corographie* (Map 14) St. Joseph II is placed due east of Orr Lake, 4.5 leagues from Ste. Marie I and five leagues from La Conception. Taking measurements from a modern map, this position is about five leagues from La Conception, seven to eight leagues from *Ihonatiria,* but only 3.5 leagues from Ste. Marie I. Because of this discrepancy some authors have placed St. Joseph II considerably further south (Jury 1965:13; Jones 1902:121). Jones revised his original estimates and then came out in favour of the Flanagan site of lot 7, concession 4, Medonte (Jones 1908:15-22). In 1947 the Flanagan site was excavated and proved not to be St. Joseph II (Jury 1948). By far the best candidate for St. Joseph II is Hunter's Fitzgerald site on the east half of lot 12, concession 4, Medonte Township (Hunter 1901:78-84). This is the largest site (15 acres) in the area in which St. Joseph II could be located. The site has an abundance of trade material, and it was well fortified by natural and man-made defences. The Fitzgerald site meets all the known requirements for St. Joseph II except its distance from Ste. Marie I. As will be shown below, this site makes even more sense when the locations of St. Michel and St. Ignace I are considered.

St. Michel (*Scanonaenrat*) was a village large and important enough to contain entirely one of the four original tribes (the *Tahontaenrat*) of the Huron confederacy. In 1639 Du Peron described it as being one league from St. Joseph II (JR 15:169), while Jérôme Lalemant wrote that the distance was one-and-one-quarter leagues from St. Joseph II (JR 17:87) the distance from Ste. Marie I is given in the *Relations* of 1645 as three leagues (JR 30:95).

The maps are conflicting on the position of St. Michel. The *Description* places the village on the north shore of what apparently is Orr Lake, while the *Corographie* places it midway between Orr and Cranberry Lakes. Taking the position of St. Joseph II into account, and the distances given in the *Relations,* St. Michel could not have been further west than somewhere on the north shore of Orr Lake. This conclusion was also reached by Jones, who argued that this was one of the few instances where Du Creux's map did not agree with the *Relations* (Jones 1908:25). Of the sites on the north

39

shore of Orr Lake, the ones that best fit the description of St. Michel are on the east halves of lots 74 and 71, concession one, Medonte Township (Hunter 1901:72).

A site that has been labelled as St. Michel is Hunter's No. 26, lot 68, concession one, Flos Township (Wright 1966:76). The site was first described by Hunter (1898:42; 1906:36) and later by Kidd (1950). Kidd was of the opinion that the site was not in a good defendable position, and is therefore perhaps early historic rather than late, when defence became more important (Kidd 1950:165). Without any explanation Wright claims that this site " . . . should be St. Michel . . . " (Wright 1966:76). The trouble is that unless one examines all sites in the immediate area in some detail, no absolute identifications can be made. For example, within a mile of Kidd's Orr Lake site are at least five other sites that have never been investigated (Hunter 1898:41-42; 1901:72-73; 1906:35-36).

Another village at times administered from St. Joseph II was St. Ignace I (*Taenhatentaron*). It was located two leagues from St. Joseph II (JR 17:-99), roughly three leagues from Ste. Marie II *via* St. Jean (JR 23:143) and six leagues from St. Jean Baptiste (JR 27:29). St. Jean, in turn, was "two good leagues" from Ste. Marie I (JR 19:179), making the distance between St. Ignace I and St. Jean about one league. Because of Iroquois harassment, this village was abandoned near the end of 1647 (JR 33:125).

The *Corographie* places St. Ignace I in its correct position, about two leagues from St. Joseph II, and three leagues from Ste. Marie I *via* St. Jean. Its distance from St. Jean Baptiste near the "Narrows" of Lake Couchiching is an exaggeration. This distance is no more than five leagues.

Of the sites in the general area described by these distances, Hunter's No. 40 (West half lot 19, concession 8, Medonte Township) seems a likely choice (Hunter 1901:87).

On the *Corographie* (Map 14), a village named *Arethsi* appears just north of St. Ignace I. On the *Description* (Map 15), it appears as a synonym for St. Ignace I. Since the Huron name for St. Ignace I was *Taenhatentaron,* the most likely explanation is that *Arethsi* was so close to the larger village that the two villages were sometimes called by the same name.

The closest site to the one tentatively labelled St. Ignace I is Hunter's No. 41, half a mile to the north east on the east half of lot 20, concession 8, Medonte Township (Hunter 1901:87).

St. Joachim is mentioned in the *Relations* of 1640 as a mission administered from St. Jean Baptiste and as a village ravaged by smallpox (JR 20:21, 41). Judging from the maps, it was on the east bank of the Sturgeon River about half way between *Arethsi* and St. Jean.

40

St. Jean was tributary to Ste. Marie I along with Ste. Anne, St. Louis and St. Denis (JR 19:167). It was about three hours or "two good leagues" from Ste. Marie I (JR 19:179), and one league from St. Ignace I. On the maps it is the northernmost village on the east side of the Sturgeon River. Bressani's map (Map 13) places both St. Jean and St. Joachim on the west bank of the Coldwater River, but this must be a mistake, judging from the written descriptions and other maps.

In the general area delimited by the maps and the *Relations* are six archaeological sites, any of which could be St. Jean and St. Joachim. Since none of these sites have been excavated, Jone's choice for St. Jean is as good as any. He places St. Jean on the west half of lot 6, concession 10, Tay Township (Jones 1908:94). St. Joachim may be the one described by Hunter on the east half of lot 2, concession 9, Tay Township (Hunter 1899:80).

St. Jean Baptiste was a large and populous village on the eastern frontier of Huronia among the *Arendaronnon* or Rock Tribe. The mission was opened in 1639 and closed at about the end of 1647, when after many defeats its citizens dispersed; some to join the Seneca Iroquois, and others to scatter among the remaining Huron villages. St. Jean Baptiste was located near a lakeshore (JR 20:31) and was reported as being twelve leagues from Ste. Marie I (JR 21:173). Its distance of six leagues from St. Ignace I has already been mentioned. These descriptions are so meagre that, were it not for the maps, we might never have known where the village was. All four maps conclusively place St. Jean Baptiste near the "Narrows" of Lake Couchiching. This location is hopelessly at odds with the estimated distance from Ste. Marie I and is closer to five, rather than six, leagues from St. Ignace I. This shows again that shorter distances were easier to estimate and more reliable than the longer ones.

On the north west quarter of lot 10, concession 3, Orillia Township, is a large site containing an abundance of French trade material (Hunter 1903:116). There seems little doubt that this is the site of St. Jean Baptiste.

Until the discovery of the *Description* (Map 15) the Huron name for St. Jean Baptiste was unknown. On this map it is identified with *Contarea* which A. E. Jones and others had postulated to be a separate village in the vicinity of St. Jean Baptiste (Jones 1908:73-84). *Contarea* is mentioned as early as 1636, and was a day's journey from *Ihonatiria* (JR 10:95). This journey would take a traveller to the eastern frontier of Huronia. Indeed, like St. Jean Baptiste, *Contarea* was a frontier village, " . . . the chief bulwark of the country . . . " and both had reputations for being " . . . impious villages . . . " and " . . . most rebellious against the truth of the faith . . . " (JR 26:175). St. Jean Baptiste, for example, had its first live convert in 1642, three years after the mission was opened; all other conversions had been among the dying, (JR 23:161). This live convert was later persecuted by his own villagers.

Jones tried to make the case that *Contarea* was destroyed in 1642 by an Iroquois raid, and since St. Jean Baptiste existed until 1647 they must have been different villages (Jones 1908:79-81). The *Relations* of 1642 are, however, quite specific that the reported destruction of *Contarea* was a false alarm (JR 23:105). In actual fact, a village was destroyed in 1642 and all but "a score of persons" killed (JR 26:175). This village is not named, and Jones thought it was *Contarea*. In the *Relations* of 1655 we discover that a large number of villagers from *Contarea* had gone over to the Iroquois and were living among them. This was precisely the fate of the residents of St. Jean Baptiste who had joined the Iroquois voluntarily (JR 36:179).

While this evidence is somewhat circumstantial, the *Description* is quite specific in identifying St. Jean Baptiste with *Contarea*. An interesting point is Bressani's identification of Lake Couchiching with *Lacus Contarea* (the "little lake"). It would be logical that the village located next to it also bore that name.

Ste. Elizabeth was a mission formed in 1640 to minister to fugitive Algonquians who had been displaced by the Iroquois from the St. Lawrence valley (JR 27:37). Because of the roving nature of the Algonquian bands, this mission was rarely in the same place in succeeding years. At various times, Algonquians were camped one-quarter of a league (JR 27:41) and one-eighth of a league from St. Jean Baptiste. The maps all place Ste. Elizabeth near the northwestern end of Lake Couchiching, but since this was a roving mission, that location must not be taken as absolute. Ste. Elizabeth may have had a different location every year, anywhere along the west shore of Lake Couchiching.

b) Ste. Marie I and the Central Area of Huronia

Ste. Marie I was established in 1639 as a central base for the missions to Huronia and as a local centre for one of the Huron tribes, the *Ataronchronon* or "Nation-Beyond-the-Silted-Lake" (JR 19:167). It was finally abandoned and burned by the Jesuit Fathers on May 15, 1649, when Iroquois ravages in the surrounding area made it impossible for them to continue their work in Huronia. The mission was moved to Christian Island (Ste. Marie II) and from there, on June 10, 1650, with a few survivors, to Quebec. The locations for these two missions are the only ones of which we can be absolutely certain. In both cases extensive French fortifications

42

have been found. Ste. Marie I is located on the north-eastern corner of Wye Lake on lot 16, concession 3, Tay Township. In 1940, the property was purchased by the Jesuits and in succeeding years the site was scientifically excavated (Kidd 1949 a; Jury, W. and E. M. Jury 1965). The second Ste. Marie is located on the south-east shore of Christian Island and recently underwent preliminary archaeological investigation (Carruthers 1965).

St. Louis was one of the missions under the jurisdiction of Ste. Marie I. Like many of the other missions it was established in 1639. On March 17, 1649, a band of Iroquois took the village and put it to the torch. The resulting smoke, and some say also the flames, could be seen from Ste. Marie I (JR 34:127; 39:249). The narrator of the *Relations* places the village one league distant from Ste. Marie I (JR 34:127), while Bressani says ". . . not more than two miles . . ." (JR 39:249). Both the *Corographie* and the *Description* place St. Louis one league east of Ste. Marie I on the lower reaches of the east bank of the Hog Creek. (Maps 14 and 15).

Due to the topography east of Ste. Marie I and the fact that the smoke and flames from the burning village could be seen from Ste. Marie I, St. Louis must have been precisely 95° east of north from Ste. Marie I. Proceeding in that direction the banks of the Hog Creek are exactly one league from Ste. Marie I. In this area are three archaeological sites, two of them half a mile east of the creek and one (the Newton site) directly on the west bank of the Hog Creek on the west half of lot 11, concession 6, Tay Township (Hunter 1899:66-69, 74-75).

In 1951 and succeeding years, excavations were made by W. Jury at the Newton site (Jury, W. and E. M. Jury 1955). This site has since been proclaimed as St. Louis and the evidence is fairly convincing, even though it is on the west side of the Hog Creek and not the east side as the maps indicate. According to Jury's excavations, the palisade demonstrates a strong French influence in that it was aligned with more or less straight sides and bastions at the corners (Jury, W. and E. M. Jury 1965:28). This type of fortification continues a Jesuit policy first attempted at La Conception (JR 10:53). An abundance of trade material was recovered and the village showed signs of having been completely burned to the ground. The troublesome conflict between the location of the Newton site and St. Louis on the maps is explained away by Jury, who claims that the site must have been moved sometime between the drawing of the maps and 1649. There is no evidence for such a move, and the Newton site shows a long period of occupance. The most likely explanation is that the village locations on the maps simply indicate the general area in which a village lay, and not necessarily an absolute location. The other two sites in the area have not been examined archaeologically. If St. Louis lay on the east side of the Hog Creek, Hunter's No. 21 seems the most likely of the two (Hunter 1899:74-75). In the meantime, Jury's evidence must stand; St. Louis has therefore been placed on the west half of lot 11, concession 6, Tay Township.

Along with St. Louis and St. Jean, three other missions, Ste. Anne, *Kaotia* and St. Denis were connected to Ste. Marie I. There are few written descriptions of these three villages; the only clues to their locations lie in the maps. St. Denis appears to have stood on the east side of Hog Creek, about a league-and-a-quarter south of St. Louis and south-east of Ste. Marie I. Ste. Anne was closer to Ste. Marie I than any of the other missions (JR 19:169). Jones thought it was *Kaotia*, which is not mentioned in the *Relations*, but the *Corographie* shows that there was another village between *Kaotia* and Ste. Marie I. Most probably this was Ste. Anne.

Two sites in the probable vicinity of Ste. Anne are Hunter's No. 11 and 12 (Hunter 1899:72). Of these, No. 12 on the east half of lot 9, concession 3, Tay Township, seems the more likely. Hunter's No. 31 on the west half of lot 3, concession 5, Tay Township, corresponds to the position St. Denis occupies on the *Corographie* (Hunter 1899:77). There are no other reported sites within a radius of one mile of this place. *Kaotia* is more problematical. Only one small site occurs within the probable area of *Kaotia*. This is Hunter's No. 17, on the west half of lot 4, concession 3, Tay Township (Hunter 1899:73). As with all the other sites mentioned, this is at best a rough guess, based on tenuous data.

La Chaudiere (Du Creux's *Caldaria*) is another village not mentioned in the *Relations*. On the *Corographie* (Map 14) it is placed about three-quarters of a league south of St. Denis and one-and-one-quarter leagues north of St. Michel on the east side of Hog Creek. On the Bressani map (Map 13) the village is given its Huron name, *Tiondatsae*. Both the French and the Huron names mean the same thing, namely a cauldron, kettle or any form resembling a kettle, *i.e., la chaudiere d'un volcan* (Encyclopédie 1753:254). (See also Appendix I: *Tiondatsae*). Judging from the *Corographie* the village stood on or near lot 2, concession 3, Tay Township, a small site described by Hunter (1899:78). Was this the village the Jesuits called *Ekhiondastsaan*? In spite of Jone's translation of the name (see Appendix I), a good case could be made that it means the same thing as *Tiondatsae* (Appendix I: *Ekhiondastsaan*). In view of the fact that the location of both villages is about half-way between *Andiatae* and *Teanaustae* and their names are similar, it is assumed that the villages are identical.

The last village to be discussed here is the second St. Ignace. The location of this village is of more than cursory interest, because it is here

44

that Fathers Brébeuf and Gabriel Lalemant met their tragic deaths on March 16 and 17, 1649. Unfortunately, a great deal of controversy surrounds the location of this village. It is therefore necessary to state the facts as precisely as they can be gleaned from the *Relations* before any interpretations can be made.

Sometime before the end of April, 1648,[1] the villagers of St. Ignace I were hunting at a place some two days journey from their village. Here they were attacked by a force of Seneca Iroquois, and, after suffering some losses, fled back to their village (JR 33:83-85). A few days later, they returned to the spot to bury their dead and collect the game that they had caught. On their way home they were set upon by a sizable force of Mohawk Iroquois and again suffered considerable losses (JR 33:89). These defeats plus the prospect of an all out attack on the village " . . . compelled those who dwelt at Saint Ignace to come nearer to us (Ste. Marie I), and to shelter themselves better against the enemy" (JR *ibid.*). The fact that St. Ignace was moved is reinforced by another passage:

> When it became necessary to demolish the Church of Saint Ignace, and the whole village commenced to disperse – owing to the losses that had fallen upon them, one after another, and the alarms that threatened them with a final misfortune . . . (JR 33:167).

The exact date of the move is not given; perhaps it was sometime in the spring of 1648 to permit time to plant the crops at the new site (*i.e.,* not later than the end of May). During July of 1648, St. Joseph II plus another village were destroyed (JR 34:87). This disaster probably led " . . . most of the people (of St. Ignace II) . . . " to abandon their village sometime before the beginning of the winter of 1648 (JR 34:125). On the 16th of March, 1649 a strong force of Iroquois took St. Ignace II by surprise (JR 34:124). Part of the village population was massacred, most were taken captive. In all about 400 people had been present in the village (JR 34:125). Three men escaped to the neighbouring village of St. Louis, one league away (JR *ibid.*). The distance of one league between St. Louis and St. Ignace II is confirmed by Bressani (JR 39:247) and Garnier (quoted by Jones 1908:109). St. Louis, as was mentioned earlier, lay one league due east of Ste. Marie I.

From a description of the attack on St. Ignace II we learn that the village was surrounded on three sides by a deep natural ditch and fortified by a strong palisade of pine posts some 15 to 16 feet in height (JR 34:124-125).

1. The *Relations* state " . . . about the end of last winter . . ." (JR 33:83). This section of the *Relations* was dated April 16, 1648 (JR 33:59).

According to Bressani the Jesuits had a hand in helping to fortify the place (JR 39:247) as they had done at La Conception and St. Louis (JR 10:53). Judging from the route taken by the fleeing villagers, there was no village between St. Ignace II and St. Louis. Later in the *Relations* we also learn that an old woman escaped from St. Ignace II to St. Michel (JR 34:137). Since she went there expressly to warn the villagers, it is doubtful if any villages existed between St. Ignace II and St. Michel.

From the foregoing statements three different interpretations have been drawn. Ridley believes that St. Ignace II never existed.[1] His reasoning is as follows: the villagers of St. Ignace I were harassed by the Iroquois in the early part of 1648 and most of them had abandoned the village by the end of that year thus accounting for the statement that only a small part of the original village population was present when the Iroquois attacked. In support of Ridley's view it must be stated that the authors of the *Relations* never state explicitly that the *village* of St. Ignace I had been moved, and they continue to use the same name until the destruction of the mission. Du Creux also makes no reference to either an actual or implied move (Du Creux 2:504-505, 517-519). The major obstacles to this theory are the distances given for St. Ignace in the early *Relations* (discussed earlier), and those given during the attack. In both cases the statements are consistent, showing that St. Ignace must have been moved closer to Ste. Marie I sometime in 1648.

Assuming, then, that St. Ignace had indeed been moved closer to Ste. Marie I, in what direction did it lie from the latter? This brings us to the controversy between Jone's interpretation (Jones 1908:104-128) and that of Jury and Fox (1947). Jones reasons that St. Ignace was moved in 1648 to within a league of St. Louis. This new location was in the uninhabited area on the west side of the Sturgeon River, south-east of St. Louis. He argues that the reason for the move was to escape the harassment of the Iroquois at the frontier, and therefore had to be west of the Sturgeon River. One league due east of St. Louis would have put St. Ignace II on the same site as St. Jean, which was impractical. It might also be added that a location south-east of St. Louis would bring St. Ignace II closer to St. Michel. Jones followed up this reasoning by making a thorough survey of all the archaeological sites within a league east to south of St. Louis. He finally decided on a site on the east half of lot 4, concession 7, Tay Township. The physical setting, the archaeological surface finds and the distance to St. Louis all agree with what is known of St. Ignace II.

1. Letter to the author dated April 3, 1967, in reply to his paper on the distribution of *Jesuit Missions* (Heidenreich 1966).

In 1932, two men, Arpin and Connon, decided to find St. Ignace II. With the help of a cyclometer they measured off three miles due east of St. Louis and landed on a site on the east halves of lots 5 and 6, concession 9, Tay Township (Fox 1941:72). Excavations were begun in the late thirties by W. J. Wintemberg, who unfortunately died before he could complete his work. Wintemberg's excavations showed that this was a site which had been fortified in the usual Huron manner and only occupied for a short time. He also unearthed two typical Huron longhouses. He did not find any European trade items, but the farmer assured him that two axes and a knife blade had been found on the site. The knife blade was analysed by the Royal Ontario Museum and evidently had been made in the 17th century (Fox 1941:75). Although some of the archaeologists were fairly certain that this was St. Ignace II, others felt that there was insufficient evidence to warrant a formal announcement.[1]

In 1946 the excavations were continued under W. Jury (Jury, W. and S. Fox 1947). In the meantime, however, a monument had been placed on the site proclaiming it as St. Ignace II (Jury, W. and S. Fox 1946:56). In other words, Jury's task was to confirm what had already been decided was the site of Brébeuf's and Gabriel Lalemant's martyrdom. If the circumstances surrounding Jury's excavations, and his reputation as an amateur archaeologist can be overlooked,[2] his results are fairly impressive. What Jury claims he found, was a site that: 1) was only occupied for a short time; 2) showed an apparant European influence on the construction of some of the houses; 3) contained a very large building which he calls a church; 4) had a palisade constructed in the typical Huron manner with a gate that was atypically Huron;[3] and 5) a site surrounded on three sides by a steep ravine (Jury, W. and S. Fox 1946:55-78).

If Jury had bothered to publish a detailed scientific report with maps and, above all, photographs, much controversy could have been avoided.

1. Wintemberg's doubts about the historical authenticity of the site rested on the fact that he could not find any trace of French trade material. Although he did not publish his misgivings, he expresses them in his field notes (Canada National Museum, MSS. Files).
2. Notice, for example, the wide discrepancies between Kidd's work on Ste. Marie II (Kidd, 1949) and Jury's reconstruction (Jury, W. and E. M. Jury, 1965). Note especially the differences between the excavated floor plans (Kidd *op. cit.*: 36) (Jury and Jury *op. cit.*, frontpiece).
3. In 1946 Jury claimed he had found a village with a typical Huron palisade following the brink of the slope surrounding the site (Jury, W. and S. Fox 1947:66). This palisade is depicted on the site map as described in the text. In a later publication E. M. Jury claims that the palisades had straight lines with bastions at the corners (Jury, E. M. 1963:100).

As it is, several questions remain unanswered. 1) In spite of the fact that Jury and Fox claim that there are no other obvious candidates for St. Ignace II within a league of St. Louis, no specific reasons are given for the elimination of a host of proven sites. Jones's St. Ignace II was brushed aside without any explanation (Fox 1941:71). 2) No reason is given why Jury and Fox thought that St. Ignace II should lie due east of St. Louis, on the east side of the Sturgeon River. As stated earlier, a location south-east of St. Louis is more sensible because it was away from the frontier and St. Jean. 3) No explanation is given why Jury's and Fox's St. Ignace II were not fortified in the manner of La Conception and St. Louis, *i.e.*, with straight-line palisades and bastions. 4) Perhaps the most serious objection is the relative lack of any trade materials. One knife blade was found in the 1946 excavations; two axes and a knife blade were apparently found by the owner of the farm while plowing. Even though St. Ignace II had only been occupied for one year, there should have been a great deal more trade material, especially if the excavations were as thorough as the report claims. This should be particularly true for a village taken by storm. Fox and Jury claim that all trade goods were carried off by the Iroquois (Fox 1941:75). There is a passage in the *Relations* stating that some of the spoils of the raid were carried off (JR 34:135); but this could hardly apply to every bead and scrap of copper. At St. Louis, for example, nails had even been found which had been used to construct some of the buildings at that site. 5) The large building excavated by Jury, if the post patterns were correctly interpreted, does not necessarily represent a European structure such as a church. In 1962 a similar house pattern was excavated at the Copeland site, which was definitely pre-contact (Channen and Clark 1965:5-7).

In conclusion it must be said that some doubt can be thrown on Jury's St. Ignace II and that a final selection of the actual site must await detailed investigations of other sites in the area, in particular Jones's on the east half of lot 4, concession 7, Tay Township.

4. THE DISTRIBUTION OF ARCHAEOLOGICAL SITES IN THE DELIMITATION OF HURONIA

a) Introduction

Since this study is only concerned with the period after 1600, it is safe to assume that Huronia can be delimited through the distribution of European trade materials.

The Huron probably started to receive French trade goods sometime in the last half of the sixteenth century. These were obtained from the Algonquians who had begun trading with French fishermen and merchants in the Tadoussac area. In 1603, for example, Champlain relates that French goods were being passed on to "the good Iroquois" (Huron) by the Algonquians (Champlain 1:164). There is no evidence to suggest that the Huron themselves came to trade with the French before 1611. Champlain writes that he met his first Huron in 1609, when the latter came to St. Eloi in Quebec to help the Algonquians and Champlain in the celebrated raid on the Mohawk (Champlain 2:67-71). Judging from Champlain's descriptions, these Huron had never seen white men before. It is interesting to note that these Huron were not interested in trade. As a matter of fact, a Huron contingent specifically interested in trade did not come to the French until June 13, 1611 (Champlain 2:186). These Huron were from the *Arendaronnon* Tribe, and in the *Relations* we learn that because they were *the first* to make the Huron-French contact it was to them that the French trade belonged under Huron law (JR 20:19). Huron trade will be discussed more fully in Chapter VII; in the meantime suffice it to say that French trade goods probably did not arrive in large quantities in Huronia until sometime after 1610. The distribution of these goods can, therefore, be used as a means of delimiting historic Huronia.

If archaeological criteria other than trade goods are used to delimit historic Huronia, the problem becomes very difficult. House patterns, projectile points, village sizes, pipe and pottery types all changed over time, but only slowly. Even if all the elements that constitute a historic site were known, it would still be impossible to delimit the occupied area because of the present lack of a representative areal sample. Such a study is possible, but would entail an enormous amount of work that a whole generation of archaeologists could not accomplish. Pottery typing according to the methods and time-scales set down by MacNeish (1952), Emerson (1956) and Wright (1966) can be used to give a rough date to a site and determine its cultural affiliations, but is not exact enough to give specific dates to sites within the contact period.

Much the same can be said for radiocarbon dating. In many respects, this is at present a somewhat overrated method for dating materials less than 1000 years old. For archaeological deposits dating to the 16th or 17th century the radiocarbon dates could be out by as much as 100 years (Garrad 1968:10; Stuiver and Suess 1967:534-540). Radiocarbon methods are constantly being refined; but until the high cost of processing a sample has been reduced and accuracy improved, the method is of only limited value for any large-scale work.

A method that shows great promise for dating contact sites is the typing of European trade goods. The type and quality of almost all trade materials changed over time; this is particularly true for beads (Quimby 1966:-81-90). At the moment, rough time scales for trade materials have been set up, but these need a great deal of refinement. Such refinement is possible and awaits competent researchers.

Of all the areas in Ontario, Simcoe County is archaeologically the best known. This is largely due to the work of A. F. Hunter (1898; 1899; 1901; 1902; 1903; 1906) who made extensive site surveys throughout the area. Hammond (1904), Jones (1908) and more recently Ridley (1947; 1966) have added to and corrected some of Hunter's work. Hopefully, some day the task of site surveying will be put on a systematic basis by a co-ordinating provincial organization.

About the turn of the last century, A. F. Hunter travelled the concession roads of Simcoe County asking farmers if they had found any Indian remains. Any reported finds were listed in a catalogue by township, concession and lot, accompanied by a short description of the finds. When a township was completed the results were published with a sketch map. In many cases, but not all, Hunter examined the site in the field to determine the accuracy of the farmers' statements. Hunter's records are particularly good for Oro, Medonte, Tay, Orillia, Flos, and Vespra Townships. Large portions of Tiny Township were not surveyed by Hunter because they were not being farmed. This is particularly true in the sandy areas of the northern parts of the Penetang Peninsula. His notes on Innisfil Township were never published, but were used in a paper by R. E. Popham (1950).

Personal experience has shown that Hunter's notes must not be considered absolutely accurate or complete. Some sites have been obliterated over the last sixty years; new ones have been found; other reported finds have simply been mistakes. In spite of these drawbacks, Hunter's site records do provide a good overall picture of the distribution of Indian sites.

To supplement Hunter's notes, a search was made through the files of the National Museum of Canada, Ottawa (Canada National Museum, MSS . Files). These files have yielded a great deal of information on actual sites visited by the archaeologists of the museum; letters sent to the museum of reported finds by farmers; and lists of artifacts in the possession of the museum from Simcoe County. All records are catalogued by township, lot and concession.

Enquiries were made at the Archaeology Division of the Royal Ontario Museum, Toronto, but the author was told by its director, Dr. W. A. Kenyon, that no material was available.

b) The Distribution of Archaeological Sites in the Delimitation of Huronia

From the site records of Hunter and others, it is possible to construct a map showing the distribution of archaeological sites in northern Simcoe County (Map 18). In order to increase the usefulness of the map an effort was made to separate those sites containing a great deal of trade materials from those containing a little, and those containing none at all. Archaeologists generally term all sites containing trade material as "contact sites;" *i.e.*, sites that existed during the period of European-Indian contact. Earlier sites are called "precontact." If a site is known to have been visited by Europeans and this has been proven through excavations, this site is termed a "historic site;" *i.e.*, Ste. Marie I and II; St. Louis and *Cahiagué*. Sometimes the term "historic site" is used to describe all sites belonging to the "historic period," *i.e.*, 1615-1650. Due to the difficulty of establishing absolute chronologies for any of these sites, this is a dangerous term. At best, it should only be used for those sites containing a great deal of trade material or Jesuit religious trinkets such as crosses and finger rings. In this study all sites for which trade material has been reported are termed "contact sites." These are subdivided, where necessary, into early or late contact sites. The term "historic site" will be avoided.

Keeping the limitations of the archaeological descriptions in mind, several useful conclusions can be drawn from the map (Map 18).

The number of contact sites drops off sharply south of a line joining Cranberry, Orr, and Bass Lakes, to the shore of Lake Simcoe near the Narrows of Lake Couchiching. A few early contact sites exist south of this line, primarily towards the eastern end of the area. Towards the north-east there are no sites of any kind below the upland areas running in a concave line from Matchedash Bay to the north-western shore of Lake Couchiching.

Within the area occupied by the contact sites, the northern portion of Tiny Township and the eastern parts of Medonte Township have fewer contact site records than the remainder of the area. In the case of Tiny Township this can be explained by the incompleteness of the archaeological record. Since there is mention of only three villages in the historical sources for all the land lying between the Coldwater River and the "Narrows" of Lake Couchiching, this area may have been largely empty during the late contact period.

It is possible, therefore, to delimit Huronia during the contact period along fairly sharply-defined lines; lines which, as will be shown in the next section of this chapter, are not too different from Huronia as delimited by the villages mentioned in the historical sources.

5. THE RECONSTRUCTION OF THE OCCUPIED AREA: A SUMMARY

On the basis of the foregoing discussion, Huronia can be delimited at least for the Jesuit period.

From 1634 to 1647, the southern frontier of Huronia lay along a line from just north of Spratt Point through Cranberry, Orr and Bass Lakes to the "Narrows" between Lake Couchiching and Lake Simcoe (Maps 17 and 19). The missions of La Conception (*Ossossane*), St. Michel (*Scanonaenrat*), St. Joseph II (*Teanaustaye*) and St. Jean Baptiste (*Contarea*) were all along the southern frontier. No known villages existed south of that line. At least one village may have been outside the south-eastern frontier. This nameless village was destroyed near St. Jean Baptiste (*Contarea*) in June, 1642, (JR 26:175) at the same time when the larger village was threatened (JR 23:105).[1]

The north-eastern frontier stretched from Matchedash Bay to Lake Couchiching along the margins of the arable soils. *Cahiagué*, which was abandoned sometime before 1623, was situated on this frontier. The rest of Huronia was surrounded by the waters of Georgian and Nottawasaga Bays. In total Huronia covered some 340 square miles.

Before 1634 the situation was probably little different (Map 19). In the south-western part of Huronia the frontier may have extended a few miles further south to account for Sagard's location of *Tequenonquiaye* later *Ossossane*. In the east there were probably more villages during Champlain's time than during the Jesuit period. The Jesuits record St. Jean Baptiste and one other village; Champlain mentioned *Cahiagué* and " . . . neighbouring villages . . . " (Champlain 3:56). Therefore the scattering of early contact sites in north-eastern Oro and South Orillia Townships, probably date from Champlain's time or earlier. Neither Champlain, Sagard or the Jesuits mention any occurrences of refugee movements from areas immediately beyond the boundaries of Huronia. What references there are, relate to population movements prior to 1600, or to the disasters of the 1640's. That such occurrences would have been noted can be seen from Lalemant's description of the arrival at *Ossossane* of a group of refugee *Wenrôh* who had been displaced from the Neutral-Iroquois frontier (JR 17:25-31).

In 1647 Iroquois incursions began in earnest. Towards the close of that year St. Jean Baptiste was abandoned. Its villagers dispersed to other Huron villages and the Iroquois. This probably meant that by the begin-

---

1. W.C. Noble (private communication) feels that this village was located on the south shore of Bass Lake.

ning of 1648 all lands east of the Coldwater River were empty of population (Map 19). St. Joseph II, now on the south-eastern frontier, was the next village to be attacked. It fell in July, 1648, accompanied by a neighbouring village which remained nameless (JR 34:87) (Map 19). Either shortly before, or shortly after the fall of St. Joseph II, St. Ignace I was abandoned. Never varying their direction of attack, the Iroquois continued to roll up the eastern frontier. In the spring of 1649 they destroyed "two or three frontier villages" in the vicinity of St. Ignace II (JR 39:247) and then the main missions of St. Ignace II and St. Louis. The "two or three frontier villages" were probably St. Jean, St. Joachim and *Arethsi*, because the frontier between St. Michel and *Ossossane* had remained untouched (Map 19). After taking St. Ignace II and St. Louis, the Iroquois withdrew. When news of these disasters reached the rest of Huronia, the remaining population scattered. According to Raguenau fifteen villages remained;[1] these were burned by their inhabitants before they fled to allied tribes (JR 34:197). By April, 1649, the only viable place of habitation left in Huronia was Ste. Marie I. On May 15th, a joint decision between the Jesuits and remaining Huron chiefs was made to remove Ste. Marie I and all Huron who were still in the country to Christian Island. By the close of 1649, the only area of Huronia still occupied was Christian Island. In June, 1650, the few who survived the winter withdrew to Quebec, leaving Huronia entirely deserted.

In summary, then, both the historical descriptions and the distribution of contact sites agree on the limits of the occupied area of 17th-century Huronia. In a later chapter it will be shown that it is doubtful whether Huronia existed as a territorial entity much before that time. In any case, the area of land termed *le pays des Hurons* or Huronia in the 17th century can be fairly rigorously delimited (Map 19). It is suggested here that the term Huronia be restricted in its definition and usage to that part of Simcoe County inhabited by the Huron between 1615 and 1650.

---

1. In all likelihood these were the villages of the *Attignaouantan*.

Chapter II

The Physical Geography of Huronia

INTRODUCTION

The purpose of this chapter is to outline the physical geography of Huronia. This will be done by describing briefly the principal physical variables of climate, drainage conditions, soils and vegetation. Throughout the discussion an attempt will be made to determine the degree to which 19th and 20th-century conditions were similar to those of the 17th century. Lastly the study area will be divided into physiographic regions.

At the outset it must be stated that it has not been the intention to write a complete physical geography of the area. An effort has been made to provide information that has a bearing on later chapters, such as the discussions on the tribal areas and agriculture.

1. APPEARANCE OF THE AREA TO EARLY TRAVELLERS

Champlain begins his description of Huronia by comparing it to the Canadian Shield. In contrast to the area to the north which ". . . is partly rugged and partly flat, uninhabited by savages, and slightly covered with trees including oaks . . ." (Champlain 3:46), Huronia was a great change. Here the country was ". . . very fine, mostly cleared, with many hills and several streams, which make it an agreeable district . . ." (Champlain, *ibid.*). Huronia was ". . . very pleasant . . ." compared to the ". . . bad country . . ." bordering Georgian Bay; it was ". . . so very fine and fertile that it is a pleasure to travel about in it . . ." (Champlain 3:47-48).

His observations regarding the local vegetation are quite good. After enumerating the most common trees, he sums it all up by stating that Huronia contained ". . . the same varieties of trees that we have in our forests in France . . ." (Champlain 3:51). While in the western part of Huronia, he commented on ". . . many great plantations of fir trees . . ." (Champlain *ibid.*); undoubtedly a reference to the pine barrens of western Tiny Township. In the same general area he described the soils as being ". . . a little sandy . . ." (Champlain *ibid.*). His references to the fact that Huronia was ". . . for the most part cleared . . ." (Champlain 3:46,122), are reinforced by a reference to the presence of ". . . good pastures in abundance . . ." (Champlain 3:130). This probably refers to abandoned cornfields that have been colonized by grasses. Specific references to vegetation and climate will be discussed later in the chapter.

Sagard described Huronia as:

> . . . a well cleared country, pretty and pleasant, and crossed by streams which empty into the great lake. There is no ugly surface of great rocks and barren mountains such as one sees in many places in Canadian and Algonquin territory. The country is full of fine hills, open fields, very beautiful broad meadows bearing much excellent hay . . . (Sagard 1939: 90).

His references to the open state of Huronia are quite numerous. In two other descriptive passages he contrasts Huronia to the Canadian Shield. After describing a quaking sedge mat, dense woods with a tangle of fallen and rotting trees, he goes on to say:

> Then there are rocks and stones and other obstacles which add to the toil of the trail, besides the innumerable mosquitoes which incessantly waged most cruel and vexatious war upon us; if it had not been for my care in protecting my eyes by means of a piece of thin stuff which I had covering my face, these fierce creatures would have blinded me many times, as I had been warned. . . . Among the Hurons, because their country is open and settled, there are not so many mosquitoes, except in the woods and places where there is no wind during the great heat of summer. (Sagard 1939: 63).

In a later passage he states that:

> Of mosquitoes and maringouins, which here we call midges and the Hurons *Yachiey*, there are not many in the fields, because their district is open country and mostly cleared. (Sagard 1939: 221).

Sagard devotes four entire chapters to the birds, land animals, fish, and vegetation of Huronia. These will be discussed in greater detail later; however, they confirm what Champlain said, namely that Huronia was in some respects very similar to France.

The descriptions of the Jesuits, while not quite as explicit as those of Sagard and Champlain, tend to confirm the impressions already gained. Huronia is described as being: ". . . tolerably level, with many meadows, many lakes . . . etc." (JR 15:153). Brébeuf writes that it has ". . . a fine situation, the greater part of it consisting of plains" (JR 8:115). The fauna was apparently very much like that of France (JR 15:153). Several Jesuits made references to the sandy soils of Huronia: ". . . the soil of this country is quite sandy . . ." (JR 8:115); and again:

. . . the soil of the Huron country and adjacent regions being sandy, if three days pass without its being watered with rain from Heaven, everything begins to fade and hang its head. (JR 10:35).

Bressani described the soil as ". . . poor, but not sterile. . ." (JR 38:241). The descriptions of the vegetation and climate will be discussed later.

In general, then, the early travellers described a country that reminded them somewhat of France. It had a similar flora and fauna, and was for the most part cleared of forest. None of the early descriptions have anything good to say about the Shield. All agree that it is a "bad country" in contrast to Huronia.

2. CLIMATE

In this section the salient features of the climate of Huronia will be described, and an effort made to compare it to the climate as depicted in the original source material. The analysis of the present climate will be based on the statistics published by the Ontario Department of Agriculture (1951 to 1960) for the town of Orillia; the work by Putnam and Chapman (1938); and the report on the *Climates of Canada for Agriculture* prepared by Chapman and Brown (1966) for ARDA.

In eastern Canada a daily mean temperature of 42°F is usually taken as the beginning of the growing season, and 38°F as the end (Chapman and Brown 1966: 6). In Huronia the growing season usually begins sometime between April 15th and April 20th, ending about October 28th to October 31st. Thus the length of the growing season is about 195 days. Killing frosts can still be expected after mid-April and before the end of October. Since the length of the frost-free period is of vital importance to corn growing, the average beginning and end of the frost-free season have been calculated. The last frosts in spring can be expected about May 16th to May 20th and the first in the fall about September 30th to October 5th. The frost-free period is therefore about 135 to 142 days. Since the Indian corn varieties matured in about 120 days, both the length of growing season and the frost-free period are adequate for corn growing.[1]

As can be expected, temperature data in the ethnohistorical sources are meager. In 1615 Champlain recorded the first frost on September 10th while just east of Lake Simcoe (Champlain 3:58). This is 17 days earlier than the average beginning of frost for that area. By October 18th of the

1. Will and Hyde give as ripening dates for Iroquois corns 100 to 132 days depending on the variety (Will and Hyde 1917: 314-315). Sagard (1939: 104) stated that corn matured in three to four months; Pehr Kalm (1935: 104) estimated a maturing date of three months.

same year he experienced his first snowfall (Champlain 3:79). Today the first snowfall cannot be expected for at least another month. According to Champlain, winter lasted about four months, from November to April ". . . when the trees begin to send out their sap and to show their buds . . ." (Champlain 3:114,168)[1]. Sagard stated that it began to get "rather cold" in November (Sagard 1939:185). The Jesuits put the length of winter at five to six months (JR 10:93,101), and summer three to four months (JR 10:91). In 1634 the first snow was recorded in the beginning of December (JR 8:143).

Another way of approaching the problem is to examine when certain activities took place. Wood was gathered before there were any leaves on the trees. This was done towards the end of March and the beginning of April (Champlain 3:156; Sagard 1939: 94). These dates agree fairly well with the present beginning of the growing season in mid April. Unfortunately, there are no specific references when corn planting began. By the beginning of June it was already in the ground (JR 10:51; 35:83-84), and by early August it was "far advanced" (Champlain 3:46). Apparently it was planted early in spring and on occasions destroyed by late frosts (JR 8:99). Among the Huron and Abenaki at Quebec, corn was planted at the beginning of June ". . . or when the snow is almost wholly melted . . ." and harvested at the end of August (JR 67:142-143). Sagard and others were under the impression that spring and summer began a bit earlier in Huronia than in Quebec (Sagard 1939: 104). The impression that one gathers from these few bits of evidence is that corn was planted sometime between the middle and end of May, and harvested towards the end of August or early September. This fits very well with the present seasonal rythm. Corn is still planted at the end of May and harvested at the end of August.

Huronia has an average annual rainfall of about 30 to 35 inches, which is fairly evenly distributed throughout the year. About 14 to 16 inches fall during the May to September growing season. According to Chapman and Brown, the area covered by Huronia has a potential evapotranspiration of 23 inches, while the average annual actual evapotranspiration is about 20 inches (Chapman and Brown 1966: Figures 17 and 20). Huronia has, therefore, a slight water deficiency of about three inches during the late summer. Such a low rate of water deficiency is not very serious in an area with water retentive soils. In Huronia, one could expect periodic droughts on some of the coarse sands cultivated by the Huron. Putnam and Chap-

1. In another passage he says "from the month of December to the end of March . . . when the snow has melted" (Champlain 3:164).

man calculated the frequency of summer (May to September) droughts for Ontario (Putnam and Chapman 1938: 428-430). Drought was calculated on the basis of one inch of rainfall or less per month. On that basis, Huronia has a drought frequency of eight to ten per cent, or roughly one serious summer drought every ten years. If 1.5 inches or less are taken as conditions of drought, which might be more realistic on coarse-textured soils, droughts could occur two or three times every ten years.

Because the Huron were almost completely reliant on agriculture, droughts were one of the major contributors to famine. Because such famines disrupted the mission activities and the Jesuits were frequently accused of being responsible for them, careful note was made in the *Relations* whenever such an event occurred. Summer droughts occurred in the following years:

1628 (JR 10:43) – "The drought was very great everywhere, but particularly so in our village (*Ihonatiria*) and its neighbourhood (Penetang Peninsula)."

1635 (JR 10:35-43) – This was the worst drought recorded by the Jesuits. No rain from the end of March to June 13th. After that it rained with a few intervals until mid July. A second drought lasted from mid July to the end of the month.

1638 (JR 17:135-137) – The drought that year affected not only Huronia, but was particularly severe among the Neutral. The latter sold some of their children to obtain corn. (JR 15:157).

1643 (JR 27:65) – A severe famine existed among the Huron and among the tribes ". . . for a hundred leagues around." Indian corn was extremely scarce. The famine was partly due to the disruption of agricultural activities by Iroquois incursions the previous year, but such raids could hardly account for the famines in areas ". . . a hundred leagues around." It is therefore assumed that conditions of drought also existed.

1649 (JR 35:85) – This year and the next were disastrous, not only because of the defeats suffered by the Huron, but also because the summer drought of 1649 killed the corn sown on Christian Island. Not enough rain fell that year to save the crop.

Since the Jesuit record in Huronia extends from 1628 to 1650,[1] we have mention of five droughts in twenty-two years, or roughly two every ten years. As stated earlier, this is approximately what one would expect

1. Except 1630-1633 when New France was in British hands.

in this century, taking 1.5 inches of rain per month on a coarse-textured soil as conducive to drought.

It is interesting to note that in Western Europe during the period, winters were slightly more severe and summers slightly moister than at present (Lamb 1963:142). Whether European observations can be transferred to North America, is questionable.

Bryson and Wendland (1967:296) postulate a cool Neo-Boreal phase (1550-1880 A.D.) in central North America somewhat similar to Lamb's European phases. During this period summer temperatures are considered to be cooler than at present, and autumns about 4°F colder. Griffin (1961:711) and Cleland (1966:35) concur with these observations on the basis of archaeological data; however, Griffin points out that these cooler conditions did not seem to have existed in Southern Ontario. His explanation for this anomaly is the modifying effect of the Great Lakes on the lands lying adjacent to their eastern and south-eastern shores.

In the absence of conflicting data and the observations presented in this chapter, one can best conclude that the climate of Huronia was very similar to the present. Winters may have been slightly longer with a slightly shorter frost-free season but not short enough to hinder agricultural activities appreciably. These observations will be strengthened in the discussion on vegetation.

3. THE NATURAL VEGETATION OF HURONIA

a) The Main Species of the Macro-Vegetation

Huronia lies in the "Huron-Ontario" section of the "Great Lakes-St. Lawrence Forest Region" (Rowe 1959:44-45). The dominant associations throughout the area are maple (*Acer saccharum*), beech (*Fagus grandifolia*) and maple, beech, basswood (*Tilia americana*). In some moister areas beech drops out of the association and is replaced by elm (*Ulmus americana*) and hemlock (*Tsuga canadensis*). White pine (*Pinus strobus*) and hemlock are found throughout the area and may be considered secondary dominants. On very droughty soils oak (*Quercus rubra, Q. alba, Q. macrocarpa*) and white pine are prevalent almost to the exclusion of all the other trees. Elm (*Ulmus americana*), poplar (*Populus grandidentata, P. balsamifera, P. tremuloides*), Ash (*Fraxinus americana, F. pennsylvanica*) and balsam fir (*Abies balsamea*) are also fairly common throughout Huronia.

In poorly-drained areas or swamps, the most common trees and shrubs are cedar (*Thuja occidentalis*), alder (*Alnus rugosa*), and in open areas willow (*Salix sp.*) and dogwood (*Cornus sp.*). Tamarak (*Larix laricina*) is scattered throughout most of the swamps.

Among the fruit-bearing trees butternut (*Juglans cinerea*), black cherry (*Prunus serotina*), pin or red cherry (*Prunus pennsylvanica*) and choke cherry (*Prunus virginiana*), are fairly common. Still found in Huronia, but at their northern limit, are the wild plum (*Prunus nigra*) and bitternut hickory (*Carya cordiformis*).

Two other fairly common trees that the Indians made use of, occurring particularly in dry open areas, are staghorn sumac (*Rhus typhina*) and the red juniper (*Juniperus virginiana*).

b) Vegetation Mentioned in the Historical Sources

Practically all the above trees and shrubs were mentioned by the early travellers in Huronia. In order to determine to what extent the composition of the natural vegetation of Huronia in the 17th century was similar to today, each plant mentioned will be examined separately.

Of the common broadleaved trees, Champlain mentioned oak, elm, and beech (Champlain 3:51). Sagard listed oak, elm and maple (Sagard 1939:-91, 240). Of the evergreens Champlain mentioned fir trees (white pine?) (Champlain 3:51) and Sagard the spruce, cedar and yew (Sagard 1939:91, 240). The fruit-bearing trees and shrubs were singled out for special mention. Champlain (3:50,60), Sagard (1939: 83, 239), and Brébeuf (JR 10:103) all list the wild grape (*Vitis Labrusca, V. aestivalis, V. riparia* or *V. vulpina*). Of the species present in Huronia, the likeliest to have been used is *Vitis Labrusca*, because it has the largest fruit (Gleason 1958, 2:517-520; Soper 1949:56). The general consensus of opinion was that these grapes were too sour to eat, but could be used to make wine (Sagard 1939:83). Strawberries (*Fragaria virginiana*), raspberries (*Rubus sp.*), and blackberries (*Rubus allegheniensis*) were all common (JR 10:103; Sagard 1939: 72,237; Champlain 3:50). Of the cherries Champlain mentioned two varieties, the "small cherry" (*Prunus pennsylvanica*) and the "wild cherry" (*Prunus serotina*) (Champlain 3:51). Both Sagard (1939: 238) and Champlain (3:50) mentioned the wild plum (*Prunus nigra*). Sagard thought this fruit almost inedible until it had been touched by frost. Blueberries (*Vaccinium sp.*) and cranberries (*Vaccinium macrocarpon* or *V. Oxycoccus*) are both mentioned (Sagard 1939: 237-238). From Sagard's description of the size of the cranberries, the variety he saw was most likely *Vaccinium macrocarpon*. Champlain (3:50) mentioned "small wild apples." Sagard (1939: 238) identifies these as the hawthorn (*Crataegus sp.*). Nut-bearing trees were listed by all the early writers. From Sagard's description these trees could only be the butternut (Sagard 1939: 238). Chestnuts (*Castanea dentata*) were not found in Huronia (Sagard, *ibid.*). Hazelnuts

(*Corylus cornuta*) occurred, but were very small (Sagard, *ibid.*). Currants (*Ribes sp.*), mulberries (*Morus rubra*) and the service berry (*Amelanchier canadensis*) were all common and considered to be good eating (Sagard *ibid.*; JR 13:13).

Except for a few references by Sagard, there is little mention of any plants beyond the common trees and shrubs. Champlain spends some time describing the mayapple (*Podophyllum peltatum*) which he regarded as "very good, almost like figs" (Champlain 3:50-51). Sagard describes leeks (*Allium tricoccum*), purslane (*Portulaca oleracea*) the Jerusalem artichoke (*Helianthus tuberosus*) and aromatic wintergreen (*Gaultheria procumbens*) (Sagard 1939:237-239). The mention of purslane is interesting because it is generally regarded as a weed that moved into Canada with European settlement (Soper 1949:35, IV). Two species singled out for special mention by Sagard (1939:240), were the plants used by the Huron for making rope. One he described as a tree from which they used the bark. This was probably basswood (*Tilia americana*). The other plant grew in "marshy spots" and was used to make hemp. This could be indian hemp (*Apocynum cannabium, A. androsaemifolium*) or swamp milkweed (*Asclepias incarnata*). The flowers which impressed Sagard the most were the pitcher plant (*Sarracenia purpurea*) and the wood lily (*Lilium philadelphicum*). Orange lilies (*Lilium canadense*) and tiger lilies (*Lilium tigrinum*) he noted quite rightly, were absent from Huronia (Sagard 1939:241).

There are a few scattered references to other plants, but because of the brevity of the descriptions, identifications are not possible. Of the plants mentioned and identified above, there is not one that does not grow in Huronia today. Some have become rare since the area was settled by Europeans (such as the wood lily); but all have been abundantly recorded during the last 100 years. If vegetation can be used as a rough indicator of climate, one can safely conclude that, on the basis of the species mentioned by the early writers, the vegetation and climate of Huronia was very much as it is today.

c) The Original Forest of Huronia

Between 1811 and 1822 Huronia was surveyed for European settlement. Because the natural vegetation growing along the survey lines had to be described in some detail, the original field notes of the surveyors allow one to make a fairly accurate map of the pre-settlement vegetation of the area.[1] Without the survey reports, such a reconstruction would be impossible, or at best a very rough guess. Relics of the original forest in Huronia are rare and tell us almost nothing of the forest composition. The area has been cut over so much that, for example, none of the large basswood trees or the vast stretches of pine barrens are left. The same is true of drainage conditions before and after settlement. Some of the creeks and springs present in 1820 are gone today, as well as lakes such as Cranberry, Lalligan and the two nameless ones on lots 7 and 15, concessions 18 and 17, Tiny Township. In some cases, old drainage channels have been obliterated; in other cases, water has been diverted. All over the area swamps have been drained and the water table has dropped.

In terms of the Indian occupancy it is particularly relevant to delimit the extent of the swamps and poorly-drained areas, because these were not used for agriculture. The height of the water table was of some importance to the raising of corn, particularly during periods of growth when the rains failed. The presence of water at a village was, of course, absolutely essential. From the surveyors' notes, one can delimit the swamp areas with some accuracy. The original drainage pattern can be outlined, at least in its rough form; and the presence of some tree species will give a fair indicator to what degree water was available for plant growth, other than rain water. Since the Huron showed a marked preference in their selection of some tree species for building materials, a map of the forest composition of the area would show to what an extent these trees could have been present in specific areas.

From the surveyors' records a map was prepared showing the pre-settlement macro-vegetation of Huronia and adjacent areas (Map 20). Since the kinds of trees mentioned by the surveyors are the same as those in the area today and those mentioned in the ethnohistoric sources, it is assumed that the 1820 conditions mirror those of the early 17th century.

One thing the survey records show very clearly is that a closed forest extended over the whole of Huronia during the early 19th century. The 170 years between the abandonment of Huronia by the Indians and the European survey of the area were therefore sufficient to allow a forest to become reestablished in even the driest sections. This shows that while periodic droughts once or twice every ten years may be disastrous for corn growth, they will not hinder the reestablishment of a macro-vegetation given enough time. Abandoned farmland in the area today shows that grasses colonise these fields first, followed by trees some thirty to forty

1. See Bibliography: Ontario Department of Lands and Forests, MSS., Book Nos. 405, 526, 560, 572, 573, 578, 652, 665, 703, 753.

years later, depending on the soil and moisture conditions. The forest conditions shown on Map 20 may therefore represent a stand which is, at least on the better-drained areas, some 130 to 140 years old. Since the Huron created changes in the original forest through selective cutting and large-scale clearing on preferred agricultural soils, the forest during Huron times was by no means the mature forest as depicted on Map 20. In all likelihood, young stands of the dominant species and grasslands (Champlain's and Sagard's "meadows" and "fields") occupied the areas of preferred soils which had been repeatedly cleared and abandoned in past times. Following this line of reasoning, it is quite likely that few of the tree stands in the preferred agricultural areas were allowed to mature beyond ten or fifteen years. The Huron had to occupy forested land, not only because the forest revitalized the soil and they did not have the tools to cope with grasslands; but also because they needed wood for burning and village construction. At *Cahiagué* alone, Dr. J. N. Emerson estimated that some 24,000 logs were used just to construct the palisade (Emerson, J. N. and W. Russell 1965: 5). Since none of these logs were over twelve inches in diameter, their collection would be an impossibility in a mature forest stand. Consequently, in order to obtain suitable building materials, areas of young forest stands were probably preferred. Such stands could probably come into existence some thirty to sixty years after an exhausted plot of land has been abandoned.

In summary, then, the well-drained uplands consisting primarily of sandy soils, which were the preferred agricultural areas, probably supported immature stands of maple, basswood, beech, elm, hemlock and pine. The poorly-drained, low-lying areas probably supported heavier stands, much like the conditions depicted on Map 20. Specific areas will be discussed in the section of physiographic regions.

4. DRAINAGE AND SOILS

a) The Height of the Water Table in 17th-Century Huronia

A question of some importance in reconstructing the physical geography of Huronia is to what extent the level of Georgian Bay has changed from the 17th century. A. F. Hunter (1911:5-7) and K. Kidd (1949:84-86) were both of the opinion that the water level in Huron times was considerably higher. Hunter estimated 12 feet and Kidd 7 to 10 feet. Jury (Jury W. and E. M. Jury 1965:62) claimed that on the basis of his excavations at Ste. Marie I he could prove that the water levels were the same.

Hunter based his estimate on the following observations:

1) The level of the trenches at Ste. Marie I were about 12 feet above the level of the Wye River in 1911. Since they once held water, the level of the Wye, and therefore Georgian Bay, must have been twelve feet higher during Huron times.

2) Ste. Marie II stands at present on a four-foot-high abandoned beach line, some 75 feet from the present shore of Georgian Bay and 10-12 feet above the present lake level. Hunter then simply assumed that the level of Georgian Bay once stood at that four-foot-high beach line. He reasoned that because Ste. Marie I was at the water's edge, so was Ste. Marie II.

3) Du Creux's (Map 12) map depicts a deeply-indented shoreline, a feature which makes a great deal of sense if one allows a 12-foot rise in the water level.

4) Bayfield's survey of Georgian Bay in 1820 shows that the water level at that time was four feet, six inches higher than in 1911. This drop of four feet in the nineteenth century is confirmed by farmers living along the shore of Georgian Bay.

Kidd based his estimate on his excavations at Ste. Marie I. In digging cross sections through the moat system, he found water laid sands in the bottom of the moat. In order to have any water in the moat system the Wye River would have had to be seven feet higher than in 1941, when it stood at 578 feet A. M. S. L. A rise of ten feet would have flooded the moat to a depth of three feet, and brought the water table to within one foot of the surface.

In 1949 Jury discovered an aqueduct which had carried spring water from the hill north-east of Ste. Marie I into the moat system. According to Jury it was now unnecessary to postulate a higher lake level; the moat could have been kept full of water from the aqueduct. Since the moat had an outlet at the Wye River, " . . . we immediately envisioned a complete canal system controlled by locks" (Jury, W. and E. M. Jury 1965:62). Jury's canal system with its three liftlocks has run into heavy criticism. As a matter of fact, no one but Jury seems to believe that it ever existed. The best review of the whole controversy is by Father W. A. Russell, a Jesuit Priest and archaeologist (Russell 1965). As at Jury's supposed site of St. Ignace II, his archaeology and documentation has been so slipshod and inadequate that one simply cannot accept his evidence regarding the lift locks. Besides the lack of evidence, the whole "lift lock theory" suffers due to its lack of logic. A system of three locks, just in order to bring a loaded canoe twenty feet from the Wye River into Ste. Marie, is a patent absurdity. Russell's theory that the aqueduct and moat system were used to drive a small mill is not only more logical, but also fits the evidence better.

Jury's major contribution is the discovery of the aqueduct which fed the moat system and the excavation of the timbers lining the retaining wall near the outlet of the system at the Wye River (Jury, W. and E. M. Jury, 1965: plate XVI). The charred tops of the timbers of the retaining wall as well as the burned remains of the feature described by Jury as "the first lock," were found eight feet below the top of the river bank. This means that the 1649 level of the Wye River stood eight feet below the present banks. Neither Kidd's nor Jury's excavations show any signs of river deposition or erosion on the site itself; one must therefore assume that the top of the river bank has maintained its level since 1649, and that the river flowed eight feet below it. Kidd's contour map (Kidd 1949:27) shows that the banks of the Wye River are at 589 feet A. M. S. L., while the Wye is at 578 feet A. M. S. L. This would place the 1649 level of the Wye at 581 feet A. M. S. L., or three feet higher than it is today.

While Jury's burned posts seem to be conclusive evidence as to where the level of the Wye River stood in 1649, it still leaves some unanswered questions. The early records pertaining to the shore of Georgian Bay definitely show that the water levels were higher in the early 1800's than they are today. In 1838, the monthly mean water level in Lake Huron was 584.69 feet A. M. S. L. (Ontario Legislature 1953:4 and plate No. 7:42). Since that time it has declined steadily to about 578 to 580 feet A. M. S. L., and has never again reached the pre-1838 levels. These observations support Hunter's insistence that during the memory of the farmers in the area the water levels in the middle of the 19th century were about four feet higher than at the turn of the century.

On the basis of this evidence, one can only conclude that the 1649 water levels stood at about 581 feet A. M. S. L.; that after the abandonment of Huronia in 1650 the water levels ascended to about 585 feet A. M. S. L., and that in the late 19th and early 20th century they dropped again to about 578 feet A. M. S. L. The 1649 water level in Lake Huron was therefore about three feet higher than today and about the same amount lower than the water levels in the first half of the 19th century.

If the 1649 water level of Lake Huron stood somewhat higher than the level in 1941, the inland water table must also have been higher. As will be shown later, there is no evidence that Huron drained swamps or lakes; or, for that matter, that they used any soils that were not well-drained. One can therefore assume that the poorly-drained areas within Huronia remained relatively unchanged well into the 19th century. This is supported by the presence of Cranberry and Lalligan Lakes on the *Corographie* (Map 14), both of which are drained today. The water table in the well-drained upland areas is more difficult to establish. All the available evidence points to the fact that it too must have been somewhat higher than today. Because the Huron needed water for cooking and drinking, their villages were always adjacent to a water supply. Today many of these archaeological sites are beside dry or intermittent creek-beds which must have held a steady water supply in Huron times. Undoubtedly the draining of the low land areas and the clearing of the well-drained upland areas in the 19th and 20th century contributed to a general lowering of the water table throughout Huronia. Huron clearing of the sandy upland areas could have contributed to local lowerings of the water table in the 17th century; but since the poorly-drained areas were not touched, both the vegetation and the water table of the upland areas probably reestablished themselves more rapidly than they do today.

In summary, then, both the Vegetation Map (Map 20) and the Soils and Drainage Map (Map 21) probably reflect 17th-century drainage conditions fairly accurately. The two maps are not at a scale where every spring or creek can be noted; but, in general, one can say that the poorly-drained areas were as extensive in the 17th century as they were in the early 19th century. Surface waters were more abundant and the water table was somewhat higher in Huron times than they are today. In the case of surface waters and the water table the 19th-century conditions probably reflect 17th-century conditions more accurately than the present conditions.

b) Soils

In choosing soils for agriculture the Huron seem to have been influenced by soil texture and drainage conditions. Eighty-seven per cent of the contact sites in Huronia are located on well-drained soils ranging in texture from sands to sandy loams (Map 21; Table 1). These soils comprise 65.81 per cent of Huronia covering some 224 square miles. Because these were by far the most important soils to the Huron, they will be examined in some detail. Information on the other soil types can be found in the *Simcoe County Soil Survey* (Canada Department of Agriculture 1962).

Two major soil series comprise virtually all of the well-drained sands, loamy sands and sandy loams of Huronia; these are the Tioga and Vasey series. According to the *Simcoe County Soil Survey* the Tioga series is a podzol developed on sands. The Tioga series includes soils of loamy sand,

66

Table 1

The Relation of Contact Sites to Soil Texture and Drainage Conditions*

	Well Drained Soils			Imperfectly Drained Soils			Poorly Drained Soils		
	% of Area	No. of Sites	% of Sites	% of Area	No. of Sites	% of Sites	% of Area	No. of Sites	% of Sites
Gravel	6.73	7	5.03	—	—	—	—	—	—
Sand and Loamy Sand	26.15	25	18.10	.04	—	—	—	—	—
Sandy Loam	39.66	95	68.46	5.60	5	3.59	3.02	—	—
Loam and Silt Loam	6.56	4	2.89	.32	1	0.72	.92	—	—
Clay and Clay Loam	—	—	—	2.01	2	1.44	3.42	—	—
Muck	—	—	—	—	—	—	4.00	—	—
Totals	79.10	131	94.48	7.97	8	5.75	11.36	—	—

*In this tabulation only contact sites were used because some of the pre–contact sites may belong to non-agriculturalists and therefore may be non–Huron.

sandy loam and fine sandy loam textures. Generally the fine earth (< 2mm) fraction contains more than 80 per cent sand, and usually over 90 per cent sand. Stone free calcareous outwash sands form the parent material on which the Tioga soils are developed. Removal of the plant cover reveals a structureless soil which is most vulnerable to erosion, particularly on steep slopes. Characteristically, the Tioga soils have a podzol profile, usually with clay illuviation into a B_t horizon. Throughout most of the profile the percentage of clay is minimal (less than 5 per cent), but may rise to 10 per cent in a B_t horizon. These soils are low in natural fertility with a small cation exchange capacity in the range of 0.7 to 7.0 m. e./100 gms.,[1] and a low moisture-holding capacity. The acidity (pH) of the parent material may range about pH 6.5 to 7.5 but in the leached A_2 horizons drop to about pH 4.5 to 5.0. Calcium is the dominant exchangeable metallic cation, the Tioga soils being particularly deficient in potassium, phosphorus and nitrogen. Tioga soils warm up quickly in the spring and are easily worked. However, their low fertility precludes any intensive agriculture without large quantities of fertilizer.

The Vasey soil series is developed on glacial till and ground moraine derived from a mixture of local limestone and granite from the shield to the north. The parent material is sandy, and the soils have a sandy loam texture. The percentage of the sand fraction can be quite variable, but is usually in the range of 60 per cent to 80 per cent. Clay fractions are only slightly higher than in the Tioga series, but the silt percentages are markedly greater. The combined silt and clay represent around 30 per cent, the silt being the larger fraction. Stoniness is variable, but generally the Vasey soils are more stoney than the soils of the Tioga series. In some areas, the land surface is studded with large ablation boulders. On the whole, the Vasey soils are less erodable, have a higher moisture-holding capacity, and are slightly more fertile than the Tioga series. The cation exchange capacity of the Vasey soils is in the order of 4 to 14 m. e./100 gms. pH values vary according to the composition of the till and are similar to those of the Tioga series. The soil profile is usually grey-brown podzolic. Although slightly more fertile than the Tioga series, the Vasey soils are also deficient in phosphorus, potassium and nitrogen.

1. The cation exchange capacity of a soil is expressed in milli-equivalents (m. e.) per 100 grams of soil. It is directly dependent on the colloidal content of a soil. A soil high in organic and clay colloids has a high exchange capacity (15 m. e./100 gms. is considered average). The cation exchange capacity of a soil can therefore be used as a rough measure of natural fertility. (Ontario Department of Agriculture n. d., Publication No. 492).

Once depleted, the recovery rate of these two soil types is extremely slow. As was mentioned in the chapter on vegetation, weeds and grasses reoccupy these soils first and trees arrive at a much later date. On lot 10, concession 14, Medonte Township, for example, a field of Tioga loamy sand has stood vacant for five years and has only been recolonized by the common weeds and a few grasses. There is no evidence of a humus layer or colonization by tree species. Even though soil fertility may be restored after thirty to sixty years or more of abandonment, soil profile development probably takes many hundreds of years. Pedological investigations at *Cahiagué* show that there was little evidence of soil profile development in a loamy sand over a time span of 350 years (Cruickshank and Heidenreich 1969:45-46). This is really not too surprising, considering the climatic regime of the area and the nature of the parent materials (*ibid.*: 45).

Again, it should be noted that it would probably take thirty to sixty years before a thoroughly depleted Vasey or Tioga soil can be used again without the benefit of a fertilizer. The question of soil depletion and rates or regeneration will be examined in detail in the chapter on agriculture.

5. PHYSIOGRAPHIC REGIONS

The area of Huron occupance, as delimited in Chapter I, can also be delimited along fairly well-defined physiographic boundaries (Map 18). The southern frontier lay along the watershed separating the lands drained by the rivers and creeks flowing into Georgian Bay and northern Nottawasaga River and the creeks flowing into Lake Simcoe. The northeastern frontier lay along the margins of the well-drained uplands between Matchedash Bay and Lake Couchiching. The rest of Huronia was surrounded by water.

a) The Southern Frontier

The south-western frontier of Huronia is sharply delimited by an extent of swampy lowlands stretching from the shore of Nottawasaga Bay to Orr Lake in the north, all the way through Flos and parts of Sunnidale and Vespra Townships in the west and south. In the east, the "Flos Lowlands" extended up the east arm of the Nottawasaga River to the headwaters of the Sturgeon and Coldwater Rivers. The eastern boundary of these lowlands terminated at the steep bluffs of the recessional shorelines of glacial Lake Algonquin which ring the edges of the "South Oro Till Plain" and the "Dry Hills of Oro." The only breaks in this otherwise flat lowland are a few patches of slightly higher-lying, better-drained soils, and the "Hillsdale Ridge."

The larger part of the "Flos Lowlands" consisted of swamp underlain by clays and silts. Prior to European settlement in the early part of the 19th century the dominant vegetation was open swamp and a thick tangle of cedar, alder and willow. Tamarack, pine, hemlock, fir and elm grew where trees could find root; all are indicators of fairly poor drainage conditions. Some of the slighly better-drained soils supported a beech-maple-basswood association with a sprinkling of elm and pine, but such areas were not very extensive.

The "Hillsdale Ridge" was an island in Lake Algonquin. It consists primarily of sandy loams grading into coarse sands and gravels along the western edge. Like all the upland areas in northern Simcoe County, springs used to issue along the outer slopes but are rare or absent to-day. Since the coarse sand and gravel portions of the ridge tend to be droughty, almost every tree species was excluded except pine. The sandy loams tended to support a mixed forest of maple, beech, basswood, elm and hemlock.

The south-eastern frontier of Huronia lay along the northern edge of a large sand and gravel kame moraine known locally as the "Dry Hills of Oro" (Hunter 1902:155). Throughout its length and breadth, this area is characterized by its varied topography and the porous surface materials. The "Dry Hills" vary between 1,000 and 1,200 feet A. M. S. L., rising some 200 to 300 feet above the valley of the Coldwater and Nottawasaga Rivers, and up to 200 feet above the "Oro Till Plain" to the south. The jumbled topography is typically that of a kame moraine, with slopes in places exceeding 20 per cent. The surface materials throughout the area are sands, loamy sands and gravels. The soils developed on these materials are podzols of the Tioga series. Because of the porous nature of the materials and their depth, there is little surface water in the "Dry Hills." In the past, springs have issued along the perimeter of the area. Some of these are reported in the survey reports, others were mentioned by Hunter; most of them are gone to-day. Perhaps the best indication of the earlier existence of springs is the string of pre-contact sites along dry creek beds on the southern margins of the "Dry Hills" (Map 18).

In pre-settlement times, the forest throughout the "Dry Hills" was an open beech, maple, basswood, pine association, showing that the water table was low, but still available to trees. In some of the dryer sections pine and oak predominated. Forest regeneration throughout the area is slow because of the infertile and porous nature of the soils. No studies have been made in the area, but some farmland, abandoned about 40 years ago, is still under a grass cover to-day.

The area south of the "Dry Hills" is termed the "Oro Till Plain." This area rises abruptly from Lake Simcoe (718 feet A. M. S. L.) to about 800 feet one-half mile inland, and from there gently to about 1,000 feet at the margins of the "Dry Hills." Throughout its area, the till plain is dotted with swampy depressions, and generally east-west trending gravel deposits. Except for the steep ascent from the lake, most of the area has a gently rolling topography, with slopes rarely exceeding 10 per cent. Outside the poorly drained areas, the soils are predominantly loams and sandy loams of the Vasey, Bondhead and Dundonald series. These soils are moderately fertile and supported a substantial mixed forest of beech, maple, basswood, hemlock and elm. Along the southern, moister margins of these till plains, ash and birch entered the association. Surface water is plentiful, and all the creeks flowing through the area have their origins near the southern margins of the "Dry Hills."

b) The North-eastern Frontier

The north-eastern frontier was marked by a more or less continuous swamp stretching along the arable uplands of Huronia from Matchedash Bay to Lake Couchiching. This swamp slowly graded into the rock knob-swamp landscape of the Canadian Shield.

The north-eastern swamp ("Coldwater Lowlands") occupies the depression of the contact zone between the Shield to the north and the limestones to the south. For the most part, the contact zone is covered by impervious lake clays; in a few places limestone outcrops come to the surface. The impervious clays and the level nature of the area are the cause of the swamp. Like most of the swamps along the margins of the Shield, this is primarily a cedar and alder swamp. Tamarack is more prevalent throughout this area than in the great swamp of the "Flos Lowlands." Scattered throughout the swamp are small islands of better-drained silt and clay loams. These supported a beech, maple, basswood association with hemlock, elm, pine and ash as secondary dominants. There are no reported Huron contact or pre-contact sites anywhere within the "Coldwater Lowlands." Some Algonquian sites have been reported along Matchedash Bay, the Severn River and the upper reaches of Lake Couchiching.

c) Huronia

Huronia is a narrow stretch of land, some forty miles long and seven to ten in width. In all it covers about 340 square miles. It consists of a series of broad, curved ridges separated by deep flat-floored valleys. The recessional shorelines marking the perimeter of the ridges indicate that these were once islands in glacial lake Algonquin and its recessional stages. Each physiographic area will be discussed in turn from east to west (Map 18).

The "Medonte-Orillia Till Upland" covers approximately 41,000 acres. Much of the area has a gently undulating topography with slopes rarely exceeding 10 per cent. The edges of the area are marked by the recessional shorelines and boulder pavements of glacial lake Algonquin, except in the south where the area abuts against the "Dry Hills." Most of the surface area is covered by a sandy till which forms the parent material of the brown podzolic and grey-brown podzolic Vasey series. These soils are well-drained, and of fair-to-moderate fertility. Tioga sands and infertile gravel soils occur as patches in the eastern half of the area.

Throughout, the "Medonte-Orillia Till Upland" is well supplied with springs and creeks. Small, swampy depressions are common along the margins of the creeks. Bass Lake, its cold waters fed by springs from the surrounding hills, occupies the south central part of the upland.

The original forest of the area was a beech maple, basswood, hemlock association. Pine and oak were more prevalent on some of the droughtier sands and gravels. A narrow, imperfectly-drained strip of land, covered by a tangle of cedar and alder separated the area from Lake Couchiching and Lake Simcoe.

The broad, flat valley of the Coldwater River separates the "Medonte-Orillia Till Uplands" from the "Mount Saint Louis Ridge." This was an area of imperfectly-to-poorly drained sands, silts and clays. The uniformity of this lowland is broken by two small islands of sandy till surrounded by boulder pavements. Prior to European settlement this valley was almost entirely occupied by a cedar and alder swamp. The swamp was continuous with the "Coldwater Lowlands" on the northeastern frontier and the "Flos Lowlands" to the southwest. Along the better-drained margins of the Coldwater valley, and extending up the slopes on either side was a heavy forest of beech, maple, pine and hemlock.

On the eastern side of the "Medonte-Orillia Upland" the land fell abruptly from the Lake Algonquin shoreline to the ill-drained silts and clays bordering Lake Couchiching and Lake Simcoe. This was generally an area of swamp interspersed with hemlock, maple and basswood.

The "Mount Saint Louis Ridge" is bounded on all sides by the slopes of the Lake Algonquin shoreline. Throughout most of its length, the bluff of the shoreline is some 200 feet high. In area the ridge covers some 15,600 acres. The topography of the ridge is gently undulating and consists almost entirely of sandy till. This till forms the parent material for the soils of the area, which tend to be boulder-studded sandy loams belonging to the Vasey series. At various depths the porous surface materials are underlain by varved clays. Consequently, a number of springs and creeks issue along the periphery of the ridge. Some of the larger creeks have cut back into the upland providing a multitude of excellent sites for Huron villages.

The original vegetation of the "Mount Saint Louis Ridge" was a heavy forest of maple, beech, and basswood. Secondary dominants were pine and to a lesser extent birch and oak. Pine was particularly prevalent on the coarse sands and gravels along the northern edge of the ridge.

The valley of the Sturgeon river separates the "Mount Saint Louis Ridge" from the "Vasey Ridge" to the west. Although narrower than the "Coldwater Valley," it is in all other respects very similar. Only the southern half of the valley was in swamp; the northern half was underlain by coarse sands and covered by a maple, basswood, pine association.

The "Vasey Ridge" covers about 28,000 acres. Like the other upland areas to the east, it consists of a thin sheet of sandy till overlying heavy clays. The surface morphology of this ridge is more varied than the previous one. This is due to the action of the Hog Creek and its tributaries, which have cut into the centre of the ridge from the north transforming the interior of the ridge into a drainage basin. The Hog Creek has thus divided the "Vasey Ridge" into two roughly equal segments. Of the two segments, about one-third of the western one consists of swamp and poorly-drained clays. The rest of the "Vasey Ridge" has soils belonging primarily to the Vasey series.

Like the other ridges, the "Vasey Ridge" is surrounded by boulder pavements and recessional shorelines. On the south it terminates at Orr Lake and the margins of the "Flos Lowlands." To the west is the valley of the Wye and to the north Hog and Sturgeon Bays.

Due to the more varied topography and drainage conditions, the original forest composition is also more varied. Basically it consisted of a maple, beech, basswood association. Pine, oak, hemlock, elm, and ash occurred according to local conditions. On the south east the "Vasey Ridge" was joined to the "Hillsdale Ridge" by a narrow strip of extremely coarse sands and gravels supporting a pure stand of pine.

Two small till islands, 2,800 and 1,800 acres in size, exist north of the "Vasey Ridge" between Midland, Hog and Sturgeon Bays. Except for their small size they are similar to the "Mount Saint Louis Ridge." They have been named the "Port McNicoll" and "Victoria Harbour" uplands (Map 18).

The Wye River lies in a narrow, swampy depression draining Cranberry and Orr Lakes through Wye Lake into Midland Bay. This valley forms an effective natural boundary to the base of the Penetang Peninsula.

The last physiographic area to be discussed here is the "Penetang Peninsula." In area it covers some 88,000 acres, which includes all but the south-eastern part of Tiny Township and all of Tay Township north of Wye Lake. In some respects is is similar to the ridges already discussed. The differences arise out of the fact that the "Penetang Peninsula" was submerged in glacial Lake Algonquin, with the result that the till areas have been water-washed and deposits of sand, silt and boulders have been left on the surface (Chapman and Putnam 1966:307). The area could be subdivided into smaller physiographic areas, but this would be of little purpose for use in later chapters.

On the western edge of the peninsula the land falls off abruptly along a 25-to-50 foot recessional shoreline to a broad beach and Nottawasaga Bay. In places this beach is up to three-quarters of a mile in width and consists for the most part of longitudinal dunes separated by small cedar swamps. Besides the usual swamp vegetation, the major tree species throughout this sandy area was pine. On the north and east coasts of the Peninsula the recessional shorelines are considerably steeper, varying from 50 to 200 feet in height. The shoreline is narrower and dunes are generally absent. The vegetation on this part of the coast was similar to the upland areas.

With exception of a few small swamps, the upland area of the "Penetang Peninsula" consists of well-drained sandy loams, sands and gravels. The topography is fairly level in the southern portion of the area and becomes gently rolling in the north. Two higher till areas, surrounded by recessional shorelines, stand out: these are Lafontaine Hill and a smaller mound east of Lalligan Lake. About 60 per cent of the soils in the area belong to the Tioga series, which are among the least fertile soils in Huronia. The Vasey series takes up about 30 per cent of the area and is slightly higher in fertility.

Several small lakes dot the interior of the Peninsula, but surface waters are not as abundant as in the areas to the east. The original vegetation reflects the generally drier conditions of this area. Both pine and oak occur as a dominant, along with the ubiquitous maple, beech, basswood association. Throughout most of the southern part of the area were extensive pine forests, interspersed with a few oaks.

Generally speaking, this is one of the least desirable areas of Huronia; perhaps this accounts for the fact that large tracts of it are still under forest to-day.

Chapter III

Tribal Socio-Political Organization, Tribal Areas Within Huronia, and Tribal Migrations

INTRODUCTION

The purpose of this chapter is to outline the social and political organization of the Huron tribes; to delineate the tribal areas within Huronia; and to trace the tribal migrations into Huronia. Such an outline is necessary to an understanding of Huron population estimates, settlement, subsistence economy, and trade.

Contrary to popular opinion, the Huron were never a single tribe with what could be termed a common national identity, but rather a confederacy of five tribes " . . . associated together for the purpose of maintaining themselves against their common enemy . . . " (JR 17:195). Differences between the five tribes seem to have been slight. At least, they did not seem to manifest themselves in markedly different geographical patterns of behavior. What differences there were, stemmed from the fact that the villagers in each tribe shared a common tribal history which expressed itself in kinship ties and intertribal politics. In most aspects of a geographical study the five Huron tribes could therefore be treated as a single group. There are, for example, few known differences between the five tribes as far as economic and settlement patterns are concerned.[1] However, to a Huron tribal differences were probably very real and important, because they reflected his social ties, his political thinking and his community history. In other words, the tribe was a socio-political unit which found geographical expression in the tribal territory, which in turn had come into being through tribal migration into Huronia. Other ways in which the socio-political structure of the Huron expressed itself, such as in settlement patterns, will be discussed in later chapters. For the moment, an attempt will be made to describe only the essential characteristics of Huron society and government, and the most immediate geographical expression of these, the tribal territory and its origin.

1. Noble (1968) has suggested minor differences in longhouse interiors and cemetery plots between the five Huron tribes.

1. SOCIO-POLITICAL ORGANIZATION OF THE HURON

a) Social Organization

i) Marriage, descent and inheritance.   Soon after reaching puberty, the Huron engaged in premarital sex, which could be initiated by either the boy or the girl (Sagard 1939:121). All sexual activity whether by the youth or adults was performed outside public view, either at night or in a private place. Eventually these relationships could result in marriage, or a more informal relationship which the Huron termed living with an *Asqua* (companion) (Sagard 1939:121). In the latter case two people would simply live together as long as it suited them, the man being obliged to furnish food and fire for the woman. Both could have sexual relations with others.

The initial step to a formal marriage involved giving presents by the boy to the girl's parents. Often this step was arranged by the parents of both parties; in any case, approval of both parents had to be sought. The boy would then spend several nights with the girl, after which she could accept or reject him. During this period the girl received gifts (Sagard 1939:-122). If the girl decided not to marry the boy, they would immediately part, each seeking another liaison. The girl and her parents would keep all presents. If the girl decided to marry, her parents would throw a feast to which the relatives and friends of both parties were invited. The father of the bride would announce the formal recognition of the marriage. Marriage could also result if, during premarital sex, a girl became pregnant. In that case her suitors would gather around and she would choose the one she liked best for her husband (Champlain 3:139-140).

The steps leading to formal marriage involved the consent of the couple and their parents. The parents tried to encourage their children to marry into prominent families, and the girl's parents in particular made sure that the prospective groom could prove himself as a warrior and provider (Sagard 1939:123-4). In spite of the role of the parents, neither the girl nor the boy could be coerced into a marriage they did not want.

Premarital sex or marriage could not take place with any person in "either a direct or collateral line, however distant the relationship might be" (JR 8:119; 10:213), or a relative within "three degrees of consanguinity" (Sagard 1939:123). Since the Huron traced matrilineal descent and had a clan system, the above quotations seem to mean that a Huron could not marry, or have sexual relations with, any person in his mother's matrilineage, nor anyone on his father's side, up to and including first cousins. Marriage with a dead brother's widow or a deceased wife's sister were strongly encouraged.

All Huron marriages were monogamous (JR 8:119; Boucher 1883:56). Divorce could be initiated by either party. A woman would simply ask her husband to remove himself from her house, which he would have to do, taking only his clothes (Sagard 1939:124; Boucher 1883:56). In the same way, a man could leave his wife after informing her and her parents, with whom he lived. Divorce was most frequent among young married couples, stemming from childlessness or inability of one to supply the needs and wants of another (Sagard 1939:124; JR 21:135; 28:51-53). Divorce was rare once a couple had children (Sagard 1939:125; Boucher 1883:-57). If a divorce seemed imminent, relatives tried to intercede to bring the couple back together. It is not clear who kept the children. Sagard (1939:125) wrote that the father took the boys and the mother the girls, while Boucher (1883:57) stated that all the children remained with the mother. In view of the residence, descent, and inheritance system, the latter seems more likely.

According to Boucher (1883:56-7) residence was matrilocal. The same can be inferred from Sagard (1939:121-5). Other evidence, however, shows that this may have been an ideal which was not always followed in practice (Richards 1967; Trigger 1969:56).

Descent and inheritance was matrilineal (Champlain 3:140; Sagard 1939:130). Children did not succeed to their father's property, but to that of their mother's brother. This practice was also followed in the inheritance of the chieftainship, which usually went to a man's nephew on his sister's side (JR 10:233; 20:215). Furthermore, in old age a man could count more on his nephews and nieces for support than his own children (JR 26:297), and it was these who publicly exhibited the greatest sorrow when a man died (JR 17:123).

ii) The family and clan. Although the Huron were monogamous and formed nuclear families, the matrilineal extended family appears to have been the fundamental social and economic unit. Each nuclear family had its own place within the longhouse, but the members of the longhouse worked together as a closely co-operating unit. In theory, if not always in practice, the extended family was made up of a senior couple, their daughters and sons-in-law with their children and any unmarried or divorced sons. The daily running of the longhouse was done by the women, probably under the direction of the senior matron who exercised considerable authority over her daughters even if these were married (Trigger 1969:-55). Major decisions were made by the male head of the household, probably in consultation with his wife and family members.

The social hierarchy above the extended family is not clear. The existence of eight clans can be inferred from the ethnohistoric sources, which mention that the Huron were composed of eight "nations," each of which had a chief (JR 33:243, 247; 38:283). Since the Huron confederacy was composed of four or five territorial tribes with a fairly well-defined political hierarchy, the clan system with its chiefs must have been a social organization which cut across tribal divisions. Judging from the way the Huron political system operated, the manner in which chiefs were appointed and councils operated, the clan system must have had mainly a ceremonial function rather than a political one.

The best evidence for the Huron clan system comes from the historic Wyandot (Trigger 1969:54-7). These had fictive, apparently exogamous kinship groupings tracing descent to a common female ancestor. Marriage was outside the clan, supporting Brébeuf's statement that one could not marry anyone on the mother's side, no matter how distant the relationship might be (JR 10:213). The historic Wyandot had eight clans: Turtle, Wolf, Bear, Beaver, Deer, Hawk, Porcupine, and Snake. Some of these animals figure prominently in the Huron creation myth (JR 10:125-139).

There is no clear-cut evidence that Huron clans were grouped into moieties or phratries. It is fairly certain, however, that localized clan segments or lineages were fundamental to political organization. The ethnohistoric sources make references to "large families" and "important families," each of which had a "distinct armorial bearing, one having a deer, another a serpent, another a crow, another thunder, which they consider a bird; and like objects" (JR 15:181). To the Jesuits each of the Huron tribes was a "collection or assemblage of grouped family stocks," among whom there was little difference except that each cherished the "names and memories" of "their different progenitors, grandfathers and great-grandfathers." Some of these "family stocks" increased through the adoption of other families; others decreased when a group left them for another family or to form a "band and a nation themselves" (JR 16:227). Large villages were divided into a number of "families" (clan segments or lineages), each having its own civil and war chief who represented them in their respective councils (JR 10:231). The relatives of the chiefs acted as their councillors (JR 10:233). Succession to a chieftainship was partly inherited, in that the men who could be considered for the chieftainship were "nephews" or "grandsons" of an existing chief; and partly elected, in that the other family members had to approve the succession.

There is nothing to indicate that the Jesuits understood, or were aware of the existence of fictive kinship. In view of the number, size and function of the "family stocks" they described, it is likely that these were clan segments based on fictive kinship (Trigger 1969:55). At the village level some lineages within each clan segment seem to have been more important than others. These furnished the chiefs who represented the larger clan segment within the village councils and at higher levels.

b) Political Organization

i) The chiefs. In theory every clan segment had a civil and a war chief. Villages therefore had as many chiefs as there were clan segments (JR 10:229-231). As mentioned earlier, the civil chief was chosen from among the best qualified candidates of a particular lineage by the members of his clan segment. He had to have shown wisdom in decision-making, skill in oratory and liberality. Usually the candidates were the old chiefs' nephews on his sisters' side of the family. If upon appointment a chief failed to meet these qualifications, he could be removed. The new chief assumed the title, duties, regalia, and name of the old chief at a special ceremony held in the spring at the grave of the previous chief (JR 23:165-9). The rules of succession regarding a war chief are not explicit, but appear to have been the same rules as those of the civil chief. A war chief had to have demonstrated bravery and leadership qualities. Neither chieftainship was lost at old age, but only upon death; unless a chief lost popular support through misconduct.

ii) The village council. Village affairs were run by two councils with separate membership and duties. The war chiefs and senior warriors met in the house of the most recognized war chief, or the initiator of a campaign, to make their plans (JR 13:59). If the meeting demanded great secrecy, it would be held in a secluded spot outside the village (JR 10:251). Civil affairs were discussed in the longhouse of the most recognized civil chief. It is probable that the council leader was chief of the most important clan segment of the village. In the summer the councils often met in the centre of the village. Meetings were held almost daily. The council could be attended by all the old men of the village, most likely those over 30 years (Sagard 1939:150), as well as the civil chiefs of the various clan segments. Women had no part in the councils. The clan segment chiefs acted as spokesmen for their relatives and initiated most discussions. Everyone who wanted to speak was given the opportunity. After a summation of all arguments by the council chief, a vote was taken. Although matters were decided by general consensus, the Jesuits felt that it was the chiefs and old men who really decided things, because the others solicited their advice and were easily swayed by their arguments (JR 10:251). After a decision was made, the council chief would announce it to the village. Decisions

79

were not binding on individuals, except insofar as they expressed the majority opinion on a matter.

The chiefs had no coercive powers, in that they lacked an army or police. Village members knew, however, that going against majority opinion would lay them open to criticism. Serious crimes, such as witchcraft with intent to kill or traitorism were punished simply by placing the criminals outside the law, whereupon anyone could kill them without fear of reprisal (JR 8:123; 10:223). Murder was probably settled by the clan segments involved, but if these could not come to a decision the village council would attempt to settle the matter (JR 10:215-223).

iii) Tribal and Confederacy councils. As noted earlier, each tribe was a collection of villages made up of clan segments. Tribal councils could be called by any chief of a clan segment whenever matters arose that involved more than the interests of his village. Such councils were therefore sporadic rather than regular affairs (JR 10:251). The meeting was announced by messenger to the villages of the tribe, or the villages involved in a particular matter. If the matter was very important, a respected old man was sent. The duty of the messenger was to inform the principal chief of the village or his deputy of the nature and place of the meeting (JR 10:253-5). The meeting place was the village of the chief who called the meeting, and he would also act as head of the council. Prior to the meeting, the clan segment chiefs who attended the meeting would consult with their relatives and village councils. The seating at the council was in terms of villages so that the chiefs and their advisers could consult with each other (JR 10:255). Prior to the meeting, the most important chiefs might be given presents, a gesture which the Jesuits believed to be a form of bribery. The meeting would begin by making certain that the main chiefs were present. If any were absent without explanation, the council was dissolved. After an exchange of greetings, the chief who had called the council would outline in detail the matter to be discussed, phrasing it in the form of a request for advice (JR 10:255). The language used in the discussions was highly ritualized, full of metaphors and circumlocutions. Every new speaker would summarize previous arguments, which would be repeated by the head of the council. In the end a majority opinion would be given which, as in village matters, was not binding on the members of the council (JR 10:251).

As at the village level, some chiefs by virtue of their reputation were considered more important than others. These men were invested with particular responsibilities and were sought out for advice on special matters. The most highly-regarded chief was considered the embodiment of the tribe. In his name, treaties were made and in formal councils his name was a synonym for the tribe (JR 10:231).

Confederacy councils were held at least once a year (Sagard 1939:150). The main function of these councils was to renew and strengthen ties of friendship between the tribes and to plan the ruination of their common enemies. The latter suggests that the confederacy was primarily a defensive alliance, although in most cases each tribe followed its own interests. Confederacy councils were usually held once a year, but special councils could be called on request of a tribal chief. Representation and seating on the council was by tribe and village (JR 15:39). Each village sent its clan segment chiefs, of whom one became the spokesman, while the rest his advisors. As in the other councils, no women were present. The meetings proceeded in the same manner as at the tribal level. The head of the council was the most respected chief of the tribe in whose territory the council was held. Again, no decisions were binding on individual members.

Government at the Confederacy level was weak and ineffectual. Policy decisions depended on all tribes agreeing, which was not always easy. Prior to the Iroquois onslaughts of the 1640's, this probably did not matter. When the Huron were faced with forces that threatened their existence, the weaknesses of these councils became apparent. They were simply not equipped to make rapid or binding decisions that would force members of the tribe or Confederacy to act in concert. In the end each village acted virtually independently of the others, enabling the Iroquois to defeat the Huron piecemeal.

2. THE DISTRIBUTION OF THE TRIBAL GROUPS

In 1639 Jérôme Lalemant listed four tribes as constituting the Huron confederacy; these were the *Attignaouantan* (Bear tribe), the *Attingneenong-nahac* (Barking Dogs), the *Arendaronnon* (Rock tribe), and the *Tahontaen-rat* (White Ears or Deer tribe) (JR 16:227).[1] In 1640 a fifth tribe was mentioned, the *Ataronchronon* (Tribe-Beyond-the-Silted-Lake) (JR 19:-167). Champlain, who was in the country for a short time, mentioned only the *Attignaouantan* (Champlain 3:46), while Sagard listed the *Attignaouan-tan*, the *Arendaronnon*, and the *Attingneenongnahac* (Sagard, 1939:91). Each of these tribes occupied their own territory within Huronia (Map 17). The villages within each tribal group were bound together by a common history, by their interrelated families, and by their councils (JR 16:229).

1. For alternate spellings and translation of tribal names, see Appendix I.

Of the five tribes the *Attignaouantan* was the largest, containing about half the population of Huronia (JR 10:77). In 1637 Le Mercier listed fourteen villages (JR 15:39), while in 1640 thirteen were reported (JR 19:209). All the *Attignaouantan* villages lay west of the Wye River, occupying entirely the physiographic area previously defined as the "Penetang Peninsula." There is no mention of any *Attignaouantan* villages east of the Wye or any non *Attignaouantan* villages west of it (Map 17). There has never been much controversy as to what villages belonged to the *Attignaouantan*. For some unexplained reason Tooker (1964:150) counts *Taenhatentaron* (St. Ignace I) and *Arethsi* among the *Attignaouantan* when the *Relations* seem to place them among the *Attingneenongnahac* (JR 19:183). The "capital" of the *Attignaouantan* shifted over time. During Champlain's visit it was probably *Carhagouha*. Le Clercq called it " . . . the most famous of their villages . . . " (Le Clercq 1881:96-97), and it was the headquarters of the Récollet mission. Sagard explained that *Quieunonascaran* was the residence of " . . . the chief of the district of the Bears . . . " (Sagard 1939:149), plus various other important sub-chiefs (Sagard 1939:91, 99, 149, 174). This fact is further evidence to prove a point made earlier that *Quieunonascaran* was but a moved *Carhagouha*. In another passage Sagard called *Tequenonquiaye* (the later *Ossossane*), the " . . . chief town of that region, and the guardian and rampart of all the towns of the Bear Nation, where they generally decide all affairs of great importance . . ." (JR 5:292). This is a clear contradiction which cannot easily be resolved. The passage naming *Tequenonquiaye* as "chief town" comes from the *Histoire* which was written after the *Long Journey*; it is possible therefore that Sagard got the two places mixed up. At any rate, during the Jesuit period *Ossossane* seems to have been the principal village of the *Attignaouantan* (JR 14:25; 17:11), a position it held until the end of Huronia.

Not only were the *Attignaouantan* the largest and most important of the Huron tribes, but along with the *Attingneenongnahac* they were the oldest residents of Huronia. Brébeuf related that those two tribes spoke " . . . with certainty of the settlements of their ancestors, and of different sites of their villages, for more than two hundred years back . . . " (JR 16:227). These two tribes termed each other "brother" and "sister" in the councils (JR 16:229). The language of the *Attignaouantan* and the *Attingneenongnahac* seems to have been identical, as well as their material culture; at least there is no evidence to suggest that there were any significant differences. This, as will be demonstrated, did not seem to have been the case with the other Huron tribes.

The *Attingneenongnahac* were made up of at least three villages (JR 19:269) and perhaps four (JR 15:39). Definite among these were *Teanaus-*

taye (St. Joseph II) (JR 19:183), *Taenhatentaron* (St. Ignace I) (JR 19:-183-185) and probably *Arethsi*. A fourth possible village is the nameless one destroyed in 1648 (JR 34:87). Jones (1908:149) seemed to think that *Ekhiondastsaan* (*Tiondatsae* or La Chaudiere) was an *Attingneenongnahac* village. It was situated on the Vasey Ridge between the *Tahontaenrat* and the *Ataronchronon*. Which tribe this village belonged to is not known.

Judging from the distribution of St. Ignace I, *Arethsi* and St. Joseph II, the area occupied by the *Attingneenongnahac* was all of the "Mount Saint Louis Ridge" south of *Arethsi*. There is no evidence to suggest that this tribe occupied any lands outside that area (Map 17).

The principal village of the *Attingneenongnahac* was always *Teanaustaye* (St. Joseph II) (JR 15:141). It was variously called " . . . the most important village of all . . . " (JR 17:11), and " . . . the largest and most populous village in all the country . . . " (JR 19:185); a position it held until its destruction in 1648 (JR 33:141). According to the Jesuit census the village contained 400 families (JR 34:87) in some eighty lodges (JR 15:153), or a population of about 2,400.

The *Tahontaenrat* (White Ears or Deer tribe) were composed of only one large village, *Scanonaenrat* (St. Michel) (JR 17:87). According to Brébeuf this was the last tribe to have migrated into Huronia. This event was supposed to have occurred sometime around 1619, or just before Sagard's visit (JR 16:227). To what extent the material culture of the *Tahontaenrat* differed from the other tribes is not known. What is known, is that their dialect was somewhat different from that of the *Attignaouantan* and the *Attingneenongnahac* (JR 10:11). The area occupied by the *Tahontaenrat* was the south third of the "Vasey Ridge" (Map 17).

The *Arendaronnon* (Rock tribe) was the easternmost tribe of Huronia (JR 20:19). During Champlain's time the principal village of the area was *Cahiagué* (Champlain 3:49). During the Jesuit period the capital had shifted to St. Jean Baptiste (*Contarea*) (JR 20:21). Since *Cahiagué* had been split into two villages and moved sometime before 1623, it is entirely possible that St. Jean Baptiste was one of these new segments.

The exact number of *Arendaronnon* villages is not known. While relating events at *Cahiagué*, Champlain speaks of " . . . neighbouring villages . . . " (Champlain 3:56), but does not say how many. In view of the size of *Cahiagué*, it is possible that there were never very many *Arendaronnon* villages. The Jesuits listed two Huron villages and one Algonquian village among their *Arendaronnon* mission. These were St. Jean Baptiste, St. Joachim and Ste. Elizabeth (JR 20:21). Another village is alluded to in a passage relating the destruction of a nameless village near St. Jean Baptiste in 1642 (JR 26:175). At a general council of the confederacy held in 1637 three tribes were present. The Bear were represented by fourteen villages and two other tribes by four each (JR 15:39). These other two tribes must have been the *Attingneenongnahac* and the *Arendaronnon*, because the *Ataronchronon* seem to have been of minor importance. Since this was a very important council, deciding in fact the fate of the Jesuits in Huronia, all villages were represented. The non-Bear villages were described as " . . . very populous villages . . . " (JR *ibid.*). One can therefore surmise that the *Arendaronnon* had four fairly populous villages, two of which were St. Joachim and St. Jean Baptiste. Ste. Elizabeth should not be counted among the *Arendaronnon* because it was made up of fugitive *Atontrataronon* Algonquians from the St. Lawrence valley (JR 27:37). Since this village was not founded until after 1640, the villagers of Ste. Elizabeth could not have been present at the council of 1637. Furthermore, it is doubtful if any Algonquians would have been permitted to partake in a general Huron council.

Like the *Tahontaenrat* it is probable that the *Arendaronnon* spoke a somewhat different dialect from the *Attingneenongnahac* and the *Attignaouantan*. Jérôme Lalemant admits that one of the reasons the Jesuits were so late in opening a mission among the *Arendaronnon* was because of language difficulties (JR 20:21). Along with the *Tahontaenrat*, the *Arendaronnon* were latecomers to Huronia. Brébeuf wrote that they entered Huronia sometime around 1590 (JR 16:227). During the Jesuit period the *Arendaronnon* occupied all of the "Medonte-Orillia Till Upland" and a small section of the "Mount Saint Louis Ridge" (Map 17). In view of the fact that all the other tribes discussed so far occupied well-defined physiographic areas, the naming of St. Joachim on the "Mount Saint Louis Ridge" as an *Arendaronnon* village is somewhat surprising. Yet St. Joachim was always administered from St. Jean Baptiste and counted among the *Arendaronnon*. Since there is no evidence to the contrary, St. Joachim must therefore be included among the *Arendaronnon* villages.

The *Ataronchronon* (Tribe-Beyond-the-Silted-Lake) are the least-known and most problematical of the Huron tribes. The Jesuits consistently speak of only four Huron tribes (JR 16:227); yet in 1639 they list a fifth, the *Ataronchronon* (JR 19:1-7). No origin for the tribe is suggested in the *Relations*. Jones postulated that the *Ataronchronon* were a " . . . congeries of other clans (clan segments?) who, in the latter years of Huronia's existence, had, in small detachments, moved nearer Fort Ste. Marie on the Wye, and had occupied the country mainly to the northeast of Mud (Wye) Lake . . . " (Jones 1908:447). This theory is not entirely without difficulties, because the earliest reference to the *Ataronchronon* is in 1637 (JR 13:61), well before the " . . . latter years of Huronia's existence . . . " In

84

all probability, the *Ataronchronon* were a fairly unimportant Huron tribe made up of clan segments from the other tribes, which for some reason wanted to establish villages of their own. That this sort of thing happened is suggested by Brébeuf (JR 16:227). There is no reason to suppose that the *Ataronchronon* were refugees.

Four major villages constituted the *Ataronchronon*; these were Ste. Anne, St. Denis, St. Jean and St. Louis, accounting in 1640 for about 1,400 souls (JR 19:167). The headquarters for the mission to the *Ataronchronon* was Ste. Marie I; however the "capital" or principal village of the tribe seems to have been St. Louis. At least it was in St. Louis that some of the important councils were held (JR 19:175). Other villages in the area occupied by the *Ataronchronon* were *Kaotia* (*Corographie*, Map 14) and *Teaontiae* (*Huronum Explicata Tabula*, Map 13). St. Francis Xavier was administered from Ste. Marie I after 1642 (JR 23:39), but appears to have been a Bear village.

Judging from the distribution of the known *Ataronchronon* villages, this tribe occupied the northern two thirds of the "Vasey Ridge" and the "Port McNicoll" and "Victoria Harbour" uplands (Map 17). Like St. Joachim of the *Arendaronnon*, St. Jean of the *Ataronchronon* lies outside a well-defined physiographic tribal area, but was always counted among the *Ataronchronon*. The southern boundary of the tribal territory of the *Ataronchronon* presents somewhat of a problem because the tribal affiliations of La Chaudiere (*Tiandatsae, Ekhiondastsaan*) are not known. Jones (1908:-149) thought that it was a village of the *Attingneenongnahac*, but this is at best a guess. It could not have been an *Attignaouantan* or *Tahontaenrat* village, because all of these are accounted for elsewhere. The *Attingneenongnahac* only had four villages, *Teanaustaye, Arethsi, Taenhatentaron* and a nameless one near *Teanaustaye* on the frontier of 1648. Jones thought that the nameless one was *Ekhiondastsaan* (La Chaudiere); but *Ekhiondastsaan* was not on the frontier or close to *Teanaustaye* and thus could not have been the nameless village destroyed in 1648. Whether *Ekhiondastsaan* was an *Ataronchronon* village is hard to say. Only four *Ataronchronon* villages are mentioned in the *Relations*, yet at least two other villages within the territory occupied by the *Ataronchronon* appear on the maps. Since there is no mention of any Huron tribes other than the five already discussed, a reasonable guess would be that La Chaudiere, *Kaotia* and *Teaontia* were all *Ataronchronon* villages in a larger tribal area. Perhaps these villages were abandoned sometime during the Jesuit period and relocated at St. Louis, Ste. Anne, St. Denis and St. Jean.

In conclusion, one could say with a fair degree of certainty that the areas occupied by the five Huron tribes can be delimited along well-defined physiographic boundaries. The only exception appears to be the northern one-third of the "Mount Saint Louis Ridge," which was jointly shared by the *Ataronchronon* and *Arendaronnon*. The southern boundary of the *Ataronchronon* presents a problem, because the exact tribal affiliations of La Chaudiere (*Ekhiondastsaan* or *Tiondatsae*) are not known.

3. TRIBAL MIGRATION INTO HURONIA ACCORDING TO ETHNOHISTORIC AND ARCHAEOLOGICAL SOURCES

A detailed prehistory of the Huron tribes is not within the scope of this study. This subject has been covered by MacNeish (1952), Emerson (1959; 1961 a; 1966; 1968), Emerson and Popham (1952), Popham (1950), Ridley (1952; 1958; 1963), Wright (1966), and Trigger (1970). Of these Wright's (1966), and Trigger's (1970) works are the most up-to-date and present a logical compromise between the views held by Emerson and Ridley. In this chapter, only the last phases of the Huron tribal migrations will be discussed.

According to Brébeuf the *Attignaouantan* and *Attingneenongnahac* had a history in Huronia that stretched back some 200 years (JR 16:227). During this time both tribes increased in numbers through the adoption of families and villages who decided to join them (JR *ibid.*). At times, some villages and families decided to leave the two mother tribes and form tribes of their own (JR *ibid.*). This could be one explanation for the formation of the *Ataronchronon*. Sometime shortly before 1600 the *Arendaronnon* migrated into Huronia and about 1620 the *Tahontaenrat* (JR *ibid.*).

In 1615, when Champlain travelled through the Kawartha Lakes system on his way to the Onondaga, he related that the Huron used to live there (Champlain 3:59; 4:248). The stated reason for their move was fear of their enemies (Champlain *ibid.*). In a later passage Champlain explains that the Onondaga once forced the Huron to move over a distance of forty to fifty leagues (Champlain 3:125; 4:304). Two interesting points can be drawn from these statements. The Onondaga lived at the south-eastern end of Lake Ontario, and even in later years always attacked Huronia from the east. The forty or fifty-league migration of Huron referred to by Champlain was therefore out of the Kawarthas, the same area the Huron stated they had formerly occupied. As a matter of fact, judging from Champlain's description of the landscape in parts of the Kawarthas, one would suspect that the forest had not yet reoccupied the abandoned corn-fields. He says for example that " . . . Along the shores (of the lakes) one would think the trees had been planted for ornament in most places . . ."

(Champlain 3:59); and again " . . . the cleared portion of these regions is quite pleasant . . . " (Champlain 3:60). Such forest conditions could persist on well-drained sandy soils up to sixty years after their abandonment. The second point to be made is that Champlain was travelling with the chief of *Cahiagué* and warriors from the *Arendaronnon*. Even though Champlain called all the Huron *Attignaouantan*, it is absolutely certain from the *Relations* that Champlain's companions were *Arendaronnon* (JR 20:19). The conclusion one could come to is that the *Arendaronnon* remembered living to the east of Huronia and were forced to migrate west up to sixty years prior to 1615, due to Onondaga attacks. This fits rather well with Brébeuf's report that the *Arendaronnon* entered Huronia some fifty years prior to 1639. It also fits with the fact that the *Arendaronnon* settled on the eastern frontier of Huronia.

It is unfortunate that the area east of Lake Simcoe is a virtual archaeological blank (Emerson 1968:63). Only three sites in the area have been excavated (McDonald-Payne, Benson and Hardrock), and only the McDonald-Payne site has been described in detail (Pendergast 1963; Emerson 1966). Of these the McDonald-Payne site in Prince Edward County dates to the early 16th century and has its strongest cultural affiliations with sites of the same period north of Toronto such as Parsons and Black Creek (Wright 1966:101). The cultural materials from the Benson site on the west shore of Balsam Lake in Victoria County and the Hardrock site from Grand Island in Balsam Lake have only been partially analyzed. Of these, the Hardrock site appears to date from the middle of the 16th century with its closest cultural relationships to sites of a similar date north of Toronto (Wright 1966:101; Emerson 1966:197-198). The Benson site is early contact with cultural similarities to some early contact sites west of Lake Simcoe (Wright *ibid*.; Emerson *ibid*.).

Inadequate data from only three sites in the area east of Lake Simcoe is hardly enough to formulate any lasting conclusions. It appears, however, that during the 16th century the eastern Ontario Iroquoian populations were shifting west and northwest. Judging from the distribution of reported finds of trade material, all of the north shore of Lake Ontario was abandoned by early contact times (Map 22).[1] Since trade material is very rare east of Lake Simcoe and never present in any large quantities on any

---

1. This map was compiled from the following sources: Boyle (1889); Canada, National Museum M. S. Files (Ontario, Simcoe, Victoria Counties); Garrad (1965; 1966); Laidlaw (1899; 1901; 1903; 1912; 1917); Lawrence, Gavillier and Morris (1909); Popham (1950). It must be emphasized that in all areas except the area of the historic Petun and Huron, trade material is rare and, when present, only in very small quantities.

particular site, one would judge that the last remnant of the eastern Ontario Iroquoians entered Huronia in early contact times, just before the end of the 16th century, forming the historic *Arendaronnon*. This coincides remarkably well with Champlain's and Brébeuf's accounts, and with the fact that no villages are mentioned east of Lake Simcoe during the historic period.

Regarding tribal movements from the south into Huronia, the ethnohistoric accounts are of little help. The most logical sequence of events is that outlined by Wright, based on the distribution of artifact assemblages, in particular pottery types (Wright 1966:78-80). Wright divides the precontact Indian population west of Lake Simcoe into Northern and Southern divisions, groupings which were not separate but very closely related. During precontact times the Southern division was slowly shifting northward. Judging from the distribution of reported trade material the southern division had migrated well north of the Holland River by the earliest contact times (Map 22). Hunter records only four occurrences of French trade goods south of Innisfil township (Simcoe County), and none of these are absolutely definite (Hunter 1889:44-45). During this time the Northern division must have been made up of the *Attignaouantan* and the *Attingneenongnahac*. The cultural material from the Southern division sites shows both Huron and Petun affinities. Wright therefore concludes that the Southern division must have split into two groups, one going on to settle in the Collingwood area and becoming the Wolf and Deer tribes of the historic Petun (*Khionontateronon*) confederacy, the other group going on to Huronia. Among the latter group were undoubtedly the *Tahontaenrat*, who were supposed to have joined the Huron confederacy some thirty years before 1639 (JR 16:227). Jérôme Lalemant reported that " . . . these nations (Huron and Petun) formerly waged cruel wars against one another; but now are on very good terms . . . " (JR 20:43). Wright speculates that these former wars could have been a result of Southern division incursions into Northern division territory (Wright 1966:79-80). All such hostilities had ceased by Champlain's time; at any rate, Petun and Huron were living at peace in 1616 (Champlain 3:95).

The most reasonable explanation for the northward and northwestward shift of the tribes that were to become the Huron and Petun confederacies, are undoubtedly the age-old rancours of intertribal warfare with the New York Iroquois tribes. This was the story told to Champlain, Sagard and the Jesuits, and there is little reason to doubt it. Intertribal warfare had been a reality for a long time before the coming of the French, although it had never reached the proportions that it did in the 1640's. The warfare prior to the 1640's consisted of raids engendered by a desire for prestige and revenge (Trigger 1960:20). Persistent, if not exactly catastrophic, pressure along the southern and southeastern frontier probably led to a slow migration to the historic occupance areas. With warfare of the type just described, rapid and long distance migrations were not necessary; but there was also no reason for the opposing groups to move closer together or even stay where they were. It is interesting to note that among the changes that were taking place in late precontact times was a trend for villages to become larger, to cluster, and to seek better defendable sites (Wright 1966:99).

Trigger (1962:137-148; 1963 a:86-101; 1968:111; 1969:24) advances the theory that pressure from the Iroquois tribes was not the only reason for the northward shift of the Huron and Petun tribes. Suitable agricultural soils and the potential for trade with the Algonquians were in Trigger's opinion at least of equal, if not greater, importance. Unfortunately, it is not possible to either prove or disprove this theory. Trigger opens his argument with the thesis that the Huron prior to the 1640's were not militarily inferior to the Iroquois tribes, and therefore warfare does not explain Huron tribal migrations (Trigger 1963a):92). Even if the Huron tribes were the military equals of the Iroquois tribes, there is absolutely no reason why villages would not want to move away from the frontier of conflict. Such movements did not have to take place in a spirit of panic resulting in long distance relocations, but could have taken place over short distances in the normal course of shifting a village. Archaeological investigations certainly seem to show that the Huron tribal migrations were a rather slow process, lasting over one hundred years. The movement to the north and northwest, the clustering of villages, their growth, and the growing regard for defendable sites, may therefore be regarded as a desire on the part of the villagers to lessen the chances of success of Iroquois raids.

The alternate motives for the migrations, suitable agricultural soils and the desire for trade with the Algonquin bands, appear to be unlikely. Northern Simcoe County is, moreover, not the only large area in southern Ontario with well-drained sandy soils. Generalized and detailed soils maps of Ontario show that suitable soils could be found almost everywhere in the province south of the Shield (Canada, Department of Agriculture 1964). There was, therefore, no lack of suitable agricultural soils south of the Shield in south central and eastern Ontario. Indeed, the very fact that agricultural Indians had occupied these areas at one time shows that farming was possible.

The theory that the Huron tribes were moving closer to the Algonquians in order to trade with them also runs into difficulties. The Huron settlements, because they were agriculturally based, were less mobile than Algonquian hunting and fishing communities. It seems unlikely that a semi-sedentary agricultural people would move their villages closer to a nomadic group in order to trade with them. The reverse seems more logical. Moreover, during the summer, when most of the trading took place, such trade was not localized at the Huron or Algonquian villages – as Trigger admits (Trigger 1960:18). In the winter at least, it seems to have been the Algonquian's practice to move to the Huron (Trigger 1963 a):92). Little is known of precontact trade relations, and the trading movements just described were those of the early contact period. Once the fur trade became more important, trading activities between the Huron and their neighbours intensified. It was then that the position of Huronia assumed strategic importance in the fur trade. It is unlikely that trade was of such magnitude, prior to direct Huron-French contact, as to promote a movement of people into Huronia. The fact that Huronia was in a strategic location helped the Huron to become middlemen in the fur trade, but this was a development of the contact period. The migrations into Huronia took place before that period.[1]

The least problematical explanation of Huron tribal migrations is still the slow but constant pressure exerted by intertribal raids on frontier villages. Military superiority of the New York Iroquois or fear of complete annihilation on the part of the Huron did not necessarily have anything to do with these movements. Most likely, individual Huron villages simply hoped to avoid the deprivations of occasional raids by moving away from an existing frontier. These tribal movements were therefore slow but steady, ultimately ending in the *cul-de-sac* between Lake Simcoe, Georgian Bay and the Canadian Shield. In the last analysis, it is probably best to attempt an explanation of Huron migrations in terms of interrelated multiple causes.

1. The growing importance of the fur trade and Huron relations with other tribes are discussed in Chapter VII.

Chapter IV

Estimated Population Size and Densities in Huronia

INTRODUCTION

In all the years that Huronia has been studied, few serious attempts have been made to estimate the total population of the area. Some writers have accepted the estimates made by Champlain and his contemporaries, others have discounted these as gross exaggerations and formulated their own in the light of what is known of other North American Indian societies. The purpose of this chapter is to examine these population estimates, and to derive a reasonable approximation for the Huron area.

1. CONTEMPORARY ESTIMATES

The first estimate of the total Huron population was given by Champlain during his 1615-1616 visit. In the 1619 edition of his diaries Champlain states that the Huron population "may amount to 30,000 souls" of whom 2,000 were "warriors" (Champlain 3:122). He stated that he got this estimate from the Huron. In 1632 Champlain's account of his visit to the Huron was republished with minor alterations. For some reason, he or his publisher reduced this figure to 20,000 (Champlain 4:302). In both cases the number of warriors is given as 2,000 and the number of villages as 18.

Sagard, whose familiarity with Champlain's writings has already been noted, gave a population estimate of 30,000 to 40,000, of whom 2,000 to 3,000 were warriors (Sagard 1939:92). His estimate of the number of villages was 25 (Sagard 1939:91). Unlike Champlain, Sagard did not travel widely in Huronia, and in compiling his book seems to have taken a great deal directly from Champlain. His population estimate is a good case in point.

The earliest Jesuit estimate was made in 1633 by Le Jeune, who placed the total Huron population at 30,000 (JR 6:59). Since Le Jeune had never been to Huronia, he could only have obtained this figure from Champlain or the Jesuits, J. Brébeuf and A. de Noue. The latter two resided among the *Attignaouantan* from 1626 to 1628.

Between 1634 and 1635 three estimates were made. All three were by Brébeuf, and all three placed the total Huron population at 30,000 (JR 7:225; 8:115; 10:313). In every case Brébeuf put the number of settlements at twenty.

In the autumn of 1634 the first outbreaks of contagious diseases were reported among the Huron (JR 8:43, 73). The Jesuits described the epidemic as measles or smallpox, but of a much more virulent variety than was known in France (JR 8:87-89). Prior to European contact smallpox and measles were unknown to the North American Indian groups; in the case of the Huron, exposure to these diseases was disastrous. In a letter dated March 28th, 1640, Jérôme Lalemant mentioned that the Huron population had fallen from 30,000 to 10,000 (JR 17:223). The letter was written to the Cardinal, Duke de Richelieu; and in it Lalemant blames the decline of the Huron population primarily on the ravages of the New York Iroquois. Since the letter was a request to the government of France to take action against the Protestant English and Dutch, as well as their Indian allies, Lalemant's explanation that the Iroquois were largely to blame for the population decline is suspect. As a matter of fact, in May of 1640, two months after his letter to Richelieu, Lalemant put the blame for the Huron population decline on the epidemics (JR 19:127). In the same passage, Lalemant makes reference to a census taken in the autumn and winter of 1639. Apparently the Jesuits took some pains to make the census as accurate as possible, because the deployment of their missionaries was to some extent dependent on the population size of the tribes and distribution of the villages. The results of the census revealed:

> . . . thirty-two hamlets and straggling villages, which comprise in all about seven hundred cabins, about two thousand fires, and about twelve thousand persons. (JR 19:127).

Unfortunately, this figure includes the neighbouring Petun (*Khionontatero-non*), who lived in the Collingwood area. Although there are no separate population estimates for the Petun, Jérôme Lalemant wrote that in 1640 the Petun resided in nine villages (JR 20:43). If one could assume that the Huron-Petun population was roughly proportional to the number of villages in each confederacy, then the Huron had a 1639 population of 8,700 and the Petun 3,300. In the light of other estimates, a post-epidemic Huron population of 8,700 seems to be slightly too low.

The last rough population estimate was made in 1645 by Jérôme Lalemant. At that time he stated that the Huron population was about 10,000 to 20,000 (JR 28:67).

After the final destruction of Huronia, two Jesuits recounted what in their opinion was the original population size of Huronia. Le Mercier, in 1653 estimated 30,000 to 35,000 (JR 42:221), and G. Druillettes in 1658 again placed the figure at 30,000 to 35,000 (JR 44:249).

Only one of the early authorities differs markedly from the other estimates. In 1691 Le Clercq wrote that at one time there had been " . . . 18 towns comprising about 10,000 souls . . . " (Le Clercq 1881:96-97). It is not exactly clear which period in Huron history Le Clercq was referring to, but it seems to have been the Récollet period prior to 1629 because he discusses Le Caron's early visit to Huronia in the same chapter. The passages Le Clercq quoted from Joseph Le Caron make no references to population estimates, so Le Clercq may even have obtained the figure of 10,000 Huron from later Jesuit estimates. It is really remarkable that Le Clercq would assign a figure of 10,000 to a pre-epidemic Huron population when all his early sources were in terms of 30,000. Perhaps he was simply using the post-epidemic Jesuit estimate without giving the matter much thought. It is doubtful if Le Caron estimated 10,000 Huron when his travelling companions, Champlain and Sagard, both put the figure at about 30,000.

In summary, there seems to be a general consensus that from 1615 to the mid-1630's the Huron population was fairly stable about 30,000 people. After 1638, due primarily to the ravages of smallpox, the population was reduced by about two-thirds to 8,700 or 10,000. Lalemant's 1645 estimate would seem to indicate that 8,700 may have been a low estimate and the actual figure was somewhat higher.

2. MODERN ESTIMATES

Most modern writers have more or less accepted the seventeenth-century estimates (Hunter 1948:3; Kidd 1949:8; Hunt 1940:40; Jury and Jury 1965:15; Wright 1966:81).

Only four authors have attempted to question the earlier Huron population estimates and devise their own. Mooney (1928:23-24) felt that the Huron population in 1600 was about 10,000 and the neighbouring Petun, 8,000. Since Mooney's work was published posthumously from an incompleted manuscript, it is not entirely clear how he derived his figures. Judging from the bibliography found with the manuscript, he did consult the *Jesuit Relations*, but apparently paid no attention to the pre-epidemic estimate of 30,000 Huron. For all intents and purposes, Mooney's estimate of 10,000 for the pre-historic Huron population can be regarded as a guess, influenced perhaps by the post-epidemic Jesuit estimates.

Kroeber (1939:140) accepted Mooney's population estimate for the Huron and attempted to justify it in terms of agricultural efficiency and socio-economic variables (Kroeber 1934:8-12; 1939:146-150). His basic premise was that the Indians of the agricultural east were not farmers but "agricultural hunters" (Kroeber 1939:150). Agricultural produce, he contended, accounted for only one-half of their diet, even though their corn yields (15 to 20 bushels per acre), were only slightly below the 1934 United States average of 25-30 bushels per acre (Kroeber 1939:146). Basically, Kroeber saw the production of corn as a means of carrying out warfare between the Iroquoian groups. Warfare in turn kept populations down, making additional agriculture unnecessary (Kroeber 1939:149). Consequently, Kroeber reasons, one should expect low population numbers and densities. His population density was computed by combining Mooney's figures for the Petun and Huron (18,000) dividing this into the "Huron-Petun culture area" (139,200 sq. km.). The result was a population density of 12.9 Indians per 100 sq. km. (Kroeber 1939:140). All things taken into consideration, Kroeber felt that this population density was about right for Indians who were primarily hunters and secondarily agriculturalists.

There is little doubt that both Mooney's and Kroeber's estimates are wrong, because they are founded on very questionable premises. Apart from the fact that the Hurons were not "agricultural hunters" but agriculturalists who derived more than 50 per cent of their diet from agricultural produce, it is very doubtful if pre-contact warfare was of such a nature that it contributed to a lack of population increase. Even if Mooney's and Kroeber's estimate of 18,000 Huron-Petun in 1600 A. D. is taken as being correct, his derivation and confidence in a population density as low as 12.9 Indians per 100 sq. km. certainly is not. Kroeber delimits a culture area of 139,200 sq. km. (53, 606 sq. mi.), stretching all the way from the Niagara escarpment to the Saguenay and from the southern edge of the Canadian Shield to the north shore of Lake Ontario and the St. Lawrence as far as the junction of the Ottawa, where the southern limits of the culture area dip south to include what are now the eastern Townships of Quebec (Kroeber 1939: Appendix Map 1). It is doubtful whether the Huron and Petun, as such, ever occupied this stretch of territory. They certainly did not occupy it all at the same time, much less in 1600 A. D. Furthermore the Huron and Petun were not a dispersed population, but one living in compact villages associated together in tribal areas, with a high predilection for certain soil types. In other words, only a portion of Kroeber's culture area ever supported the Huron and Petun at any one time. Therefore a density of 12.9 Indians per 100 sq. km. does not make any sense, and one should expect considerably higher population densities.

The actual area occupied by the Huron in the early 17th century has already been delimited. This was an area of some 883 sq. km. (340 sq. mi.). To this one can add a generous 195 sq. km. (75 sq. mi.) for the Petun area, resulting in a total area of 1,078 sq. km. (415 sq. mi.) from which the Huron and Petun derived most of their sustenance. Even if Mooney's estimate of 18,000 Huron and Petun is taken as accurate, this would mean a population density of 16.7 persons per sq. km. (43.4 per sq. mi.), or 1,670 people per 100 sq. km. When Huron soil preferences and their degree of agricultural efficiency are taken into consideration, the actual population density is somewhat higher. Clearly, then, Kroeber's justification of Mooney's estimates is founded on several misconceptions; and this in turn throws considerable doubt on Mooney's original estimate.

Only one writer has tried to make a serious case for a higher Huron population estimate. Robert Popham (1950:86-87) came to the conclusion that the pre-1636 Huron population could have been as high as 45,000 to 50,000. He accepts the figure of 30,000 for the conventional Huronia, but claims that on the basis of the presence of trade goods on ten village sites in Innisfil Township Simcoe County the whole area west of Lake Simcoe was also occupied in early historic times, but overlooked by Champlain and the Jesuits. Popham therefore reasoned that the whole of Simcoe county was occupied prior to 1636. His final figure was derived by estimating a population density of 55 people per square mile over "conventional Huronia" and then extending this figure over the whole of the County.

A basic criticism can be levelled at this estimate: it concerns Popham's definition of the occupied area. The figure of 55 people per square mile was based on the assumption that the early estimates of 30,000 Huron applied to Simcoe County north of Kempenfeldt Bay and that Champlain, Sagard and the Jesuits simply did not know of the Huron in Innisfil or adjacent townships. That this assumption is highly unlikely has already been discussed earlier. There were probably no major areas of settlement south of the Cranberry, Bass and Orr Lake frontier; the Innisfil area was abandoned at some time before Champlain's arrival and the displaced population formed the bulk of the Petun and some of the Huron tribes. In view of Champlain's and the Jesuit's knowledge of the Petun and even the Neutral, it does not seem possible that they could have overlooked ten Huron settlements in Innisfil Township; a supposed population equal to that of the Petun and one-third to one-quarter the size of the Huron.

95

Recently, Trigger (1969: 12-13) calculated a total Huron population of 18,000. His estimate was based on the post-epidemic Jesuit census, and on known epidemic death rates from uninoculated Indian populations. An estimate based on similar sources to that of Trigger will be discussed later in this chapter.

3. EVALUATION OF CONTEMPORARY ESTIMATES AND NEW APPROXIMATIONS

a) Evaluation

One of the really remarkable things about the early population estimates is the way in which the figure 30,000 was accepted by all the early writers up to the Jesuit census of 1639. From the manner in which this figure was used there seems little doubt that Sagard and the Jesuits were simply using Champlain's writings. Champlain's 1632 revision (or misprint) to 20,000 people did not seem to have been taken into account. The universal acceptance of a population estimate of 30,000 could mean four things: 1) everyone agreed that 30,000 was a reasonable estimate; 2) a second estimate was not attempted because the later writers were not acquainted with the whole of Huronia; 3) Champlain's estimate suited the political and other motives of the Jesuits; and 4) during the fifteen to twenty years after Champlain's visit, the figure had become so accepted that no one really thought about revising it.

It has already been stated that Champlain's estimates regarding long distances must be regarded with caution. There is no reason to suppose that his population estimates were any more accurate, particularily when he seems to have obtained the figure from the Huron themselves. Sagard almost certainly did not travel much in Huronia, and in all probability simply copied from Champlain. The Jesuits, however, were a different matter. Several of them were familiar enough with Huronia to have made independent estimates before their census of 1639. Yet they seem to have relied solely on Champlain's figure of 30,000 Huron.

Some ethnologists such as Kroeber (1939:177-180) and Stewart (1949:656-657) have rejected missionary estimates as being exaggerations. Other writers have shown that in many cases missionary estimates were actually much more accurate than those of Kroeber and his colleagues (Dobyns 1966:395-416). In attempting to justify the mission to the Huron and seeking aid for such an enterprise, the Jesuits would certainly gain from inflated population estimates; yet there is no evidence that they would deliberately falsify documents that were sent to their

Superior in Quebec and ultimately back to France and Rome. One is, therefore, inclined to believe that the original estimate of 30,000 was simply accepted as reasonably accurate; and that the question was of little concern until the mission had to be reorganized in 1639, at which time a more accurate census had to be made.

For reasons already stated, the 1639 census count of 8,700 to 10,000 people is probably the most accurate estimate for the post-epidemic Huron population. An attempt will now be made to use this estimate and other methods to arrive at some understanding of the pre-epidemic Huron population.

b) New Approximations

A method that has been widely used to estimate pre-European Indian populations is the death rate due to contagious diseases applied to more accurate post-epidemic population counts (Dobyns 1966:410-412). According to the Jesuits, smallpox was the primary agent that reduced the Huron population (JR 8:87-89). This disease affected in particular the old and young (JR 17:11), thus removing not only a percentage of the population, but also two particular segments of the social structure, the children and the old people. It is impossible to estimate a rate of decline among the Huron from contemporary documents. Numbers of dead or dying are given for a brief period such as a month, or single visit by a missionary, but never over an extended period of time (JR 17:25, 61). The Jesuits estimated that by 1640 the Huron population had declined by about two-thirds (JR 17:223).

Studies made on more complete data from uninoculated Indian populations suggest a smallpox death rate of 75 per cent among California groups (Cook 1955:322), while among the Assiniboine a death rate of 66 per cent has been recorded (Dobyns 1966:411). In 1780 David Thompson observed the catastrophic effects of smallpox among the Chippewa, Blackfeet and Snake Indians. In a relatively short time the disease had decimated about three-fifths of the Plains Indian population (Thompson 1962:236). In addition to his personal observations, Thompson quotes the Blackfeet's own estimate that more than half of their population had died (Thompson 1962:245). Other studies list death rates of 50 per cent among the Chickasaw, Catawba and Cherokee in mid-18th century Georgia and South Carolina (Duffy 1951:335, 338); and, slightly later, a similar death rate among the Pueblo of New Mexico (Aberle, *et al.*, 1940:167).

The studies cited above all deal with unvaccinated aboriginal American populations who apparently experienced smallpox for the first time. These populations range from hunters and gatherers to agriculturalists and from western Canada to the southeastern and southwestern United States. A death rate of 50 to 70 per cent among such populations appears to be common. It is interesting to note that, as late as 1924, a smallpox epidemic in Windsor, Ontario, carried with it a mortality rate of 71 per cent among the unvaccinated infected population (Heagerty 1928:95).

In view of these figures, similar death rates among the Huron would not be unexpected. If the 1639 census of 8,700 to 10,000 Huron is taken as reasonably accurate of the post-epidemic population, the following pre-epidemic estimates can be made (Table 2).

Table 2

Huron Population Estimates Based
on Smallpox Death Rates

Death Rate	1639 Census of Post-Epidemic Population	Pre-Epidemic Estimate
50%	8,700	17,400
60%	8,700	21,750
70%	8,700	25,660
50%	10,000	20,000
60%	10,000	25,000
70%	10,000	33,300

With 9,000 Huron as an average post-epidemic population and an average death rate of 60 per cent, the resulting population before the mid 1630's could have been in the order of 22,500. Trigger (1969:12-13) arrived at a pre-epidemic figure of 18,000 also using epidemic death rates.

A method for estimating aboriginal populations occasionally used, is to take estimates of the total number of warriors in a tribe and multiply this figure by the average number of people in a family (MacLeod 1928: 545-546). The only estimates of warrior totals for Huronia are Champlain's figure of 2,000 (Champlain 3:122) and Sagard's figures of 2,000 to 3,000 (Sagard 1939:92).

References to the average number of people per family are scarce. Virtually nothing is known about family size, birth rates, death rates and

98

average life spans. Ragueneau cites one case in which 8 to 10 families made up 60 to 80 people. (JR 35:87), or six to ten people per family. In 1657-58 Druillettes described several agricultural tribes in the western Great Lakes area with a similar socio-economic structure to the Huron. After stating that for every man " . . . there are at least three or four other persons, namely, women and children . . . " (JR 44:245), he goes on to describe some of these tribes and villages in greater detail (JR 44:245-247). From his descriptions one can gather that the average family size was roughly in the order of four to six people including the men. All these estimates are within the range of five to eight members per Huron family set by Trigger (1969:13).

Studies done on other shifting agriculturalists suggest the following family sizes: Gabel (1967:32) takes an average of five people; Sahlins (1968:30) estimates five to eight; Cowgill (1962:277) actually worked out the average size of a household among shifting cultivators in the Maya Lowlands as six people, and Howells (1960:168) used a family figure of five to estimate Pecos Pueblo populations.

From the 1639 Jesuit census of the Huron and Petun one can derive an average family size of three, which is obviously much too low in view of these other estimates. This low figure is explained by the Jesuits as being due to smallpox, in that prior to the epidemics the longhouses and villages were much more populous (JR 19:127). If the aforementioned smallpox death rate of 50 to 70 per cent is applied to the average post-epidemic family size of three, one would get a pre-epidemic family size of six to eight people.

Taking all these estimates into consideration, a Huron family size of four to eight people does not seem unreasonable. Applying an average of six members per family to Champlain's and Sagard's estimated 2,000 to 3,000 warriors one would get total population estimates of 12,000 to 18,000 Huron, providing that each family furnished one warrior.

David Thompson's observations among pre-epidemic Mandan populations in 1797-98, tends to reinforce the opinion that one warrior for every six or seven people in an agricultural North American Indian group is a reasonable estimate (Thompson 1962:173). In all he visited two groups of 1,520 and 1,330 people, with 220 and 190 warriors respectively, or one warrior to about seven people. Family sizes seemed to have varied up to ten people.

Even if the size of the average Huron family has been correctly estimated, little confidence can be placed in the resulting total population estimate unless we have independent means of checking Champlain's and Sagard's warrior figures. Of all the early writers, Champlain was probably the best informed on the fighting potential of the Huron because he tried to raise an army among them in 1615. This army was composed of at least 500 men (Champlain 3:60), although 2,500 had been promised (Champlain, 3:32). Since the 1615 campaign had first been called off and then hastily revived, only 500 warriors turned up. According to Sagard this was about the average number of Huron who went to war every year (Sagard 1939:152). In the case of the 1615 expedition, most of the warriors came from *Cahiagué* and the neighbouring villages (Champlain 3:56), so presumably they were mainly *Arendaronnon*. If the other tribes could put up a similar number of warriors, a total warrior population of 2,000 to 3,000 does not seem unreasonable.

A third method of gaining an understanding of the total Huron population is to estimate the population size of the individual villages that made up the five tribes. In a few cases the populations of villages can be estimated; in other cases an idea of their size can be gained from the importance with which the Jesuits regarded them. While this method is, of course, fairly subjective, it tends to support the earlier estimates.

Champlain (3:122) estimated 18 villages; Sagard 25 (Sagard 1939:91); Le Clercq (1881:96-97) gave a figure of 18 (probably from Le Caron or Champlain); Brébeuf (JR 8:115) listed 20 in 1634 and the same number in 1636 (JR 10:313). The 1640 census lists 32 villages and hamlets of which 9 belonged to the Petun (JR 19:125-127). The discrepancies between the various estimates are understandable, in view of the fact that villages shifted periodically and occasionally split into two or more villages or sometimes combined into one.

Using the *Relations* and *Maps,* a careful tribe-by-tribe inventory can be made of the names and number of villages belonging to each tribe during the Jesuit period (Table 3). Each village will be rated in relation to the largest villages and according to the scraps of information that can be gathered about them in the *Relations*.

The Jesuits regarded *Teanaustaye* (St. Joseph II) as the largest village in Huronia (JR 17:11; 19:185; 33:141), and the size of the others can be estimated in relation to this one. *Teanaustaye* was composed of 80 cabins (JR 15:153) and 400 families (JR 34:87). This works out to five families per longhouse, which is about right, considering the Jesuit estimate of an average of three hearths per longhouse and two families per hearth (JR 19:127). Longhouses varied enormously in size (JR 16:243), but judging from excavations in Huronia a longhouse containing six families seems about average (Emerson 1961 b):62-64). At six persons per family, *Teanaustaye* could have contained about 2,400 people.

One of the other large villages was *Ossossane* with 40 longhouses (JR 15:153), or a population of about 1,500 people. St. Jean Baptiste and St. Michel were at least as large as *Ossossane* because like *Ossossane*, they were the principal villages of their respective tribes. Accordingly *Teanaustaye* will be given an arbitrary rating of four, signifying it as the most important and the largest village in Huronia with a population of 2,400. *Ossossane*, St. Michel and St. Jean Baptiste will be given ratings of three to four, but less than four, with populations varying between 1,500 to 1,800. The other villages will be rated from one to three depending on their "importance." A rating of one will carry an arbitrary population figure of 300 and a rating of two a population of 600. In archaeological terms, a village containing 300 people in about six longhouses can be considered small. It is doubtful whether there were any villages smaller than this during the historic period.

Two other fragments of information that we have is that the *Attignaouantan* made up about half of the Huron population (JR 10:77), and that the *Ataronchronon* had a post-epidemic population of 1,400 (JR 19:167).

The village-by-village tabulation results in a total Huron population of 20,400 (Table 3). Such a series of estimates is, of course, fraught with difficulties and open to challenge. In the light of available knowledge however, it is difficult to see where these estimates could be refined. Closer approximations might be made if the exact location and size of every village were known. In that case, estimates could be made on the basis of numbers of families per longhouse and numbers of longhouses per acre. The latter ratio could be established through a comparison of excavated sites. As yet, not enough sites have been excavated to establish good longhouse-per-acre ratios. Only many years of diligent digging will allow one to make less subjective estimates of Huron populations.

There are a number of other methods of estimating populations which can be used with varying degrees of success. Most, however, require specific information, which is never available for all the Huron villages. Howells (1960:158-176) estimated prehistoric Indian populations from skeletal evidence. His method can be reduced to the relationship: $P \times R/100 = S/T$; where P is the population of a village; $R/100$ the estimated death rate in people per 100 per year; S the number of skeletons in the cemetery; T the number of years a village was in existence. Only a few Huron ossuaries have been excavated, such as the two at *Cahiagué* (Hunter 1901:98; Harris 1949:73), containing 550 skeletons; *Ossossane* with an estimated 1,000 skeletons (Quimby 1966:110); and *Teanaustaye* with 500 to 1,000 skeletons (Hunter 1901:80). The problem is that, even if one knew variables such as the death rate and the length of time a village was

101

Table 3

Huron Population Estimates Based
on Village Totals

Tribe	Village	Rating	Population
Attingneenongnahac	Teanaustaye	4	2,400
	Taenhatentaron	2-3	800
	Arethsi	1	300
	Nameless one	1	300
Subtotal			3,800
Arendaronnon	St. Jean Baptiste	3	1,800
	St. Joachim	2-3	800
	Nameless one	2	600
	Nameless two	1	300
Subtotal			3,500
Tahontaenrat	St. Michel	3	1,800
Subtotal			1,800
Ataronchronon	St. Louis	2	600
	St. Anne	2	600
	St. Denis	2	600
	St. Jean	2	600
	Kaotia	2	600
Subtotal			3,000
Attignaouantan	Ossossane	3	1,500
	Andiatae	2-3	800
	Angoutenc	2-3	800
	Arendaonatia	1	300
	Anonatea	1	300
	Arent	2	600
	Arontaen	2	600
	Karenhassa	1-2	400
	Iaenhouton	1	300
	Ihonatiria	1	300
	Oenrio	1	300
	Onnentisati	1	300
	Quieunonascaran	3	1,500
	Tondakea	1	300
Subtotal			8,300
Huron Total			20,400

in existence, we still do not know whether all the skeletons in an ossuary came from the same village. In the case of *Ossossane*, for example, eight or nine villages buried their dead together in one ossuary (JR 10:291). The *Teanaustaye* ossuary presents a different problem, in that the skeletal population represents part of a massacre. Population estimates from skeletal remains are possible in the future, but must be subject to the most careful evaluation.

c) *Summary*

By the use of three standard methods of estimating pre-contact Indian populations, the Huron population prior to the onslaught of European diseases could have been as low as 14,000 and as high as 33,300. The median figures for all three estimates run from 16,000 to 22,500 with an average of 20,200, which is close to the figure obtained by totalling the estimated village populations. On the basis of these figures, it would seem that the original estimate of 30,000 Huron, recorded by Champlain and accepted by later writers, is about one-third too large.

In view of the preceding discussion, the author will henceforth use the figure of 21,000 Huron to describe the pre-epidemic Huron population, and 9,000 as the post-epidemic population. For particular tribal areas and villages, the figures compiled in Table 3 will be used. On the whole, it is felt that the tribal totals are more accurate than figures for individual villages.

4. POPULATION DENSITIES

Using a population total of 21,000 Huron in a culture area of 340 square miles, one would arrive at a population density of 62 people per square mile (2400 per 100 sq. km.). This figure is well within the range of population densities that have been computed for shifting agriculturalists. Under tropical conditions such densities can vary upwards to 200 people per square mile (Cowgill 1962; Dumond 1961). Since little or nothing is known about population densities among shifting agriculturalists in mid-latitude areas, comparative figures are not available.

Population densities for the individual tribal areas vary between 52 and 233 people per square mile (Table 4). Figure 1 depicts the relation between the total tribal area and the estimated population. The Product Moment Coefficient of Correlation (Spiegel 1961:244-245) between these two variables is 0.94, which is statistically significant at the 0.01 level using Student's test (Spiegel 1961:247). If population is correlated with only arable soils in each tribal area, the correlation coefficient is 0.95. The

103

Table 4

Population Densities in Huron Tribal Areas

Tribal Area	Population Estimate	Area (acres)	Area (sq.mi.)	Density (P/sq.mi.)	Arable Area (acres)	Arable Area (sq.mi.)	Density (P/sq.mi.)
Attingneenongnahae	3,800	10,422	16.3	233	9,976	15.6	243
Arendaronnon	3,500	43,521	68.0	52	36,016	56.3	62
Tahontaenrat	1,800	9,313	14.6	124	8,058	12.6	143
Ataronchronon	3,000	25,934	40.5	71	23,233	36.3	83
Attignaouantan	8,300	88,176	137.8	60	77,598	121.3	68
Huronia Total	20,400	177,366	277.2	74	154,881	242.2	84

difference between these two correlations is insignificant, because the tribal areas are situated on the well-drained upland areas of Huronia, with about an equal proportion of agriculturally usable and non-usable soils.

Since the Huron showed a marked preference for certain soil types an attempt was made to correlate tribal population estimates with tribal areas adjusted to a scale of preference in soil types. An index of preference was calculated in the following way for each soil type: Index of preference for soil type x = % of total sites on soil type x / % of soil type x in total area. The computed indices show that the sandy loams were in considerably higher demand than the other usable agricultural soils (Table 5), demonstrating that Huron agricultural technology limited the variety of soils that could be used, but that within these limitations the Huron showed a marked preference for the more fertile soils. Assuming that higher population densities among agriculturalists are partly a reflection of soil productivity, the total area of each soil type in each tribal area, if adjusted to the index of preference, should reflect more uniform population density figures. Table 6 shows that this assumption is fairly true, in that the population densities now vary between 51 and 149 people per square mile. The Product Moment Correlation Coefficient between the estimated population and the adjusted area figures is now 0.97 (Figure 2).

Table 5

Indices of Preference for Well-Drained Soils

Soil type	Index of preference
Gravels	.7
Sands and loamy sands	.7
Sandy loams	1.7
Loam and silt loam	.4
Clay and clay loam	.0

The close correlations between tribal area and population, and the significance of preferred soils in this correlation, can be attributed to a fairly close adjustment to an agricultural resource base. The relatively higher population density for the *Attingneenongnahac* is explainable either as an error in the original population estimate, or in terms of an adjustment of tribal boundaries. Admittedly, the population figure for the *Attingneenongnahac* is only an estimate, but so are the figures for the other four

105

tribes. One would, therefore, assume that any error of estimate is spread fairly evenly over the five groups, and does not favour one by as much as 100 to 150 per cent. What is more likely is that an adjustment of territorial boundaries took place, necessitating a higher *Attingneenongnahac* population concentration. The likelihood that this in fact took place can be deduced from the tribal history of the Huron confederacy. The *Attingneenongnahac*, it will be recalled, once shared Huronia with the *Attingnaouantan*. The three tribes that moved into the country just before the French arrival, moved into the south, central and eastern sections of Huronia, thus surrounding the *Attingneenongnahac* on three sides. It is, therefore, likely that the redistribution of land affected the *Attingneenongnahac* more than the *Attignaouantan* and necessitated a shrinking of tribal boundaries.

Table 6

Population Densities in Adjusted Huron Tribal Areas

Tribal Area	Population Estimate	Adjusted Area (acres)	Adjusted Area (sq.mi.)	Density (P/sq.mi.)
Attingneenongnahac	3,800	16,314	25.5	149
Arendaronnon	3,500	41,106	64.2	56
Tahontaenrat	1,800	11,931	18.6	97
Ataronchronon	3,000	33,819	52.8	51
Attignaouantan	8,300	83,973	131.2	64

In summary, then, the overall population density of Huronia before the 1630's was in the order of 62 people per square mile, using a culture area of 340 square miles and a population of 21,000. The population densities of individual tribal areas varied from a low of 52 people per square mile to 233 per square mile. In making this estimate the lowlands adjacent to the tribal areas were omitted. A narrower range of population densities was obtained when the soils of each tribal area were weighted according to a scale of preference. In this case the variation was between 51 and 149 people per square mile. The close relationship between population and the size and productivity of the tribal area is probably due to a fairly close adjustment to an agricultural resource base.

Chapter V

Features of Settlement

INTRODUCTION

Among geographers there is a surprising degree of unanimity as to what is included under a study of settlement. Broeck and Webb (1968:340), for example, define settlement in the following manner:

> The word settlement indicates to the geographer all man-made facilities resulting from the process of settling, including the establishments that shelter people and their possessions, the roads that connect, and the fences that part them.

A more complete definition is given by Kohn (1954:125):

> In general, settlement geography has to do with facilities men build in the process of occupying an area. These facilities are designed and grouped to serve specific purposes, and so carry functional meanings. Their exterior forms reflect architectural styles of the time and culture from which they spring. Their distribution produces discernible patterns in the landscape. Once created, they are apt to outlast both the function for which they were originally designed and the architectural fashions of their time. For these reasons they reflect changes in man's occupance of an area and are often the only existing landscape expressions of the past.

To demonstrate the degree of unanimity between geographers, anthropologists and archaeologists as to the content of settlement pattern analysis, the following statement by an anthropologist might serve as comparison to those of Kohn and Broeck:

> As I see it, this (the study of settlement) would include a description of (1) the nature of the individual domestic house type or types; (2) the spatial arrangement of these domestic house types with respect to one another within the village or community unit; (3) the relationship of domestic house types to other special architectural features, such as temples, palaces, ball courts, kivas, and so on; (4) the over-all

107

village or community plan; and (5) the spatial relationships of the villages or communities to one another over as large an area as is feasible. (Vogt 1956:174).

While there is a large degree of agreement between the disciplines as to the categories which should be considered in an analysis of settlement, their final objectives are somewhat different. Most geographers have been primarily interested in the spatial aspects of settlement as indicators of culture areas, culture change, economic patterns and environmental relations. Among anthropologists the emphasis has been somewhat different, in that settlement has also been used to derive inferences about social, political and religious organization (Vogt 1956:173-175; Willey and Phillips 1962:48-49; Trigger 1967b:151-152). Through the nature of their disciplines, the geographer ultimately describes human spatial organization and the anthropologist, human social organization. Since geography, anthropology and archaeology consider phenomena that result from human behavior, the seeming differences between these disciplines are actually more apparent than real. In the last analysis all of these disciplines look at man as the possessor of learned behavior, interacting with other men and his cultural and natural environment. Some of the relations between these disciplines have been summarized by Mikesell (1967).

One of the organizational problems that must be dealt with in most settlement studies, is whether subsistence systems should be discussed as an aspect of settlement or given separate treatment. This question becomes particularly crucial in any discussion of the relation of habitation units or agglomerations to the natural environment. That a dilemma should exist is quite natural because the actual settlements, the subsistence systems and the natural environment are interrelated. Some authors have tried to solve their dilemma by assuming that any one factor, usually technology or environment, acts as a determining agent on the rest.

For the sake of convenience and clarity, subsistence systems have been separated from settlement in this study. Under the general term "settlement" the author understands the general categories proposed by Kohn and Vogt, leaving subsistence economies to a later chapter. For the moment, environmental factors have only been considered in as much as they pertain to the actual selection of a village site, or the availability and nature of construction materials. Wider environmental relations will be considered under subsistence economies.

The only departure from the usual organization of a chapter on aspects of settlement is a discussion of the size, function and distribution of settlements after a consideration of the smallest unit of settlement, the dwelling, and before a discussion of the total village complex (morphology). The logic behind such an organization was an awareness that while the basic dwelling unit may have been similar for all types of settlements, the morphology of the village may have been different depending on the size and function of the villages. Conversely, it is difficult to consider the size of villages without first considering the basic dwelling unit. The most logical organization was therefore considered to be (1) placing the settlement into its natural setting; (2) a discussion of the basic habitation unit; (3) a consideration of the size, function and distribution of settlements; (4) the morphology of the settlement; and (5) the lines of communication between settlements. It is hoped, therefore, that this chapter is a description of "the facilities the Huron build in the process of occupying an area." The manner in which they exploit that area is left to the next chapter.

1. FACTORS INFLUENCING THE SELECTION OF PERMANENT VILLAGE SITES

a) Water Availability

To the Huron, the selection of a village site was anything but a haphazard affair. As a matter of fact, considerable care seems to have been exercised in regard to a choice of location. Each site had to have a combination of specific requirements among which water availability, soil type, defendability and surrounding vegetation seem to have been the most important. Of the early writers Sagard alludes to the concern the Huron had with picking a site:

> This [a site] they know very well how to choose, taking care that it shall be adjoining some good stream, on a spot slightly elevated and surrounded by a natural moat if possible. . . . (Sagard 1939:92).

There is no doubt that a permanent and readily-available water supply was of paramount importance. There is no known site in Huronia that is not immediately adjacent to a spring, creek or some other supply of water. Palisaded villages were usually placed on the edge of a stream bank, thus having the double advantage of being near water and on a slight slope for defence. In the case of unpalisaded villages the individual longhouses were scattered along the stream bank or in some cases around the head of a spring (for example, the Fournier site, Tay Township, Concession 3, lot 16, E. half; Russell 1967:2). In some cases even the larger villages seem to have been built around the head of a spring; at least Champlain reported this for an Onondaga village he attacked in 1615 (Champlain 3:70).

Proximity to a permanent water supply was, of course, mandatory because the Huron did not have the technology to dig wells or transport water over great distances. Water had to be carried in fragile earthenware or bark vessels. There is no evidence that it might have been stored in any quantities, except perhaps on the galleries of the palisade, to quench fires in case the village was attacked (Champlain 3:122; Sagard 1939:92).

b) Soil Preferences

The Huron's preference for certain soil conditions has already been noted (Table 1). In all 94.5 per cent of the 139 sites examined occur on well-drained soils ranging from gravels to silt loams. Together these soils comprise 79 per cent of Huronia. The soils preferred most were well-drained sandy loams, covering 40 per cent of Huronia and having 68.5 per cent of the sites. These were, of course, among the more fertile soils within the agricultural technological capabilities of the Hurons.

At the risk of belabouring the obvious, the data in Table 1 was tested by Chi-square (X^2) in order to determine that the coincidence of soil types to sites was not due to chance (Gregory 1963:151-157). A X^2 value of 31.5 was obtained which, with 12 degrees of freedom, yields a probability value of less than 0.01. On the basis of these relationships it seems that the frequency occurrence of village sites is not related to the frequency occurrence of the soil types. One must, therefore, conclude that soil type was a major factor which the Huron took into consideration when choosing a site. Such a high degree of soil selection, and an awareness of relative soil fertility within the range of soil possibilities, is not uncommon among shifting agriculturalists (Narr 1956:139; Gabel 1967:31; Stevens 1964:-267; Flannery, et al., 1967:448-449).

c) The Influence of Slope on Site Selection

The influence of slope on site selection is more difficult to evaluate. Judging from Sagard's brief statement, quoted at the beginning of this chapter, the Huron made an effort to locate their villages on sites that had reasonably good natural defences, such as a break-in-slope. Judging from the descriptions of Huron-Iroquois warfare, the success of an attack depended more on surprise than on a prolonged siege. One would therefore expect that a mere break-in-slope was not a major obstacle to the successful conquest of a village. A break-in-slope would have to be reinforced by a palisade in order to be really effective (Hunter 1901:66-67).

110

In his travels Champlain visited 18 villages, of which six were palisaded (Champlain 3:122). Brébeuf stated that of the twenty villages he saw ". . . some villages tolerably well fortified" (JR 10:51; 11:7). He goes on to say that in case of an attack those Huron who could retreated to the fortified villages; the others hid in the forest (JR 10:51). Sagard stated that as a rule the villages closest to the frontier were the best-fortified (Sagard 1939:92).

In his site surveys in Simcoe County, Hunter lists ten sites out of 75 in Medonte township and eight sites out of 69 in Oro township which he feels were chosen with defensive requirements in mind (Hunter 1901:67; Hunter 1902:159). Judging from field work done by the author in Medonte township, Hunter's figures for sites with obvious defensive advantages should be doubled. The overwhelming impression is, however, that sites occurred on breaks-in slope simply because they were placed beside a spring or creek which happened to issue along the recessional shorelines of glacial Lake Algonquin. The scarcity of sites on the gently rolling uplands away from the break-in-slope near the recessional shorelines is easily explainable by a lack of surface water on the uplands rather than a lack of defendable sites (Map 18). The absence of palisades at many otherwise defendable sites would tend to support this view.

In general, only the largest sites and especially those of the historic period seem to have been placed deliberately on defendable sites. Of these *Cahiagué* (Concession, 14, lot 10, Medonte Township), St. Joseph II (Concession 4, lot 12, Medonte), St. Louis (Concession 6, lot 2, Tay) and *Ossossane* (early 1630's) (Concession 7, lot 16, Tiny) are particularly good examples. From the historical descriptions we can infer that the following villages were palisaded: *Carhagouha* (Champlain 3:48), *Ossossane* (late 1630's) (JR 10:53), *Quieunonascaran* (Sagard 1939:156). St. Ignace II (JR 34:123), St. Jean Baptiste (JR 20:31-33), St. Joseph II (JR 39:239) and St. Louis (JR 34:125). These were without exception the largest and most important villages in Huronia. If the actual locations of these villages are correct, the site of each one seems to have natural defences developed to an unusually high degree; that is, breaks-in-slope occur on two or more sides of the village. This is not true for smaller village sites in Huronia, where a break-in-slope may occur on only one side of a village.

From this discussion, one might infer that a defensive position beside a break-in-slope was important in the locational requirements of the larger more important villages, and that in the majority of cases a position beside a break-in-slope simply meant that the site was located near a source of water.

111

It is interesting to note that among some of the New York Iroquois during the contact and historic period, a defendable position seems to have been of major importance (Parker 1916:490-491; Houghton 1916:-513; Ritchie 1965:317; Jameson 1909:140-157). This characteristic of the League Iroquois village sites may reflect the fact that they were embroiled in wars with every Indian group on the entire perimeter of their frontier. As early as 1615 Champlain remarked that on the whole, the League Iroquois knew how to choose and build better defences than the Huron (Champlain 3:70). This observation was echoed by several writers after him (Hennepin 1903,1:116; Morgan 1962:313-315).

d) Vegetation Preferences

Although certain species of trees were preferred as building materials and firewood, macro-vegetational patterns seem to have no obvious relation to the distribution of sites (Map 20). Any seeming relationships can be explained in terms of soil type and drainage conditions. The preferred species were: cedar, birch, elm, pine, and oak. Of these, the first three are widely distributed in Huronia, so that almost any site would have access to them. Cedar and elm bark were a major construction material in the building of longhouses. Both are ubiquitous throughout the area; cedar in the swamps and elm on the moister, heavier soils. Birch bark was probably used in small quantities for the construction of utensils and canoes, and can easily be transported over some distance if it is scarce near a site. Pine, a preferred source for resin, firewood and palisades, is more common in the western end of the Huronia; but there does not seem to be any obvious relationship between the location of sites and occurrence of stands of pine. In general, the areas of pure pine in Tiny Township seem to have been avoided; but this can be related to the coarse sands, gravels, and lack of surface water in the area. As stated earlier, these physical conditions are probably responsible for the pine stands.

Oak is regionally concentrated in the western end of Huronia (Map 20). Similar to pine, this tree can exist on the droughtier sands and gravels in Tiny Township. Apart from its acorns, oaks did not have any particular value to the Huron. Acorns seem to have been collected and consumed only in times of dire famine (JR 27:65; 34:197, 215, 225; 35:21, 23, 99). In 1649, for example, the refugee group on Christian Island scattered in the forest to collect acorns. Before winter they had put in a supply of 500-600 bushels (JR 35:99). The only references to acorns list them as a famine food. It is therefore doubtful if areas of oak were especially sought as village sites.

Some sites in Huronia were placed adjacent to small huckleberry marshes.[1] While huckleberries and other fruits were part of the diet obtained by gathering, it hardly seems possible that the presence of a berry site was a major site requirement. In all likelihood, such sites became a factor if all the other site prerequisites were present. The possibility that these small marshes were ponds during Huron times, cannot be discounted.

There is a strong possibility that far more important than any single species or association of species, was the actual size composition of a particular timber stand. Huron technology in coping with large trees was limited, and the nature of the construction of their villages demanded enormous quantities of logs under ten inches in diameter. It is therefore postulated that areas of secondary growth were sought. This hypothesis will be elaborated later in this chapter.

e) Proximity to Navigable Waterways

In his study of Iroquois sites, Houghton (1916:513) stated that navigable streams and lakes were generally avoided during the contact and early historic period; presumably because these provided easy avenues of attack. Parker (1920, Pt. 1:122) concurs with some of Houghton's observations and adds that most villages prior to the historic period were two to twenty miles inland from Lake Ontario on hilltops, but often within easy reach of navigable streams. If sites near navigable waterways were generally avoided among the New York Iroquois, this does not seem to have been the case among the Huron during the same period. Where sites occur near lakes and streams, they were often as close as preferred soil type and drainage conditions permitted. Since Huronia is dissected by a number of navigable streams (to canoes), and almost surrounded by water, it would be difficult to avoid placing a village within an easy walk of a navigable waterway. As a matter of fact, no Huron village, no matter where it was located, was more than a five-hours' walk from either of the large lakes.

Prior to the historic period, a location near a navigable body of water does not seem to have been of too much importance (Map 18). Fishing, clam-gathering, and trading were seasonal affairs carried on by small groups of people. As trade with the French increased, the location of a village near a stream or lake may have become more important. At any rate, during the historic period most of the villages were as close to navigable water as soil resources permitted (Map 17). At the same time,

1. See, for example: Hunter's No. 38 and 41, Tay, Lot 5, Conc. 10 and Lot 3, Conc. 9 (1899:80); Hunter's No. 10 and 11, Medonte, Lot 17, Conc. 3 and Lot 16, Conc. 3 (1901:74).

it must be pointed out that in locating on the bluffs overlooking navigable waterways, none of the other site requirements were sacrificed. In view of the Huron dependence on agriculture, a location near a lakeshore or large stream, while desirable, could only have been of secondary importance.

f) Summary

The two most important factors in selecting a site were water availability and soils. It would be pointless to try to separate these into more and less important. No village could function without either of these resources. Other factors such as natural defences, types of vegetation and proximity to navigable waterways seem to have been of secondary importance, and in some cases of no importance at all. For reasons stated in previous chapters, it is likely that areas of immature tree growth may have been preferred over mature stands. It is entirely possible that some socio-religious factors may have been operative in site selection; if this was so, there is no record of it.

During the historic period a preferred village location seems to have been on a bluff, beside a spring, overlooking a navigable waterway, with a large hinterland of arable soils.

2. THE VILLAGE

a) The Longhouse

Any discussion of the Huron village must by necessity begin with a description of the basic dwelling unit, the longhouse. The importance of the longhouse to an understanding of the Iroquoian tribes has been pointed out by almost every writer on the subject (Morgan 1962:313-319; Morgan 1965:64-67, 124-133; Fenton 1951; Trigger 1963a; Richards 1967). Not only was the size and importance of a village described in terms of the number of longhouses, but the longhouse was also a reflection of the size of the extended families and the physical manifestations of the social system. Emerson (1961b:62) calls the longhouse the

> . . . key to an understanding of Iroquois culture. It was much more than just a dwelling place – it was the basis of the Iroquois philosophy of life – and the concept of the longhouse underlay every aspect of Iroquois social, political and military life.

This discussion will begin with the physical nature of the longhouse.

i) The size of the longhouse. Since the longhouse varied in length according to the number of hearths located in it, and since the number of hearths was a reflection of the number of nuclear families, therefore the longhouse varied in length according to the size of an extended family group (Morgan 1962:315-316; 1965:64-65; Johnston 1964:24-25; JR 16:243; 35:87; Sagard 1939:94). Champlain (3:123) described the longhouse as being "twenty-five to thirty fathoms long more or less, and six wide. . . ." Sagard (1939:93) concurs with this description. Among the Jesuits du Peron wrote that ". . . some of them (the longhouses) are 70 feet long. . ." (JR 15:153). Brébeuf (JR 8:107) was more specific, stating that:

> there are cabins or arbours of various sizes, some two brasses in length, others of ten, others of twenty, of thirty, or forty; the usual width is about four brasses, their height is about the same.

Bressani (JR 38:247) gives exactly the same description as Brébeuf.

Translated into modern measurements, this would mean that the Huron longhouses varied in length from 12 to 220 feet, with a width and height of 20 to 33 feet (Table 7). The average width would therefore have been in the order of 27 feet and the length about 100 feet.

Among the New York Iroquois, longhouses were recorded with similar dimensions to the Huron ones. In 1634 an anonymous Dutch trader placed the average width of a longhouse at 22 to 23 feet and their length ranging from ten to 100 paces (*ca.* 25-250 feet), with an average of about sixty paces (*ca.* 150 feet) (Jameson 1909:141-144). Among the Seneca in 1677, Greenhalgh stated that the average longhouse was fifty to sixty feet long (O'Callaghan 1849:13), while Morgan (1962:315) felt that the usual length was 50 to 130 feet.

Archaeological work shows that the size of longhouses did indeed vary considerably. Emerson places the average longhouse at about 120 by 30 feet, varying all the way up to 180 feet and more in length (Emerson 1961b:62-63). Jury, in his investigations at St. Louis, found that the average size of the longhouses was about 50 by 20 feet (Jury and Jury 1955:-55). Since other aspects of St. Louis show a strong French influence, the longhouses may not be typical of the contract period. At the supposed site of St. Ignace II, Jury found that the average longhouse was about 90 by 30 feet (Jury and Fox 1947:64-69). At the late prehistoric sites of McKenzie and Hardrock, Emerson excavated two longhouses 174 by 28 feet and 150 by 24 feet respectively (Emerson 1954:163, 187). Going back earlier in time, at the Lalonde period Forget site, Jury excavated twelve longhouses averaging about 28 to 100 feet, while the Lalonde Copeland site furnished four longhouses, 88 by 24 feet, 45 by 20 feet, 42 by 30 feet and

Table 7

Contemporary Size Estimates of
Huron Longhouses

Author	Length (feet)	Width (feet)	Height (feet)
Champlain	± 125-160	30-33	?
Sagard	± 125-160	30-33	?
Du Peron	± 70	?	?
Brébeuf	12-50-110-165-220	20-24	20-24
Bressani	12-50-110-165-220	20-24	20-24

one very unusual one measuring 90 by 55 feet (Channen and Clarke 1965:5-10). Personal observations at the excavations of *Cahiagué*, confirmed by Dr. J. N. Emerson, would place the average *Cahiagué* longhouses at about 90 by 25 feet. Longhouses similar to the Huron ones in size have also been excavated on New York Iroquois sites (Ritchie 1965; Funk 1967:8184; Hayes 1967:91-97; Tuck 1967:75-79; White 1967:-85-89).

Taking all things into consideration, the archaeological excavations validate the ethnohistoric accounts to a considerable degree. Huron longhouses varied in length from about 30 to over 180 feet with a fairly constant width of about 25 to 30 feet. An average size of 80 by 28 feet does not seem unreasonable. New York Iroquois longhouses were about the same average size, but on occasions seem to have reached greater length. The fairly uniform width and height of all the houses is probably related to the limitations of the construction materials and the methods of construction.

ii) Interior arrangement of the longhouse. The information on the interior of the longhouses gained from the ethnohistoric accounts and archaeology is also fairly consistent. According to the ethnohistoric accounts the hearths were set in a passageway some ten to twelve feet in width running down the centre of the longhouse (Champlain 3:123; Sagard 1939:94). Storage areas or vestibules were placed at both ends of the longhouse (Champlain 3:123; Sagard 1939:95; JR 8:107) with additional storage facilities under long sleeping platforms which ran along both sides of the lodge (Sagard 1939:95; JR 8:107-109). The average longhouse seemed to have three or four fires with two families to a fire, one at either side of the central passage (Sagard 1939:94; JR 15:153; 16:243; 35:87), although longhouses with up to twelve fires were reported (Champlain 3:123-124; Sagard 1939:94).

One writer, Jérôme Lalemant, mentioned that the fires were usually placed two or three paces apart (five to eight feet) (JR 17:177). Among the New York Iroquois Lafitau described each fire as adding about 20 to 25 feet to a longhouse (Johnston 1964:24). A Dutch trader among the Mohawk wrote that, on the average, there was about 17 to 20 feet of space per fire (Jameson 1909:144). Morgan (1962:315) felt that this distance was more like ten to twelve feet. In view of the fact that the longhouse underwent great changes in the 18th and 19th centuries, Morgan's figures probably do not reflect the early 17th-century longhouse.

Archaeological information on the interior of Huron longhouses is meagre. Except for two plans (Emerson and Russell 1965), none of the *Cahiagué* work has been published. The results from Jury's Forget excavation are unpublished and his work at the supposed site of St. Ignace II (Jury and Fox 1947) and St. Louis (Jury and Jury 1955) is too unreliable to be of much use. Some information is available from the Hardrock and McKenzie sites (Emerson 1954) and the 16th-century Copeland site (Channen and Clarke 1965).

Judging from the longhouses excavated so far, two types of fireplaces were present. At *Cahiagué,* Hardrock, McKenzie and two of the four Copeland structures, large oval hearths were located down the central passage of each longhouse. These hearths varied from seven to ten feet in length and three to four feet in width. Their spacing down the centre of the longhouse was about five to ten feet apart. The usual deposit in these hearths is a light grey ash, although patches of bright orange and red fused sand and ashes are often found within the hearth area. Besides these central hearths, virtually every longhouse had a large number of smaller fireplaces scattered along each side of the longhouse. In the case of two of the four Copeland structures (which are very unusual in many respects), the central hearths were absent. Instead, smaller fireplaces were placed at random throughout the longhouse.

The large central hearths were probably the fireplaces reported by the early travellers. Taking their length and spacing into account, each family would, on the average, have fifteen linear feet of living space (ranges from 12 to 20 feet). This average comes very close to the estimates made by Lafitau and other travellers. The linear frontage along the central hearth would probably vary with the size of the family. The depth of the living space from the edge of the fire to the longhouse walls averaged about eleven feet. Thus each family could expect to have about 180 square feet of living space (ranges from 140 to 240 square feet). Excavations at the New York Iroquois sites show that the spacing of fireplaces and the amount of living space were in every respect similar. At an average of six people per family, this would give each individual about 30 square feet. Since the longhouse was really used only during the winter and at night, 30 square feet per person seems to be adequate.

In interpreting the two types of fireplaces, the following theory might be offered. The large central hearths were mainly used during the winter. Their principal function was to keep the longhouses warm. The smaller fireplaces and patches of fused ash and orange sand within the large hearths were the cooking fires. Judging from the number and spacing of the small fireplaces, each nuclear family cooked for itself and had at least one to two of these fires within their own living area. During the winter the central hearths provided heat. In addition to the smaller fires, during mealtimes the large fire was probably allowed to die down and concentrated at smaller areas within the large hearth for cooking purposes. While the large hearth was burning, the fire was kept within the hearth area by large logs (Sagard 1939:94).

Most of the early travellers report that each side of the longhouse was lined with sleeping platforms (Sagard 1939:93; Champlain 3:123; JR 17:-203). These platforms were wide enough to sleep on and raised about four to five feet above the ground. In the summer the platforms were used for sleeping and in order to escape the dust and fleas on the longhouse floors (Champlain 3:123; Sagard 1939:93; JR 10:91). In the winter everyone slept huddled together on floormats and sheets of bark in front of the fire. The space beneath the platforms was used to store dry wood (JR 8:109).

There is no direct evidence that the interior of Huron lodges was divided into family compartments such as the ones described by Lafitau (Johnston 1964:25) and Morgan (1962:315; 1965:126). Archaeologically, both sidewall sleeping platforms and family cubicles have been described for the New York Iroquois (Ritchie 1965:308; Funk 1967:83; Hayes 1967:93). For the Huron such evidence is as yet inconclusive (Emerson, 1961b:64; Noble 1969:20). If these compartments were constructed of sheets of bark or skins suspended from a few posts, conclusive evidence as to their existence may be very difficult to determine.

The ethnohistoric sources mention that large storage areas were located at each end of the longhouse (Champlain 3:123; Sagard 1939:94-95; JR 8:107; Johnston 1964:26). According to Sagard (1939:94-95) and Lafitau (Johnston 1964:26) two types of storage areas were present; an interior "lobby" or anteroom used for storing casks of corn, and an exterior vestibule which served as a wood shed. The exterior vestibule could be closed in the winter with sheets of bark. These storage areas have been excavated at the Copeland site (Channen and Clark 1965), at Hardrock (Emerson 1954:201-202) and at *Cahiagué* (Emerson 1961b:63; Emerson and Russell 1965:Fig. II-III). Most often, however, storage areas were only present at the end of the longhouse. On the average, the interior storage area was about five to fifteen feet in length and extended the width of the longhouse. Similar storage areas have been found in New York Iroquois longhouses (Hayes 1967:93; White 1967:87).

The most serious storage problem was the yearly corn harvest. Not only did the Huron have to store large quantities of corn, but the corn had to be kept dry, away from mice and other vermin and as safe from fires as possible. In most cases, the larger part of the harvest seems to have been stored in large bark casks in the aforementioned storage areas. During harvest the corn was taken from the fields, tied in bundles and hung on racks along the interior of the longhouse walls to dry. When the corn was dry, it was shelled and put into the casks (Sagard 1939:104). Brébeuf reported that some of these corn bins held 50 to 60 bushels of shelled corn (JR 8:95). Since these bins were exposed to fire and mice, part of the harvest was stored in underground storage pits (Sagard 1939:95). Archaeologically, these storage pits are one of the most common features associated with Iroquoian longhouses. Most often they occur scattered almost at random along both sides of the longhouse. At times they are also found outside the longhouse (Funk 1967:83). Their number per longhouse varies from a few to several hundred, and on the average they are about three feet in diameter and four feet deep. The interior of the pits was lined with bark and grass. The enormous number of pits associated with some longhouses probably means that in some cases most of the corn may have been stored in subsurface pits. In other cases, the large bark casks described in the ethnohistoric sources were used, as well as storage pits. A likely explanation for the pits, at least in the cases where they are found in conjunction with corn bins and storage areas, is that this is where seed corn was stored. Fires were a serious problem and sometimes contributed to famine (JR 8:93, 105; 10:35; 14:43-45). In instances where fires destroyed a longhouse or group of houses, the families of the surviving longhouses would contribute corn to their unfortunate neighbours (JR 14:45; 8:95); but in spite of this the protection of seed corn was a matter of great importance.

One further method of providing storage facilities was to suspend two poles along the middle of the longhouse from which pots could be hung (Champlain 3:123; Sagard 1939:95). Apparently this was one of the few ways in which clothing and food could be kept safe from mice.

Most varieties of fish were dried or smoked and stored in bark casks within the longhouse. Whitefish were sometimes reduced to oil and stored in earthenware vessels (Sagard 1939:186). One variety of fish, the *Eincha-ton*,[1] was not cleaned, but simply strung onto cords and suspended from the roof of the longhouse (Sagard 1939:95).

iii) Construction of the longhouse. To all the European visitors the Huron longhouses reminded them of "arcades," "bowers," or "garden arbours" (Champlain 3:122-123; Sagard 1939:93; JR 8:105; 15:153); *i.e.,* a long rectangular structure with a vaulted roof (Figures 3 and 4). The exact construction of the longhouse can be inferred from archaeological excavations and the ethnohistoric sources. The outer walls of structure were usually made up of a double row of staggered saplings some two to four inches in diameter (Figure 4). The saplings in each row were set about 18 inches apart and were driven some two to two and a half feet into the ground (Emerson 1954:201; Emerson 1961b:63; Emerson and Russell 1965:Fig. II-III). The two rows composing the outer walls were then bent towards each other and tied together along the top (Kinietz 1940:41-42). Sheets of bark were fastened between the poles of the frame in such a way that they overlapped like roofing tiles (Champlain 3:123; Sagard 1939:93; JR 8:105; Johnston 1964:25). The preferred construction material seems to have been cedar bark, although elm, ash, fir and spruce bark were also used (JR 8:105; 14:43-45). Among the New York Iroquois, elm bark appears to have been the usual construction material (Johnston 1964:25). To give the structure added strength, saplings running the length of the lodge were lashed to the exterior frame, bark siding and roofing. The interior of the longhouse was kept rigid by large central support posts slightly offset from the centre line (Emerson 1961b:64). Doors were placed on either or both ends of the longhouse, or on the sides near the ends (Emerson 1954:164, 202; 1961b:63). The only other openings in the structure were a few holes in the roof to permit smoke to escape (Champlain 3:124; Sagard 1939:95; JR 8:107). All openings could be closed by sheets of bark or skins (Sagard 1939:81; Johnston 1964:25, 26). Although the Huron longhouses appear to have been constructed with a vaulted roof, the majority of longhouses in at least one Mohawk village in 1634 were reported as having flat roofs (Jameson 1909:141).

Judging from Lafitau's excellent description of the Iroquois longhouse, the best time for building was in the spring when the sap was rising in the

1. From the description given the *Einchaton* (*Leinchaton*) could be the catfish or bullhead. Sagard mentioned that it was about a foot and a half long, and resembled the French *barbeau* (barbel).

trees and bark and boughs were pliable (Johnston 1964:25). In Huronia we know of at least one village undergoing spring construction (JR 8:101). In January 1616 Champlain came across two villages under construction in the Petun country, but these may have been villages not finished the previous year (Champlain 3:96). Late summer and fall were apparently poor construction periods because bark stripped from the trees at that time tended to be dry and crack easily (Sagard 1939:81).

According to Sagard (1939:79), the erection of the longhouses seems to have been semi-communal affairs, much like the "bees" among the 18th and 19th-century settlers of Ontario. The decision to help a family, the amount of help and probably the place where the longhouse was to be erected, was decided by the village council. The decision was then advertised throughout the village by a "town-crier" so that all able-bodied men could attend. Communal help was apparently extended to a point where it was felt that the family for whom the longhouse was intended, could finish it themselves. The same kind of service was given to the Récollets at *Quieunonascaran* (Sagard 1939:79) and later to the Jesuits at *Ihonatiria* (JR 8:107) and *Ossossane* (JR 12:257). In the case of the Jesuits their Huron help was given presents, while the Récollets were asked to plead with their God to make the rain stop when it was threatening the harvest. In both cases then, favours were expected. From the difficulties encountered by the Récollets with some of their help, one would gather that aid in erecting a longhouse was usually extended primarily to relatives (Sagard 1939:-78).

iv) Functional differences between longhouses. The primary function of all longhouses was to serve as residence for its inhabitants. In addition to this function, at least two structures were singled out for additional functions.

The longhouse of the principal village chief was built ". . . much larger than the others, sometimes making it as much as twenty-five or thirty brasses (125-180 feet) in length" (JR 10:181). This structure served as dwelling of the chief and meeting place of the village and other councils (JR 10:233; 13:59; Sagard 1939:149). The same longhouse may have been used as a place of village entertainment such as feasts and dances (Sagard 1939:115).

A second large longhouse was set aside as residence for the principal war chief. Here all war councils were held (JR 13:59) and prisoners brought back for torture (JR 13:59; 15:173).

It is doubtful if every village had such structures. Some sources state that only the "principal villages," perhaps tribal "capitals," had multi-functional longhouses (JR 10:231). Archaeologically, except on the basis of unusual size, such longhouses may be difficult to define. Judging from a few meagre descriptions, the interior of the chief's houses differed little from any other longhouse (JR 13:61). As yet, no unusual differences have been noted in the interior arrangement of Huron longhouses which would enable one to classify some of the council houses.

v) The quality of life in the longhouse. To most of the Europeans in Huronia, life in a longhouse was an unpleasant experience that took some time getting used to, or had to be endured stoically. The houses were dusty and filled with smoke (Champlain 3:124; Sagard 1939:94-95; JR 10:91-93). The smoke problem was so serious that many Huron suffered from serious eye troubles. Besides smoke, the interior of the longhouses smelled of rotting fish and urine (Sagard 1939:93, 95, 227). The general hustle and bustle in the cabins and an almost complete lack of privacy made religious instruction difficult: a reason why the Jesuits later insisted on having separate cabins, and a church if possible, outside the village proper (JR 10:79; 17:197). One of the greatest complaints was that the Huron, their belongings and the longhouses were infested with fleas (Champlain 3:123; Sagard 1939:93, 227-228; JR 10:91; Johnston 1964:27). Several writers mentioned that unlike some of the other inconveniences, this was one also keenly felt by the Huron. During the summer months mosquitoes and "sandflies" (probably black flies) were an added problem. Mice abounded in and about the longhouses, and were difficult to keep away from stored food and clothing (Champlain 3:123; Sagard 1939:227). An added source of annoyment was the freedom exercized by children and their seeming lack of respect for the Jesuits and their own elders. In the winter most of these problems were compounded because all activity was concentrated in the longhouses. Writing in 1639, Jérôme Lalemant stated that to some Jesuits, martyrdom by a hatchet blow might be preferable to spending the rest of their lives among the Huron. His description of life in a Huron longhouse is worth quoting because it is an excellent example of what a highly-educated and refined European thought he had to put up with (JR 17:13-15):

> If you go to visit them in their cabins – and you must go there oftener than once a day, if you would perform your duty as you ought, – you will find there a miniature picture of Hell, – seeing nothing ordinarily but fire and smoke, and on every side naked bodies, black and half roasted, mingled pell-mell with the dogs, which are held as dear as the children of the house, and share the beds, plates and food of their masters. Everything is in a cloud of dust, and, if you go within, you will not reach the end of the cabin before you are completely be-fouled with soot, filth and dirt.

Other descriptions of this sort can be found in Brébeuf's "Important Advice For Those Whom It Shall Please God To Call To New France, And Especially To The Country Of The Hurons" (JR 10:87-115).

As "outsiders" or at best "participant observers," the Jesuits and others were of course primarily aware of the personal discomforts of longhouse life. The Huron probably saw matters in quite a different light; or, as Champlain put it, their life may seem wretched to a European but the Huron seemed happy "and believe that none more excellent can be found" (Champlain 3:125).

In actual fact, communal life with one's nearest kin in a longhouse offered social and economic benefits that an outsider could only be dimly aware of. These benefits derived mainly from the fact that the members of the longhouse were completely interdependent. Furthermore, the system of marriages outside the kin group spread this interdependency to other kin groups, tying longhouses and ultimately villages together. The longhouse was therefore the physical symbol of social and psychological security, not only at the family level, but ultimately at the village and tribal level. No one needed to feel that he was alone in his house, village or tribe, as long as he met his obligations and responsibilities to his relations and his neighbours.

Communal longhouse life also had obvious economic benefits. Since the extended families of each longhouse shared the larger part of their produce, the aged and the incapacitated were taken care of. Time and again, the missionaries stated that as long as some corn was in the village, no one went hungry (Sagard 1939: 88-89). A corollary to communal life and food sharing is the sharing of economic risk. A potential disaster such as a crop failure in one part of the village fields was not as severe to any one family as it might have been if the bulk of the corn produce was not shared. One further economic advantage of longhouse life was that it permitted a greater diversity of activities. No nuclear family could by itself undertake the tasks of agriculture, trading, hunting, gathering and warfare. Job sharing at the family level, and for some activities at the village level, made diversity possible.

vi) Summary and discussion. The average longhouse was about 80 by 28 feet (2,200 square feet) in size. It contained about three central fire places with two families to a fire. Each family had roughly 180 square feet of living space, leaving 45 per cent of the longhouse in storage areas and about 5 per cent taken up by hearths. On the basis of three hearths per longhouse, two families per hearth and six members per family, the average longhouse could have contained about 36 people. Thus each person had about 30 square feet of living space and 45 square feet of longhouse floor area.

In his study on the relation between floor area and settlement population, Naroll demonstrates that an allometric relationship exists between these two traits among prehistoric societies. Taking 18 societies, a loglog regression was run and tested at a .0005 level of significance. The coefficient of correlation was in the order of 0.88 (Naroll, 1962:588). On the basis of the regression, Naroll concludes that a relationship of one person per ten square meters of floor area is the expected. Unfortunately, Naroll made no distinction between hunters and gatherers, pastoralists, specialized gatherers and agriculturalists. His ratios might have been slightly different if societies at various socioeconomic levels and in different environmental areas had been treated separately. Naroll's ratio for the Iroquois (one person to four square meters of floor area) was taken from Morgan (1962:315-319) and probably represents the Iroquois in the 18th century. On the basis of the preceding discussion an average of one person to six square meters of floor area seems to have been common for the Huron. This ratio is well within the range of deviations on Naroll's scattergram (Naroll 1962:588, Fig. 1), demonstrating that a ratio of one Huron to 45 square feet of longhouse is a valid estimate in the light of other societies.

In social terms the longhouse represented the physical manifestation of the primary social and economic unit. It was at this level and in these surroundings that the Huron values of family solidarity, economic cooperation and rule by the mutual agreement of adults found their basic expression. The longhouse was in many ways a miniature village because the values of the longhouse were projected to the village level through kinship ties and the necessity for economic and social cooperation. Ultimately the ties binding longhouse to village passed beyond the village level to other villages at the tribal level. It is therefore no accident that the decision-making process at the village and tribal levels were in a sense a reflection of longhouse rules and values. The longhouse was, in fact, a highly sophisticated reflection of Huron cultural values.

To Europeans, whose value system placed a premium on the nuclear family, a high degree of privacy, personal comfort, cleanliness and orderliness, life in a Huron longhouse must have seemed chaotic and almost unbearable. Yet, in spite of these cultural differences and the obvious repugnance the missionaries felt towards many Huron cultural values, they recognized and commented on such values as family solidarity and charity towards one's neighbours, both of which the Huron possessed to a high degree.

b) The Size, Function and Distribution of Settlements

i) The size of settlements. Beyond the longhouse, the basic unit of settlement was the village. Just as the longhouse was the physical expression of the extended family, so was the village the expression of a number of closely co-operating lineages. In sociological terms the Huron village is a good example of Murdock's definition of "community," namely " . . . the maximal group of persons who normally reside together in face-to-face association" (Murdock 1949:79). The village was a place where:

> Every member is ordinarily acquainted more or less intimately with every other member, and has learned through association to adapt his behavior to that of each of his fellows, so that the group is bound together by a complex network of interpersonal relationships. (Murdock 1949:82).

Spatially, the Huron village can be defined as a cluster of longhouses which in some cases were surrounded by a palisade. Since Huron villages were usually some distance from each other due to the intervening agricultural lands and forests, there is little difficulty in defining the extent of a single village. In practical terms, a village may be delimited by the distribution of its garbage dumps (middens), which were piled against, or just beyond, the palisades; or, if palisades were absent, just beyond the longhouses. It is in this manner that the extent of most of the known Huron villages have been defined.

According to the ethnohistoric sources, Huron settlements varied in size from what were loosely described as collections of "poor hovels" (*pauvres bicoques*) (JR 5:258) and "villages" (*village*), to "large villages" or "small towns" (*bourgade*) (JR 19:126), and finally "towns" (*bourg* or *ville*) (JR 19:126; Sagard 1939:319). Most often the term "village" was used; sometimes preceded by the words "large" (*grand*) or "small" (*petit*). Although these terms are not very specific, they do point out the fact that Huron villages varied somewhat in size.

The usual practice of early travellers was to give the size of a village in terms of the number of longhouses in it. The largest of the Huron villages were said to have contained " . . . fifty, sixty and one hundred cabins . . . " (JR 10:210); although Champlain relates that one village, *Cahiagué*, had " . . . two hundred fairly large lodges . . . " (Champlain 3:49). Excavations have shown that *Cahiagué* was a double village composed of five and 9.5 acre segments (Cruickshank and Heidenreich 1969:39). Future excavations will probably show that two hundred longhouses was an exaggeration. During the Jesuit period St. Joseph II was the largest village with about 80 lodges (JR 15:153). Only one known village exceeded St. Joseph II in size, and that was the ill-fated refugee village on Christian Island, consisting of slightly more than 100 lodges (JR 35:87). The circumstances under which this village was created and the short term of its existence (1649-1650) would hardly allow one to call this a typical large village. Population estimates for these villages were discussed previously, none of the ethnohistoric accounts list any areal measurements for the Huron villages.

More is known about the size of villages among the New York Iroquois. Table 8 summarizes several of these accounts. Only travellers' descriptions of roughly the Huron period were consulted here. It was felt that the 1677 figures by Greenhalgh were close enough in time to be indicative of the pre-1650 period.

Three conclusions may be drawn from these figures: a) village sizes varied between members of the Iroquois Confederacy, Mohawk villages being on the average smaller; b) villages rarely exceeded 100 longhouses; c) New York Iroquois villages lie within the size range of Huron villages.

Judging from documented site surveys of 47 Huron villages, the average Huron village covered some four to six acres (Figure 5). Occasionally a village was as large as eight or ten acres; and, at least on two occasions, as large as fifteen acres. Surface finds in Huronia and adjacent areas indicate that some "villages" were smaller than one acre. These may have been isolated cabins or groups of longhouses used during the summer months by the women and children who tended fields too far removed from the main village for daily travel (JR 20:39). It is interesting to note that Neutral villages were roughly in the same size range as the Huron ones. Most Neutral contact sites rarely attained ten acres, five to eight acres appeared to have been common (Noble: private communication, March 12, 1969). In spite of the data compiled in Figure 5 the average Huron village may have been somewhat smaller than five acres. A figure of four acres is probably more meaningful. Most of the sites included in the surveys are well-known sites to archaeologists and farmers because they captured local interest. The impression gained from Hunter's surveys (Hunter 1898; 1899; 1901; 1902; 1903; 1906; 1911) and field work by the author, is that many small sites have been obliterated by farming. The data presented in Figure 5 may, therefore, be slightly biased in favour of the larger sites; and an average of four acres per site seems more reasonable.

The field surveys also indicate that the size difference between pre-contact and contact sites is only slight. Except for a few very large contact sites such as St. Joseph II, there is no size difference at all. This would

126

Table 8

Size of New York Iroquois Villages
Observed by Early Travellers

Tribe	Name of Village	Date of Observation	Size in No. of Longhouses	Palisades	Authority
Mohawk	Onekagoncka	1634	36	?	Jameson 1909: 140
Mohawk	Canowarode	1634	6	?	Jameson 1909: 141
Mohawk	Schatsyerosy	1634	12	?	Jameson 1909: 142
Mohawk	Canagere	1634	16	No	Jameson 1909: 143
Mohawk	Schanidisse	1634	32	?	Jameson 1909: 144
Mohawk	Osquage	1634	9	?	Jameson 1909: 144
Mohawk	Te-nontoge	1634	55	Yes	Jameson 1909: 145
Mohawk	Cahaniaga	1677	24	Yes	O'Callaghan 1849: 11
Mohawk	Canagora	1677	16	Yes	O'Callaghan 1849: 11
Mohawk	Canajorha	1677	16	Yes	O'Callaghan 1849: 11
Mohawk	Tionondogue	1677	30	Yes	O'Callaghan 1849: 12
Mohawk	?	1677	10	No	O'Callaghan 1849: 12
Oneida	Sinneken	1634	66	Yes	Jameson 1909: 149
Oneida	?	1677	100	Yes	O'Callaghan 1849: 12
Onondaga	?	1677	140	No	O'Callaghan 1849: 12
Onondaga	?	1677	24	No	O'Callaghan 1849: 12
Seneca	Canagorah	1677	150	No	O'Callaghan 1849: 13
Seneca	Tiotohattan	1677	120	No	O'Callaghan 1849: 13
Seneca	Canoenada	1677	30	No	O'Callaghan 1849: 13
Seneca	Keint-he	1677	24	No	O'Callaghan 1849: 13

strongly suggest that economic efficiency and social complexity did not increase enough during contact times to affect village size except in a very few cases. Indeed, as will be pointed out later in this chapter, large villages, even during contact times, tended to be unstable and to break up in smaller units.

A further impression gained from the field surveys is that there were some differences in village size between the tribal areas. On the whole, the *Attignaouantan* and *Arendaronnon* villages were smaller than those of the *Ataronchronon, Tahontaenrat* and *Attingneenongnahac*. Some archaeologists have theorized that this size difference may be due to different social conditions between these tribes.[1] There is as yet no evidence that social conditions between the tribes were different but a good case can be made that some villages had more stable social conditions than others. In other words, there may have been village differences, but not tribal ones. Another factor permitting larger villages in some areas may be soil conditions. There are no sites larger than five acres in size on any soil type other than the more fertile sandy loams. Since the occupied areas of the *Ataronchronon*, *Tahontaenrat* and *Attingneenongnahac* are almost totally composed of the more desirable soils, one would think that these areas offer a greater opportunity for the development of larger villages.

In view of the fact that few villages have been excavated, very little can be said about the average number of longhouses per acre. Some of the sites listed in Table 9 have been excavated, the others are known sites whose extent and number of longhouses have been reliably described. Based on this small sample, the average village contained only about five to six longhouses to the acre (Figure 6). A high coefficient of correlation of 0.96 was obtained from this small sample, which is significant at the 0.1 per cent level using Student's "t" test (Figure 6). If five to six longhouses per acre is a reasonable estimate, and the average longhouse covered 2,200 square feet (80 × 28 feet), then only about 25 per cent to 30 per cent of a village area was taken up by longhouses. As a matter of fact in the three excavated villages the longhouses took up 25 per cent to 29 per cent of the village areas. On this basis it is possible that village population densities were in the order of 180 to 220 people per acre, and that each person had about 160 square feet of village space in addition to his 45 square feet of longhouse floor area. This amount of living space seems to be adequate to permit a smooth functioning of Huron social and economic conditions.

It would be interesting to see whether any differences in house density existed between unpalisaded and palisaded villages. Unfortunately, there is not sufficient data to allow such comparisons. Except for the two largest villages in the sample (Table 9), all the others were palisaded. One might reason that palisaded villages were more tightly built-up in order to conserve the labour and construction material that went into the palisade. However, Huron social interaction demanded fairly close proximity of all longhouses within a village. It is, therefore, likely that the difference in house density between villages was not too great, whether they were palisaded or not.

1. This hypothesis was presented by A. Tyyska and W. Hurley at the second annual meeting of the Canadian Archaeological Association, March 14 to 16, 1969.

Table 9

The Number of Longhouses Per Site

Tribe	Name Village	No. of Longhouses	Size of Site (acres)	Longhouses per acre	Excavated
Huron	MacKenzie	17	4.5	4	yes
	Forget	12	1.8	5	yes
	Hunter's #36	29	5.7	5	yes
	St. Joseph II	80	15	6	no
	Ossossane	40	5	8	no
Oneida	Sinneken	66	9.5	7	no
Seneca	Canagorah	150	20	7.5	no
	Tiotohattan	120	30	4	no

Of necessity, this discussion was somewhat hypothetical. Only years of archaeological research will allow one to accumulate data which will permit a refinement of longhouse site densities. These figures do, however, point out that estimates such as Champlain's 200 longhouses at *Cahiagué* must be viewed very carefully. Unless this village was totally different from the ones examined so far, it is unlikely that the double village totalling 15 acres now believed to be *Cahiagué* ever contained more than 100 longhouses unless they were unusually small.

ii) Social limitations on the size of settlements   On the basis of the discussion so far, is it possible to theorize on the optimum size of Huron villages? Of the 47 sites whose size is known, only twelve were larger than five acres (Figure 5). Since the sample of 47 sites includes most of the largest sites in Huronia, the number of sites that exceed six acres is very small. Converted into population numbers, it seems that few villages exceeded 1,000 to 1,200 people. This would suggest that village populations reached a certain level and for some reason rarely exceeded this level. Leaving economic and environmental considerations aside until Huron agriculture has been discussed, a fairly good case can be made for an optimum population figure of 1,000 to 1,200 (five to six acre site) on a sociological basis.

A closer examination of some of the larger known villages reveals two interesting phenomena: 1) large villages tended to be unstable, and ultimately split into smaller villages; and 2) large villages were often composed of two or more small villages located adjacent to each other. A few examples can be cited. When *Toanche* was moved in the 1620's, it was split

129

into two villages, *Oenrio* and *Ihonatiria* (JR 14:23). When a proposal was made by the Jesuits to reunite the villages, the leaders of the two places could not come to an agreement (JR 14:25,33). Similarly *Ossossane* seems to have split into smaller villages, or at least lost some of its population prior to their move in 1636. Brébeuf relates that for the "feast-of-the-dead" in 1636, people from " . . . eight or nine" villages returned to *Ossossane* to bury their dead (JR 10:291). At least *Iahenhouton* was an offshoot of *Ossossane* (JR 14:15-17). In the case of *Quieunonascaran* this does not seem to have been one large village at all, but ". . . three little hamlets . . ." so close to each other that they went by the same name (JR 13:125). The same appears to have been true for St. Ignace I and *Arethsi* which appear on some maps as separate villages close together, and on the *Description* as *St. Ignace ou Arethsi* (Map 15). Perhaps the best example is *Cahiagué* ("The-places-divided-in-two"), the largest village in Huronia during Champlain's time. Its name suggests that there were two villages going by the same name. This has now been confirmed archaeologically. Sagard stated that when the village was moved sometime prior to his visit, it was split into two separate villages (Sagard 1939:92). The reasons given for the move were soil and wood exhaustion in the vicinity of the village. As a matter of fact, soil and wood exhaustion are given as the major reasons for most shifts in village locale by the early writers (Sagard 1939:-93; JR 11: 7; 15:153).

While some of the shifts in village locale might be explained in terms of soil and wood exhaustion, these factors do not explain the splitting-up of villages or the existence of double and triple villages. As far as agricultural, forest and game resources are concerned, it makes no difference whether a village exists as a single large unit or as two units six-hundred feet apart, as was the case at *Cahiagué*.

The splitting of villages, the existence of double and triple villages and the stabilization of most villages at 1,000 to 1,200 people makes a good deal of sense in the light of Huron social behavior. Since the smooth functioning of a village depended on mutual agreement rather than laws or coercion it follows that the more interrelated the families of a village are, or the smaller the population of a village, the more smoothly it would function. In other words, village co-operation increases as population numbers decrease, and lack of co-operation increases when more and more people are involved. This becomes painfully obvious when one examines the behavior of Huron warriors in large scale warfare, such as Champlain's 1615 attack on the Onondaga (Champlain 3:72-73) or the behavior exhibited in village, tribal and confederacy councils. Generally speaking, the Huron simply did not have the social mechanisms to cope

130

with large numbers of people if these did not wish to co-operate. The dichotomy between the necessity to co-operate and the tendency towards individual or family action has been described in very lucid terms by Trigger:

> The masculine (Huron) ideal stressed a pride in personal independence which tolerated a minimum of coercion. But on the other hand the need for defence, and later trading alliances, had created an area thickly settled with crowded towns. This and the communal life of the longhouse necessitated much cooperation. Huron society was striving for cooperation without organic integration. (Trigger 1963 b:166),

In a highly interesting paper, Naroll made an attempt to correlate the population of the largest settlements of thirty pre-urban societies with the diversity and complexity of their social organization (Naroll 1956). His findings suggested among other things ". . . that when settlements contain more than about five hundred people they must have authoritative officials, and if they contain over a thousand, some kind of specialized organization or corps of officials to perform police functions. . ." (Naroll 1956:690). It is clear that the Huron had "authoritative officials" in their settlements, but specialized police functions were all but absent. The lack of Huron social cohesion once large numbers of people were involved and the fact that few villages were over 1,200 in population seems to suggest that the Huron followed a pattern similar to the societies studied by Naroll. The same factors would account for the splitting of large villages and the tendency for villages to remain separate entities even when they located close together. Since Huron villages tended to be made up of a number of lineages who united for the duration of the village (Trigger 1963 b:157), the likelihood of splits occurring between lineages would be greater in the larger villages. Consequently, the chances of two or three villages uniting to form one single large village were even more remote.

It would be very interesting to find out how many of the large Iroquoian sites reported for Ontario are in actual fact multiple villages. The site of *Cahiagué*, for example, was long supposed to be the largest village in Huronia covering some 25 acres. Once the perimeter of the village was excavated, it turned out to be two villages of five and 9.5 acres each, with a vacant space of 8.5 acres between them. On theoretical grounds one might expect the larger villages to have been similar to *Cahiagué,* especially those reported to be over ten acres; but, as yet, none besides *Cahiagué* have been sufficiently excavated.

131

On theoretical grounds those villages containing more than 1,200 people (larger than six acres) must have had a somewhat different social organization than the smaller villages. In some cases these large villages were noted as being the residence of the "great men" of a tribe, and may therefore have been large villages simply because of the more effective leadership qualities of some of its citizens. *Cahiagué* under Atironta (Darontal) was a case in point (Sagard 1939:91; Champlain 3:81), and his successor Atironta (Aeoptahon) at St. Jean Baptiste (JR 20:35; 23:167; 27:289-291). Similarly *Quieunonascaran* under Auoindaon and Onoratandi (Sagard 1939:91, 99, 174), *Ossossane* under Ontitarac and Anenkhiondic (JR 10:289; 14:33; 15:39) and Endahiaconc at *Teanaustaye* (Sagard 1939:91; JR 13:125; 28:85-89), were known as powerful men and good leaders. As a matter of fact, there does not seem to be any record of any "great men" living in small villages. Highly-regarded men such as these did not have to "rule" by advice and persuasion alone, because disruptive elements in a village could be accused of witchcraft and executed (Trigger 1963 b:166-167).

Theoretically, then, Huron villages could reach populations of 1,000-1,200 under normal social conditions. In the case of some villages, larger populations were possible under more effective leadership: leaders who, because of the esteem in which they were held, could use their talents and socially accepted methods of control to greater effect in permitting larger villages to function smoothly.

Clustering of villages resulting in larger-than-normal aggregate populations might occur in areas of favourable environmental potential for defensive or social reasons. In at least one case, both defensive and social reasons were given to the Jesuits as advantages for combining several villages (JR 10:241). In this case it was pointed out that more warriors would be available to ward off enemy attacks and that a better pool of village leaders would be available to protect the rights of the Jesuits. Clustering of villages or the formation of larger villages may therefore be regarded as a striving for protection from forces outside and within the village. In all of this, multiple villages would have some advantages over single large villages. It is more difficult to attack two villages close together (such as *Cahiagué*) and they are more easily defended than one large single village. Two villages must be taken separately and can give each other aid, while one large village need only be breached at one point. Clustered villages could also preserve a great deal of village autonomy by each having its own council for domestic affairs, yet drawing on the special talents of a respected chief from one of the village segments in time of war or social tension. In the case of one large village the chances of divisive quarrels arising would be greater, simply because of the closer proximity of the village members. The only size limitation to village clusters in which each village is largely autonomous would be set by the quality of the natural environment, while a large single village would suffer from heightened chances of intra-village quarrels.

Since the largest villages seem to be of the contact period, one can reason that, other than the factors already discussed, a number of factors may have been operative that are peculiar to the contact period. Growing defensive needs could have been a reason, but this does not seem too likely until the advent of increasing Iroquois raids in the 1640's. Since at least two and maybe three tribes arrived in Huronia at the beginning of the contact period, the increasingly closer proximity of villages might have made it easier for villages to join together for brief periods of time. A further cause that might be advanced, is that some small villages decided to band together into larger villages in order to better organize and carry out trading expeditions. At first the yearly fur brigades going to the St. Lawrence area seem to have been organized on a village basis. Later, as Iroquois raids and Algonquian tolls increased, the village contingents joined together into larger flotillas. Sagard, for example, went to Huronia in the canoes from *Ossossane* (Sagard 1939:70) and left in those from *Quieunonascaran* (Sagard 1939:251), while Brûlé travelled with those from *Toanche* (Sagard 1939:246). Similarly the Jesuits mentioned that they travelled with Huron from a particular village (JR 5:263; 14:55). At all times, the larger the flotilla was, the safer it was from Iroquois attacks and the more readily it could pass through the toll blockades set up by the bands along the Ottawa-Lake Nipissing-French River route. Larger villages could therefore organize more successful fur brigades. As French-Huron trade increased, it would therefore be advantageous for villages to join together into larger units. It should be mentioned, however, that if considerations of trade were ever a factor in creating large villages, there are no records of it. The largest Huron villages all existed before the arrival of the Jesuits, and some even before the arrival of Champlain and Sagard.

In summary, Huron villages were fairly compact agglomerations of longhouses, rarely exceeding six acres in area and 1,200 in population. A strong factor keeping village populations to a level of 1,200 may have been complexities of village life and the lack of social institutions to cope with them. The existence of a few large and multiple villages, in substantially the same environment as the smaller villages, seems to rule out the quality of the environment as placing limits on settlement sizes well above 1,200 people. Technological limitations and environmental potential

133

probably became more dominant factors in placing a maximum size on the large single and multiple villages.

Perhaps the most plausible explanation for the rise of a few large villages, is simply that after the new tribes moved into Huronia in the latter part of the 16th and early part of the 17th centuries, the closer proximity of the villages and the more restricted area of village movement, made the brief union of several villages more possible. The presence of effective leadership in these larger villages allowed them to function and may have been a strong factor in the original creation of larger villages. As French-Huron trade and Iroquois attacks increased, the large villages could assume a greater importance by becoming regional strongholds, mission centres, political foci in their respective tribal areas, and more effective trading villages. While the Jesuits were in favour of the creation of larger villages, there is no proof that any of their exhortations were ever accepted. While the Huron may have accepted Jesuit suggestions on how to palisade their villages more effectively, there is not a shred of evidence that the Jesuits influenced them in a decision to build large villages. There is also no evidence that some villages became large because they were regional markets for trade goods. Huron economics, as will be discussed later, operated on a different level.

iii) The function of settlements.   The primary function of all Huron villages, large or small, can be categorized as a residence for the village population, a storage area for food products and a place for social interaction. Some of the larger villages also served as strongholds in time of attack and as a residence for influential men in tribal affairs. During the French period a few villages had the additional function of serving as a base of operations for mission activities. Economic functions for the villages are difficult to define because the Huron did not have a market-oriented economy. There were, as far as is known, no central places that served as local markets for foreign or domestic goods. Trade and exchange was a function of certain lineages or clan segments, rather than villages. From these families goods filtered out to other families or individuals in a variety of ways, none of them involving fixed or temporary market sites. For these reasons economic functions will be discussed in a later chapter. All of these functions have been mentioned in earlier chapters; the residential and mission functions however, need some clarification.

A frequent misconception about Huron villages is that they served as year-round dormitories for their inhabitants. The truth of the matter was that from spring to late autumn the villages were devoid of most of the men and a large portion of the women, children and the old people. It was for this reason that most of the mission activities were concentrated in the winter months:

> ... during the whole Summer and Autumn, they are for the most part either in their rural cabins, taking care of their crops, or on the lake fishing, or trading; which makes it not a little convenient to instruct them. (JR 8:143).

or:

> Their trading expeditions and the farms take everyone, men, women, and children – almost no-one remains in the villages (JR 10:53).

Similar statements can be found in other parts of the *Relations* (JR 16:- 249; 17:103; 19:125). Because some of the fields were too far from the main village, temporary longhouses were erected (JR 8:143; 14:49; 20:39, 45). Similar temporary villages and cabins were erected on fishing expeditions (Sagard 1939:185), hunting excursions (Champlain 3:82-83; JR 33:- 83) and as a base of operation for war parties (Champlain 3:74). These are all activities that would take a good portion of the population out of the villages during the spring, summer, and autumn. This yearly cycle made the Huron more vulnerable to attack during the organized Iroquois warfare in the 1640's (JR 33:259). Some of these temporary camps have been archaeologically identified by Pendergast (1962:21-34; 1966; 1969).

In the early 1630's the presence of a permanent Jesuit mission at a village was regarded by the Huron as an important function. With the return of the Jesuits to Huronia, several villages vied for the privilege of housing them (JR 8:51, 71, 85, 101, 105; 10:235-249). The reasons for this are not too difficult to determine. The presence of a Jesuit gave a village chief and the inhabitants of a village prestige among their neighbours (JR 10:237). The Huron also regarded the presence of a priest in their village as a means of gaining favour with French officials and traders in Quebec (Trigger 1968:120, 125-127). At times such favours were sought overtly (JR 13:25, 125). Champlain had made it very plain to the Huron that French goodwill depended on how they received the Jesuits in their villages (JR 8:49-51). This threat was reiterated by others in later years (JR 21:143-145). The Huron therefore thought that the presence of priests in a village would give that village trading advantages. Once in a village, the Jesuits were expected to reciprocate Huron hospitality with gifts of trade goods (JR 8:93-97, 105; 10:249; 15:157). Similar gifts, especially tobacco, were made to those who listened to the sermons and became baptized (JR 8:145; 13:141; 17:95; 18:19-21; 23:129). In a minor way then, the Jesuits became linked with trade and assured a small inflow

135

of trade goods into a village. The villages in which the Jesuits were located therefore assumed a secondary function some of the other villages did not have. The fact that the Jesuits ultimately settled in the larger, more important villages simply strengthened the functional importance of these villages. There were no functional rivals to the large villages until the establishment of Ste. Marie I. By that time, of course, priests were no longer welcome in any but a few Huron villages.

Ste. Marie I was created in 1639 out of the missions at *Ossossane* and *Teanaustaye* (JR 19:133). The original aim was to build a mission from which the total Jesuit effort could be co-ordinated. The location was deliberately chosen for its central position in Huronia (JR 19:133), some distance from the nearest Huron villages. It was easily accessible to all parts of Huronia and Georgian Bay, yet was far enough from the neighbouring villages to escape the daily interruptions and "impertinences" the Jesuits had had to deal with at the Huron villages. While originally Ste. Marie I was only intended to be the administrative centre of the Huron and Petun mission, it quickly assumed a larger regional role. As a physical outpost of France, it became a disseminator of French culture. Here the Huron could see French architecture, fortifications and craft specialists at work. Kidd states that some effort was made to introduce the Huron to European agricultural methods at Ste. Marie I (Kidd 1949:12). While this may be true, there does not seem to be any corroborating evidence. With the building of a hospital in 1642-43, Ste. Marie I assumed regional medical functions, absent from the other villages. By 1643 Jérôme Lalemant was calling St. Marie I ". . . the continual resort of all the neighbouring tribes. . ." (JR 26:201). It was especially for the Christian converts that Ste. Marie I assumed a dominant role. For them the complex on the Wye River became a place for devotion, handouts in time of need, and a refuge from persecution (JR 21:141-143; 23:41; 26:201, 211; 27:65; 33:77). By 1647 St. Marie I had in fact emerged as the functional nucleus of the country, with the Jesuits as the most effective leaders (Trigger 1960:39).

Whether Ste. Marie I served as a trading post is doubtful. Earlier experiences had shown the Jesuits that the presence of French traders in Huronia was not desirable from a religious point of view (JR 6:83; 14:19; 17:45; 22:311). To the Jesuits it was preferable that they themselves would seek to encourage Huron-French trade, but that the actual trading be carried on at the posts on the St. Lawrence. As far as is known, French traders did not come to Ste. Marie I, and the place was never used as a trading post. Therefore, like the Huron villages, St. Marie I did not serve any commercial function.

In summary, one can fairly state that functional differences between Huron villages were slight. What functional differences there were rested on the fact that some villages were regional strongholds and a few were the residences of the tribal leaders. French trade could have made the *Arendaronnon* villages, particularly *Cahiagué*, centres for the distribution of French trade goods. It was the *Arendaronnon* who had pioneered French-Huron trade and consequently to them that this line of trade properly belonged under Huron law (JR 10:223; 20:19). It was, however, decided that French-Huron trade was so important that all villages were given the right to participate in it (JR 20:19). This development, plus the absence of a market-oriented economy ruled out economic functions as a basis for differentiating villages.

iv) The distribution of settlements. Theoretically, the distribution of Huron villages is dependent on the distribution of agriculturally usable soils, water resources and other site requirements discussed earlier. If these site requirements are more or less equally available, villages can only be as close together as the size of the agricultural umland necessary to support them and the area available for periodic shifts in village locale. The size of the agricultural umland and the area available for shifts in village locale would in turn be dependent on the population size of the villages, the natural productivity of the soils and the density of settlement. Because Huron villages varied in size and periodically shifted their site, one could not expect a uniform distribution of sites, even if site requirements were evenly distributed or village territories became formalized due to population pressure. In other words, an even distribution of villages could only result if villages became fixed in their location. This would involve fundamental changes in the nature of Huron agriculture, village life and economy. An even distribution of villages in Huronia could only occur by chance. If site requirements had a clustered or random distribution, an even distribution of settlements would be even less likely.

Whether site requirements were clustered evenly, or randomly distributed, villages could only be as close together as the extent of their village umland. The spatial relation of villages would change periodically as village sites shifted. In all cases, the site to which a village shifted would be dependent on the availability of the right site requirements as close as possible to the old site to minimize the work involved in moving the village. Because distances were short within each tribal area, and because each village was virtually independent of every other village, distances between villages need not be a factor in a new location. Since only land under *active* cultivation was regarded as the private property of village families (Sagard 1939:103), a relocated village could go anywhere within the tribal territory, just as long as it did not encroach on the cultivated lands of another village.

On the basis of this reasoning, whether the major site requirements were evenly or randomly distributed, one would expect an almost random distribution of villages in Huronia. During the Jesuit period villages varied in size up to about 2,400 people and with them the size of their agricultural umland. Villages shifted about every ten to thirty years (Champlain 3:124; Sagard 1939:92), although every eight to twelve years seems more likely (JR 10:275; 11:7; 15:153; 19:133). Finally and most importantly, water resources and soil conditions, specifically the more desirable soils, were neither evenly distributed (except in the tribal area of the *Attingneenongnahac*) nor clustered. Consequently, one would expect that Huron villages had a more or less random spatial pattern, even though the overall population of the occupied area may have reached an optimum level.

Keeping the limitations of the data on the distribution of Huron villages in mind (Map 17), an attempt was made to derive a quantitative description of the distributional pattern. Using a standard method of Nearest Neighbour Analysis (Duncan 1957:33; Haggett 1965:232), an index of 1.15 was obtained for all villages west of the Coldwater River for whom the data was more complete. Since index values using this test can range from zero (clustered distribution) to 1.0 (random distribution) to 2.15 (even distribution), an index of 1.15 would seem to indicate an almost random distribution of villages, which is what was expected. There is little doubt that this randomness is a reflection of the random to uniform distribution of site requirements and the independent, self-sufficient nature of the villages.

The most striking thing about the location of the functionally more important villages, *Ossossane* (La Conception), *Scanonaenrat* (St. Michel), *Teanaustaye* (St. Joseph) and *Contarea* (St. Jean Baptiste), is that they are all on the periphery of their respective tribal areas and along the southern frontier of Huronia. This is to be expected, in view of the fact that the major regional function served by these villages was as a stronghold against enemy attack and seat of the influential war and tribal leaders.

The location of Ste. Marie I could not have been better chosen. As mentioned earlier, its chief function was as administrative centre for the missionary activity to the Huron villages. The major locational requirements were access to Georgian Bay, peace and quiet from the nearest Huron village, but, above all, minimum travel distance to the largest number of people. With these criteria in mind, the only site the Jesuits could have chosen was in fact the site they did choose. Any site along the Wye River, between Wye Lake and Midland Bay is the point of minimum travel time to the maximum number of villages. Only the thinly-populated *Arendaronnon* mission lies outside of this area (Map 17). Maximum travel time to the farthest villages (except St. Jean Baptiste) was only four leagues or about four hours.

c) Morphology of the Village

i) The palisade. Unlike European Neolithic societies such as the Danubians, where the palisade was as much a defensive measure as a cattle enclosure, or Neolithic African groups, where the palisade or thorn hedge was a cattle enclosure as well as protection against marauding carnivores, the Huron palisade served only one function. It was a defensive measure against enemy attacks. The Huron did not have any domesticated animals except the dog, and there were no wild animals in Ontario that might pose a threat to humans.

The fact that not all villages were palisaded has already been observed. As far as can be determined, only the more important villages were protected or those closest to the frontier. In case of an attack, the inhabitants from the smaller villages or those villages that could not be fortified, destroyed their villages and fled to the larger palisaded villages where they would build lodges for themselves and help in further fortifications (Sagard 1939:92, 155; JR 10:51). Those that could not make it to a larger village hid in the forest (JR 10:51). It can be reasoned therefore, that the presence or absence of a palisade was a function of need, balanced against the availability of building supplies and labour. Frontier villages undoubtedly had a greater need for defences than villages further removed from the frontier (as events in the 1640's demonstrated).

The descriptions of palisades in the ethnohistoric sources are fairly uniform:

> . . . fortified by wooden palisades in three tiers, interlaced into one another, on top of which, they have galleries which they furnish with stones for hurling, and water to extinguish the fire that their enemies might lay against their palisades. (Champlain 3:122).

> or:

> Some of these (villages) are not shut in, while the others are fortified by strong wooden palisades in three rows, interlaced into one another and reinforced within by large sheets of bark to a height of eight or nine feet, and at the bottom there are great trunks of trees placed lengthwise, resting on short forks made from tree trunks. Then above

these palisades there are galleries or watchtowers, which they call *Ondaqua,* and these they stock with stones in war time to hurl upon the enemy, and water to put out the fire that might be laid against their palisades. The Hurons mount up to them by means of a ladder, very ill made and difficult to climb, and defend their ramparts with great courage and skill. (Sagard 1939:91-92).

More specifically, *Carhagouha* had a ". . . triple wooden palisade thirty-five feet high" (Champlain 3:48). St. Ignace II was ". . . surrounded with a stockade of pine-trees, from fifteen to sixteen feet in height . . ." (JR 34:123-125), and St. Louis was ". . . fortified with a fairly good stockade" (JR 34:125; 39-249). A few contemporary drawings mirror these descriptions (Figure 7).

Archaeologically, as much is known about the palisades as about the longhouses. In general, the palisade followed the edge of the slope on which the village was situated. To the rear of the slope the palisade was built in an arc encircling the village into a rough oval. If the village stood on an interfluve, the palisade was built along the break of slope. In no case was a palisade constructed in the form of a recognizable, straight-line geometrical figure. Since palisades enclosed the occupied portion of a village, Huron villages were roughly oval in shape (Figure 8).

Of the palisades, or portions of palisades, excavated so far, most consisted of multiple rows of staggered posts. Individual posts usually varied from three to five inches in diameter and were spaced six to twelve inches apart. A second row, when present, was usually placed two to two and a half feet from the first row (Figure 9). Judging from various excavations, the base of the posts was roughly tapered and driven into the ground anywhere up to twenty inches. Presumably, branches were woven between the uprights and logs and bark placed between the rows.

The most detailed work on Huron palisades has been done at *Cahiagué* (Emerson and Russell 1965). This was a massive enclosure varying between three and seven rows of posts. At the northern village segment three to four rows were built along the brow of the slopes, and four to five rows along the flat southern approaches. The southern village segment was protected by five to seven rows along the unprotected northern perimeter, four to five rows on the unprotected southern perimeter and three to four rows along the east and west ravines (Figure 8). This general pattern is repeated at other sites, namely that the flat approaches to a village were more heavily fortified than the perimeters along breaks in slope. The *Cahiagué* palisades also show that when more than two rows of posts are present, one of the interior rows is composed of heavier logs up to ten inches in diameter, spaced some two to three feet apart.

140

As yet there is no evidence from any excavated site that posts were driven into the ground at an angle, as pictured on Bressani's map (Figure 7). The usual type of construction seems to have been a tightly interwoven series of uprights with each row about two and a half feet apart. The standard four row palisade at *Cahiagué* was therefore some 7.5 feet thick (Figure 9).

As yet no "galleries" or "watchtowers" have been described in the archaeological literature. This does not mean that they were a figment of Champlain's and Sagard's imagination. In all probability, galleries and watchtowers were built on top of the five to seven feet of space between the outer and inner walls of the palisade (Figure 9). There is no reason why a separate structure should be erected to serve these purposes. On one or two rowed palisades such superstructures may have been absent.

In their discussion on the *Cahiagué* palisade, Emerson and Russell (1965:16-18) proposed a type of palisade that differs radically from the standard descriptions. Basically, their conception of a palisade is a series of palisade lines consisting of staggered uprights with no interwoven branches, logs, galleries or towers. Because the rows were staggered, an arrow would have trouble penetrating the defenses and a defender could simply step between the rows and fire back. This "open" type of palisade would also have made gates unnecessary. The trouble with this theory is that such a defensive system would only work if the attacker was content to stay at a distance and shoot arrows at the palisade. It would be absolutely useless in a surprise attack (the usual method of warfare), or once the enemy had reached the first palisade line. Interwoven branches, the inter-lacing of the various rows, logs and sheets of bark are not the type of evidence one could expect to find archaeologically. It is therefore difficult to say that they did not exist. The ethnohistoric descriptions and the rather obvious defects in the Emerson-Russell palisade would seem to mitigate against its existence in that form.

Not enough village sites have been dug to say anything definite about the number and construction of village gates. Sagard stated that the "gates and entrances" could be "closed with bars." One could not enter a gate "striding straight in," but was "forced to pass turning side-ways" (Sagard 1939:92). Two gates answering this description were apparently found by Jury at Hunters Village Site No. 36, Tay Twp. (Jury and Fox 1947:61, 66). Preliminary analysis of the post-hole patterns at the north central palisade segment of the southern village component at *Cahiagué* strongly suggests a similar structure to the ones found by Jury and described by Sagard (Personal observation). Apparently the outer opening of the gate led into a walled passage at right angles to the main palisade. At intervals barriers were erected across the passage, all but closing it. Such a passage would have to be negotiated in a zig-zag pattern and could easily be blocked, as described by Sagard. Another possibility arising out of Sagard's description would be simply to build a second palisade system behind and parallel to an opening in the primary palisade system. This would be a simpler, but equally as effective a gate as the ones found by Jury.

The number of gates at a village is not known. Jury's village had two; other villages have not been sufficiently excavated. The Jesuits describe the presence of two gates at St. Joseph II (JR 39:239-241). The existence of two gates allowed a part of the population to escape after the Iroquois attackers had taken possession of the main gate during the attack of the village in 1648. The difficulty met by the Huron in attempting to escape from villages that had been surprised and breached by attackers suggests that gates were a necessary means for getting out of a palisaded village. It was not a mere matter of walking between rows of stakes as suggested by Emerson and Russell. This is further illustrated by the fact that the Iroquois armies had to dig and chop their way into St. Louis after several other attempts at storming the place had failed (JR 34:127).

There is little evidence that the Huron built earthworks or ditches around the perimeter of their palisade as added defensive measures. This practice has been reported at some of the League Iroquois villages (Houghton 1916:513; Parker 1920:120-122). Only one site in Huronia was reported to have had a defensive ditch; the large contact site of St. Joseph II on lot 12, concession 4, Medonte Township. Hunter reports that he, and others, managed to define a trench about 50 yards in length running between the heads of two ravines thus providing added defences at the only part on the village perimeter that was not adjacent to a ravine. The ditch was slighly curved, with the concave side facing the interior of the village (Hunter 1901:78-79).

On the whole, Europeans were not impressed by Huron fortifications. Champlain, for example, remarked that the fortifications of the League Iroquois were considerably better (Champlain 3:70), and as early as 1636 the Jesuits were instructing the Huron in the basic principles of European fortifications (JR 10:53).

Against Iroquois method of warfare the usual Huron palisade was probably reasonably effective. Its principal drawback was that it could be set on fire. Unless the village was attacked in a large force and by surprise, it could withstand an attack by any small, disorganized group of warriors of the size of the Huron and Iroquois war parties in the 1630's. As the League Iroquois armies got larger and better organized, the traditional

Huron palisade proved to have additional weaknesses: the main one being that the palisade lines were curved instead of straight. It was this weakness that the Jesuits were trying to rectify at Ossossane:

> We have told them also that henceforth they should make their forts square, and arrange their stakes in straight lines; and that, by means of four little towers at the four corners, four Frenchmen might easily with their arquebuses or muskets defend the whole village. They are greatly delighted with this advice, and have already begun to practice it at la Rochelle (*Ossossane*) . . . . (JR 10:53).

The extent to which this advice was followed is unknown. The Jesuits themselves state that they had a hand in fortifying St. Ignace II (JR 39:-247), the village on Christian Island (JR 35:85); and Jury appears to have found a palisade at St. Louis showing a strong French influence (Jury and Jury 1965:28).

ii) The distribution of longhouses within the village. One of the really surprising things about the extent of Iroquoian archaeology is the lack of any studies on the total layout of villages. At least something is known about every aspect of a village (houses, palisade, middens and cemeteries); but virtually nothing is known about the internal arrangement (morphology) of the village. In one of the few statements on the subject, Ritchie (1956:-78) wrote that Iroquoian towns:

> . . . would probably equate rather closely in size and general arrangement with the Late Mississippi towns of the Southeast, except that the former lacked the temple mounds, chief's houses, charnel houses and other elements of the south-eastern ceremonial complex. The council house of the Iroquois – the focus of political and religious activities – affords the closest parallel. Even at the present day, Iroquoian houses on the reservation tend to cluster around the council house.

In the meantime little additional work has been published to gain a deeper insight into Iroquoian village morphology. Recently some anthropologists have drawn attention to the general lack of prehistoric settlement pattern studies (Chang 1967:15–17; 1968:2–4) and Iroquoian settlements in particular (Trigger 1967b:153). During the Mid-1960's settlement studies were launched by the University of Western Ontario at the Forget and the University of Toronto at *Cahiagué* and the Maurice, Robitaille, Charlebois and Lichtenfeldt sites, all in Huronia. As Yet, no definitive results have been published from these sites (Tyyska 1969).

For the Huron, the ethnohistoric sources are of little use. Beyond stating that houses were usually placed three to four yards apart ". . . for fear of fire which they greatly dread" (Champlain 3:125), and that the villages had "streets" and "public places" (*correfours*) (Sagard 1939:203; JR 15:157; 16:247), nothing else has been written.

Slightly more is known about the village morphology of other Iroquoian tribes, and there is no reason to believe that they were substantially different from the Huron. During his visit to *Hochelaga* (1535–St. Lawrence Iroquois), Cartier describes a typical Iroquoian village, roughly circular in shape, surrounded by a strong palisade with one gate, containing fifty longhouses (Lescarbot 2:116–117). On his arrival at the village he was taken to:

> . . . the middle of the town, where between the houses is an open square, a stone's throw or thereabouts in breadth. (Lescarbot 2:112, 443).

The use of this square was evidently for public meetings and festivals. A picture of *Hochelaga* appeared in Ramusio's *Delle Navigationi et Viagi*, but is probably nothing more than a graphic rendering of Cartier's description, heavily influenced by 16th-century European ideas of town planning.

Much the same could be said about Champlain's celebrated picture of the Onondaga village he attacked in 1615, were it not that unlike the drawing of *Hochelaga*, which cannot be attributed to Cartier, Champlain refers to the picture of the Onondaga village in his text. In view of the accuracy of Champlain's maps, it is difficult to dismiss his drawings entirely. In view of other descriptions of Iroquoian villages, some of the essentials of Champlain's picture are probably correct. What he appears to have seen was a heavily-fortified village built close to the edge of two parallel creeks and a larger body of water. The centre of the village had an open area around which the longhouses were placed in groups. The space between the grouped longhouses he interpreted as "streets." Similar to other illustrators of his time, Champlain made the village rather spacious, and the morphology more geometric than it probably was. Nineteen years after Champlain a Dutch traveller visited a Mohawk village with ". . . thirty–six houses, in rows like streets, so we could pass nicely." (Jameson 1909:140–141).

Among the very few illustrations of Iroquoian villages is one that is supposed to represent the chief village of the Susquehanna (*Andaste*). It appears on a map engraved in 1720 by H. Moll (*A New Map of the North Parts of America Claimed by France* – Public Archives of Canada, Ottawa). The problem with this picture is that it seems to be a reverse image of John White's well known sketch of the North Carolina *Powhatan* village of *Pomeiock*, visited by the English in 1585. Over the years *Pomeiock* has been copied and re-copied so often that it has become generally accepted as a standard illustration of any eastern woodlands village. Like the Iroquoian tribes, the *Powhatan* lived in communal longhouses and in palisaded and non-palisaded villages (Birket-Smith 1963:157–178; Morgan 1965:119–124). The village of *Secotan,* also illustrated by John White, is an example of the latter. In the case of the palisaded village the essential characteristics are an open central area and a loose arrangement of houses about it, while the unpalisaded village is simply a random agglomeration of longhouses. Other illustrations and verbal descriptions of Iroquoian villages and those of neighbouring groups show similar characteristics.

Thus far, only two Huron villages have been more or less completely excavated; Forget (unpublished), and Hunter's No. 36 in Tay Township, the supposed site of St. Ignace II (Jury and Fox 1947). Both of these villages were excavated by W. Jury, whose work, as mentioned earlier, must be viewed with some caution. Be that as it may, one can at least say that both villages have open areas. In the case of Hunter's No. 36, an unusually large longhouse is situated on the edge of an open central area. The other longhouses are loosely spaced about the open area much like the Susquehana and *Powhatan* villages. One is tempted to visualize related groups of longhouses within the total village pattern, and it is unfortunate that the original excavations were not exact enough to permit one to do this. In the case of Forget (Figure 8), at least one open area is present. However, no report on the village has as yet been published.

Personal observations from numerous field seasons at *Cahiagué* and conversations with archaeologists Dr. J. N. Emerson and Mr. A. Tyyska leave one with the firm conviction that longhouses were deliberately placed parallel to each other, interspersed with small open areas (Figure 8). On the basis of the distribution of pottery types, pipe styles and trade goods, Mr. Tyyska feels that the inhabitants of the longhouses surrounding each open area had close relations and may have belonged to the same lineage or clan segment (Tyyska 1968). A great deal of further study at *Cahiagué* and other sites will be needed to validate these preliminary observations.

On the basis of the little that is known about the morphology of the Huron village and a body of theory built up from cross-cultural studies among American Indian societies, one can at least hypothesize what the Huron village may have been like. Basically there seem to be three morphological types: the dispersed village with no palisade, compact palisaded villages, and multiple villages.

The dispersed village was simply a loose agglomeration of longhouses along the edge of a watercourse without any particular plan. Villages such as these have been observed in Huronia, but none have been excavated. Judging from its name, *Arethsi* ("The Straggling Village") seems to have been such a place, perhaps much like the Powhatan village of *Secotan*. In Chang's (1958:306) classification of Neolithic villages this type would come closest to his unplanned village.

In Huronia as elsewhere, compact palisaded villages varied in size and complexity. The main determinant was probably whether one or more lineage or clan segment was present. Chang (1958:306) found that mono-lineage communities were ". . . often composed of houses arranged in a circle around a small plaza which sometimes contains a men's house or the chief's house." When more than one lineage was present,

> . . . each localized in one segment of the community. The segments are in effect small, planned, sometimes fenced villages with dwelling houses arranged in a pattern, centering on a plaza, a men's house, or other special buildings; in many cases, each segment is a communal house. The segments are further arranged either regularly or irregularly into a community, which sometimes has an additional common plaza and some community buildings or, occasionally, a big enclosure. The segmented community pattern seems to indicate the existence of several lineages, each occupying a segment. (Chang 1958:306–307).

Since both monolineage and multilineage villages existed among the Huron, the chances are that morphological patterns will be found corresponding somewhat to Chang's definitions. Forget, for example, is probably representative of the smaller monolineage communities, while Hunter's No. 36, with its central open area and large, centrally-located house, as well as some indication of longhouse grouping, seems to have been one of the more complex multilineage villages. This was certainly the case at *Cahiagué,* where there is evidence of grouping of longhouses about open areas. In addition, of course, *Cahiagué* was a multiple village and therefore represents the ultimate in the organizational complexity of Huron villages.

At present little more can be said about Huron village morphology. This is one area of Iroquoian research that shows great promise for the future. In all likelihood, however, it will be a long time before anything definitive is known simply because a number of whole villages must be carefully excavated; and that is an enormous task."

iii) The disposal of garbage. The most distinctive archaeological feature of Huron village sites are its garbage dumps (middens). Since they are the only visible surface feature at a site, it is virtually impossible to locate a site where the middens are indistinct or absent. Middens contain most of the artifact material of a site. They can be used to delimit the extent of a site; they furnish information on the diet of the inhabitants; and, because they were deposited on the land surface, they sometimes cover undisturbed soil profiles dating to the period of Indian occupation. In view of the importance of middens to archaeologists, it is surprising that none has ever attempted an analysis of them. As yet, the archaeologist has been solely concerned in extracting artifact material from the middens. Layering in middens; the material itself; the position of middens in relation to each other and the longhouses; differences in the artifactual material between middens (often as high as between contemporary sites): all of these have been almost entirely ignored. An analysis of midden material is beyond the scope of this study, but future work should prove this to be a fruitful area of research.

In appearance, middens vary from low mounds up to four feet in depth to scattered surface deposits only a few inches deep. The area covered by the deposits can vary up to several hundred square yards. The interior of some middens is layered in a series of lenses of varying thickness. In colour the lenses vary from light grey to black depending on the amount of ash and charcoal present. The predominant material in the middens is woodash, mixed with small amounts of fine sand and silt. The consistency of the midden material is therefore light; when dry, it easily becomes windborne. Besides the usual artifact material, carbonized cultigens, fishbones and animal bones are also present in varying amounts. The pH (acidity) of the bulk of a midden varies between 7.0 and 8.5, usually increasing with depth. A few areas within a midden can be as low as pH 4.5. In general, the black layers with a high percentage of charcoal and the light grey layers of almost pure woodash have the highest pH readings.

From the position of the middens one would gather that, in most cases, garbage was simply dumped on the periphery of the village. Only in the case of large villages can middens be found within the village proper. As a matter of fact, the writer has never seen a village in which a person had to walk more than one hundred feet to the nearest garbage dump. It would therefore be more correct to say that garbage was simply dumped within a convenient distance of a longhouse. This does not mean that garbage disposal was a random process. The middens are well-defined areas and the space between them almost free of any refuse. The sum total of the evidence seems to be that longhouses, including the hearth areas, were cleaned out periodically and the garbage disposed of in predetermined places. The layering in the middens may represent such periodic house-cleaning.

There is little indication from archaeological or ethnological sources how villagers disposed of human waste. Sagard (1939:93, 227) noted that Huron children, and no doubt the many village dogs, urinated on the longhouse floors. While neither Sagard, nor anyone else, commented on the behavior of adults around the village, he did note that while travelling the Huron

> . . . used to stoop down in some place apart with a decency and modesty that were anything but savage. (Sagard 1939:60).

If the Huron behaved differently around their villages, it was not mentioned in the ethnohistoric sources. Soil chemical analysis at the Maurice and Robitaille sites in the Penetang penisula indicate a high phosphorus content throughout the village and especially in the middens (Heidenreich, et al., 1971). While the phosphorus content of an undisturbed soil was in the neighbourhood of 400 to 500 ppm. (depth 10″), in the village it would vary between 700 and 2,000 ppm and in the middens up to 4,500 ppm. Since excrement is high in phosphorus, the high values within the village might be due to an indiscriminate disposal of human waste. Further chemical analysis in the future will hopefully solve the problem.

On the whole the middens, composed primarily of ash, charcoal and rotting vegetable remains, need not to have been either offensive or a health problem to the villagers. Few animal and fish remains found their way into the middens, and what little was thrown out was probably eaten by the dogs. There is no reason to suppose that the accumulations of garbage ". . . rendered it impossible for them (the Huron) to remain long in one place" (Hunter 1948:4); at least this was never cited as a cause for shifting a village. As a matter of fact, the subject of refuse is never mentioned in any of the ethnohistoric sources. In all probability, Huron domestic habits were not too different from those in rural France of the 17th century. An any rate, the total lack of any references to waste disposal and accumulation seems to indicate that the early writers did not observe anything unusual or particularly offensive about Huron habits.

iv) The cemetery. The disposal of the dead formed an extremely important part of the Huron cultural system. The size, location and types of cemeteries were an important aspect of any settlement. The social, religious and ceremonial aspects of death and burial were minutely described by Champlain (3:160–163), Sagard (1939:205–214) and in various parts of the *Relations*. These aspects have been summarized by Tooker (1964:128–

148

140) and Trigger (1969:102–112). Although most Huron ossuaries have been dug and looted, only three contact ossuaries have been excavated by the archaeologists (Maurice Site, Tiny Twp.; *Cahiagué*, Medonte Twp.; *Ossossane*, Tiny Twp.). The *Ossossane* excavation was published by Kidd (1953:359–379), a part of the *Cahiagué* report exists in manuscript form (Harris, n. d.:17pp) and a preliminary study of the Maurice ossuary has been made by Jerkic (1969). Notes on less scientifically-excavated ossuaries can be found scattered throughout Hunter's reports on the townships in Simcoe County. For the purposes of this study, the ossuary will be treated as much as possible as an aspect of settlement, without the accompanying social, religious and ceremonial ramifications.

Basically, the burial of the dead seems to have been a two-stage affair. Upon the death of a villager, his family put the body on a mat in a flexed position (JR 10:267) and wrapped it in a robe (Sagard 1939:205). A feast was prepared and residents from the village of the deceased as well as neighbouring villages invited (JR 10:269). Those present at the feast were most likely relatives or close friends. After these ceremonies and a lengthy funeral oration the body was placed in a temporary grave. In most cases, the grave consisted of a platform raised on posts over six feet above the ground (Sagard 1939:207; Champlain 3:160). On occasions, the body was interred in a grave below ground level (Champlain 3:160; Sagard 1939:-208). In the latter case, a shrine was built over the grave and the whole encircled by a fence. The usual distance of the cemetery to the village was "... a harquebus-shot ..." away, or some 300-400 yards (Sagard 1939:-207).

Periodically all the bodies were disinterred and reburied in a mass grave during the "Feast-of-the-Dead." Champlain (3:161) and Bressani (JR 39:-31) stated that this event occured every eight to ten years. Sagard (1939:-211) put the time at every ten years, while the Jesuits mention a time span of about twelve years (JR 10:143, 275, 281). On most occasions this seems to have been a tribal affair (JR 10:261, 279). A tribal council was held and the representatives from various villages would decide which village would be chosen for the honour of holding the "Feast" (Champlain 3:161; Sagard 1939:211; JR 10:261). The actual spot where the mass grave was dug was usually anywhere from 200 yards to half a mile from the designated village. On some occasions, when the tribal council could not arrive on a compromise site, each group of dissident villages would hold their own "Feast-of-the-Dead" (JR 10:279). Judging from the mumber of contact ossuaries in Huronia, such disagreements were either more numerous than the ethnohistoric sources seem to imply, or burial practices changed somewhat after the mid-1630's when the Jesuit observations were made.

It is, however, safe to say that not every village had a "Feast-of-the-Dead" and therefore an ossuary connected with it.

Prior to the "Feast" the bodies were taken from the temporary graves and stripped of all remaining flesh. The bones were then bundled up and transported to the designated site, where among much feasting, dancing and speeches they were placed into a mass grave. The whole ceremony could, on occasion, last up to two weeks. The final mass grave was usually a round pit, varying in size with the number of bodies and grave goods to be placed in it. The one at *Ossossane,* for example, was some 20 feet in diameter and five feet deep (Kidd 1953:365), containing about 1,000 skeletons.When the ceremony was finished the pit was covered with skins, logs, tree bark, and finally earth. The grave was then marked with a solid wooden fence (Sagard 1939:212).

Judging from the "Feast-of-the-Dead" witnessed by Brébeuf at *Ossossane,* the village at which the "Feast" was held was moved after the ceremonies were completed (JR 10:291–293, 299). Although concrete evidence that the "Feast-of-the-Dead" was accompanied by village movement is lacking, it seems more than a coincidence that the time interval given for the "Feast" was the same as the usual period of village movement, namely every eight to twelve years (JR 15:153; 16:229; 19:133). In one passage, Brébeuf discusses both the "Feast" and village movement, but does not make it clear if the two events coincided:

> The graves are not permanent; as their villages are stationary only during a few years, while the supplies of the forest last, the bodies only remain in the Cemeteries until the feast of the dead, which usually takes place every twelve years. (JR 10:275)

One further piece of supporting evidence is that the souls of those who were too weak to undertake the long journey to the village of the dead after interment in the ossuary, used the abandoned cornfields of the living to plant their corn (JR 10:145). This they could hardly do if the village cornfields were still in use after the "Feast-of-the-Dead." Whether villages other than the one at which the "Feast" was held were also moved is doubtful. At least there is no evidence to warrant such a conclusion.

People who did not die a natural death, or infants, were buried separately from the others (Tooker 1964:132; JR 39:31); but there does not seem to be any point in discussing these practices here. An interesting possibility is that with the growth of the Huron Christian community in the 1640's, some Christian burial practices may have been carried out. Even the Jesuits were astonished when in 1643 a council of Christians at St. Joseph II decided that it was not proper that they be buried with their pagan relatives. (JR 23:31). Patches of single burials are quite common in central and eastern Huronia, but generally absent in the west (Hunter 1901:71; 1909:161). In some cases these may be Christian burials; but judging from the age of some of the sites, it is more likely that ossuary burial was originally not common to all the Huron tribes but a practice that became more common with residence in Huronia. It seems unlikely that the large numbers of single burials reported at some sites were the result of forgetfulness or village movement prior to the "Feast-of-the-Dead." Ossuaries appear to be rare, and single burials the rule, in the areas east of Lake Simcoe (Hunter 1901:71; Laidlaw 1899, 1901, 1903, 1912, 1917). The most likely explanation for the single burials in central and eastern Huronia seems therefore that this was a practice introduced to Huronia through pre-contact tribal migrations, but proceeded to be replaced by ossuary burial.

In summary, care for the dead was highly developed among the Hurons. A special area was set aside a short distance from the village as a temporary, and in some cases permanent, graveyard. The graveyard was held in deep respect and was often frequented by mourners (JR 39:31). If a fire broke out in the village and threatened the graveyard, the graves were protected first (Sagard 1939:209; JR 39:31). Among some of the Huron tribes, certainly among the *Attignaouantan* and *Attingneenongnahac,* the villages of each tribe got together every eight to twelve years and decided on a place to bury their dead in a common grave. Not only was this a religious ceremony but also an occasion to symbolize tribal union through common burial, renew friendships and act as a general catharsis of personal grief (Sagard 1939:213–214). In all likelihood, the village at which the "Feast-of-the-Dead" was held, was moved to a new location just before or immediately after the ceremonies were completed.

v) Labour and time involved in erecting a village. The clearing of land, the construction of longhouses and the erection of a palisade were all properly speaking, men's work. The amount of work involved and the length of time taken to complete it would depend on the size of the village to be constructed, the urgency of the job, the quantity of materials available and the number of men in the community. Assuming that the number of available men is directly related to the size of a village, and that the erection of a village was a matter of high urgency, the major variable influencing the amount of work put into the job and the length of time taken to complete it was the availability of building materials.

Judging from archaeological investigations and contemporary descriptions, the universal construction materials were posts from three to ten

151

inches in diameter up to thirty feet long, and sheets of elm and cedar bark. With a polished stone axe or adze of the type used by most Neolithic peoples including the Huron, a man could remove a conifer some seven inches in diameter in about five to seven minutes (Clark 1945:68), and a hardwood about twelve inches in diameter in thirty minutes (Iversen 1956:38). The maximum amount of time spent on cutting a tree of the type used in Huron construction should therefore not take more than twenty minutes. Since the vast majority of the posts used were in the order of four to five inches in diameter, an average cutting time of ten minutes is fairly realistic.

During contact times the iron axe became immensely popular and must have reduced the work of tree-fellings. The popularity of the axe as a trade item is attested to by the literature of the period and also by the fact that in the latter part of the 19th-century iron axes were found in such quantities that scrap iron dealers thought it worth their while to make regular visits to Simcoe County farmers (Hunter 1889:1; 1901:73). Even though the standard French trade axe was made of soft iron and not particularly well constructed, it would be fair to say that it enabled the Huron to cut their tree felling time by at least one half. Providing that enough building material was available, the iron axe probably enabled the Huron to construct such strong and massive palisades like the ones at *Cahiagué,* which apparently are not found at pre-contact sites.

The amount of wood needed for a large village of, for example, six acres, housing 1,000 people in 36 longhouses surrounded by a single palisade, can be roughly calculated:

Palisade – 3,600 stakes (5″ diameter; 15′–30′ long).
Longhouses (exterior walls) – 16,000 poles (4″–5″ diameter; 10′–30′ long).
Longhouses (interior support posts) – 250 posts (10″ diameter; 15′–20′ long).
Longhouses (elm or cedar bark) – 4,500 sq. ft. per longhouse, or 162,000 sq. ft. for 36 longhouses.

In examining this list, the immediate problem is that these materials are not readily available in a mature forest. All the necessary building materials came from logs under twelve inches in diameter. Even the bark for the longhouses could be obtained from small trees, since an elm or cedar ten inches in diameter could furnish a piece of bark 30 inches by at least five to eight feet. A mature forest might furnish enough building material if only the branches from large trees are used; but the job of first cutting down the large trees and then stripping them of their branches would be an almost impossible task. Moreover, the bark from a mature elm or cedar is difficult to remove, not very pliable and tends to split; while branches, often being crooked, are definitely inferior to young trees and saplings as palisade and longhouse material. The chances, therefore, are that the Huron located their villages in areas of secondary forest growth; areas of long abandoned cornfields that contained a good stand of trees under ten inches in diameter. Because Huronia was fairly densely settled, and had been occupied by agriculturalists well before the beginning of the 17th century, there should not have been any dearth of areas in immature forest growth.

In an immature forest, containing primarily trees under ten inches in diameter, one might expect a density of about one tree per hundred square feet or 435 trees per acre. Proximity to swampy depressions, creek beds and the better-drained upland areas in Huronia would assure a variety of habitats in which immature cedar, elm and the other tree types can be found. At any rate, the wood required for a six-acre site could be found on about 46 acres surrounding a village, or within a 800 foot radius. If the village was in the centre of the area, the farthest limits of the area necessary to furnish the building materials are no more than a thirty-minute walk.

Out of a population of 1,000 people, one might expect 200 able-bodied men. The amount of time taken to cut a tree under ten inches in diameter, transport it to the construction site and place it in position, should not take on the average more than one hour. If 200 men are engaged in this task, working in teams of three, for only six hours a day, the entire village could be build in fifty days. Placing the stripped bark on the longhouse frames might take another twenty days, but a village could be finished for occupation well within three months. Starting in the spring a village could be finished mid-summer. At the same time as the land was being stripped for building materials, it could be burnt over and the women could start the planting. The late summer and fall would therefore be free for the traditional seasonal activities of hunting, fishing and harvesting.

There is, of course, no reason why the beginning of construction should wait until spring. This was the best time for obtaining bark for roofing and siding the longhouses (Johnston 1964:25), but the actual clearing of the land and cutting of timber could take place in the late winter. In at least two instances, this seems to have been the case (Champlain 3:96; JR 12:77).

Actual references to the time it took to erect a village are almost nonexistent. Ste. Marie II on Christian Island comprising about 100 longhouses (probably small ones) was completed during the spring and summer of

1649 (JR 34:215, 225; 35:27, 83-87), but because of the circumstances surrounding the creation of this village it could hardly be called a typical example. In another reference we know of one longhouse being constructed in three days (JR 10:249). In view of the considerable work involved in building a new village, it is possible that palisade posts and other materials which were still in good condition were moved from the old village and reused at the new one. Observations at several archaeological sites of post-holes seem to indicate that sometimes posts were simply left to rot in the ground, but often were pulled out prior to a move. For example, in places at *Cahiagué* the remains of cedar palisade posts have been found, in other places post-hole patterns consisted of a very light humic soil (completely decayed posts); but most often the post patterns were simply an infill from the upper four to five inches of the soil section. Where palisades ran through midden areas, post holes are often filled with midden material. In the latter two cases the presence of topsoil or midden material in the post holes can be interpreted as the removal of posts during the relocation of a village.

A great deal of work must be done before anything definite can be stated as to how common a practice the physical moving of a village actually was. It stands to reason, however, that whenever possible previously-utilized building materials were treated economically, especially when a village move was only over a short distance.

In the building of very large villages, the amount of work involved must have been somewhat greater than in the case of the hypothetical six-acre village discussed above, in spite of the proportionally larger population. This is primarily because the wood must be brought in from a greater distance and because these villages were often more heavily fortified. Suppose, for example, that the double village of *Cahiagué* comprising a total of 15 acres, contained about 100 longhouses and a combined total of 3,600 people of whom 700 were men. On the basis of several seasons' excavations, Emerson and Russell (1965:5) calculated that the palisade was composed of about 24,000 posts. The hundred longhouses could take up roughly 50,000 posts and 450,000 square feet of elm and cedar bark. On the basis of the previous estimates, about 170 acres of young trees would be needed to furnish enough wood for such a village. Due to the greater travel time and the fact that an average of four rows of palisade were erected, the completion of the village would now take about 100 days (three men per post working six hours per day, at 1.75 hours per post). Added to that the time taken to cover the longhouses with bark, and in spite of the extra men, the village must have taken more than a normal working year to complete. In all probability the longhouses and one palisade row (or section of palisade) were completed first, the rest being finished the following year. This might account for the irregularities in the *Cahiagué* palisade found by Emerson and Russell (1965:15).

The hypothesis that any average village could be largely, and in most cases completely built in three to five months rests rather heavily on the existence of a good stand of immature trees in the vicinity of the village site. The existence of numerous pre-contact and early contact sites in Huronia seems to justify the opinion that large areas of secondary forest growth must have been in existence. For example, *Ossossane* is surrounded by three sites predating it by 60 to 80 years; *Cahiagué* is very close to a Lalonde site some 70 years earlier; St. Joseph II is near two sites predating it by some 40 years. An inventory of all sites is not possible because the archaeological record is not complete; but in many cases such as the ones cited above, the existence of timber of the kind hypothesized is not only possible, but under local soil conditions more than highly probable.

3. COMMUNICATION BETWEEN VILLAGES

All communication between villages in Huronia was by foot over a network of narrow trails. There is no evidence that canoes were used for any other purpose than fishing or long-distance trade. Even to the Neutral or Petun, travel was overland (JR 18:39; 20:45; 21:205). According to the French, all trails, whether they ran between villages in Huronia or to points outside Huronia, were difficult to negotiate (JR 13:181; 17:17; 20:99). Until one found out through experience exactly where a trail led to, it was easy to get lost on the many forks and branches (Sagard 1939:-69).

If Huron trails were difficult to negotiate at the best of times, they were almost impossible in the winter because the snow tended to obliterate them (JR 20:45). Snowshoes and toboggans eased the difficulties of travel somewhat (Sagard 1939:83, 93), but by and large winter travel was avoided as much as possible (JR 20:45). The difficulties of winter travel are illustrated by Le Mercier's rather graphic description that it took a group of Jesuits the better part of a December day to cover the four leagues (twelve miles) between *Ihonatiria* and *Ossossane* (JR 13:181). In his statement he also points out that this travel time was not unusual for winter months. Except for occasional hunting and ice fishing or socializing with neighbouring villages, there was really no reason why the Huron should have indulged in much winter travel.

The amount of regular intervillage travel is difficult to estimate. During the spring, summer and fall, most of the travelling seems to have been to the village fields or points outside of Huronia. Travel between villages was primarily for socializing or political activities which took place mainly in the fall.

While travel between villages may not have been very frequent, a network of trails did exist. In the opinion of A.F. Hunter, some of the main Huron trails were kept open by Algonquian hunters after the fall of Huronia and were used by European settlers in the 19th century (Hunter 1948:5-6). During his research into the history of Simcoe County, Hunter took considerable pains to map existing Indian trails from settlers' accounts and his own observations (Map 23).[1] His belief that at least some of these trails date back to the Huron, finds strong support in that most of them connect major contact sites or lie along routes mentioned by the Jesuits.

Incomplete as Map 23 must be, a few general observations can be made. Wherever possible the trails followed the high ground avoiding swamps or crossing them at their narrowest extent. Three of the four frontier villages lie at points where a number of trails intersect. In each case it is likely that the villages generated the trails rather than the trails attracting the villages. *Ossossane* was the major connecting point between Huronia and the Petun (JR 20:45) and on a major trail to the Neutral (JR 17:27). St. Joseph II was the principal point of departure to the Neutral from central and eastern Huronia (JR 21:205), while St. Jean Baptiste on the "Narrows" of Lake Couchiching was the last village to all points east of Huronia. On the whole, the network of trails has a marked north-south orientation. This is to be expected in view of the shape of Huronia. Of the east-west trails, one ran along the southern frontier connecting *Ossossane* to St. Jean Baptiste. At St. Joseph II the frontier trail met a major one coming from the farthest north-western extremity of Huronia, the *Pagus Etondatrateus* ("Land's End"), opposite Christian Island. The northern trail, and probably one of the most important, ran from *Toanche* and *Ihonatiria* to St. Jean Baptiste.

In all, there seem to have been about 200 miles of trails, of which the east-west trails comprise 92 miles and the north-south trails 108 miles. Although there is no evidence for it, small trails probably connected every village to its nearest neighbour. If this was the case, these trails would add only 20 miles to the known 200-mile trail network.

The picture thus presented, while it is probably incomplete, appears to be a trail network that reflects the spatial behaviour of the Huron. Trails

1. The map was compiled from Hunter (1898; 1899; 1901; 1902; 1903; 1906), and from the routes taken by the Jesuits on their travels.

connect villages to their nearest neighbour representing avenues of maximum inter-action. Routes directly connecting villages beyond their neighbours are very few. The degree of connectivity between villages can be tested by comparing the existing number of routes with the maximum number of routes theoretically possible (Abler, Adams and Gould 1971: 259). On a scale running from 0.048 (minimum connectivity) to 1.0 (maximum connectivity) the Huron trail-network has a connectivity index of 0.083, indicating an extremely low. degree of regional connectivity. In view of the self-sufficient nature of the villages, and the absence of a market-oriented economy and strong central places, this was to be expected.

A few of the trails may not have been Huron, particularly the ones on the west banks of the Coldwater and Sturgeon Rivers, which do not pass by any late Huron villages. Similarly, the trail from St. Joachim to Matchedash Bay is probably Algonquian, because the area about Matchedash Bay was an Algonquian camping area well into the 19th century. The other trails appear to be reasonably accurate. Most follow "natural routes of travel" to anyone acquainted with the area. On the whole it is difficult to see how this map could be improved upon, unless more detailed 17th-century maps are found. Such a discovery is, however, most unlikely.

Chapter VI

The Huron Subsistence Economy

INTRODUCTION

The Huron economy can be divided into two aspects: those that relate directly to subsistence and contribute the largest part to the Huron diet, *i.e.,* agriculture, fishing, hunting and gathering; and those that relate to trade. Huron trade will be treated in a separate chapter for two reasons: first, the contribution of trade to the diet can be regarded as a supplement which increased during times of famine, but was never too important in feeding the bulk of the Huron population; second, Huron trade is inseparable from Huron external politics and the two must be treated together in assessing the wider impact of Huronia. The term "subsistence economy" is therefore taken as relating to those activities other than trade that are concerned with the production of sustenance from the natural environment. By necessity the separation of trade from other subsistence activities is somewhat artificial because Huron food surpluses formed a part of the Huron export. Trade must therefore be kept in mind in assessing Huron agriculture. Since the Huron themselves seem to have regarded trade primarily as an aspect of external politics and intertribal relations, it seemed to be convenient to treat the subject in the same manner.

Huron subsistence activities revolved primarily around the growing of corn and catching of fish. The primary importance of corn and fish were illustrated to Ragueneau when the Huron told him of the existence of:

> ... a phantom in the woods of prodigious size, who bears in one hand ears of Indian corn, and, in the other, a great abundance of fish; who says that it is he alone who had created men, who has taught them to till the earth, and who has stocked all the lakes and the seas with fish, so that nothing might fail for the livelihood of men. (JR 30:27).

This was the Hurons' answer to the Jesuit's claim that their God had created man and provided for his livelihood. A multitude of other references attest to the fact that the Huron had a well-developed agricultural economy, supplemented largely by fish and lesser amounts of meat.

Even though the Huron practiced slash-and-burn agriculture in the true sense of the word, *svedjebruk* (Mead 1953:44) or *swedje-land* (Büsching 1787 :449), the productivity of this system should not be underrated. "Primitive agriculture" is definitely a misnomer. Even though the Huron did not know the science behind what they were doing, they utilized virtually every known means of producing good yields that is possible without manuring, crop rotation and agricultural machinery. The net result was an economy that was able to feed some 21,000 people on a territory of 340 square miles.

By necessity, some aspects of this chapter are highly speculative. Years of experimental agriculture would be necessary to test some of the estimates made about soil productivity, the effect of burning, yields and forest regeneration. As a matter of fact, it would be an interesting experiment to test the Huron agricultural cycle. At the moment too little is known about soil and crop behaviour under an agricultural system such as that of the Huron.

1. COMPOSITION OF THE DIET AND HEALTH

In order to gain some understanding of the degree to which the Huron relied on certain foods, it is necessary to make an estimate of the composition of their diet. Such an estimate is also fundamental to any discussion of village fields, agricultural techniques and yields. Due to the nature of the evidence any estimates of diet are open to some argument, and the literature on the subject has varied widely. Kroeber (1939:146), for example, wrote that the Huron probably obtained about 50 per cent of their diet from agricultural products, while Popham (1950:88) estimated that corn alone supplied 75 per cent of the total diet. Neither author attempts to justify his estimates or shows how they were derived. It is therefore necessary to quote at some length from the diaries of contemporary observers before any estimates can be justified.

If there is one thing that the ethnohistoric sources describe adequately, it is the Huron diet. The reason for this is, of course, a natural curiosity in other peoples' food habits; but it is also because the French travellers had to subsist on the same diet, and it was a diet that took some time getting used to.

The unanimous opinion was that corn formed the overwhelming staple in every season. Champlain (3:125) called corn " . . . their principal food and usual sustenance . . . ", an observation with which Sagard concurs (Sagard 1939:80, 105-106). The Jesuits without exception mirror the observations of Champlain and Sagard in describing corn as the "chief of their riches", and "the sole staff of life" (JR 10:93, 101; 11:7; 15:153, 159; 19:129; 27:65; 29:247; 33:77; 35:153). Corn formed the basis of anything that was eaten. All the other foods, with rare exceptions, were mixed into the ubiquitous corn soup (*sagamite*) or baked into the occasional corn bread. The dependence on corn was so complete that a crop failure meant starvation.

Champlain considered beans almost as important as corn (Champlain 3:125), however, the Jesuits and Sagard scarcely mention them. Sagard wrote that beans were added to the corn bread or soup " . . . if they have any . . . " (Sagard 1939:105). His only other mention of beans was that he saw a field full of them on his arrival (Sagard 1939:70). There is, however, a possibility that these were wild beans, which, like the wild peas he saw, fooled him at first sight (Sagard 1939:90-91). The Jesuits, in all their discussion of Huron diet, mention beans only three times (JR 15:153; 21:195; 38:245). As a matter of fact, Bressani was under the impression that beans were introduced by the French (JR 38:245). In the middens carbonized beans are by no means rare. They turn up about as frequently as squash remnants, but are outnumbered by carbonized corn fragments by at least 100 to one.

During the late summer and fall squash was as important as beans and perhaps more so. It is mentioned by Champlain (3:47; 50, 31), Sagard (1939:72, 107, 240) and the Jesuits (JR 10:103; 11:7; 13-41, 47; 15:153; 20:81; 21:195). Brébeuf went so far as to write that:

> . . . the squashes last sometimes four and five months, and are so abundant that they are to be had almost for nothing, and so good that, on being cooked in ashes, they are eaten as apples in France (JR 10:103).

It is not always certain whether the writers were referring to pumpkins or squashes because they used the same term, *citrouille,* to describe both. Boucher (1896:144) describes the *citrouille* as:

> . . . of a species different from those of France; they are smaller, and not so unsubstantial; their flesh is firmer and less watery, and of a better flavour.

This is a description of squash. One might also gather from Brébeuf's statement that it was squash that he was describing because of the long period of availability.

The only other cultivated plants mentioned were tobacco and sunflowers. Champlain (3:50) relates that the sunflower was mainly used for hair and body oil. From the only reference to sunflowers in the *Relations*

(37:105) one would gather that they were gathered wild rather than grown purposefully. Tobacco was only grown in limited quantities by the Huron; most of it seems to have been imported from the Petun.

Except in times of famine, gathering does not seem to have been very important. Various fruits formed the bulk of the gathered vegetable products (Champlain 3:50-51; Sagard 1939:72, 74, 83, 238, 239; JR 10:103; 13:13, 41, 47, 85; 35:87). These were often backed into the cornmeal, or mixed with the corn gruel. Acorns, roots and herbs were eaten only rarely (Sagard 1939:108) although there were plenty about (Sagard 1939:237-241). The few references to gathered vegetable foods in the *Relations* definitely associate them with times of famine (JR 27:65; 35:87).

One of the really startling facts about the Huron diet is the lack of meat. This was first observed by Champlain and reiterated by every writer after him (Champlain 3:126; Sagard 1939:82, 106 107; JR 7:223; 13:109, 113; 17:17, 143; 38:245). Bressani, for example, was of the opinion that the Huron " . . . hunted only for pleasure or on extraordinary occasions . . . " (JR 38:245). About the only time of the year that meat seems to have been generally available was during the fall and early winter (JR 13:109, 113; 17:141-143). In a sense, this is an expected pattern. During the spring and summer the men were either preparing the fields or were away on fishing, war or trading expeditions and in the winter travel was difficult. Late fall was the traditional time for hunting and about the only time, apart from winter, that enough men were about for the task. The reported lack of meat is certainly mirrored by the lack of animal bones in Huron middens. This could be partially accounted for by butchering practices if the animals were cut up before the meat was brought to the village. But in that case at least some bone material should be present. Yet the few scraps of bone that are found can in no way be related to any selective process such as butchering practices would imply.

Fish and other aquatic animals such as turtles and clams seem to have been considerably more important than meat. Fish were easier to catch and could be stored longer by reducing them to oil, smoking or drying them. Where fish is mentioned, it is mentioned as a major addition to the usual corn gruel (Champlain 3:137, 129; Sagard 1939:71, 106-107; JR 10:93, 101; 15:159; 21:195; 30:27; 33:77; 35:175). Clams and turtles could be gathered along the lakeshores and streams during the summer, but regular expeditions were not undertaken to obtain them. While bone material is scarce at all sites and fish bones fairly plentiful, turtle bones and clam shells are more variable. An impression gained by the author is that clam shells for example are more plentiful on precontact sites, and on contact sites near favourable aquatic habitats. This impression would have to be supported by future field work.

Apart from the occasional feasts or in times of overabundance, the Huron ate regularly twice a day; in the morning and late afternoon to early evening (Champlain 3:130; JR 8:113; 15:183). The same eating pattern was observed when travelling (JR 7:223). The amount of food consumed must have varied widely, but Sagard relates that the usual meal was about the amount one could get into an alms-dish (Sagard 1939:72). As the amount of food intake must have varied from day to day, so it did with the seasons. Corn and beans were dried, stored and eaten the year round. Squash and wild fruits were available from mid-summer to the fall. Fish was caught the year round, but most often in the spring, fall and early winter. Meat was available only sporadically but most often in the fall (Table 10).

Table 10

Seasonal Availability of Main Food Sources

	Spring	Summer Early	Summer Late	Autumn	Winter
Corn	x	x	x	xx	x
Beans	x	x	x	xx	x
Squash	—	—	x	xx	—
Fish	x	x	x	xx	xx
Meat	x	—	—	x	x
Gathered Food	—	—	x	x	—

Note: — denotes generally absent
x denotes generally available
xx denotes an abundance

From the preceding descriptions, a hypothetical daily diet has been constructed which seems representative of the yearly food intake (Table 11). The percentage figures given are a balance between calorie values and relative weight of the food source. In their descriptions the Jesuits were, of course, describing bulk. In order to make a more accurate assessment of dietary intake and food value, the bulk estimates must be compared and adjusted to calorie values. Popham (1950:88-89) estimated the dietary intake of the Huron (men, women and children) to be about 3,500 calories per day. Wolf (1966:4-5) puts the average daily caloric intake for Neolithic societies at about 2,500. Considering the figures compiled by Rose (1939:54) for work expended by men, women and children, 3,000 calories per day for the Huron seems more realistic. During some parts of the year the calorie intake would probably be higher and during other times, particularly during spring and winter, the calorie intake could be expected to be lower.

Of the total diet, 65% was assigned to corn. In view of Popham's (1950:88) estimate of 75%, this figure might seem low. If more than 65% of the diet was corn, it becomes difficult to account for the other food products the Huron ate. An intake of 65% seems therefore a bit more reasonable. In terms of weight, this would mean that the Huron had a daily consumption of 1.3 lbs. of corn. In view of other corn-growing Neolithic societies this figure is eminently reasonable. Cowgill (1962:- 277) for example quotes averages from Central America ranging from 1.3 to 2 lbs. per person per day.

Table 11

The Average Daily Huron Diet Expressed in
Calories and Weight Equivalents

Food	% cals. in diet	Calories*	Wt. in ounces*
Corn	65%	1,950	19.3
Squash	2%	50	4.6
Beans	13%	400	4.0
Fish	9%	300	5.8
Meat	6%	150	3.2
Gathered Fruits	5%	150	7.8
Totals	100%	3,000	44.7

*Note: Calorie values and weight equivalents have been compiled from Rose (1939:542-591). Corn was calculated as "yellow uncooked cornmeal"; beans as "dried kidney beans"; squash as "steamed pumpkin"; fish as "steamed white fish"; meat as "cooked round beef"; gathered fruits as "blueberries." It was felt that these came closest to the foods used by the Huron. Caloric loss due to cooking would be kept to a minimum because the Hurons ate most meals in soup form.

Other cultivated vegetables were given 15% of the daily diet, of which 13% was assigned to beans and 2% to squash. Beans were available most of the year, while squash was primarily eaten during the autumn. From the descriptions of the way in which squash was eaten, one might gather that it supplemented the usual diet rather than being an integral part of it. Squash is also a bulky food, with a relatively low caloric value. In the

163

light of the descriptions, one third of a pound of squash per day seems about right. All of this would, of course, be eaten during the season when it is available, thus accounting for the descriptions of large amounts.

Fish and meat were given a value of 15%. Because fish was listed as being more important than meat, it is given 9% and meat 6%. Fish was available during the larger part of the year in dried or fresh form. It could also be obtained in larger quantities than meat. Meat is more difficult to dry and there is no evidence that the Huron stored it for any length of time. In a sense meat can be regarded in somewhat the same way as the availability and consumption of squash. When a bear, deer or moose was caught the whole animal was eaten almost at once (JR 8:127; 10:179-191, 213; 15:113; 17:163; 23:63). This was usually an occasion for a feast, or at least made a feast for some other purpose possible. During these occasions a large number of people in addition to the family of the hunter were invited. The feast would then go on until the animals were consumed. During these occasional periods of plenty, considerably more than the normal amount was eaten. Like the figures for squash, the figures for meat therefore represent an average for the year. The daily meat intake therefore fluctuated between zero on most days and well above the combined calorie intake of the other foods on a few days.

The 5% estimate for gathered foods is the most problematical. During times of famine this figure could be expanded to take the place of corn and beans. Under no circumstances, however, could a Huron population of 21,000 subsist very long on gathered produce. Judging from the few records of severe famines an attempt was made to purchase food from neighbouring villages or tribes, (JR 8:97; 15:157; 35:99) or the men had to make a greater effort at hunting (JR 26:311). Regular gathering seems to have been largely confined to wild fruits and berries. Long lists of edible wild plants could be compiled but their significance in the regular diet seems to be small. It is also doubtful if much time was available from the tending and harvesting of the cornfields for extensive gathering. Berries were, of course, dried and stored for the winter.

On the whole, the Huron seem to have been remarkably healthy. The most complete descriptions of Huron health and disease are given by Champlain (3:135-136), Sagard (1939:192-204), Ragueneau (JR 33:199-209) and Bressani (JR 38:257-259). Du Peron (JR 15:155) described them as " . . . robust, all are much taller than the French," while Bressani (JR 38:257) wrote that " . . . they are more healthy than we." In none of these writings are any descriptions of diseases that are attributable to undernourishment or vitamin deficiencies.

The most complete studies done on contact Huron skeletal material are those by Dr. R. I. Harris (n. d.; 1949:71-75) on the 250 skeletons from the *Cahiagué* ossuary. His conclusions are that there is no evidence of either scurvy or rickets, both caused by vitamin deficiencies (Harris, n. d.:11). Caries are almost absent (Harris, n. d.:10). Some tooth crowns show a great deal of wear, and many jaws have missing teeth; both can be attributed to old age and abnormal tooth wear due to a gritty diet (Harris, n. d.:10-11). One skeleton had evidence of tuberculosis and many suffered from osteo-arthritis of the spine. Tuberculosis, Harris feels, must have been contracted from the French; while arthritis, although only present in the spine, may be a symptom of old age (Harris 1949:74; n. d.:14). Another common ailment were squatting facets, a deformation in the ankle caused by spending a great deal of time in a squatting position (Harris 1949:74-75). Some of the skeletons showed evidence of flat feet (Harris, n. d.:9).

Clearly much more work must be done and published on Huron skeletal material. For the present, though, it seems that the Huron were a remarkably healthy lot. Using Rose's (1939:542-591) tables of the nutritive value of various foods, an attempt was made to calculate whether there were any serious deficiencies in the Huron diet (Table 12). According to the system used by Rose, a healthy 3,000 calorie diet should include 30 shares of each of the elements listed in Table 12. On the basis of this evaluation, the Huron diet is slightly below normal in calcium and Vitamin C (ascorbic acid).

Using a different method for assessing the nutrient value of Huron foods, somewhat similar results were obtained (Table 13). This assessment was based on Bogert, Briggs and Calloway (1966:556-579) and Wilson, Fisher and Fuqua (1967:535-559). Again, the Huron diet is apparently low in calcium and Vitamin C (ascorbic acid).

Additional calcium was probably obtained by gathering calcium rich foods such as clams, nuts and crabs. In some areas of the world it has been shown that calcium is also unintentionally added to food through the local water supply and grain milling practices (Bogert, *et al.,* 1966:154). The water supply in Huronia is high in calcium carbonate. In addition, "stone powder" found its way into the diet from milling stones and clay vessels, both with high contents of calcium carbonate. A third source of calcium, and perphaps the most obvious, is the utilization of calcium in producing Vitamin D from sunlight. People who are exposed to sunlight most of their lives can adjust to a much lower total intake of calcium (200-400 mg. daily) because Vitamin D (synthesized by sunlight) improves the body's efficiency in calcium absorption when concentrations of available calcium

Table 12

Nutritive Value of Huron Diet
Nutritive Value of Food in Shares

Food Material	Calories	Protein	Calcium	Phosphorous	Iron	Vitamin A	Vitamin B	Vitamin C
Corn	1,950	19.0	3.8	18.6	11.4	32.3	67.3	—
Squash	50	0.8	2.2	2.3	4.0	trc.	trc.	7.
Beans	400	9.2	7.6	12.8	18.4	0.8	29.2	—
Fish	300	26.7	6.6	15.6	4.2	—	trc.	—
Meat	150	12.0	0.8	7.4	9.0	trc.	trc.	—
Fruit	150	0.6	2.4	1.1	4.1	0.6	—	16.
Totals	3,000	68.3	23.4	57.8	51.1	33.7	96.5	24.(

Table 13
Recommended Daily Intake of Nutrients Compared
with Huron Intake

a) Recommended Intake

	Calories	Protein	Calcium	Iron	Vitamin A	Thiamine	Riboflavin	Niacin	Ascorbic Acid
		gm.	mg.	mg.	I.U.	mg.	mg.	mg.	mg.
Daily Food	3,000	70	800	10	5,000	1.2	1.7	19	70

b) Huron Intake

	Calories	Protein	Calcium	Iron	Vitamin A	Thiamine	Riboflavin	Niacin	Ascorbic Acid
Corn	1,950	55.0	120	14.0	3,000	2.25	0.7	12.0	—
Squash	50	1.4	38	0.6	9,723	0.05	0.8	0.9	8
Beans	400	6.0	38	2.0	220	0.14	0.1	1.0	14
Fish	300	40.0	—	1.8	240	0.24	0.1	14.7	—
Meat	150	25.0	11	3.2	10	0.06	0.2	4.5	—
Fruit	150	1.6	34	2.3	224	0.06	1.0	0.8	32
Totals	3,000	129.0	230	23.9	13,417	2.80	2.9	33.9	54

are low (Bogert, *et al.,* 1966:154; Wilson, *et al.,* 1967:140). Since pregnant and nursing women and young children need more than a normal amount of calcium and Vitamin D, the average amounts in the Huron diet may be a bit low. There is, however, as yet no evidence of calcium deficiencies or rickets in Huron skeletal material.

A lack of Vitamin C (ascorbic acid) is a prime cause of scurvy. As is well known, scurvy was a disease the Indians knew about and were able to cure. Both Cartier (Lescarbot 2:153) and Champlain (3:264-265) were taught by Indians along the St. Lawrence how to treat scurvy by preparing a drink from cedar and hemlock boughs. A daily intake of 30 mg. of Vitamin C is usually enough to cure and prevent scurvy (Bogert 1966:217). The slightly lower-than-recommended intake among the Huron probably posed no serious problems to the average person because the onset of disease was noticeable and could be cured. For pregnant and nursing women however, the lower-than-normal dosage might be serious because during this time they need a larger than normal dose. While the intake of Vitamin C might be high enough to prevent scurvy in the mother, the child or fetus could be affected. This was particularly true during the latter part of the winter and early spring when normal Vitamin-C-bearing foods were not generally available (Champlain 2:59-63). Again, it must be pointed out that as yet there is no evidence from Huron skeletal material that they suffered from Vitamin C shortages.

A disease that often afflicts people with a high maize diet is pellagra (Bogert 1966:254; Wilson 1967:272-275). The symptoms of the disease are severe skin disorders, diarrhea, insomnia, irritability, depression and finally dementia, paralysis and death (Wilson 1967:273). The cause of the disease is an absence of niacin and one of the amino acids, tryptophan. Corn is low in both niacin and tryptophan. From the *Relations* it is not possible to detect the disease because the descriptions are poor and some of the symptoms are similar to those described by the Jesuits for smallpox. Insomnia, irritability, depression and dementia were all reported for the Huron, but it is more than probable that these were culturally induced. Theoretically, the Huron intake of meat and especially fish should contain more than enough niacin to prevent pellagra. This is especially true since the Huron had the habit of eating the whole fish or animal including entrails, liver and kidneys, which are all rich in niacin. Turkeys and other fowl are an added source of niacin.

On the whole the theoretical daily diet, in spite of its high corn content, seems to have been adequate enough for the Huron, so that they did not suffer any observable dietary diseases. If dietary problems existed, the most likely areas of the population so affected were probably infants, pregnant women and their fetuses. The degree to which Huron children suffered from malnutrition and the magnitude of the infant mortality rate can only be guessed at. On the whole children were highly desired, especially girls (JR 15:181), and well cared for. None of the early writers mention a high infant mortality rate among the Huron although they reported high infant mortality rates among the Algonquians (JR 1:259). Instead of a high infant mortality rate Sagard (1939:127) describes a birth rate lower than that of France. While the good friar attributes the low birth rate to sexual license, a more probable explanation was the fact that the Huron abstained from sexual intercourse with their wives during the nursing period which, according to Brébeuf, could last as long as two to three years (JR 10:127).

On the basis of the preceding pages one might argue that malnutrition and infant mortality were not serious during normal conditions. As far as can be determined, the usual Huron diet was healthy, if a bit low in calcium and Vitamin C. In times of famine, however, one could expect serious dietary deficiencies. These would probably effect pregnant women and infants more than the rest of the population. Rather than overall dietary deficiencies or a high birth and mortality rate, the natural population increase was probably controlled by factors such as sexual abstinence during the nursing period and high infant mortality rates during famine periods. On the whole, there does not seem to be any reason to suppose that the Huron suffered from any illness attributable to their normal diet.

2. AGRICULTURE

a) Land Ownership

References regarding Huron practices of land ownership are few, and in some respects inconclusive. The most complete description is by Sagard (1939:103):

> It is their custom for every family (*mesnage*) to live on its fishing, hunting and planting, since they have as much land as they need; for all the forests, meadows and uncleared land are common property, and anyone is allowed to clear and sow as much as he will and can, and according to his needs; and this cleared land remains in his possession for as many years as he continues to cultivate and make use of it. After it is altogether abandoned by its owner then anyone who wishes uses it, but not otherwise.

Champlain (3:155-156) describes a similar practice:

168

Their custom is that each household lives on what it can get by fishing and sowing, having as much land as it needs.

On the surface these references seem to be fairly straightforward. The problem is that Champlain and Sagard were using the word *mesnage* which could mean "family" or "household". Since several nuclear families comprising an extended family lived together in one longhouse; it is important to know which meaning of the word was used to describe landownership. Herman (1956:1045) pointed out the same dilemma in determining the ownership of other aspects of Huron property. From the passage by Sagard one would think that land was owned by individuals or the nuclear family to which the individual belonged. In another passage Sagard (1939:94, 321) definitely refers to the nuclear family by the name *mesnage.* The few references in the *Relations* seem to support Sagard's inferences that individuals owned their own fields which they cultivated for their families (JR 20:79; 38:271). Several references allude to women working in *their* fields (JR 13:11). Whether it was the women who actually owned the land they were working or the men, is not known.

If one takes the point of view that land was individually owned, it becomes difficult to explain why other practices related to the land were longhouse (extended family) affairs. Land clearance for example, was carried on by groups of people (Champlain 3:156); and, as mentioned in a previous chapter, the bulk of the produce was stored in bins shared by the entire longhouse. Similarly other subsistence activities such as fishing, hunting and gathering firewood seem to have been largely group activities. Individual ownership of land is also difficult to explain in terms of the strong feelings of communal responsibility, and the fact that a disinterested attitude towards ownership *per se* was encouraged (Herman 1956:-1057).

Among the New York Iroquois it was the women who owned the land (Tooker 1964:60; Synderman 1951:15-34). Two classes of landownership were recognized; individually-owned fields which the women worked for their families (Parker 1910:29, 92), and communal fields worked by the women for the whole village under the supervision of a senior matron (Parker 1910:29-30). Participation in working of the communal fields was not mandatory, but the results were only shared by those who had contributed to the labour (Parker 1910:29). Morgan (1962:326) relates that, similar to the Huron, all unused land among the Iroquois was common property; and abandoned land reverted to common property that anyone could take up. Land under active cultivation belonged to an individual whose rights to that land were protected by common consent.

169

While most of the references regarding Iroquoian property rights seem to imply individual ownership, Driver (1964:255) feels that agricultural land was not individually owned, but that each field was owned and operated by the extended family of a longhouse. In view of the close cooperation between members of the extended family and their sharing of other tasks, Driver's suggestion has some merit. At the moment, however, there does not seem to be any evidence that the Huron operated in this manner. Moreover, there are no references that any fields were owned and operated in common, either on a village, clan, lineage or extended family basis.

Going strictly by the available evidence for the Huron, however little it may be, one must come to the conclusion that all land under active use for agricultural purposes was the property of the person or nuclear family that used it. The land continued to remain a person's property until he gave it up by ceasing to cultivate it, whereupon anyone could take it over. All land not actively cultivated was common property. Commonly-operated fields either on a village or extended family basis may have existed as among the League Iroquois, but if they did there is no record of it. Feelings of communal responsibility towards the extended family were satisfied by giving mutual aid in clearing the fields, sharing a large portion of the produce and probably in weeding the fields and harvesting crops. Part of the agricultural produce had to be pooled in any case for use in trade, since trade was an affair involving the larger family, rather than just an individual.

Several important implications can be drawn from the preceding discussion and the reference from Sagard. Because only land that was actually being used could be considered a person's property and unused land reverted to the "public domain", vacant land could not be accumulated as wealth, sold or inherited. It would therefore be impossible for a landed class to exist or even come into being. The size of individual fields would therefore vary according to the needs and initiative of a person and his family. The entire village lands should be a fairly close reflection of the size of the village polulation and the quality of the natural environment. Ultimately the result of such landholding practices would be an equitable distribution of land, closely adjusted to the needs and initiative of a family. It would also be difficult to envision a regular cycle of field rotation related to some sort of fallowing system, since the fallow land, not being actively used, could be considered abandoned land and therefore free for anyone to use. Wealth and status, while not measured in terms of land, could accrue from land by the accumulation of a surplus. The surplus could then be disposed of by giving feasts, gifts to the not so fortunate, community payments and for trade. Prestige and social status was therefore measured in terms of generosity; and, as often happened, the most industrious were the most wealthy, the most generous and the most respected men in the community (Herman 1956:1054-1055). It should be added that community feeling assured that the system of generosity and prestige operated the way it did. The industrious, fortunate or wealthy were expected to be generous. Failure to do so could result in jealousy and ill will (JR 8:95). But, by and large, public pressure to share wealth did not seem to be necessary for ". . . every man taxes himself freely with what he can pay and without any complusion gives of his means according to his convenience and goodwill" (Sagard 1939:267). In another passage Sagard (1939:89) observed that gifts and food were given to such an extent that no one ever went hungry. Champlain (3:164-165) and the Jesuits (JR 8:95, 127; 10:213, 215, 303-305; 28:49-51; 33:207) made similar observations.

Land therefore seems to have been individually owned and partially operated by the larger family through mutual aid. The products of the land, however, were shared either with the extended family or with the larger community through gift giving, feasts or other institutionalized methods. The results of such generosity were prestige in the community and any honours such as official appointments that the community might wish to bestow. In a sense, therefore, it was necessary for individuals to own their own fields and produce the surplus necessary for gift-giving in order to gain public standing. Besides prowess in hunting, fishing and war, a disposable agricultural surplus was the only other means of achieving personal standing in a community, either by giving the surplus away or by trading it for other products that could be redistributed. Such a system would be difficult to envision if land was owned and operated communally and all the proceeds shared *directly.* It is possible therefore to reconcile individual ownership of land and feelings of communal responsibility. As a matter of fact, individual ownership of land seems to be necessary in order to exercise communal responsibility as the Huron saw it and reap the benefits of generosity.

b) Major Crop Types

The most complete description of Huron corn is given by Sagard (1939:- 104):

> . . . there comes up from a single grain only one shoot or stalk, and the stalk bears two or three ears, each ear yielding a hundred, two hundred, sometimes four hundred grains, and there are some that

yield more. The stalk grows as high as a man and higher, and is very thick. It does not grow so well and so high, nor is the ear so big or the grain so good, in Canada [Quebec] or France as there [Huronia]. The grain ripens in four months, or in three in some places.

From the *Relations* one would gather that corn was planted sometime during the latter part of May (JR 13:251) and harvested in the beginning of September (JR 13:85), lending support to Sagard's growing period of about three months.

The earliest and most complete description of Iroquois maize grown in Canada was made by Peter Kalm between 1748 and 1751 (Kalm 1935:-98-117). Kalm describes two main varieties grown in Canada; a small three month variety (Kalm 1935:104) which prefers sandy soils (Kalm 1935:116), and a larger variety taking up to six months to ripen (Kalm 1935:103). The Indians seemed to prefer the three-month variety (Kalm 1935:104) which was also the one most often grown in Canada (Kalm 1935:103). He also observed that commonly each stalk produced two or three ears, each ear containing about 300 kernels (Kalm 1935:109). On the whole, the larger variety produced greater yields, but because the smaller variety could be planted closer together, per-acre yields were similar (Kalm 1935:104). As one proceeded north, the differences between the two major varieties became less (Kalm 1935:103). Similar observations to Kalm's were made by other early travellers (Anderson and Brown 1952:2-8).

According to a number of studies done on Indian corn varieties from the Great Lakes area, which botanists feel have not been appreciably altered by the great experiments in hybridization during the last hundred years, two main varieties were present; *Zea mays amylacea* (flour or bread corn) and *Zea mays indurata* (flint or hominy corn) (Anderson and Brown 1952; Brown and Anderson 1947; Hill 1952; Parker 1910; Waugh 1916; Will and Hyde 1917; Zirkle 1969). Some other varieties may have been present such as pop corn, but never in appreciable quantities. The Indians subdivided the two main varieties according to colour and slight differences in the hardness of the kernels. From the studies cited above, the main morphological distinctions of the two principal varieties can be tabulated (Table 14). This tabulation comes close to Kalm's observations, but Sagard's description indicates that the average cob may have been somewhat smaller. A point to notice is that corn matured in the time given by the early writers and usually had two cobs per stalk.

Table 14

Morphological Differences Between Flint and Flour Corn

Morphological Distinctions	Zea mays amylacea (Flour Corn)	Zea mays indurata (Flint Corn)
Number of rows	8	8
Length of cob	4″ to 8″	4″ to 11″
Number of kernels per row	20 to 45	25 to 60
Number of kernels per cob	160 to 360	200 to 660
Number of cobs per stalk	2 to 3	2
Length of growing period	130 days	100 days

Detailed studies on Huron corn remains have not been published.[1] Personal observations, principally at *Cahiagué,* would lead one to the conclusions that the average corn cob was about three to five inches long, eight-rowed, though occasionally reaching ten rows. A four-inch cob with about 200 kernels seems to be the average, confirming Sagard's observations. Although the length of the cob is considerably shorter than modern varieties, the size of the kernels is the same. From the charred remains only two varieties could be distinguished, flour and flint corn. Of these, the latter outnumbered the former about three to one. The larger proportion of flint corns is probably accounted for by the fact that it is a hardier variety than flour corn. Since the average length of the frost freeperiod in Huronia is about 130-140 days, a predominance of flint corn would be expected (Chapman and Brown 1966: Figure 12).

Less is know about Huron beans and squashes. Champlain (3: 125) mentions the *febues du bresil* (red beans) while Boucher (1896:144) identifies Huron beans as *haricots* (kidney beans). Beans found on Huron sites tend to be kidney shaped, and about one quarter inch long. Being charred, their colour is impossible to determine. Most likely, the main variety was the kidney bean (*Phaseolus vulgaris*). Judging from Boucher's (1896:144) description of squash, the Huron grew the summer squash (*Cucurbita polymorpha*). This fits with a Jesuit description that some squash was available in early August (JR 20:79).

1. Noble's (1968) thesis is the only work that attempts a study of corn remains from Ontario archaeological sites.

c) Preparing the Land, Planting and Taking Care of the Fields

i) Preparing the fields.   Huron agricultural methods were fairly typical of swidden farming. Champlain and Sagard provide the most complete descriptions on the manner of field preparation and planting:

> A party of them will strip the trees of all their branches which they burn at the foot of the said tree to kill it. They clear up the ground thoroughly between the trees and then sow their corn a pace apart putting in each spot about ten grains, and thus continuing until they have enough for three or four years provision, for fear lest they should have a bad year (Champlain 3:156).

Sagard's statement adds some information not mentioned by Champlain:

> They cut down the trees at the height of two or three feet from the ground, then they strip off the branches, which they burn at the stump of the same trees in order to kill them, and in the course of time they remove the roots. Then the women clean up the ground between the trees thoroughly, and at distances a pace apart dig round holes or pits. In each of these they sow nine or ten grains of maize, which they have picked out, sorted, and soaked in water for a few days, and so they keep on until they have sown enough to provide food for two or three years, either for fear that some bad season may visit them or else in order to trade it to other nations for furs and other things they need; and every year they sow their corn thus in the same places and spots, which they freshed with their little wooden spade, shaped like an ear with the handle at the end. The rest of the land is not tilled, but only cleansed of noxious weeds, so that it seems as if it were all paths, so careful are they to keep it quite clean; and this made me, as I went alone sometimes from one village to another, lose my way usually in these cornfields more often than in the meadows and forests (Sagard 1939:103-104).

Only one point must be added, and that is that the Huron had no knowledge of fertilizers. Sagard for example, stated that the villages had to be moved periodically when the local wood resources were exhausted or when:

> . . . the land is so exhausted that their corn can no longer be grown in the usual perfection for lack of manure; because they do not understand cultivating the ground nor putting the seed anywhere else than in the usual holes. (Sagard 1939:93).

These observations were echoed by the Jesuits (JR 11:7; 15:153).

From the foregoing descriptions, later accounts and early settlers observations, a fairly-detailed reconstruction of Huron agricultural procedures is possible.

The first step was the removal of trees and brushwood. As mentioned in a previous chapter, it is more than highly probable that areas of young trees were sought, not only because they were easier to remove, but also because that kind of wood was needed in large quantities. Clearing a virgin forest must have been a terrible job which was rarely attempted. A good indication of the difficulties involved in clearing a virgin forest is the description of the abortive settlement on Christian Island. Ragueneau described it as: "These grand forests, which, since the Creation of the world, had not been felled by the hand of any man" (JR 35:85). Later in the same passage he blames the lack of corn in the village partially on the Hurons inability to clear enough land in " . . . a thick forest unprepared in any way for tillage" (JR 35:87).

The usual procedure in land-clearing was to chop down the smaller trees, stripping the larger ones of their branches and girdling them. The ground was then thoroughly cleaned of grass, weeds and shrubs. This debris was then piled against the stumps and larger trees that could not be felled, and burned. There is no evidence that the Huron, or for that matter any of the Iroquoian groups simply set the forest on fire to clear land for agriculture. Such a procedure would have been disastrous in view of the fact that nearby villages were built of wood, since the Huron did not have the ability to control large fires. The time of year when most of the clearing operations went on, was apparently in the spring, just before the seed was planted. This coincided with the period (March and April) when the women gathered their supply of firewood; and it is not unreasonable to suppose that the two tasks, land clearance by the men and firewood gathering by the women, were related (Champlain 3:156; Sagard 1939:-94). One last aspect of forest clearance may have been the removal of the smaller stumps and large dead trees. Parker (1910:22) stated that dead trees in the cornfields were not regarded safe and were removed as soon as possible.

ii) Preparing the seed and planting. The second step was the preparation of seeds for planting. Several authors noted that corn seeds were first soaked in water or a bed of moist bark (Sagard 1939:103; Lafitau 1724, 2:76-78; Kalm 1935:107). Kalm observed that this practice made the corn come up several days earlier. In fact, soaking the corn in the warmth of a longhouse would cause the kernels to germinate. The fact that the kernels used for seed were carefully selected beforehand, shows that the

175

Huron had a good working knowledge of crop improvement; or, at least, crop maintainance practices. If, as is probable, the larger seeds were selected for seed, the Huron, consciously or unconsciously, selected for quality and yield. It is therefore not really surprising that corn culture was so highly developed. The really great improvements in corn breeding in Ontario came when Europeans introduced fertilizer and began to understand the mechanisms of hybridization through seed selection and cross-pollination.

After the seed was soaked in water, the women departed into the fields and began the actual planting. Both Sagard and Champlain related that up to ten grains were placed into the ground at distances about a pace apart. DeRasieres (Jameson 1909:107) among the New England tribes in 1628 mentioned that about five to six seeds were planted in each spot about two-and-a-half feet apart. Kalm (1935:105-106) among the Iroquois in 1748-51 reported that four to five kernels were planted in one spot, usually three to four feet apart for the variety of corn grown in Canada.

As the corn grew, earth was carefully hoed up around the plants. Parker relates that the first hoeing occurred when the corn was a "span high," with a second final hoeing when the plants were "knee high" (Parker 1910:29). The same practice was later copied by Europeans, who used both the hoe to heap earth around the growing corn, and the plough (Kalm 1935:105, 107). As late as 1954, the old Iroquoian method of corn growing was still recommended to Canadian farmers:

> Planting [of corn] is done either in hills or rows. Hills are usually spaced three or three and a half feet apart. Usually four or five seeds are sown and when the young plants emerge the three strongest plants are left to grow, the others are pulled out. (Ferguson 1954:24).

Kalm (1935:106, 107) also reported that the usual number of stalks per corn hill was about three to four.

Once the corn hills were established, it was the universal practice to use the same hills over and over again until the land was exhausted. (Sagard 1939:104; Waugh 1916:17).

Because the same hills were reused year after year, they became a remarkably persistent feature in the landscape of the north-eastern United States and Canada. Corn hills have been described and measured in every State from Massachusetts to Michigan (Delabarre and Wilder 1920; Hinsdale 1928). In Ontario they were described by Hunter (1898:13, 37, 41; 1899:58, 65, 67, 69, 73-74, 75, 76, 77, 78; 1901:76, 85, 87), Wintemberg (1930) and Lee (1958:10-11). Hinsdale (1928:32, 36) and Delabarre and Wilder (1920:213, 221) observed that corn hills were both regularly and irregularly distributed. The latter authors postulated that the irregularly distributed corn hills were on land that had not been cleared of tree stumps, but that after the stumps had been removed, the cornhills were placed in regular rows (Delabarre and Wilder 1920:225). None of the corn hills seen in Ontario have been described as having any regularity in the manner of their distributional pattern.

On Table 15 the observations by various authors have been summarized regarding the size and spacing of corn hills. In a later chapter this information will be used to attempt a reconstruction of Huron corn yields. Only one contemporary picture exists of Iroquoian corn hills (Lafitau 1724, 2:155). The spacing between the hills as pictured by Lafitau is about three to four feet.

If the spacing of corn hills is taken at three to four feet, theoretically there could have been as many as 2,500 to 4,700 corn hills to the acre. Most of the best documented sources, including the Ontario ones, seem to settle on a figure of slightly less than four feet between corn hills. If 3.75 feet are taken as a reasonable average, a completely utilized field would have about 3,000 corn hills to the acre. Of course, not all the land could be used because of stumps, rocks and other debris. In the previous chapter an average of 435 trees per acre was considered a reasonable estimate for a youthful forest. If each of these takes up the area of a potential corn hill and a few more are taken up by rocks and other obstacles, a final figure of 2,500 corn hills per acre does not seem unreasonable. This figure is fairly close to the 2,600 corn hills per acre counted by Delabarre and Wilder (1920:213).

After the corn had been planted and grown up to about two inches (Jameson 1909:107), one or two weeks according to Kalm (1935:106), beans were planted in the same hills. Corn, beans and squash were always grown together. This practice was sanctified in Iroquoian mythology (Waugh 1916:3, 103-104; Parker 1910:27, 38; Tooker 1964:60). The extent to which beans were interplanted is not known. In New England both Champlain (1:328) and De Rasieres (Jameson 1909:107) observed that three to four beans were planted in every hill. Among the Iroquois, Parker (1910:27) noted that beans were planted in every seventh hill. In view of the relative importance of beans to corn among the Huron it is not likely that beans were planted in every hill. In actual fact, beans in every seventh hill is extremely close to the ratio of beans to corn in the Huron diet discussed earlier.

Among the Iroquois squash was also planted in the corn hills (Parker 1910:91; Waugh 1916:113). The number of corn hills involved and the extent to which the Huron practiced this is not known.

Table 15

The Size and Spacing of Corn Hills

Authority	Diameter of corn hills (feet)	Dist. between centre of corn hills (feet)
Kalm 1935:105-106	?	3-4
Sagard 1939:103	?	(1 pace)
Champlain Vol. 1:328	?	3
Champlain Vol. 3:156	?	(1 pace)
Jameson 1909:107	?	2.5
Wintemberg 1930	3	3
Lee 1958:11	2.5	5
Delabarre and Wilder 1920:214	2+	4±
Hinsdale 1920:31	1.5	3
Hinsdale 1920:36	2	4
Aller 1954:68	4	6
Personal Observation	3	4

iii) Tending the fields and common pests.   After the planting was finished and the corn hills hoed up, the women and children spent the bulk of their time up to harvest tending the fields (JR 8:143; 10:53; 13:11). Most of their time was spent on weeding (Sagard 1939:104) and chasing birds away (Sagard 1939:220; JR 10:145). The Huron considered birds such a pest, that they even asked the priests how they could get rid of them (Sagard 1939:220). Particularly troublesome seem to have been "cranes", "geese" and "crows". The "cranes" mentioned by Sagard could have been the migratory sandhill crane (*Grus canadensis*) now extirpated from the area (Devitt 1943:285).[1] Sagard's geese were probably the

1. The editors of Sagard's *Long Journey* (1939:220) state that Sagard's "crane" was the Great Blue Heron (*Ardea herodias*). This is unlikely for two reasons; the heron subsists on a diet of fish, insects, mice, amphibians and the like and does not usually move in large flocks as described by Sagard. Cornfields are definitely not its habitat (Martin, *et. al.,* 1951:78-79; Taverner 1919:82; Devitt 1943:-257). The sandhill crane on the other hand, although now rare in Ontario flocks in fairly large numbers and is known to have a high corn diet when he can get it (Martin, *et. al.,* 1951:80, 81; Taverner 1919:85-86; Walkinshaw 1949:38-42, 44-48). At the Robitaille site, a late contact Huron village, the Sandhill crane constitutes the largest amount of avian bone material (Savage 1971).

Canada goose (*Branta canadensis*). Crows (*Corvus brachyrhynchos*) were a serious pest not only among the Huron, but also among the Iroquois (Kalm 1935:106, 114-116). Kalm devoted several pages to descriptions of ingenious ways the Iroquois had of getting rid of them. Grasshoppers and caterpillars were also considered pests (JR 10:195; 14:105; 18:85). One woman even came to Le Mercier with a grasshopper she had caught begging him ". . . to teach her some contrivance for killing the little creatures that eat the corn. . ." (JR 14:105). According to Kalm (1935:-115-116) one of the worst pests the Iroquois had to contend with were squirrels. Waugh (1916:36-37) adds blackbirds, the raccoon, woodchuck and jay to the list of pests feeding on corn. Blackbirds (*Euphagus carolinus* and *Quiscalus quiscula*) and jays (*Cyanocitta cristata*) are extremely common in Huronia (Devitt 1943:45-46; 1944:90-91), as are raccoons (*Procyon lotor*) and woodchucks (*Marmota monax*). Among the squirrels, Sagard mentioned several varieties, but none in connection with corn growing. Of the squirrels most damaging to corn, the eastern fox squirrel (*Sciurus niger*), is absent in Huronia, but common in the Iroquois country (Martin, *et al.,* 1951). A list of animals was prepared whose diet shows a marked preference for corn. This list was checked against the occurrence of birds and mammals in Huronia. Only those animals common to Huronia in the past and present were retained on the list (Table 16). The result is a formidable array of potential pests the Huron had to deal with. Of these, the crows, blackbirds, grackles and raccoons are considered the most injurious (Martin *et al.,* 1951:465-466). Sagard's mention of crows probably includes blackbirds and grackles. Raccoons were also considered injurious to corn by Kalm (1964:243). That this animal was not mentioned by the Jesuits or Sagard is unusual except that perhaps, due to its nocturnal habits, the priests were not aware of it.

The extent to which these animals damaged a corn crop is difficult to estimate. Judging from Kalm's (1935:115) descriptions and the fact that the Huron women spent the entire summer in the fields, damage could have been considerable.

iv) Harvest. By early August corn was well advanced (Champlain 3:46) and by the end of August and early September it was ready for harvesting (JR 13:85). Like other agricultural work, harvesting was the responsibility of the women (Champlain 3:136; Sagard 1939:101, 104). The ripe corn cobs were picked in the fields and taken back to the longhouse. There the husks were pulled back exposing the grain. The next step was to tie several cobs together into a large bunch and hang them on the longhouse walls and ceiling to dry. When dry the grain was shelled, cleaned and stored

179

Table 16

Common Animal Pests in Corn Fields

Animal	Amount of Corn in diet	Reference (Martin, et al, 1951)
Sandhill crane (*Grus canadensis*)	25%-50%	:80-81, 465
Mourning dove (*Zepaidura macroura*)	10%-25%	:111-112, 465
Bobwhite quail (*Colinus virginianus*)	25%-50%	:100, 465
Rusty blackbird (*Euphagus carolinus*)	10%-25%	:173, 465
Crow (*Corvus brachyrynchos*)	25%-50%	:135, 465
Grackle (*Quiscalus quiscula*)	50%+	:174, 465
Blue jay (*Cyanocitta cristata*)	10%-25%	:131, 465
Raccoon (*Procyon lotor*)	25%-50%	:221, 466

in the bark casks discussed in the previous chapter. In addition to the harvesting procedure just described, the Iroquois, and perhaps also the Huron, sometimes pulled up the stalks with the cobs attached, tied them into bundles and propped them up in the field to dry (Parker 1910:31; Waugh 1916:39).

Once out of the fields and in the bark casks, the corn was subject to the onslaughts of mice, who were there " . . . in thousands . . . without number" (Sagard 1939:227). Sagard lists two common mice in and about the longhouses; one about the size of the common European mouse (probably a species of *Peromyscus*) and the *Tackro*, " . . . twice as big as the common mouse and not as big as rats" (Sagard 1939:227). The ubiquitous meadow mouse (*Microtus sp.*) well known as a corn-eater, fits the description of the latter. Both of these rodents were eaten by the Huron.

Among the Iroquois the end of the harvest was marked by thanksgiving ceremonies (Waugh 1916:38-39). The Huron had thanksgiving ceremonies (JR 10:177), but none of the ones described can be specifically associated with the corn harvest.

d) The Effects of Huron Agriculture on the Land

All of the early writers were in agreement that Huron agricultural practices were deleterious to the soil, forcing abandonment due to soil and wood exhaustion after a number of years of continuous cultivation. Both Sagard (1939:92) and Champlain (3:124) wrote that abandonment took place after ten, fifteen or thirty years. The Jesuits who were no doubt better informed, having lived longer among the Huron, stated that the land held out for twelve years at the most (JR 15:153), but most often only for eight to ten years (JR 15:153; 19:133). In view of the soils chosen by the Huron for corn culture, eight to twelve years of continuous cropping on the same cornhills seems like an exaggeration. Most farmers in the area today estimate that a sandy loam or loamy sand would not support a corn crop for more than four to six years without fertilizer. Since the Huron did not fertilize their fields or practice any recognizable form of crop rotation or purposeful fallowing, other answers must be found for an observed period of cultivation up to twelve years. Essentially, the answer must lie in a combination of factors, chief of which are Huron agricultural practices, the effect of burning on the soil, demands placed by corn on soil and the natural fertility of the soil itself.

i) The demands of corn on soil. Except for periodic droughts, moisture and temperature requirements for corn-growing are adequate anywhere in Huronia. As a matter of fact, in the first half of the 17th century some corn was grown as far north as Lake Nipissing and adjacent areas (Champlain 2:275, 276; Sagard 1939:66-67; JR 21:239-241; 23:255).

The literature on corn-soil relationships is vast. For the purposes of this chapter only a brief summary is given. Corn grows best on deep, moisture-retentive, yet well-drained loams. Providing the proper nutrient levels can be maintained, it also grows well on sandy loams and sands. Corn grows best in soils with a pH range of 5.5 to 7.0 (Thompson 1952:110); therefore podzols tend to be slightly too acidic especially in the upper horizons. Both on the Vasey and Tioga soil series in Huronia, especially the latter, the soil pH must be raised for maximum corn production.

Good corn production is heavily dependent on available nitrogen, phosphorus and potassium, all of which are deficient in the Vasey and Tioga sandy loams and loamy sands used by the Huron (Canada, Department of Agriculture 1962:33, 45). It was on the basis of this information that farmers in Huronia today estimated that the Huron would not get a crop off their fields after four to six years unless they used fertilizer. A deficiency in any of these elements causes discolouration of the leaves, reduction in the growth rate and small, imperfectly-shaped ears. Yields will drop markedly as these symptoms appear and finally the fields will cease to be productive (Sprague and Larson 1966:3-4).

One of the major problems with the sandy soils in Huronia is that they are not particularly rich in organic matter. Since organic matter is the major supplier of soil nitrogen, any process that removes organic matter from the soil is ultimately deleterious to corn-growing. The same is true for available phosphorus, which is present in the mineral content and organic matter of the soil. Phosphorus can be depleted extremely quickly if organic matter and fine soil particles are somehow removed, as through erosion of the surface layers of a soil (United States Department of Agriculture 1938:383). Unfortunately, the parent materials of the sandy soils in Huronia are deficient not only in organic matter, but also in the fine soil particles; and are therefore low in phosphorus to begin with (Chapman and Putnam 1937:178). Potassium is present in the soil minerals, particularly feldspar, and is released to plants through the slow process of chemical weathering. Corn places fairly heavy demands on available potassium and the amount of corn that can be grown without potassic fertilizers is limited. Because soil development is very slow in Huronia, potassium is not replaced very quickly.

The rate at which corn removes nutrients and the rate of nutrient replacement through natural agencies must be established experimentally for a particular locality. Even if absolute amounts of necessary nutrients are known for a soil, danger points are reached long before total amounts have been removed by a corn crop. Danger points and rates of removal have not been established for soils in Huronia. However, the statements by local farmers that the loamy sands cease to be productive after four to five years, the sandy loams after five to six years and the sands after about three years of continuous corn culture, seem to be fairly reliable indicators of rates of nutrient loss. The Simcoe County Soil Survey rates the Vasey sandy loam as "fair" for corn and the Tioga sandy loam and loamy sand as "fair to poor" (Canada, Department of Agriculture 1962:84-85). Both need yearly applications of nitrogen, potassium and phosphorus.

ii) The effect of burning on soil fertility.   Since the Huron burned their land to remove brushwood, weeds and probably the previous year's corn stalks, an assessment must be made of what burning does to the soil.

All authors who have written on the subject agree that burning raises the pH of a soil (Fowells and Stephenson 1934:175; Ahlgren and Ahlgren 1960:495; Vogl 1969:253-254; Kivekas 1941:194). Wood ash is rich in magnesium, calcium, potassium and phosphorus in addition to which ashes from corn cobs and stalks are very high in potash (United States Department of Agriculture 1938:518-519; Ahlgren and Ahlgren 1960:517; Vogl 1969:254). Studies done by Vogl (1969:253) in Wisconsin indicate a raise in soil pH from 5.5 and 6.0 to as much as 8.0 and 8.5 after burning. Studies done in Sweden under similar leaching conditions as Huronia show that the increased pH is still detectable after ten years (Ahlgren and

Ahlgren 1960:495). Potassium has been shown to increase after burning by over 150 per cent in Oregon and Washington, dropping to about 100 per cent after two years; calcium increased by 300 per cent to 800 per cent and phosphorus increased by "marked amounts" (Ahlgren and Ahlgren 1960:499-500). Both Oregon and Washington have climatic conditions promoting higher rates of leaching than in Huronia.

The effect of burning on the production of available nitrogen is less specific. Some authors report a significant loss in nitrogen, others report a significant gain (Ahlgren and Ahlgren 1960:497-498). The differences between these studies seem to be largely a result of how soon the study was done after a burn and how severe the burn was. A severe burn destroys soil organic matter and with it available nitrogen. The result is a net loss if tests are made immediately after the burn (Fowells and Stephenson 1934:175). In the longer run, however, because burning increases the pH of the soil, it stimulates bacterial activity and therefore increases nitrification (Ahlgren and Ahlgren 1960:498-499; Fowells and Stephenson 1934:181; Kivekas 1941:194; Vogl 1969:254). The net result is a rise in nitrogen, well above the original levels. Some authors report detectable increases in soil nitrogen five to twenty-five years after a burn depending on the soil type.

In general, most authors agree that the immediate effect of burning is a rise in soil fertility (Fowells and Stephenson 1934:181; Kivekas 1941:-194; Ahlgren and Ahlgren 1960:493-494). Some studies cited by Ahlgren and Ahlgren (1960:493, 498) mention specifically that yields from corn and legumes increased after burning. In the long run, however, the effect of continuous burning cannot be anything but detrimental. Continued productivity of forest soils is dependent on organic matter, which is reduced by each successive burning. In the meantime little organic matter is added to the soil. The short-term result of fire is therefore increased fertility due to the release of plant nutrients, an increased soil pH and a stimulation of nitrification. The long-term result is a thorough depletion of a given soil and a long period of recovery. A further long-term danger of burning is that because organic matter is destroyed the soil surface becomes more succeptible to erosion.

The length of time during which soil fertility is increased after burning is impossible to estimate and must be derived experimentally. About the only thing that could be stated with certainty is that burning enabled the Huron to cultivate their soils longer than the four to six years estimated by present farmers in the area. At the same time, the soil recovery rate would also have been longer than soils that had not been repeatedly burned.

iii) Other Huron farming practices related to crop productivity.   Besides burning unwanted brush and crop residues, the Huron also spent a great deal of time weeding their fields (Sagard 1939:104). Weeding was a common practice among all the Eastern Woodland Indians (Jameson 1909:107; Waugh 1916:20). Weeding is of great importance to corn growing, not only because weeds affect yields, but also because they could conceivably make a corn field unfit for crop growing, by becoming so firmly established that it is difficult to get rid of them with crude hoes and digging sticks. The Ontario Department of Agriculture (*n. d.,* a) has estimated that losses in corn yield from an unweeded field could be in the order of ten to thirty per cent. Because the Huron weeded their fields diligently they were probably aware of the adverse effects of weeds.

A second practice that served to increase yields was the growing of beans and corn together in the same corn hill. The role of nitrogen fixation by bacteria at the roots of leguminous plants is well known. This accounts for one of the greatest supplies of fixed nitrogen available to plants (United States Department of Agriculture 1938:364). Whether the Huron knew that the interplanting of beans was beneficial to corn growing or just a convenient method of providing a prop for the bean vines, is not known. One would think that generations of experience and observation had shown that corn hills with beans gave better yields for a longer period of time. The very fact that at least the Seneca considered beans and corn inseparable, believing that a spiritual union occurred when the two were planted together, indicates an awareness of the beneficial effects of planting these crops together (Parker 1910:27). If, as among the Seneca, beans were planted in every seventh corn hill, the effect would be to slow down soil nitrogen exhaustion. Since it is unlikely that the same corn hills were planted with beans in succeeding years, the beneficial effects of nitrogen fixation would be spread over the entire corn field. Except to say that bean planting is beneficial to corn growing and would set back nitrogen exhaustion, it is not possible to estimate an exact number of years over which corn growing could be extended.

One last Huron agricultural practice that had potential benefits to corn growing was the method of planting corn, beans and squash in hills. Any removal of the natural vegetation cover through burning exposes the soil on the resulting clearings to the dangers of erosion. Because the Huron did not have the plough, soil disturbance was kept at a minimum. In spite of that, however, sheet wash could ultimately destroy a field in very short order. The amount of soil that can be removed by erosion from an unprotected field is staggering. Experiments conducted by the Ontario Department of Agriculture (1952:23-24) demonstrate that 90 to 100 tons of soil can be removed from an acre of silt loams with a 14-16 per cent slope in one year. Similar experiments in the United States on a silt loam under corn, not contour-ploughed, with a 12 per cent slope, demonstrated a soil loss of 99 tons per acre including 40 per cent of the yearly rainfall of 38 inches lost as runoff (Russell 1961:630). At the same time yields dropped 20 per cent with three inches of surface soil removed and 88 per cent with all of the surface soil removed (Ontario Department of Agriculture 1952: 21). Contour ploughing on a 10 per cent slope reduced soil loss from 77 tons per acre to 29 tons per acre (Ontario Department of Agriculture 1952:23). It is inconceivable that the Huron would have obtained even three successive crops from a field had they not practiced soil conservation procedures. The actual village sites, particularly on sloping ground, often show signs of considerable erosion (Cruickshank and Heidenreich 1969:- 46). At the Robitaille site (lot 17, concession 20, Tiny Township), sheet erosion on parts of the site has lowered the soil surface by approximately ten to twenty inches to the transition zone between the B and C horizons, creating aluvial fans in adjoining creek valleys (Heidenreich, *et al.,* 1971). The adjoining corn fields show no evidence of erosion except where fields adjoin steep slopes. Observations will, of course, vary with the slope on which the corn hills were planted; but the net effect of irregularly-spaced mounds over a sandy surface should be almost as effective as contour ploughing, thus reducing soil loss. Along with a reduction of soil loss one could also except a reduction of surface runoff and therefore maximization of available moisture.

The fact that the Huron did not have the plough or indeed any animals to pull a plough, meant that surface soil disturbance was kept at a minimum. The digging stick was merely used to poke a few holes into the ground to receive seeds, and the crude hoes were used to heap up a small mound around the growing corn. Apart from these hills, the remainder of the soil was not loosened. As a matter of fact, the areas between the hills became hard-packed paths as the women walked between the hills tending the corn (Delabarre and Wilder 1920:211).

The minimization of soil surface disturbance due to the use of the digging stick probably had one further effect besides reducing the danger of erosion. Ploughing tends to loosen the soil to a depth of about ten inches, thus increasing the rate of soil leaching. By comparison, leaching should not be as rapid in the top layers of a soil profile under Huron methods of agriculture.

A further effect of hilling up corn during the period of early growth is a reduction of the effect of late frosts. The area between the hills would act as a pocket to trap cold air. In later years, after the hills were well-established, being up to a foot in height, none but severe frosts need to have affected corn growth.

iv) Estimates of the length of time fields could be used under Huron agricultural practices. Although there seems to be little doubt that Huron agricultural practices prolonged soil fertility, it is difficult to estimate by how much. Most studies done on other shifting cultivators in temperate forest lands either avoid a discussion of cultivating periods (Narr 1956:134-151) or assume that such periods were similar to cultivation cycles in the tropics (Guyan 1954:123). In parts of the Soviet Union were slash-and-burn agriculture was carried on up to the 19th century, guesses as to the length of time a piece of land was cultivated, range from three to six years, depending on the soil type (Smith 1959:53). Only a few scholars have attempted to estimate cultivation periods from empirical observations in northern latitudes. Using strictly archaeological evidence, Piggott (1965:-52) estimated that the Neolithic Danubian settlements of south central Germany occupied an area for about ten years, returning after a fifty-year fallow period during which the land had recovered. In Finland, Mead (1953:46) has documentary evidence of continuous cultivation on the same plot up to ten years. On the basis of his work on early European agriculture in Ontario, which was in some respects strikingly similar to Huron methods, Schott believed that the Jesuit estimates of cultivation periods up to 10 or 12 years were reasonable (Schott 1936:47). On the better soils early Ontario farmers used Indian methods for two to four years until the stumps were removed, and then the plough for up to twenty-five years without fertilizer, manure or fallowing (Schott 1936: 169-171).

There are several problems in using examples from European cultures. In some respects the Danubians come closest to the Huron, because both were digging-stick and hoe cultivators. However, the Danubians also had domesticated animals and may have abandoned land earlier than the Huron in order to create grazing areas. In the case of the examples from Finland and the Soviet Union, not only domesticated animals but also the plough were present. In both cases, rotation patterns existed where continuous cultivation was followed by an equal number of years of grazing. The use of the plough may have led to more rapid soil exhaustion. The Huron, of course, did not have the plough nor the necessity of creating grazing areas.

In the light of the discussion of Huron farming methods and Schott's study, the Jesuit observations of cultivation periods ranging from eight to twelve years seem to be valid. One might conclude, therefore, that the effect of Huron clearance and farming methods served to double the time span one could expect from continuously cultivated land. Sands might have been cultivated for five to six years, loamy sands from six to eight years, and sandy loams from eight to twelve years.

v) Rates of forest regeneration. Rates of forest and soil regeneration vary principally with the type of soil involved, the size of the area to be recolonised and the amount of previous disturbance. Among the Huron, we are dealing with thoroughly depleted sandy soils that had been burned regularly, and fields probably ranging in size from small patches of several acres to fields several hundred acres in size. Since the Huron were selective in their use of construction materials and firewood, potential seed sources in the form of residual stands between the fields and in poorly-drained areas would have undergone selective cutting. In each of the tribal areas small poorly-drained patches, creek valleys and other uncultivable land are quite common over short distances. Tree stands among the corn fields would therefore have been frequent.

Several of the early writers noticed that Huronia abounded in open grassy areas (Sagard 1939:90; JR 8:115; Boucher 1883:23). Unlike some parts of Ontario, none of these grassy areas could be considered "natural." Eight years after Huronia was abandoned, when Radisson paddled along the shore of the Penetang peninsula, these open areas were still visible (Adams 1961:86-87). There can be no doubt that the early explorers were referring to abandoned corn fields that have been recolonised by grasses and weeds. By 1820, a closed forest extended over the entire area previously cultivated by the Huron.

Plant succession on abandoned farmland in Huronia can be easily observed; actual rates of succession are more difficult to establish. By the time of field abandonment, the initially beneficial effects of burning would have passed and can therefore be ignored in this discussion. By the time of abandonment, dormant seeds would have been destroyed as well as any small amounts of organic matter normally remaining in the soils of an abandoned field.

The first plants to enter a sandy soil in Huronia are annuals and biennials commonly called "weeds" by farmers. These are followed two or three years later by a few species of grass and other perrennials. It was this stage that was observed by Sagard, Radisson and others. After a number of years colonies of sumach (*Rhus typhina*), hawthorn (*Crataegus sp.*), poison ivy (*Rhus radicans*), various raspberries (*Rubus sp.*) and cherries (*Prunus pennsylvanica, P. Virginiana*) begin to appear from the edge of the woods. Just preceding these shrubs, and intermingled among them on most sites, one

187

of the most common plants is bracken fern (*Pteridium aquilinum*). Some trees begin to appear during the early stages of shrub growth; notably the elm (*Ulmus americana*). The next trees to follow are all fairly intolerant species such as poplar (*Populus tremuloides, P. grandidentata* and *P. balsamifera*), birch (*Betula papyrifera*) and white pine (*Pinus Strobus*). Judging from the Forest composition in 1820, the last trees to become re-established are maple (*Acer sacchurum*), beech (*Fagus grandifolia*) basswood (*Tilia americana*) and hemlock (*Tsuga canadensis*). Because of its greater need for sunlight and greater drought resistance, oak (*Quercus alba, Q. rubra* and *Q. macrocarpa*) could be expected to colonise some areas before the more tolerant trees arrive.

Studies done on the rates of succession on abandoned farmland are fairly numerous. One of the best for the purposes of this study was conducted in Michigan involving a variety of soil conditions including depleted sandy loams (Beckwith 1954:349-376). The successional stages observed by Beckwith are in every way comparable to those observed in Huronia. On sandy loams, abandoned after having been repeatedly planted with small grains, grasses and other perennials begin to appear after two to three years (Beckwith 1954:365). Prior to that time, the abandoned fields were dominated by annuals and biennials. Grasses may predominate on the poorer soils for 15 to 20 years after abandonment (Beckwith 1954:367). Shrubs may make an appearance as early as 10 to 15 years after abandonment, but do not form a conspicuous part of the vegetation until 15 to 20 years after abandonment (Beckwith 1954:368). Intolerant trees became dominant 20 to 25 years after abandonment (Beckwith 1954:370). After a similar successional pattern in Huronia, one might expect an immature forest composed of trees four to ten inches in diameter after 35 to 40 years.

Since the plant succession described above was that on a sandy loam, 35 to 40 years must be regarded as a minimum time span for a plant succession useable by the Huron. On a loamy sand such a succession could take 50 years or more. All the soils used by the Huron, therefore, need a fairly long period of recovery before they could be used again. Unfortunately, there is no information on the early survey records of northern Simcoe County that would allow one to reconstruct the density and basal diameters of tree stands at the time of European settlement. With such information it might have been possible to detect former areas of Indian clearance. Without such data one can only say that 170 years were long enough for a closed forest to have become re-established.

vi) Potential of preferred soils for Huron agriculture: a summary. In the preceding pages, a case was made for the accuracy of the Jesuit observations that some of the better soils supported agriculture for up to twelve years, and some of the poorer soils up to five or six years. These estimates, and estimates for soil recovery rates, are listed in Table 17. The implication to be drawn from this table is that a sandy loam for example, was cultivated for about eight to twelve years. During this time yields declined steadily, until by the end of the period the originally-cleared fields ceased to be productive. After the sandy loams were abandoned, it took at least 35 years for trees with a basal diameter of four to ten inches to become re-established. On the poorer soils, cultivation periods were shorter and recovery periods longer.

Theoretical as the figures in Table 17 may be, it is felt that they are reasonable in the light of present knowledge. A refinement of these figures, particularly the length of the cultivation periods, should someday be attempted experimentally.

e) Corn Production in Huronia

i) Estimates of corn yields. Only two authors who have written on the Huron have given what they believed were reasonable estimates for Huron corn yields. Both estimates can be described as educated guesses. Kroeber, whose interpretation of Huron agriculture must be considered problematical, gave a figure of about 15 to 20 bushels per acre (Kroeber 1939:146).[1] Popham (1950:88) thought that 30 to 35 bushels per acre would be reasonable yield, but because the Huron could not clear and plant a complete acre, they probably only got 20 bushels per acre. Neither author discussed declining yields on partially-exhausted soils. Both probably regarded their figures as averages rather than highs or lows.

Two authors have calculated actual yields from 19th-century Indian corn fields. In 1878 the Sioux at the Crow Creek Reserve in South Dakota got 20 bushels per acre (Will and Hyde 1917:142). One corn variety on the same reserve got yields as high as 40 bushels per acre. The Sac and Fox got 20 bushels per acre in 1874; the Yankton Sioux, 30 bushels per acre in 1867 ("a good year") and the Santee in 1878, 25 bushels per acre. Will and Hyde (1917:298) felt that the Iroquois yields were similar to the Mandan at 40 bushels per acre.

In view of the fact that early colonists in New England and Ontario used methods similar to those of the Huron, some of their yields might be

1. All figures on yield in this discussion are in bushels of shelled corn per acre at a moisture content of 15%; one bushel equals 56 lbs.

Table 17

Cultivation Periods and Recovery Rates of
Preferred Soils in Huronia

Soil Textural Type (Well-drained)	Length of Cultivation Period (years)	Length of Recovery Period (years)
Gravel and sand	5-6	60+
Loamy sand	6-8	50+
Sandy loam	8-12	35+

examined. Using documentary evidence, Bidwell and Falconer (1925:-101) gave average yields for Connecticut and New York in the early 19th century as 25 bushels per acre. Yields were reported for some Ontario Counties between 1847 and 1852 (Table 18). In the case of Hastings County the yields in some townships were unusually low due to late frosts (Upper Canada, Board of Agriculture 1856:234). The yields in Bruce County were considered low because the farmers " . . . did not take good care of their crop . . ." (Upper Canada, Board of Agriculture 1856:647). The average for Upper Canada in 1852 was 24 bushels per acre (Upper Canada, Board of Agriculture 1856:441, 459).

The problem with the figures listed in Table 18 is that we are not told how many years the fields from which the figures have been derived had been under cultivation. Several references show that the methods employed were similar to those of the Huron (Upper Canada, Board of Agriculture 1856:371, 646). Because these figures are County averages, one must assume that fields in various stages of land exhaustion were represented. In that case, yields averaged 24 bushels per acre with a maximum of about 33 bushels and a minimum of about 9 bushels per acre.

An interesting point to notice, which can be used as a warning in using comparative material across different environments, is that according to figures compiled by Cowgill in the Yucatan and Watters in Mexico, Venezuela and Peru average corn yields were considerably lower than in Ontario. Both gave average yields of about 14 to 18 bushels per acre (Cowgill 1962:276, 277; Watters 1966:5). In both cases fields were abandoned when yields dropped by 50 to 75 per cent or five to nine bushels per acre (Cowgill 1962:276-277; Watters 1966:9-10).

Table 18

Average Corn Yields in Ontario Counties, 1847-1852
(Taken from: Upper Canada, Board of Agriculture 1856)

County	Year	Yield (bu/acre)	Page Ref.
York, Ontario & Peel	1847	27	:331
York, Ontario & Peel	1849	27	:331
York, Ontario & Peel	1851	33.5	:331
Peel	1851	31	:363
Hastings	1851	17 (8.7-23.7)	:237
Prince Edward	1852	31	:363
Carleton	1852	22	:459
Bruce	1852	18	:647

In the whole of the *Jesuit Relations* there is only one reference that gives any indication of Huron yields. Du Peron wrote that the Huron corn " . . . sometimes yields one hundred grains for one" (JR 15:157). One hundred grains for one must refer to yield as related to the amount of seed used and not yield as related to the number of seeds that produced plants, because considerably more than one hundred grains were carried by one corn plant. The amount of seed used can be calculated by multiplying the weight of the number of seeds usually placed in a corn hill by the number of corn hills per acre. The result is 15 pounds of seed per acre.[1] If, as Du Peron stated, the Huron got a yield one hundred times greater, then the final yield was 1,500 pounds or 27 bushels to the acre. This figure compares favourably with yields obtained by early Ontario settlers.

Yields may be calculated in another way. As previously discussed, the average corn cob was about four inches long, containing 200 kernels which weighed about 2.0 ounces. If the average corn hill produced three stalks with two ears each, the resultant yield would be 33 bushels per

1. The average number of corn hills per acre was previously estimated at 2,500 and about ten seeds were placed into a corn hill. The weight of 200 corn kernels at a moisture content of 15 per cent was calculated experimentally at about 2.0 ounces.

acre.[2] This figure must be considered somewhat high because spoilage due to birds, insects and rodents would take a toll before the corn could be harvested. The amount lost before harvest is difficult to estimate. Rather arbitrarily, a figure of 20 per cent has been taken, bringing average yields down to 26 bushels per acre of harvestable corn and in line with Du Peron's estimate.

Sagard's statement that the Huron sometimes got 100 kernels on a cob can be taken as a measure of declining yields. One hundred kernels per cob would give them 16 bushesls per acre which, with a 20 per cent loss would bring the harvestable yield to 12.8 bushels per acre. If the Huron, like other shifting agriculturalists, waited until their average harvestable yields had declined by 60 to 75 per cent , their fields were abandoned once yields reached seven to eleven bushels per acre.

Sagard's report that some ears had up to 400 kernels was undoubtedly true; but this would hardly be a field average, even under the most favourable conditions. A cob holding 400 kernels would have to be about eight inches long. Such cobs have not been found on Huron sites but cobs longer than this have been excavated on Iroquoian sites predating the 17th century (Stockhouse and Corl 1962:6). In any case, a field yielding such cobs would have given the Hurons 67 bushels per acre. Such yields were not really reached until the introduction of hybrids.

The rate at which yields declined is difficult to estimate. Following the reasoning put forth so far, sandy loams were abandoned after eight to twelve years when:

. . . the land long tilled produced scanty crops (JR 11:7).

or:

. . . when the land is so exhausted that their corn can no longer be grown in the usual perfection (Sagard 1939:93).

Other reasons for land abandonment will be discussed later, in the meantime the observation by the priests seem to indicate that after ten years the land still produced corn, but that the crops were not worth picking. It stands to reason that land would have to be abandoned some-time before an absolute minimum is reached. It is therefore probable that, like other corn growers, the Huron abandoned their land after yields had

---

2. Yield (bushels) = number of corn hills per acre (2,500) x number of plants per corn hill (3) x number of cobs per plant (2) x weight of kernels per cob (2.0 oz.) divided by the number of pounds of corn in a bushel at a moisture content of 15 per cent, (56 lbs.). The numerator of the fraction must first be converted to pounds.

fallen 60 or 75 per cent from the average to seven or ten bushels. If eight bushels is considered cause for land abandonment, the figure is identical to yields justifying land abandonment among other corn cultivators.

By the time eight bushels per acre are reached on the original fields a number of other factors must have come into play, such as an extension of the fields during the years of declining yields and fire wood exhaustion. These will be discussed below.

If eight bushels are reached after ten years on a sandy loam and 27 bushels are an average, the absolute maximum during the first years of cultivation would be 46 bushels per acre. The average of 27 bushels would have been obtained after five or six years, assuming a steady year by year decline to eight bushels after ten years.

The situation just described may be considered very hypothetical, not only because of the assumptions built into it, but also because of the nature of the data used and the number of unforeseen factors that could and probably did play a role in upsetting the system. One of the most complicated of these factors is the proportion of corn lost to predators. Throughout the discussion a 20 per cent loss was assumed. In any year this loss could have been greater or less. In view of the care taken by Huron women of the crops, a figure of 20 per cent seems justified. The average yield computed here may seem high compared to the opinion most scholars seem to have of the efficiency of Iroquoian agriculture. It is difficult to see how this average yield can be reduced. If Ontario farmers in the first half of the 19th century averaged 20 to 25 bushels to the acre, 27 bushels among the Huron seems reasonable. Corn was not as important to the early Ontario settlers as it was to the Huron, and although methods were similar, the Huron spent considerably more effort in tending their fields than the 19th century farmer. It is therefore felt that the Huron yields here computed, while they may vary greatly in any one year due to unforeseen circumstances, are fairly reasonable.

One would not expect average yields on gravels, sands, and loamy sands to be of the same magnitude as on sandy loams. Maximum and average yields would be expected to be lower. Rates of decline have already been described, and eight bushels after five years seems reasonable for a coarse sand. What a maximum or average crop was, is difficult to say. If crops declined on a coarse sand at the same rate as on a sandy loam a maximum yield of 24 bushels could be expected with an average of 16 bushels after three years.

ii) Yearly Huron corn requirements. In an earlier chapter it was estimated that Huron corn requirements came to about 1.3 pounds per person per day. This figure represents the subsistence needs of a person, but is not representative of his total needs. Champlain (3:156) claimed that the Hurons strove to create a fairly large surplus " . . . for fear lest they should have a bad year." (Sagard 1939:103) also stated that they sow:

> . . . enough to provide food for two or three years, either for fear that some bad season may visit them or else in order to trade it to other nations for furs and other things they need.

Brébeuf even went so far as to call Huronia " . . . the granary of most of the Algonquins" (JR 8:115). Several references attest to the fact that corn was a major item of trade with the Algonquians (JR 11:7; 13:249).

What is difficult to reconcile, is Champlain's and Sagard's claim that the Huron strove to create a surplus to stave off starvation in case of crop failure, the fact that the Huron traded corn to the Algonquians and the manner in which the Huron viewed a potential crop failure. A potential crop failure was so serious that thought had to be given to trading food surpluses from neighbouring tribes. In other words, it is unlikely that they created a surplus for lean years as well as for trade. Any surplus from a fall harvest must have been traded during the late fall and winter to the Algonquians, leaving just enough corn for seed and food until the next harvest. One possible way of reconciling Champlain's and Sagard's observations with later accounts is that in the early years of contact and in precontact times corn surpluses were stored for lean years and only a small fraction was traded. As the Huron demand for furs increased during contact times more corn was needed as a trade item, with the result that the entire surplus above subsistence and seed needs was traded off. Numerous references, to be discussed later, show that the Algonquians were primarily interested in corn as a trade item. In return they supplied furs, meat and fish.

One thing that emerges from this discussion is that the Huron recognized the desirability of producing some measure of corn above their subsistence needs. If they simply counted on an accidental bumper crop for trading purposes, it is doubtful if Champlain and the others would have stated specifically that the Huron strove to create a surplus. It is also doubtful if regular trade could have been performed simply on the basis of an unexpected windfall. Recognizing, therefore, that a surplus was produced with intent, the question becomes: how much extra corn was grown? This question is, of course, impossible to answer with any degree of certitude. Champlain's and Sagard's statements must be vastly exaggerated, because they seem to indicate that each year the Huron grew enough corn to feed two to three times their own population. Even if "most of the Algonquins" subsisted entirely on Huron corn, the Huron would not have had to grow nearly as much as described by Sagard and Champlain.

A solution to the problem of surplus is really not possible. One must therefore hazard a guess. If Huron needs are 1.3 pounds of corn per person per day, 472 pounds or 8.4 bushels are needed a year. If a surplus was created, enabling each person to contribute one half a bushel towards trade, overall Huron needs would be about 1.4 pounds per day or 9 bushels per person per year. This would give a village of 1,000 people a stock of 500 bushels for trading purposes. The whole of Huronia would therefore have a stock of 10,500 bushels for trade, an amount which seems more than adequate, considering storage problems and the extent of the trade involved.

A figure of 1.4 pounds of corn per person per day is still well below the figure of two pounds per person derived by Popham (1950:89). If the Huron used two pounds of corn a day it becomes difficult to see what they did with it. Storage problems alone would be enormous. At 1.4 pounds per person per day, the average family of six would have to produce and store 54 bushels of corn per year. A longhouse composed of six families would therefore need 324 bushels of corn a year for subsistence, seed and trading purposes. Since one bushel of dried shelled corn takes up about 1.25 cubic feet (Ontario Department of Agriculture, n.d., a:32), the 324 bushels could be stored in four bins eight feet high and four feet in diameter. In view of the descriptions of corn bins and the area reserved for storage purposes in a longhouse, not only for corn but fish and beans as well, this figure seems about right.

At nine bushels of corn per person per year, the yearly corn requirements for a population of 21,000 Huron would be in the order of 189,000 bushels.

f) Huron Land Requirements for Agriculture

Assuming a fixed need of nine bushels per person per year, Huron land requirements must have increased yearly due to declining yields on the originally cleared fields. The whole cycle of land use was characterized by the re-use of the originally cleared land until that land failed to produce. The point at which the original plot ceased to be effective for Huron needs was previously set at about eight bushels per acre. Additional land could be gained by stumping as mentioned by (Sagard 1939:103). Inevitably, though, more land had to be cleared to keep pace with declining yields. This could be done by extending the original fields or by clearing new patches wherever land was available. The exact procedure for gaining new land is not known. Two plausible approaches might be advanced. For the first of these, one might reason that in the initial year enough land was cleared as close to the village as possible to meet the requirements of each family. As yields declined, the original fields were extended until they reached a neighbour's plot or some natural obstacle. Additional patches would then have to be cleared farther from the village. An alternate method would have been for each family to select an area large enough and sufficiently far removed from neighbouring fields and uncultivatable areas so that the necessary yearly extensions of land would not lead to a proliferation of new fields, but simply an extension of the old. While the latter method has the advantage of keeping the number of fields to a minimum, it imposes longer travel times on villagers whose fields are farthest from the village. This method also assumes that individuals could lay some sort of claim to unused land until their fields grew to make use of it. Under Huron land-holding practices no one could lay claim to unused land. In view of the proliferation of cultivated patches among other shifting cultivators, the first of the two methods mentioned seems the more probable. One would reason, therefore, that by the time the original plot was thoroughly depleted several other plots existed, compounding the problems of adequate maintenance and supervision.

In calculating Huron land requirements two important points must be kept in mind. First, the land requirements for one person, or a village, will vary with the number of years a plot or plots have been under cultivation. As the first plot loses fertility and yields decline, more land is added in the second year. The second year's addition will however, have the original fertility of the first plot. In the third year, land must be added to take care of a two-year's decline from the first plot and a one-year decline from the second year's addition. The third year's increment will, however, have the original fertility of the land. And so on, until the area is abandoned. The second point to notice is that rates of decline, and therefore land requirements, will be different for different soil types.

Keeping the above points in mind, calculations were made to obtain the yearly land requirements for one person on the three major soil types utilized by the Huron, during any year of continuous occupation (Figure 10). In calculating the figures for the graph two assumptions had to be made; first, the yearly need at nine bushels per person is constant throughout each cycle; second, yields decline at a predictable rate as discussed earlier. If either of these factors vary at an unpredictable rate, no estimates of land requirements are possible. The data on Figure 10 therefore depicts the increasing land needs of a person whose yearly need is nine bushels of corn. The yearly gains in fertility from newly-added land are taken into account, as well as the yearly losses from land cleared in previous years. This is a much more realistic method of calculating land needs than the usual method of dividing the average yield into the yearly need.

The disadvantages of using a coarse sand or gravel rather than a sandy loam are immediately apparent. Twice as much land must be cleared the first year, and about three times as much added every year to keep up with declining yields. In the end the coarse sand or gravel can only be cultivated half as long as the sandy loam. In view of the large disadvantages of this soil type over the others, it is surprising that any village sites occur on it at all. A family of six would have to clear 2.25 acres in the first year, and by the end of the five-year cycle would have a total of 4 acres under cultivation to bring in an annual crop of 54 bushels.

The loamy sands, utilized by about 18 per cent of the Huron villages are somewhat better. A family of six would need to clear 1.6 acres in the first year and have 2.9 acres under cultivation after seven years. On the sandy loams a family of six would need 1.14 acres in the first year and 2.2 acres after ten years. This soil type supported about 72 per cent of the villages in Huronia.

In order to calculate the total amount of land in Huronia under crops in any one year, three assumptions are made; the first is that the number of people dependent on each soil type is roughly proportional to the percentage of village sites on each soil type (Table 1); two, that the silt loams, being higher in natural fertility than either loamy sands or coarse sands can be added to the sandy loams; and three, that because of the likelihood that all the plots are at different stages in their cycle toward abandonment, land requirements can be calculated from the mid-point of each cycle. The result is that, in any given year, about 6,500 acres in Huronia were under crops (Table 19). Since beans and squash were grown on the same fields, no additional land was needed. It is interesting to note that on the basis of observations on Iroquois reservations in New York State, Fenton feels that a population of 20,000 Huron could have supported themselves from 7,000 acres under active cultivation (Trigger 1969:28).

In order to estimate the total land taken up by agriculture in Huronia, the "fallow" period must be taken into consideration. The minimum length of the fallow period on each soil type was estimated previously. The land taken up by fallow can be calculated by determining the amount of land used by each cycle and multiplying it by the number of cycles that were run during a fallow period; or:

Amount of fallow land (acres) = F/C × N

- where F is the fallow period in years
- where C is the length of one cycle in years
- where N is the land used up in one cycle.

In order to find the total land in use, one additional cycle must be added. This is the land last put under crops before returning to the fallow land:

Total Huron land needs (acres) $= (F/C \times N) + N$

On this basis, the total Huron land needs for a population of 21,000 are close to 50,000 acres (Table 20), or about 2.3 acres per person. The amount of land available to the Huron from the three preferred soil types was previously calculated at 157,861 acres (Table 20). The Huron, therefore, used about one-third of the soils available to them under their system of agriculture.

Does this mean that Huronia was underpopulated and could have supported three times as many people? Probably not. In order to support 60,000 people, the area would have had to be used at its maximum carrying capacity relative to the Huron ability to produce food. This is, of course, impossible. No socio-economic group such as the Huron could ever live up to the maximum carrying capacity of their territory. The implication of maximum carrying capacity is that the Huron would have had to make optimum use of their soils. There would have had to be long-range regional planning of soil resources: a perfectly balanced cycle of cropping and fallowing and a soil resource base that was equally usuable and so distributed that maximum use could be made of it. It would also mean that no droughts, falling water tables, wars or bumper years for crop pests upset the system. For these and many other reasons no population can ever live up to the "carrying capacity" of the territory it inhabits. Furthermore, it should also be added here that the calculations of total land needs were based on a minimum fallow period. Depending on ground water conditions, the extent of original clearings in an area, and on many other conditions, some fields might have taken more then 35, 50 or 60 years to recover. The figures on Huron land requirements may therefore be underestimated, rather than overestimated. In other words, it is very doubtful if Huronia could ever have supported anything approaching 60,000 people under Huron subsistence techniques. Rather than being underpopulated, it is much more likely that the area was approaching a population maximum. This was suggested earlier by the close correlation between the amount of preferred soils in each tribal area and its population (Figures 1 and 2).

198

Table 19

Average Yearly Land Requirements for Crops in Huronia

Soil Type	Population	Average Crop Acreage
Coarse sands and gravels	1,050	543
Loamy sand	3,780	1,406
Sandy loam and silt loam	16,170	4,495
Totals	21,000	6,444

Table 20

Total Huron Land Requirements

Soil Types	Population on each soil type	Length of one cycle (yrs.)	Length of fallow (yrs.)	Land used in one cycle (acres)	Amount of land in fallow (acres)	Total Huron land needs (acres)	Total land available in Huronia (acres)
Coarse Sands and Gravel	1,050	5	60	694	8,328	9,022	14,652
Loamy Sand	3,780	7	50	1,833	12,831	14,664	56,906
Sandy Loam and Silt Loam	16,170	10	35	5,821	20,374	26,195	86,303
Totals	21,000			8,348	41,533	49,881	157,861

Of all the tribal groups the *Attingneenongnahac* must have been particularly pressed for land. It will be recalled that this group occupied an area 10,422 acres of which 9,976 were sandy loams (Table 4). With a population of 3,800 this tribe had the highest population density of any tribe in the area. The total land requirements for 3,800 people on a sandy loam are 7,776 acres, showing that the *Attingneenongnahac* used 78 per cent of their available soil resources. As stated earlier, the high population density of the *Attingneenongnahac* was probably the result of crowding which occurred when some land was given over to the three tribes that arrived in the late 16th and early 17th century. Such a high proportion of soil resource use should therefore not be considered normal. If the population total dependent on each soil type in the other tribal areas was known similar calculations could be made.

3. GATHERING, HUNTING AND FISHING

The relative importance of gathering, hunting and fishing was described in the first part of this chapter. This section is intended to be an elaboration of some aspects of these activities, particularly the manner in which they were carried out and the time of year in which these activities took place.

a) Gathering

As an activity, the gathering of wild vegetable products was carried on from spring to late fall whenever time or opportunity permitted. A description of the different plant varieties available to the Huron has been compiled by Yarnell (1964:44-88) and it would serve little purpose to compile an identical list here.

In general the food plants were used as an addition to the usual corn dishes to give them a greater variety in flavour. Particularly important were fruits such as raspberries, cranberries, cherries, grapes, wild plums and mayapples. Other vegetable products such as the Jerusalem artichoke, various vetches and wild leeks were also gathered. All of these were discussed in Chapter II.

Special mention must be made of the gathering of "hemp". This seems to have been a communal activity involving, in one case, about forty women (JR 26:203-205). In all, four types of plants seem to have been used. Sagard (1939:240) mentions a type of "hemp" growing in " . . . marshy damp spots . . . " which was probably swamp milkweed (*Asclepias incarnata*), while Lalemant (JR 23:55) wrote that the Huron women gathered hemp on " . . . the untilled plains . . . " The latter reference must refer to spreading dogbane (*Apocynum androsaemifolium*) and Indian hemp

(*Apocynum cannabium*). Hemp was collected in the late summer and fabricated into twine and various products during the winter (Sagard 1939: 98; JR 23:55, 241). "Hemp" was also obtained from the bark of a tree called *Atti* by the Huron (Sagard 1939:240). The bark was removed in strips and boiled to separate the fibres. From the description, the tree could have been basswood (*Tilia americana*).

In view of the abundance of maples in Huronia, it is possible that the Huron also gathered maple sap. For the Huron, this activity is only mentioned by Le Clercq (1881:208); although the Jesuits recorded it among the tribes of the St. Lawrence Valley (JR 6:273). From the manner in which the Huron prized the sugar brought in by the Jesuits, one might almost suspect that maple sugar was unknown to them (JR 14:31, 41, 57). Since all the neighbouring tribes made use of maple sap, it would be reasonable to suppose that Huron did likewise. Whether any of the Indian groups reduced maple sap to sugar, is not known.

On a few occasions Hunter (1898:37; 1899:65) noticed small groves of cherry trees growing at Huron village sites. It is doubtful if these were deliberately planted by the villagers. What is more likely, is that some of the seeds that found their way into the garbage dumps managed to germinate and take root. Cherry trees could have been quite common on abandoned sites, but since the wild cherry grows best in a fairly open habitat, it is likely that the cherries were displaced once the forest had closed up after Huronia was abandoned. Orchards of fruit trees were reported for the Iroquois, but how early they were deliberately planting trees is not known (Cook 1887:73; Parker 1910:19).

An interesting observation is that most of the gathered produce grows in open fields or the edge of the forest. With their clearing of the woodland and abandoning of fields, the Huron were therefore modifying their environment to accommodate a greater number and variety of useful plant species.

b) Hunting

The dog was the only domesticated animal the Huron had. Sagard (1939: 226) described them as being about the size of a moderately-sized mastiff with upright ears and a pointed snout. He also noted that they howled rather than barked. Like most breeds of Indian dogs, the Huron variety was probably part timber or brush wolf. Dogs were not only pets and companions (JR 14:33-35), but also a valuable asset in hunting. However, the greatest use of the dog seems to have been as a source of meat. Both Sagard (1939:226) and LeJeune (JR 7:223) stated that the Huron raised them like sheep as a meat supply. Most references seem to agree that dogs were principally eaten at feasts or ceremonies (Champlain 3:129; Sagard 1939:220, 226; JR 9:111; 21:161; 23:173). The animals were simply left to roam through the villages and longhouses feeding off refuse and leftovers.

Contrary to popular opinion, the turkey (*Meleagris gallopavo*) was not domesticated (Sagard 1939:220). As a matter of fact, it was rare in Huronia but more plentiful in the Petun area and among the Neutral (Sagard 1939:220; JR 21:197). This was a remarkably astute observation, because the turkey is at its northern limits in Southern Ontario; and even in the early part of the last century it was only found in the southern parts of Simcoe County (Snyder 1951:93). Another reason for the scarcity of the turkey in Huronia could have been the fact that its habitat is a mature forest. In other words, one would not expect the turkey to be common in cleared areas and as far north as Huronia. It is interesting that Sagard 1939:220) considered the turkey and a number of varieties of geese potential domesticates, but the Huron were not " . . . willing to give themselves the trouble . . . ."

While on the subject of domestication it is noteworthy that Champlain was of the opinion that once the Huron had been shown the value of domesticated animals, and certain species had been introduced, " . . . they would be careful of them and would keep them quite well . . . " (Champlain 3:130). Because of the large tracts of grassland in Huronia, Champlain thought that feeding " . . . horses, cows, sheep, pigs and other kinds (of animals) . . . " should pose no particular problem (Champlain 3:-130-131). Champlain's opinions were based on an observation that the Huron sometimes kept and fed caged black bears (*Ursus americanus*) for two or three years, fattening them for special feasts (Champlain 3:130). This practice was also observed by Sagard (1939:220), and by some Dutch travellers among the Iroquois (Jameson 1909:143). Since the Jesuits did not comment on such a practice, it is fair to conclude that keeping bears in pens was not very common.

In spite of the general lack of meat in the Huron diet, several authors also mention that Huronia did not seem to lack in game (Sagard 1939:-222; JR 7:7). Animals that were considered rare or absent in Huronia were the moose, bison, wolf, caribou and lynx (Sagard 1939:223-225). Deer were more plentiful outside Huronia, especially towards the country of the Neutral (Sagard 1939:225, 227; JR 21:197; 27:289-291). Bears, foxes, martens, hares and a multitude of birds and smaller mammals were considered plentiful (Sagard 1939:217-228). As far as is known, the only mammals or birds that were not eaten were the crow (Sagard 1939:221) and probably the skunk (Sagard 1939:224).

The stated absence of moose (*Alces americana*) bison (*Bison bison*), wolf (*Canis lupus*), woodland caribou (*Rangifer caribou*) and lynx or bobcat (*Lynx canadensis, L. rufus*) in Huronia is interesting, because it supports the contention that environmental conditions in the early 17th century and the present were similar. Some bones from these animals are present in middens on earlier sites south of Huronia. Thus, for example, the caribou is present at the Lawson site near Chatham, Ontario, tentatively dated at 1500 A. D. (Wright 1966; Noble 1968). Moose remains have been found at the Roebuck site near Prescott (ca. 1450 A. D.), at the Middleport site west of Hamilton (ca. 1350 A. D.) and at the MacKenzie site near Wood-bridge (ca. 1550 A. D.) (Emerson, *et al.,* 1961 b:96-98). Bison was found at the Roebuck site. The presence of bison skins among the Huron was reported by Champlain (3:105) and Sagard (1939:225), but, as Champlain observed, these were traded from Indian groups in the northwest. Boucher (1896:137) also points out that the bison was absent in eastern Canada. Moose and caribou seem to have migrated out of Southern Ontario into the Shield by Huron times. Both the lynx and bobcat should have been present in Huronia (Peterson 1966:280-286). Sagard's "leopards" (Sagard 1939:223-224), the cougar (*Felis concolor*), as he noted, was rare to absent in Huronia (Peterson 1966:276-277). Sagard's observation that the wolf was rare in Huronia probably means that this shy creature was not often seen. The timber wolf (*Canis Lupus*) is more prevalent on the Shield, but the brush wolf (*Canis latrans*) was once fairly common in Southern Ontario (Peterson 1966:197-203). Both of those animals tend to avoid human contact and would be extremely difficult for Indians to hunt.

Frequencies of animal bone material have not been published for Huron contact sites. Reports are, however, available for two early contact Petun sites whose economy and settlement patterns were almost identical to the Huron. Judging from the presence of trade goods at these sites, the Sidey-Mackay site probably dates to the earliest period of contact, and the MacMurchie site a little later. Both predate Champlain's visit to the area. The frequency of bone material at the two sites is listed in Table 21 (Bell 1953:71; Emerson, *et al.,* 1961 b:101). An interesting comparison is the Lalonde period Copeland site north of Barrie (Channen and Clarke 1965: 14). Over the hundred years represented by the three sites, deer is replaced by beaver (*Castor canadensis*), and later by beaver and muskrat (*Ondatra zibethicus*) in order of importance. This is undoubtedly a reflection of the growing importance of the fur trade.

Unfortunately, no attempt has ever been made to determine the age, size, or number of individuals of each species present. The orders of

Table 21

Bone Material at Three Sites Near Huronia
in Order of Relative Abundance

Coperland (pre-contact, *ca.* 1500)	Sidey-MacKay (early contact, *ca.* 1580)	MacMurchie (contact, *ca.* 1600)
Virginia deer	beaver	beaver
beaver	Virginia deer	muskrat
black bear	black bear	Virginia deer
red fox	dog	black bear
dog	woodchuck	dog

importance represented by Table 21 reflect the percentage of bone material of an animal related to the total bone material at the site. Because one deer or one bear supplies considerably more meat than several beaver or muskrats, one cannot really say that deer and bear ceased to be the major meat-producing mammals.

The ethnohistoric sources state quite clearly that deer and bear were the major food animals (Champlain 3:81; JR 23:63). These were followed by the dog (Sagard 1939:220). Beyond these three animals anything that had meat on it, from birds to mice, was eaten (Sagard 1939:217-228). The general lack of meat in the diet can best be explained in terms of a variety of factors which were somewhat different for different animals. Chief among these factors where the abundance of the animal, hunting methods, and the seasonality of the hunt.

Unlike the deer, the black bear was not subject to seasonal hunting or organized mass hunts. Bear seem to have been hunted by individuals or small groups of men on occasions when one was scented by a dog or when one was known to be about (JR 15:99; 14:33-35). Huronia and adjacent areas were a perfect habitat for the black bear, but population densities must have been low compared to other meat and fur-bearing animals. The black bear is omnivorous, preferring substantial wooded areas, especially near large streams. They tend to be solitary, moving in fairly well-defined territories (Peterson 1966:221). Population densities in a deciduous forest have been estimated at two to five bears per ten square miles (Shelford 1963:29). The low population densities and solitary nature of this animal would dictate the hunting procedures described in the ethnohistoric sources. The tractability of the young and their omnivorous diet would make it fairly easy to raise cubs in captivity for special feasts. In view of the low density of black bears and their relatively low reproductive rate,[1] one would expect that over the years of hunting this animal would have been more prevalent outside of Huronia. In other words, the bear could not have been a major food source for 21,000 people. The fact that it was considered a close second in importance to deer as a meat supply serves to point out that meat could not have been too important in the Huron diet.

The major source of meat for the Huron were deer. Deer were hunted in snares (JR 23:157), in traps (JR 30:53), by individuals using the bow (JR 26:313), and most commonly in large organized communal drives (Champlain 3:60-61, 81-85; JR 15:183; 22:273; 33:83). Two types of communal drives were described. Both of these methods involved a large number of people who were placed in a line through the woods driving the animals ahead of them. In one case, the animals were driven towards a peninsula and eventually into the water, where they were killed from canoes (Champlain 3:60-61; JR 22:273). In the other case, the animals were driven into a triangular enclosure with a compound at its apex. When the animals reached the compound it was closed, and the animals killed with bow and spear (Champlain 3:81-85). In the communal hunt witnessed by Champlain in the Belleville area, 120 deer were caught by 500 men in 38 days. A similar deer hunt was described by Ragueneau a two days journey south of St. Ignace I (JR 33:83). This hunt involved 300 people, including women. Although hunting was a man's occupation, women were taken along to help cut up the meat and transport it back to the village (JR 33:89).

Unlike the hunting of other animals, deer hunting had a definite seasonal pattern. The best time for these mass hunts was the late fall (Champlain 3:60-61, 81-85; Sagard 1939:82; JR 8:149; 13:109, 113; 39:207), towards the middle or end of October. The other period for hunting was the late winter. Most hunters returned during Lent, just before Easter (Sagard 1939:82; JR 15:183; 17:143). February was considered to be a bit early for hunting (JR 13:263), so most of this activity seems to have taken place in March.

Sagard and the Jesuits mention two types of deer. The most plentiful of these was the *Sconoton* (*Skenonton*) which was judged to be a little smaller than the ones the priests were familiar with from Europe (Sagard 1939:

1. Females start breeding when they are three years old. They breed only every other year and usually produce two cubs (Peterson 1966:221).

225). This was undoubtedly the Virginia or white-tailed deer (*Odocoileus virginianus*). The other variety was larger and sometimes called "stags" or "elks" (Sagard 1939:225; JR 29:221). From the descriptions this would be the American elk or wapiti (*Cervus canadensis*).

Although the general habitat of the white-tailed deer and the wapiti are the same, the wapiti is less specialized in the food it eats (Peterson 1966:-321). Both the deer and wapiti thrive best in areas of second growth timber, on the edge of the forest or in natural openings. Both tend to avoid heavy forested areas. The wapiti will eat a great variety of grasses, herbs, shrubs and trees (Peterson 1966:321). By contrast, the white-tailed deer tends to avoid grasses, concentrating on small trees and shrubs such as the maple, cedar, yew, hemlock, sumac, various ashes, basswood, dogwood, willow and others (Taylor 1956:199-200). When acorns are available, white-tailed deer prefer these to all other foods (Taylor 1956:197). In the summer both species can be found scattered throughout their range. During this time single deer or a doe with her offspring travel more or less alone within a restricted territory. At this time deer have their widest distribution and lowest density. In the fall deer tend to congregate in mast-producing areas such as heavy concentrations of oak and/or, chestnuts (Taylor 1956:141). This usually happens in October and marks a period of high concentration of deer in a particular habitat. In late October and the beginning of November the rutting season starts, lasting until the end of November (Peterson 1966:324). Although the animals are still in the mast-producing area, feeding becomes of secondary importance and mobility is high (Taylor 1956:142). In the winter deer seek sheltered areas and if the snow gets deep, they will "yard" (Taylor 1956:143). At this time cedar swamps are a favourite habitat and as a result of "yarding", it is in late winter that deer achieve high local densities and limited mobility. Mobility may even be more impaired in early spring, when deep snows become crusted with rising daytime temperatures. During this period food is also at its lowest (Peterson 1956:325). There is some evidence that deer will migrate when weather conditions become uncomfortable or food becomes scarce (Taylor 1956:158).

The habits of deer described above account to a large extent for the seasonality of Huron hunting and for the areas described as having large deer populations. The late winter and late fall produced large local concentrations of deer, and Huron communal hunting expeditions coincided perfectly with these periods. In the summer when deer were scattered the Huron men were away trading. During this time occasional animals might be snared, trapped or shot with the bow and arrow.

206

As observed earlier, deer were considered to be more abundant outside of Huronia, which is reflected by the observation that large hunting expeditions had to be carried on outside the area. In view of the fact that deer prefer areas of forest regeneration, forest edges and openings, one would think that Huronia proper was a perfect habitat for them. The answer seems to lie in a variety of factors. Huronia was heavily settled and large areas were burned every year. Given a choice, deer tend to avoid human beings and live in terror of fire and smoke (Taylor 1956:164). While large areas within Huronia provided an excellent habitat, the previously abandoned lands to the south and south-east provided similar habitats without yearly fires or settlement. Mast-producing areas were also more prevalent south of Huronia, particularly the open oak woodlands of the Oakridges moraine and the oak-chestnut areas along the north shore of Lake Erie. The prevalence of this type of habitat would explain the two fall mass hunts observed by Champlain in the Rice Lake area, Ragueneau's observations on the large hunt a two days journey south of St. Ignace I; and Sagard's comment that deer were more plentiful in the Neutral area.

There are only three references that give any indication of the numbers of deer taken. The communal hunt described by Champlain involving 500 men produced 120 deer in 38 days (Champlain 3:85). A winter hunt carried out by the villagers of *Contarea,* had a yield of 20 deer and four bears (JR 10:181). Judging from the size of some feasts prompted by hunting successes, 30 deer were an above average take (JR 10:179).

The low Huron meat intake in as far as bears were concerned, has already been discussed. Deer meat was only readily available in the late winter and fall in what appear to be not very large amounts. A take of 20 deer and four bears for a village the size of *Contarea* is not large. Neither is a take of 120 deer for 500 men in 38 days. Huron hunting methods, the seasonality of hunting and the seasonal availability of game seem to have been the factors responsible for the low meat intake in the Huron diet.

It is doubtful if the beaver was ever very plentiful in the occupied areas of Huronia. Certainly by the time the fur trade was well on the way beaver were absent in Huronia. In 1623 Sagard wrote that ". . . such a quantity of them (beaver) is brought every year (to the St. Lawrence area) that I cannot think that the end is in sight" (Sagard 1939:232). In 1634 Le Jeune commented that:

> There is a danger that they will finally exterminate the species in this Region (the Shield area), as has happened among the Hurons, who have not a single Beaver, going elsewhere to buy the skins they bring to the storehouse of these Gentlemen (the traders). (JR 8:57).

The habitat of the beaver is well known. It always lives in waterways such as streams and lakes where poplar and other deciduous trees and shrubs are present. Because of its restricted habitat and distinctive signs of its presence, the beaver is easily hunted, and is over-exploited. Beaver hunting was, of course, carried on in the winter when the animals were in their huts and the fur was at its best (Sagard 1939:233). Since not all beaver live in huts (some live in burrows along stream banks), it was probably difficult to exterminate them completely in Huronia and adjacent areas. Left alone for a few years, bank beaver tend to replenish their population fairly rapidly. By the latter part of the 17th century, and perhaps earlier, beaver had repopulated Southern Ontario and were hunted by the League Iroquois. Some of the main beaver-hunting areas were mapped by Lahontan, including the Holland marsh, the swampy areas of Lake St. Clair along the Sydenham and Thames rivers, the swamps at the headwaters of the Grand river and Spencer creek, and areas on the south side of the Ottawa near the Rideau. The high incidence of beaver on the early contact sites probably reflects a peak of beaver hunting in and near Huronia which dropped later during the contact period. It is therefore doubtful if beaver figured in the Huron diet to any extent during the 17th century.

The importance of smaller mammals in the diet was probably low. Most, such as foxes, squirrels, mink, marten, and otter would have been difficult for the Huron to catch. Snares were set, but according to Sagard ". . . not often, because the cords are neither good nor strong enough, and the animals break and cut them easily when they find themselves trapped" (Sagard 1939:223). Sagard made this statement in connection with hares and rabbits (probably *Lepus americanus,* the snowshoe hare, and *Sylvilagus floridanus,* the cottontail rabbit). One would expect that if these were difficult to snare, other mammals common to Huronia, with the exception of the woodchuck, would be even more difficult to catch. Bones from small mammals are infrequent on Huron sites, emphasizing the point that Huron hunting techniques were simply not sophisticated enough to exploit them as a meat resource. Although the paucity of bones from larger mammals may be partially a reflection of butchering techniques, this would not explain the scarcity of bones from the smaller mammals.

c) Fishing

Fishing was an activity that was carried on virtually throughout the year. There are descriptions of winter fishing (Champlain 3:166-168; JR 35:-175), spring fishing (JR 14:57; 17:197; 19:171-175), summer fishing (JR

208

8:143; 16:249; 17:51) and autumn fishing (Champlain 3:56-57; Sagard 1939:185-189; JR 8:143; 13:115; 15:113). The two peak seasons seem to have been the late winter to early spring, and the fall from late September to the beginning of December. These peak periods are the same as those for the hunting season. This may mean that some villagers went fishing, while others went hunting; or that there were regional differences in Huronia, those villages close to the fishing grounds placing a greater emphasis on fishing than hunting. The data is unfortunately insufficient to make a case for either one or the other. Preliminary excavations at some sites in the Penetang Peninsula seems to suggest that these placed a greater emphasis on fishing compared to sites in central Huronia.

The principal food fish of the Huron were whitefish, trout, sturgeon, pike and at certain times of the year two fish called the *Auhaitsiq* and the *Einchataon* (Sagard 1939:230-231). Similar to the hunting periods, the peak periods for fishing were closely adjusted to the movements of the fish.

The whitefish *(Coregonus culpeaformis)* spawns in Georgian Bay from the middle of November to mid-December and in Lake Simcoe from the beginning to the end of November (MacKay 1963:131). Spawning takes place in shallow waters, over rocky shoals, gravels and sand. Throughout the winter it inhabits fairly shallow waters reappearing on the shoals as the ice breaks up (MacKay 1963:127, 130). By the end of May they seek deep waters. The lake trout (*Salvelinus namaycush*) inhabits rocky shallows in the spring as the ice melts and seeks deeper waters by May (MacKay 1963:-121-122). Between mid-October and late November, it spawns on the rocky and sandy shoals of Georgian Bay. Spawning in Lake Simcoe takes place between mid-October and early November (MacKay 1963:122). Its movements and habitat are therefore similar to the whitefish. These were the principal fish caught during late autumn fishing among the islands in Georgian Bay (Sagard 1939:230). By late November, as Sagard correctly observed, these fish departed from the shoal areas and the Huron returned to their villages (Sagard 1939:189).

Sturgeon, pike and maskinonge, the other major food fish, spawned in the spring. The sturgeon (*Acipenser fulvescens*) ascends streams or shallow lake waters, spawning during the latter part of May and early June (MacKay 1936:32). During the summer and fall it feeds in fairly shallow waters. From various descriptions of pike, both the northern pike (*Esox lucius*) and the maskinonge (*Esox masquinongy*) must have been caught (Champlain 3:45-46; Sagard 1939:230). Both of these fish spawn as soon as the ice melts in shallow, weedy waters, small streams and creeks, and along grassy margins of lakes (MacKay 1936:194, 204), during the sum-

209

mer the pike stays in shallow weedy waters while the maskinonge descends to slightly deeper areas. In the fall the maskinonge returns to shallow waters.

What Sagard described as the *Auhaitsiq* was a fish "similar to the herring but smaller." It was only available during certain times of the year, when it was caught in "immense numbers" by means of seine nets. Many people co-operated in the catch, and it was later divided among the participants. These fish were eaten fresh or smoked (Sagard 1939:231). This inadequate description fits almost any small to medium-sized "herring" like fish such as the smelt (*Osmerus modax*), alewife (*Pomolobus pseudoharengus*), mooneye (*Hiodon tergisus*), shad (*Dorosoma cepedianum*) and the cisco (*Coregonus artedii*). Of these, the mooneye and shad do not commonly occur in Lakes Simcoe and Huron (Scott 1954:12, 16). The smelt and alewife are probably too small to have been caught in seine nets; besides, they seem to be 20th-century introductions to Lake Huron (Scott 1954: 15, 17; Hubbs and Lagler 1947:43, 57). The shallow water cisco seems to fit Sagard's description best. Superficially it resembles the herring more than any other Great Lakes fish. It moves in large schools and is found in shallow waters from late fall, when it spawns, to the late spring. During the summer this fish seeks deep, cold waters.

The last important food fish described by Sagard was the *Einchataon*. This fish has already been mentioned in connection with longhouse storage facilities. The *Einchataon* was a fish up to one-and-one-half feet long and resembled the French *barbeau* (barbel). The fish was not cleaned, but hung in bunches along the inside of the longhouse roof. It was caught in the late fall and was a major food source during the winter (Sagard 1939:95, 230-231).

Of the common fish in the Great Lakes, only the sturgeon, catfish and burbot have barbels. The sturgeon was described by Sagard in an earlier passage and is a much larger fish than the *Einchataon*. The burbot (*Lota lota*) is a fairly large fish which would have been available to the Huron only through ice fishing. It also resembles the cod more than it does the *barbeau*. Of the catfishes the channel catfish (*Ictalurus punctatus*) is the largest; it spawns in the spring and is caught in commercial quantities (MacKay 1963:178-183). The more common brown bullhead (*Ictalurus nebulosus*) is smaller than the channel catfish; it also spawns in the spring and travels in schools (MacKay 1963:184). A fish that resembles the French *barbeau* (*Barbus barbus*) is the common sucker (*Catostomus commersonnii*) except that it does not have barbels (Sterba 1963: 237-238, Figure 298). The sucker is, however, most abundant when spawning in the early spring and not in the late fall, which is when the Huron caught the *Einchataon*.

None of the fish listed above answer Sagard's description adequately. Of these, the catfish comes perhaps the closest. The fact that the Huron caught the *Einchataon* in the late fall after the trout and whitefish had gone corresponds to the habits of the catfish, who seek out the spawning areas to feed on the eggs.

Most of the fishing was carried on with nets and seems to have been very efficient. Expeditions were sent among the islands of Georgian Bay, Lake Simcoe and the smaller lakes within Huronia. The "Narrows" between Lake Couchiching and Lake Simcoe were an important fishing station. When lake fishing, a seine or gill net was used, and was set into the water in the evening and taken up in the morning (Sagard 1939:186). Some of the larger whitefish were boiled and the resulting oil skimmed off and stored in gourds.[1]

Winter fishing was also done with a seine (Champlain 3:167-168; JR 35:175). The net was spread under the ice by passing it from one hole to another in a large arc, returning at the end to the original hole. Net sinkers kept the net in a vertical position. When the net reached the bottom, the two ends were drawn together and the net hauled onto the ice through a large main hole (Champlain 3:167-168).

Some fishing was carried on with a line and hook (Champlain 3:167; Sagard 1939:189) – but apparently not very successfully, because lines could not be made strong enough to hold large fish (Sagard 1939:189).

Champlain's description of the fishing station at the "Narrows" is interesting and has been confirmed archaeologically. Apparently the "Narrows" were closed with a series of stakes except for a few openings where nets were set (Champlain 3:56-57; Kenyon 1966:1-4). Champlain described the catches as being very plentiful, and there is no reason to doubt him. Even today the "Narrows" are a well-known fishing place, particularly during spring spawning runs of walleye (*Stizostedion vitreum*) suckers, pike and sturgeon.

The seasonal abundance of the common fish in the lower Georgian Bay and Lake Simcoe area has been compiled in Figure 12. From this Figure, it is apparent that the outstanding fishing season is the late fall. The three most important fish are all present at the same time in the same general habitat. All three school in large numbers and are easily caught in seine nets. By contrast, the spring fishing season is of longer duration because spawning times overlap from March to early June. The spring fish also do

1. Sagard describes these storage vessels as ". . . the rind of a certain fruit that comes from a foreign country . . ." (Sagard 1939:186). It reminded him of calabashes.

not school in the same numbers as the fall fish, nor do they spawn in open waters. The best chance the Huron would have had to catch any of these fish would have been by closing off small weedy bays, creeks and rivers with nets and weirs. The "Narrows" between Lake Couchiching and Lake Simcoe were an ideal place for this type of spring fishing. Summer fishing could not have been too fruitful. Fishing by the line or spearing were probably the most promising methods. Winter fishing, like spring fishing must have been a cold, uncomfortable experience. Excellent catches of whitefish, cisco and burbot could have been made with the methods described by Champlain.

Brief mention should be made of various amphibians and reptiles present in Huronia. Sagard noted the presence of turtles, snakes and various kinds of frogs. Of these, turtles were eaten and certain snakes hunted for their skin (Sagard 1939:235-236). Whether snakes were eaten is not known. Several interesting observations have been made in a study of turtle remains, from archaeological sites (Bleakney 1958:1-5). Of eight common species only three turn up in very small quantities on Indian sites; the Midland Painted Turtle (*Chrysemys picta marginalis*), the Snapping Turtle (*Chelydra serpentina*) and Blandings Turtle (*Emys blandingi*). All three are inhabitants of shallow, weedy waters. The author concludes that turtles were not actively pursued for food, but were probably collected incidentally as the opportunity presented itself; for example, by children playing at the edge of ponds (Bleakney 1958:4). If the Indians had hunted turtles diligently, more species and bone fragments should have been present. These observations concur with personal observations at several Huron sites. Turtle bones, while not rare, do not occur in the quantities one would expect from their abundance in Huronia.

One frog that was evidently eaten was the green bullfrog (*Rana catesbeiana*). Sagard (1939:236) gives an excellent description of it, so that a definite identification can be made (Logier 1937:12-13). Sagard adds that he did not try them because he was not convinced they were "clean".

In providing a food-supply, fishing had several distinct advantages over hunting. Pound for pound, fish were more plentiful, easier to catch, and more predictable in their habitat and habits. Moreover, fish could be dried and stored. There is no evidence that the Huron had the ability to preserve and store meat for any length of time. As observed earlier, meat was invariably eaten immediately after the animal was killed. Fish was therefore a staple, and game a seasonal supplement. The Huron subsistence economy should therefore be regarded as an agriculture-fishing complex and not as an agriculture-hunting complex as Kroeber (1939:150) had proposed. Future archaeological work should test the possibility of minor regional variations.

212

4. THE PROBLEM OF VILLAGE MOVEMENT

Throughout this study, reference has been made to the fact that the Huron shifted the locale of their villages periodically. Sagard and the Jesuits were of the opinion that soil and firewood depletion in the neighbourhood of the village were responsible for these moves (Sagard 1939:92-93; JR 10:275; 11:7; 15:153; 19:133). According to Champlain such a move was one to three leagues from the old site (Champlain 3:124-125). As stated earlier, these moves usually occurred after eight to twelve years.

These observations are interesting because they seem to indicate that a village was moved when the original fields, those first cleared and closest to a village, were exhausted. After six to twelve years, depending on the soil type, the soils on the major fields would have been exhausted and the soils on the smaller yearly extensions would have been in various stages of nutrient depletion. Except for the small yearly extensions to keep up with declining yields, apparently no major clearing operations were carried out once a village was built and the first fields cleared. By the time the original fields gave out, almost twice as much land stood under crops than in the first year of clearance; all of it had been added piecemeal. By the end of the cycle there was, therefore, one main depleted field, and again as much in small parcels adjacent to the main field or further removed; all were in various states of exhaustion. The question now becomes, why was not more land cleared further from the village after the closest fields were depleted? Was distance to outlying fields a factor?

The distance of village to the fields is dependent on the size of the village, the soil type utilized and the amount of arable land near the village. Since these variables could all vary independently of each other, it would be best to look at a few examples. On a sandy loam a village of 1,000 people would need 360 acres of land to produce a bare minimum for subsistence (Figure 10). If only half of the village umland were arable, which is not uncommon in Huronia, the farthest fields after ten years would not lie further than 0.60 miles from the village. For smaller villages, the distance from village to the productive fields would, of course, be less. On a coarse sand a village of 1,000 would have an umland of 0.80 miles after six years. A village such as St. Joseph II, with a population of 2,400 living on a sandy loam, would have an umland of 0.90 miles after ten years, while *Ossossane* with a population of 1,500 on a loamy sand would have an umland of 0.84 miles after seven years. *Cahiagué*, with an estimated population of 3,200 and an umland of sandy loams would have its fields in a radius of 1.1 miles after ten years. It would seem, therefore, that the village fields of even the largest villages were not located much

213

more than a mile from the village, even if only 50 per cent of an umland were arable. The interesting thing is that few, if any, Huron village of the contact period could ever cultivate their umland, because they were located on the abandoned Lake Algonquin shorelines. The land below the shorelines was invariably in swamp. Rather than cultivating an umland, they cultivated a hinterland. *Ossossane* therefore had a semicircular hinterland of 1.4 miles; St. Joseph II a hinterland of 1.3 miles and *Cahiagué* a hinterland of 1.5 miles (Figure 11). Since these were the largest villages in Huronia, one can surmise that the Huron did not wish to cultivate fields that were more than about one and a half miles from their village. Because most of the villages were much smaller than *Ossossane*, St. Joseph II and *Cahiagué*, one wonders if simple distance of village to fields was a factor in village abandonment. If soil exhaustion did play a role, and all the ethnohistoric sources said it did, it was not a simple relationship between the location of productive fields and their distance from the village. A series of other factors must have come into play.

The problem takes on a different perspective when one realizes that only women worked in the fields. In the case of St. Joseph II, out of a population of 2,400 perhaps 500 were women capable of performing agricultural labour. At the end of ten years these 500 women had to tend 860 acres of plots scattered over 2.7 square miles, even though the farthest fields were only 1.3 miles from the village. In view of the task of weeding and hoeing these fields, and above all the problem of keeping birds and animals away, this must have been a fearful job. Thus, while the actual walking distance to the fields was never very long for any village large or small, the problem of looking after an increasing number of scattered plots with a limited number of women would affect each village equally whether it was large or small. In other words, the distance of village to productive fields was not as serious as the ratio of women to productive land scattered over a large area. This ratio would affect all villages, large or small. Therefore, by the time the closest fields were exhausted, which were the largest contiguous fields, the other more scattered plots could not be supervised adequately and the village had to be relocated.

By the time a village had existed for six to twelve years and the nearest fields were exhausted, three other related problems may have played a part in village abandonment. One of these has already been mentioned, and that was the problem of bird, animal and insect pests. Not only were these a problem in the fields but, as mentioned earlier, also in the village. After six to ten years of continuous occupance the villages must have accumulated a substantial population of mice (Champlain 3:123; Sagard 1939:227). Except for their dogs, the Huron had no way of ridding themselves of these rodents. In some Central American countries rodents and other pests have been cited as causes for land abandonment (Watters 1966:10); and there is no reason to suppose that the situation in Huronia was any different. A second problem, once the women got too scattered over the fields, was one of protection. Iroquois raids were a constant summer threat and there were never enough Huron men who could be induced to stay in Huronia to protect the villages and women in the fields. As long as the women were within the shadow of the village, they could flee there for protection. Once they moved away from the closest fields they could no longer be adequately protected. Several references state clearly that it was usually among villagers working in the fields, particularly the women, that the greatest casualties occurred (JR 10:95; 27:65; 29:249). A third problem was one of getting adequate supplies of firewood. Both Sagard (1939:92-93) and Brébeuf (JR 11:7) cited distance to firewood as a cause for village relocation. Gathering firewood was also the women's job (Champlain 3:136, 156; Sagard 1939:101). Apparently only good dry wood was used. The Huron preferred:

> . . . to go far in search of it rather than to take green wood or what makes smoke; for this reason they always keep up a clear fire with a small quantity of fuel; and if they do not find trees that are quite dry they fell those which have dry branches. . . . We were not so particular, and were satisfied with what was nearest to our hut, so not to spend our whole time in this occupation. (Sagard 1939:94).

Champlain's (3:156) statement that it took only two days to gather a year's supply of firewood seems absurd, when other writers stated that distance to firewood was a reason for village abandonment. Perhaps Champlain was referring to a recently-erected village. With gradual land clearing and yearly burning, one could reason that by eight to twelve years good firewood had to be obtained from areas beyond the cleared fields. Since all the firewood was carried to the village on the backs of the women, this could have become quite a troublesome job once the forested areas were more than a mile from the village.

A number of other reasons for periodic village relocations could be cited. Fear of enemy attack appears to have been one (Champlain 3:124-125). Sagard (1939:155) noted that this was especially true for frontier villages. At least *Toanché* and St. Ignace I were moved for such a reason. In the case of *Toanché* it was because the inhabitants feared French revenge for Brulé's murder, and in the case of St. Ignace I it was fear of an Iroquois attack. Occasional fires may have led to village relocation, especially if such a fire occurred several years after initial settlement. By that time new construction materials may have been difficult to obtain near the village.

The possibility that social tensions led to a splitting and movement of the larger villages was mentioned in the previous chapter. Social tension is also seen as a primary factor in limiting the size of Huron villages. In view of the efficiency of Huron agriculture and fishing, and providing a village had an arable hinterland of at least one mile in depth, there is no reason why environmental factors should have played a role in keeping the great bulk of the villages below a level of 1,000 people. The discovery of manuring or a rational pattern of fallowing might have given villages a greater degree of permanency in an area, but these factors could not by themselves lead to larger villages. Larger villages would necessitate social mechanism that the Huron did not possess. The very existence of a few large villages demonstrates that with existing agricultural practices villages larger than 1,000 people were possible.

In summary, it is postulated that village movement was a phenomenen that arose out of a combination of factors. Chief of these was soil depletion on the fields closest to the village and the resultant scattering of a limited number of women over a large area made up of a great number of small, family-sized corn patches. The scattering of the labour force made working the fields difficult, especially the control of pests. At the same time, protection of the women from enemy raids became next to impossible as long as the bulk of the men were engaged in summer trading and fishing. The exhaustion of firewood within carrying distance of the village is seen as another contributory cause in village abandonment.

5. THE SEASONAL CYCLE

The Huron subsistence system may be summarized in a general statement encompassing two fundamental aspects of a geographical study: the relationship between man and environment and man's spatial behaviour. What follows is such a statement built around Huron seasonal activities (Figure 12 and 13).

The Jesuits recognized that Huron activities followed a standardized pattern:

> They regulate the seasons of the year by the wild beasts, the fish, the birds and the vegetation (JR 15:157).

It is this pattern of spatial activities that will be generalized from the earlier chapters.

216

The seasonal cycle of Huron activities began in early March when some of the men went deer hunting in places where deer had "yarded". On returning from the hunt the men went fishing until mid-May to take advantage of the spring spawning runs. As soon as the ice broke up, the Algonquian groups who had wintered among the Huron departed. During this period the women went to gather firewood and probably maple sap. By mid-May the fields were prepared by burning them over, an activity that mainly women participated in, unless new fields had to be cleared. Planting was done by the women in late May. At this time some of the men departed for war and others went off to the Algonquians, Petun and Neutral to trade. A predetermined number of men stayed behind to protect the villages from possible enemy raids. These engaged in summer fishing, odd jobs around the village and some work in the fields. If the Huron had news of a large impending raid, more men would stay home until the threat had passed.

Throughout the summer the women lived in the fields, hoeing the corn, pulling weeds and attempting to chase pests from the crops. During the late summer some gathering took place, notably berries and indian hemp. Children probably helped gather berries, particularly the girls. During the early summer the men completed their trading with the Algonquian bands and began to make their way to the St. Lawrence, where they generally arrived towards the end of July or early August. Back at home small Iroquois war parties made surprise raids on unsuspecting women working in the fields or men hunting and fishing away from the village. Similar raids were carried out by Huron in the territory of their enemies.

Towards the end of August and early September the corn was harvested, dried and stored away. Shortly after this activity was completed the men returned from trading and war. From late September to early December some of the men went fishing. Others went hunting in the mast-producing areas of Ontario, where the deer gathered for the rutting season. Mass hunts were carried out, involving a large segment of the male and female population of a village. Since the rutting season ended in November, the returning hunters could engage in the late fall and early winter spawning runs for whitefish, lake trout and cisco. Most of the fish caught would be dried and stored for the winter.

During the late fall various Algonquian bands settled near the Huron villages to spend the winter. The Nipissing usually settled among the *Attignaouantan* in western Huronia, and various Ottawa Valley Algonquians among the *Arendaronnon* in eastern Huronia. Once Ste. Marie was established, a number of Algonquian groups from various parts of Ontario wintered there. Similarly, the Ottawa regularly wintered among the

Petun. On their way to Huronia the Algonquian bands would lay in a supply of fish and furs to barter for corn and other items. Much of Huron-Algonquian trade was probably carried out during the winter in Huronia.

By late November and early December everyone was back in the village. This was a period of socializing. A variety of feasts took place to celebrate a successful harvest, hunting, fishing and trading. These feasts were accompanied by gambling and gift-giving. If war had been success-ful, captives were tortured to highlight the social activities. Few economic activities took place in the winter. Among these was ice-fishing and trading with the Algonquian visitors. The women would weave mats, manufacture fishnets and prepare corn for the next season's trade.

Roughly every eight to twelve years this cycle of seasonal activities would be modified for every village through village relocation and the great feast-of-the-dead. Sometimes only one village would be involved, but most commonly several villages would undergo these activities together. Relocation could result in the splitting up of larger villages, or the temporary union of smaller villages. It was a year of social realign-ments and social reaffirmations.

Chapter VII

External Relations and Trade

INTRODUCTION

Few aspects pertaining to the Huron have been discussed as frequently as their role as traders. Of these studies, Biggar's (1901) volume and the first three chapters of Innis' (1930) study laid the foundations for later works such as Hunt's (1940) thesis on the interrelationship of war and trade in the Great Lakes area, and Rich's (1967) updating of previous work. The most recent statement on the subject is Trigger's (1968) excellent paper, bringing some anthropological theory into the discussion as well as a more critical reading of the primary sources.

Due to the unreliability of some of the secondary sources, a detailed discussion of these will be generally avoided. In the case of Hunt's (1940) book, for example, a major discussion of this work would result in an unnecessarily long and complicated chapter overshadowing the main purpose of this section. Instead, the primary documents, maps, and archaeological material will be re-examined to construct as plausible a picture as possible of the growth of the Huron trade network, the social and economic significance of trade, and the interrelated facets of inter-tribal politics and war that were a part of trade. In keeping with the theme of the study, the emphasis will be placed on the organization and development of trade by the Huron, rather than the organizational problems of the French fur traders.

The interpretation of Huron trade presented in this chapter differs somewhat from the accepted picture. For example, this writer could find no evidence for the widespread pre-contact Huron trade network envisaged by Hunt. Instead, it seems that Huron trade developed slowly out of close relations with Algonquian groups into a vast carrying trade that involved not only the Algonquian but also the Petun, Neutral and western Montagnais. The maximum development of this trade network was not reached until late 1630's and early 1640's when the Algonquian bands between Huronia and the St. Lawrence were decimated by disease and war. Prior to that time the Algonquians were a major factor in the eastern Canadian trade network with a substantial trade of their own; a trade they jealously guarded. In order to present a plausible picture for these and other interpretations it is necessary to examine the original sources on a year-by-year basis. Only then is the slow development, ultimate extent and nature of Huron trade apparent. That previous writers on the subject did not do this is not surprising, in view of the tediousness of the task.

The development of Huron trade falls into five major sections: pre-contact trade, the early French contact period, the period to the English conquest (1629), the period up to the early 1640's and the period ending with the fall of Huronia. The periods beginning with the first French-Huron contact are examined on a yearly basis. Documentation is, of course, not available for every year; but overall trends in the development and nature of Huron trade can be established. Each yearly outline is followed by a summary and discussion of the period. As pointed out earlier, only major differences between this and previous work are discussed.

1. THE POLITICAL AND SOCIAL BASIS OF TRADE

Two closely related elements of Huron life were external politics and trade. As a rule, the Huron did not trade with tribes with whom they were at war, or strangers with whom they had no peace treaties. The conclusion of some sort of peace treaty was therefore a prerequisite to trade. This point is extremely well illustrated by the early contacts between the Huron and Champlain. Before any trading was done the Huron insisted on a military alliance (Champlain 3:69-71). When other French traders came to trade with the Huron, Champlain had to explain that they were all from the same nation and that no separate alliances were necessary (Champlain 2:188-189, 193-204). Throughout his lifetime Champlain remained in a special position with the Huron because he alone of all the traders observed the reciprocal relationships of alliance in war and relations in trade. Similar relations were observed between the Huron and Algonquians. Not only were these trading partners but also military allies (Champlain 1:164; 2:68). The Montagnais were wedded to the military alliance through the Algonquians (Champlain 1:103; 2:122), which later led to a profitable Huron-Montagnais trade.

Another illustration of the close relationship between politics and trade was the constant attempt to suppress murder, and therefore war, between tribes. Murder was a matter that affected not only the relatives of the deceased, but the entire tribe (JR 10:225). In order to avoid serious ruptures between tribes heavy payments were made to assuage the feelings of the tribe that had been wronged. Among the Huron more was paid when a Huron murdered a foreigner than one of his own kind:

220

. . . because they say that otherwise murders would be too frequent, trade would be prevented, and wars would too easily arise between different nations (JR 33:245).

The size of the payment seems to have been directly related to the value the Huron placed on the trade contacts with that group (JR 38:283-285). In the case of the murder of a French *donné*[1] by some Huron the ensuing payment was much higher than it would have been if a member of a friendly tribe had been murdered (JR 33:239-249). Earlier, in the case of the murder of Brulé, the Huron had automatically assumed that their trade connections with the French had been put on a very insecure basis. Some were afraid to come and trade at Quebec (JR 8:103), others were easily dissuaded from going on the St. Lawrence when some Allumette told the Huron fur brigade that the French meant to avenge Brulé's death (JR 5:230; 8:103). Another example in which murder and wounding threatened trade and peaceful relations was an incident between the Huron and Algonquians at *Cahiagué* in 1615 (Champlain 3:101-114). Champlain regarded the matter very seriously, because in the opinion of both Huron and Algonquians non-settlement of the alleged wrongs would result in war between the two groups and therefore in a complete halt in French-Huron-Algonquian trade (Champlain 3:103). The matter was finally settled through Champlain's diplomacy and heavy payments by the protagonists.

In order to ensure healthy relations between tribes, people were sometimes exchanged (JR 12:79). These could act as trade contacts, hostages, and spies. It is interesting to note that when Champlain wanted to place French youths among the Huron and Algonquians, these groups expected some of their members to be placed with the French (Champlain 2:-138-142, 186-188, 201-202). The fact that Champlain wanted to exchange people clearly inspired trust and helped cement relations.

Once trading relations had been established with another group, not all Huron could take advantage of these relations. Trade was in the hands of the person ("master of the route") who pioneered the route and established the first contacts (JR 10:223-225). The only people who could share in this trade automatically were the children of the "master" and members of his lineage and perhaps clan segment:

1. The *donné* (literally "a given man") was a layman who had donated his services free of charge to the Jesuit Order for a specified period of time. He had no priestly function but acted as a servant to a priest. The function of the *donné*, the nature of his vow and specific individuals are discussed in the *Relations* (JR 21:293-307; 33:253; 42:265).

The children share the rights of their parents in this respect (trade), as do those who bear the same name (JR 10:225).

Non-lineage members might be permitted to share a trade route providing proper payment was first made (JR: *ibid.*). In the case of French-Huron trade, the trading rights belonged to certain lineages among the *Arendaronnon* because it was they who had first contacted Champlain. However, in view of the importance of the trade, the *Arendaronnon* decided to share it with the other Huron tribes (JR 20:19).

Encroachment on another lineage's trade route was only tolerated if the offending member did not get caught in the act (JR 10:225). If he was caught in the act of trading, he was treated as a thief and might barely get away with his life. If he managed to get back to the village undetected, complaints would result but no prosecution would ensue.

In order that Huronia was not left unprotected, the chiefs and their councils had to decide who and how many men could go on the yearly trading expeditions (Champlain 3:166; Sagard 1939:99). In keeping with other council decisions, the decision as to who could go trading was not binding, but contravention of the decision could result in strong village disapproval; and as a rule these decisions were accepted (Sagard 1939:-99). In later years as French-Huron trade grew stronger, it became more and more difficult to keep some men at home to protect the villages (JR 10:51; 14:57). In 1637 for example, some of the ". . . old men and those most influential in the country . . . " were accused of starting rumours of an impending Iroquois attack in order to keep enough men in the villages (JR 14:39).

The establishment of political alliances and trade between tribes did not extend to unhindered passage across the territory of an allied tribe. In some cases, where tribes permitted passage, payment had to be made. Forcing a passage could, of course, lead to a war. In the case of the troublesome Allumette, for example, the Jesuits observed that the Huron would not force their way across Allumette territory in spite of Huron numerical superiority (JR 9:275), and in spite of the exorbitant tolls the Allumette were charging (JR 10:77). In the case of the Petun and Neutral, transit across Huron territory was strictly forbidden by the Huron and no Petun or Neutral ever attempted to force their way (JR 21:177, 203-205). Huron observation of these rules, even in the case of weaker allies, was probably prompted by a feeling of self-preservation. If they broke the rules others could do the same, leading to a collapse of the intricate system of alliances and a termination of trade.

A discussion of these trading regulations leads to some interesting conclusions. Essentially the stability of the Huron trading system depended on peaceful relations, not only with trading partners but also with any intervening tribes. Prior to trade, peace treaties had to be negotiated. Judging from Champlain's descriptions, such peace negotiations were elaborate affairs in which gifts and sometimes people were exchanged. In all probability, such treaties were renewed every year. The fragile nature of inter-tribal relations is illustrated by the fact that a single murder could result in almost instant hostility. The customary means of preventing open war was to pay off the aggrieved party. While inter-tribal trade seems to have been in the hands of lineages, the whole tribe would be held responsible for their actions. Treaties seem to have been made in the name of the tribe, while the lineage who pioneered the new route had the rights to the trade. Such a system of regulations was exceedingly sophisticated. The fact that the tribe stood behind the individual trading families helped to assure them a measure of safety away from home. While an individual trader might be charged exorbitant transit fees or occasionally mistreated, his life was usually safe. The spectre of intertribal war as the result of one murder was enough to assure the lives of the traders. Monopolistic control over trade routes by the men who had pioneered them would encourage a proliferation of Huron trade contacts with every neighbouring tribe. Such a regulation would encourage each Huron lineage to seek its own trade contacts until all neighbouring groups had been contacted. If a group found that the trade they had opened up was too large to handle, others could buy their way into the route. It would be difficult to think of a more efficient trading system for a group that had a barter economy and acted essentially as middlemen between the French, a host of small Algonquian tribes and a large number of Neutral and Petun villages. Private trading rights assured contact with a maximum number of foreign tribes; it assured a lack of competition and therefore high prices to the Huron traders, who distributed high value French goods and their own manufactured products. The whole system was backed by the entire tribe, who stood collectively behind each trader.

Another interesting facet of Huron trade was the means by which the proceeds of trade were redistributed in Huronia. While a barter economy existed between the Huron and non-Huron tribes, there is no evidence of any kind of barter system between the Huron. There is no evidence that goods and services were redistributed in Huronia through commercial transactions or any kind of marketing system. Indeed, there is no evidence of the existence of market places, or a hierarchy of villages based on marketing principles. Goods and services were exchanged on an entirely different basis. The Huron system comes close to Dalton's definition of a reciprocity economy, " . . . that is, material gift and counter gift-giving induced by social obligation derived, typically, from kinship. . . " (Le Clair and Schneider 1968:153).

Unquestionably, the prime means by which goods were redistributed was through gift-giving. All members of a lineage would automatically share in the goods an individual member accumulated (JR 10:223-225). This observation seems to have been validated archaeologically, since marked differences in the quantity of trade goods occur between long-houses within the same village (Tyyska 1968:8). Some lineages had more trade goods than others. Beyond the lineage, goods were diffused through a variety of institutionalized gift giving ceremonies. Gifts were exchanged when people visited each other (Sagard 1939:140); gifts were given in marriage to the prospective bride and her parents (Champlain 3:138; Sagard 1939:122-123; JR 14:19); rich presents were given in name-giving ceremonies when a youth succeeded to the name of a deceased member of the community (Sagard 1939:209-210; JR 23:167-169).

Curing ceremonies and burial ceremonies were other occasions on which large presents were distributed. In order to be cured of a sickness, either real or imaginary, the afflicted person could demand anything he desired in order to cure his illness (JR 14:27). At times these "illnesses" took the form of regular "festivals," during which an effort was made to drive all "evil spirits" out of the body and soul of the afflicted and out of the village. During these "festivals" the "afflicted" could ask for anything they wanted and most often their desires were fulfilled (Champlain 3:149, 164-165; Sagard 1939:118-119, 203; JR 10:175-177; 23:53). These curing ceremonies seem to have been an attempt to cure psychosomatic illnesses through the identification and subsequent possession of desired objects. On the occasion of a death of a member of a community, his property was given to his sister's sons and daughters (Champlain 3:140; Sagard 1939:130). Others would heap gifts on the bereaved and the body of the deceased, a ceremony in which:

> . . . they spare nothing, not even the most avaricious. We (the Jesuits) have seen several stripped, or almost so, of all their goods, because several of their friends were dead, to whose souls they made presents JR 8:121).

The great "feast-of-the-dead" resulted in a universal exchange of goods, some of which were buried in the ossuary (Champlain 3:161-163; Sagard 1939:172-173; JR 10:265-271; 23:31).

Since the Huron were inveterate gamblers, games of chance were a further means of distributing goods (Champlain 3:166; Sagard 1939:-96-98). As a matter of fact, Le Jeune commented that some Huron undertook the trading voyage to Quebec only to gamble, and that some lost their merchandise through gambling even before they got to Quebec (JR 5:241). In some of the games, whole villages would play against each other, with heavy betting on both sides (Champlain 3:166, JR 10:187). Stakes were high, and when an individual ran out of goods he would on occasions gamble his own scalp and fingers (JR 16:201). Some large losses were observed by the Jesuits. In one case a man lost a beaver robe, four hundred glass beads, and then hanged himself (JR 10:81). On another occasion, one village lost thirty collars of 1,000 beads each, in addition to all moveable property including tobacco pouches, robes, shoes and leggings (JR 17:205). Losses in the value of two to three hundred écus[1] were not uncommon (JR 15:155). Along with frequent feasts, festivals and gift giving, gambling was a prime means of redistributing wealth.

In order to have some accumulation of goods at hand in case of public emergencies, each village and probably each lineage, set up a public "treasury". Each person contributed what he could and the lot was under the supervision of a chief (Sagard 1939:266-267; JR 28:87). Such accumulations of capital were necessary to make treaties, exchange prisoners or pay off blood feuds arising out of murder (Sagard 1939:163-164; JR 10:217-221; 33:229-249). In a case cited by Champlain some Algonquians had to pay fifty wampum belts and ". . . a great number of kettles and hatchets and two female prisoners (Iroquois) . . . " (Champlain 3:102-103) for a Huron they had killed. Other examples are cited by Brébeuf (JR 10:215-223), demonstrating clearly that no one person could pay the quantity of goods usually demanded for a murder. Capital goods had to be accumulated by a lineage and a village to prevent inter village and inter-tribal blood feuds.

One of the prime motives for the accumulation of wealth was to give it away. This enhanced the giver's social status in the eyes of his villagers. One of the qualities a leader had to have was liberality (JR 10:231). Gift-giving and a generous disposition were therefore a means of acquiring prestige and ultimately, perhaps, political power. War chiefs in particular had to be wealthy, because they were obliged to give feasts and

---

1. The écus was worth about three francs, while the franc and the livre were about equal in value (JR 1:313; 4:269). One pound of beaver was worth about ten livres (JR 28:235). Gambling losses could therefore have been equivalent to seventy-five pounds of beaver, which could conceivably be the profit from an entire summer's trading.

presents in order to drum up enthusiasm for a campaign (Sagard 1939:-151-152; JR 10:181). Although political eminence was primarily achieved through real ability measured in terms of success at trading, good advice, valour or liberality, it could also be achieved through bribery (JR 10:235). It would therefore stand to reason that a person with proven ability as a trader had a good chance of acquiring a chieftainship, and that the acquisition and judicious disposal of trade goods was one of the roads to political power.

The means by which goods were redistributed among the Huron also provides a partial explanation of why goods were acquired. A Huron was expected to give gifts, to participate in ceremonies and to take part in gambling. He therefore had to acquire goods to fulfil his social obligations; the more successfully he fulfilled these obligations, the more recognized he became in the community. There were, of course, other reasons for participating in trade. To some trading was an adventure or a challenge akin to a raid in enemy territory (Trigger 1968:113; JR 5:241). In addition to important social motives for the acquisition of socially valued products, French trade goods were valued because they were durable utilitarian goods. French trade goods in order of popularity seem to have been hatchets, knives, kettles and iron arrow points. Beads were very popular, but seem to have been largely given as presents to the Huron. Other items were blankets, capes, shirts, fish hooks, pocket knives, rings, awls and sword blades (JR 5:263-265; 10:53; 12:119-121, 249, 257; 15:159). All of these items, with the exception of the textiles, have been amply confirmed by archaeology.

French trade goods were, of course, valued by those tribes that did not have any close connections with the French. They were therefore useful in expanding trade with the Petun and Neutral, for products the Huron desired to trade somewhere else.

All of these points will be examined later in this chapter. In the meantime it is important to reiterate that the motives behind Huron trade were not only the acquisition of utilitarian objects. If utilitarian value was the only concern, the Huron market could have been quickly saturated. The acquisition of trade goods to further social ambitions and the expansion of trade to neighbouring tribes were equally important. This will be re-examined later. If the Huron had had a money economy, or a social structure based on accumulated wealth or land, the situation might have been different. However, land could not be bought or sold; prestige arose not out of accumulated wealth, but out of socially-accepted means of redistributing wealth. Since goods were in constant exchange (some went out of exchange through ossuary burial, others simply wore out), those people who had lost their goods or given them away had to acquire new ones. The surest way of acquiring large quantities of goods was through trade. Thus trade was perpetuated; and the proceeds of trade were useful not only as utilitarian objects, but also in meeting social obligations. Huron social institutions helped to keep the whole system going.

2. PRE-CONTACT TRADE

The extent of Huron trade with neighbouring tribes prior to their contact with the French in 1609 is largely a matter of conjecture. Pre-European Huron sites yield very few evidences of trade with other tribes (Wintemberg 1926:37). The only articles that turn up with any regularity, and that can be considered foreign to Huronia, are shell objects and chert. To these can be added the occasional piece of catlinite and native copper.

Catlinite (pipestone), a fine grained reddish stone, is occasionally found in the form of small beads and ornaments. It was mined and utilized primarily by the Siouan Indians of Southwestern Minnesota and South Dakota. In all probability, the few pieces that found their way to Huronia came to them *via* the Puan, who lived on the western shores of Lake Michigan (Map 24). Because only small amounts of catlinite occur on Huron sites, it is not likely that the Huron had direct contact with the Puan. Probably intervening Algonquian bands, such as the Ottawa or Nipissing, acted as middlemen between the two groups. Ottawa relations with western tribes can be ascertained from Champlain, who stated that they carried shields made of buffalo hide (Champlain 3:45); and Sagard, who noted that the Ottawa had extensive relations with tribes to the north and west (Sagard 1939:64-66). There is no evidence that the Huron had any direct contact with any of the western tribes until perhaps after the fur trade was well developed. But even this is doubtful.

Small amounts of native copper could have filtered down to the Huron from the upper Lake Superior and western Lake Michigan area, where the mineral was once mined. The active exploitation of copper had ceased by about 1500 B.C. with the disappearance of the Old Copper Culture (Quimby 1960:63); but small bits and pieces could still have been mined and traded by Ottawa and Nipissing traders who had contacts in these areas. Some Algonquian traders told Champlain in 1603 that the Huron knew of the existence of a northern copper mine (Champlain 1:164), yet the only proof Champlain ever got from this copper-producing area was from an Algonquian man seven years later, who had obtained it there himself (Champlain 2:123). Again, judging from the small amount of native copper that has turned up on Huron sites, it is doubtful if they exploited these sources of copper directly.

Flint, or rather chert, had to be imported because there are no significant chert formations in Huronia. No study on Huron chert artifacts has been made, but none of the material need have come from a greater distance than the Niagara Escarpment (Ingham and Dunikowska-Konuiszy 1965). Chert was probably one of the items obtained from the Neutral and Petun.

Shell artifacts, primarily in the form of wampum beads are the only concrete evidence of possible long distance trade in any quantities. Most of these beads were manufactured from the columella of shells such as *Marginella apicina* and *Fulgor perversa* (Wintemberg 1926:37, 44). These shells are native to the shores of the American south Atlantic and Gulf States. The probable direct Huron source for these shells, besides the usual neighbouring trading partners, were the Andaste (*Susquehannock*). As early as 1615 Champlain mentioned the loose Huron military alliance with the Andaste (Champlain 3:53-55). He even sent Brulé to them in order to get help in the forthcoming raid on the Onondaga (Champlain 3:213-226). In later years several attempts were made to link up with the Andaste showing that Huron-Andaste relations had existed for a long time (JR 30:253; 33:73, 133). On his trip, Brulé noted that the Andaste had access to the sea (Champlain 3:218). Since the use of wampum beads was widespread among the Indians of north-eastern North America, much of the Huron beads could have come from various sources, and probably did. The route to the Andaste was dangerous and long. It skirted the edge of the territory occupied by the Seneca (Champlain 3:55; JR 33:131-133) and at least on one occasion the trip took some fifty days to complete (JR 33:129) (Map 24). It is doubtful if any quantity of goods came over this route during the Huron-Iroquois wars. The Neutral, who had similar trade connections (JR 21:201), and some of the eastern Algonquian tribes were probably the best sources for sea shells.

The most likely indicators of pre-contact Huron trade are the observations of Champlain and Sagard in 1615-1616 and 1623. Essentially, these observations convey the impression that Huron trade with the Petun and Neutral was less developed than trade with the Algonquian groups. The Neutral were mentioned primarily as growers and exporters of tobacco (Champlain 3:99; Sagard 1939:158). Although the Huron were officially at peace with the Neutral in 1615, the chances are that this had not always been the case. In 1623, for example, members of the Huron *Attignaouantan* were trying to organize a war against the Neutral, which might have succeeded were it not for the intervention of the Récollets (Sagard 1939: 151, 157). If the Huron were that careless about the possibilities of a Neutral-Huron war in 1623, their trade contacts could not have been highly valued at that time, and might have been only weakly developed prior to contact. Except for tobacco, of which the Huron did not grow much, it would be difficult to think of any products except luxuries that the two groups could have exchanged. Their subsistence economies were, of course, very similar. More extensive trade seems to have developed as a result of the fur trade.

The situation between the Huron and the Petun seems to have been similar. Champlain noted that the two groups were at peace, but the *Relations* point out that this peace had a recent origin (JR 20:43). Like the Neutral the Petun were known for their tobacco " . . . in which they have a great trade with other tribes" (Champlain 6:248). Other than tobacco, the subsistence economy of the Petun was identical to that of the Huron (Champlain 3:95-96).

Huron trade of Algonquian products to the Petun and Neutral seems to have been unlikely. The Ottawa (*Cheveux Relevés* or *Ondatahouats*), an Algonquian group allied to the Neutral in a war against the Fire Nation (*Assistaeronon*) (Champlain 3:97, 99) and living as close neighbours to the western villages of the Petun, probably supplied all the Algonquian products the Petun and Neutral needed. Both Champlain (6:248-249) and Sagard (1939:67) considered the Ottawa great traders, dealing in dried berries, reed mats and other products for fur, wampum, nets and pigment. Their trade network appears to have extended to the north to the *Saulteur* and Ojibwa bands along the east and northeast shore of Lake Superior, and north west to the Puan (Sagard 1939:64; JR14:155). Both Champlain and Sagard estimated that the Ottawa travelled 400 to 500 leagues to go to trade. Until late in the contact period, Ottawa connections to the east seem to have been minimal. In 1615 Champlain tried to persuade them to trade at Quebec (Champlain 3:96-97), but in 1623 the Ottawa were still getting their French trade goods from the Huron near the mouth of the French River (Sagard 1939:66). Ottawa-Neutral trade appears to have been highly developed; probably more developed than Huron-Neutral trade. Ottawa-Neutral political ties were of course much closer than Neutral-Huron ties. The former had a political-military alliance against the *Assistaeronon* west of Lake St. Clair, while the latter merely tolerated each other in their respective territories (Champlain 3:99-100). It is interesting to note that it was the Ottawa who tried to dissuade Champlain from visiting and establishing trade contacts with the Neutral (Champlain 3:100). As will be shown later, as the fur trade developed it was the Huron that took over the role of primary traders with the Neutral and Petun.

Pre-contact Huron trade seems to have been strongest with some of the Algonquian groups, notably the Nipissing. Ridley's (1954) excavations at

229

the Frank Bay Site on the south shore of Lake Nipissing show beyond the shadow of a doubt that Huron and proto Huron contacts with the bands of this area were of considerable antiquity. Since some of the Nipissing wintered regularly among the Huron, it is not entirely clear whether the Huron material goods found at the Frank Bay Site were brought there by Nipissing returning from Huronia or by Huron trading among the Nipissing. In all probability both situations occurred. The point is that Huron-Nipissing relations predated European contact by a considerable margin.

Champlain (3:39-40) and Sagard (1939:64) found the Nipissing friendly, kind and polite. Apparently they were one of the few Algonquian bands who had no objections to the French passing through their territory to the Huron. Other Algonquian bands along the Ottawa-Lake Nipissing route, particularly the Allumette, tried to hinder French-Nipissing and French-Huron contact from the beginning of the contact period. In 1609 they tried to stop the Huron from coming to the St. Lawrence (Champlain 2:71) and in 1613 they prevented Champlain from going to the Nipissing (Champlain 2:285). This can be interpreted as meaning that until the contact period Nipissing, and therefore Huron connections with the eastern Algonquian bands, the Montagnais and the St. Lawrence valley, were through a series of middlemen, notably the Allumette. Travel across the territory of the Algonquian Ottawa River groups was discouraged. According to Champlain (3:39-40) and Sagard (1939:86-87) the Nipissing did their trading with groups a month's journey to the north. These bands were in turn trading with Europeans on Hudson Bay. The Nipissing even offered to take Champlain on one of their northern trips (Champlain 3:101, 104). The impression one gets is that the lower Ottawa River Algonquians acted as middlemen between the Nipissing and the French prior to 1609. Trade goods were passed on to the Nipissing who in turn traded them to the north and north west for furs (Champlain 3:39-40; 4:287) and to the south to the Huron.

Ridley's archaeological proof of a longstanding tie between the Huron and Nipissing is mirrored by Champlain's early observations. The explorer noted that the Nipissing wintered among the Huron in 1615-1616 (Champlain 3:101, 104). Sagard noted the same thing in 1623 (Sagard 1939:86). References from the *Relations* to be examined later, show that this was a yearly affair. In their contact with the Huron the Nipissing exchanged skins (Champlain 4:309-310) and probably fish (Champlain 4:287; JR 21:239) for corn, corn meal, wampum and fishing nets (Champlain 3:131). The contention that the relationship between the Nipissing and Huron had been a longstanding one is further illustrated by the fact that the Nipissing spoke Huron as well as Algonquian (Sagard 1939:86).

The Huron's ignorance of Algonquian was described by Sagard as either indifference or lack of need. If Huron pre-contact trade had ranged beyond the Nipissing a knowledge of Algonquian would have been essential. Such a lack of knowledge seems to indicate that Huron trade contacts were mainly confined to neighbouring Algonquian bands, in particular the Nipissing and Ottawa who regularly wintered in or near Huronia and therefore spoke Huron. Later, when the Huron expanded the fur trade, their language was used widely in the Great Lakes area.

Huron pottery material has been found as far north as the mouth of the Michipicoten River (Ridley 1961; Wright 1963; Wright 1965). Judging from the quantities found, it is likely that at least some Huron travelled that far north. It is not clear whether these trips were as a result of the developing fur trade, or whether some Huron were regularly travelling that far in pre-contact times. The few pieces of Iroquoian pottery found in the Lake Abitibi area appear to be late Algonquian copies of Huron pottery (Lee 1964:40-41). In view of the development of the fur trade and the lack of motive for pre-contact long distance travel, it seems more likely that direct Huron contact to the Lake Superior area was a result of the fur trade.

Huron knowledge of routes to the Iroquois country appear to have been good through the excursions of their war parties (Champlain 2:110). Even though the Huron were aware of the routes to the south and southeast to the St. Lawrence area, they did not use them as trade routes because of potential Iroquois attacks (Champlain 3:80-81). As a matter of fact, in 1639 the Huron told the Jesuits that they would have come to the French before 1609 if they had known a safe route (JR 16:229). The "safe route", as it finally turned out, was the Ottawa River route which prior to contact times seems to have been little-used by the Huron.

In summarising this section, it must be pointed out that the best evidence for Huron pre-contact trade is with their immediate neighbours. Of these, the Petun and Neutral seem to be of secondary importance. Part of the explanation seems to be 16th-century hostilities, similar subsistence economies and probable trade on the part of the Petun and Neutral with the Ottawa. Routes to the southeast and east via the Kawartha Lakes and the upper St. Lawrence were known, but were not used for trading because of Iroquois hostilities. Similarly the route to the Andaste was known, but little used. Huron contacts to the northeast along the Ottawa seem to have been slight, except through a string of Algonquian middlemen. There is no evidence that trade was carried on into western Lake Huron and Lake Michigan. Ottawa and Neutral hostilities with the *Assistaeronon* probably prevented Huron trade in the Michigan Peninsula; and Ottawa-

Nipissing trade with the Puan in the Green Bay area of Wisconsin prevented the Huron from making contacts there. Due to the distances
involved and the reality of close contact with the Nipissing, Huron trade
in the Michigan and Wisconsin areas would seem rather pointless. Only
to the north can a good case for large-scale Huron trade be made. This
trade involved a close relationship with the Nipissing and, to some extent,
the Ottawa. These Algonquian bands seemed to have had extensive connections with Siouan and Ojibwa groups to the north and northwest. To
what extent the Huron travelled the trading routes north of Lake Nipissing, and from the French River to the Sault and beyond into Lake Superior
and Lake Michigan is unknown. On the basis of Huron pottery at several
sites up to the mouth of the Michipicoten River, some Huron may have
travelled that far. This might account for the stories Champlain heard of
Huron knowledge of a northern copper mine.

The number of Huron involved in summer trade outside of Huronia
is likely to have been small in terms of the later fur trade. Trade was in
the hands of small groups of individuals and lineages with monopolistic
rights to certain routes. It is difficult to envision a large percentage of the
male population of Huronia taking part in such a trade. Moreover, the
Nipissing and some other Algonquian groups such as the *Iroquet* were
wintering regularly among the Huron. It is at this time that trade could
most conveniently be carried on. The long-distance summer trade to the
north was probably motivated by trade for exotic rather than utilitarian
products, and by the desire for adventure and prestige.

Prior to the fur trade, there does not seem to have been any pressing
need for the Huron to undertake voyages of the kind they participated in
during the 1630's and 1640's. All evidence seems to point to gradual
expansion of the Huron trade network from the neighbouring Iroquoian
and Algonquian groups, to include most of the Algonquian and some of
the Montagnais bands of Ontario and Quebec. The nature of Huron trade
and its gradual expansion can best be illustrated by studying it over time
on a year-by-year-basis. Of crucial importance is an understanding of the
beginnings of French contact.

3. THE EARLY CONTACT PERIOD

There is no evidence to suggest that the Huron got any quantity of French
trade goods until late in the sixteenth century. Hunt's elaborate thesis of
a 16th-century Indian trade network carrying European goods from the
Atlantic coast " . . . swiftly throughout the region . . ." just does not seem
to be true (Hunt 1940:13-18). The earliest Huron and Petun sites con-

taining some trade material date towards the end of the 16th century (Wright 1966:74-75, 101). The first trade goods may have trickled in earlier, but only in very small quantities. This is not to deny that some trading had been going on along the Atlantic coast of Canada since before Cartier's visit to the St. Lawrence in 1535. However, the quantity of goods involved does not seem to have been large enough to have had much effect on the tribes of the Great Lakes area. It is probable that most trade goods prior to the latter part of the 16th century were absorbed by the various Montagnais and Algonquian bands, a small residue finding its way to Huronia. It is interesting to note that Lescarbot (3:25-26) definitely puts the beginning of the fur trade to de Mont's efforts in the Tadoussac area. This could not have been earlier than 1599. Prior to that time ". . .Tadoussac had hardly been heard of; at most the savages, and then only those of the neighbourhood, came perfunctorily to find the codfishers in the neighbourhood of Bacallaos (Newfoundland), and there bartered almost for nothing such things as they had" (Lescarbot, *ibid*).

The Huron definitely got their first trade goods from Algonquian traders before 1603 (Champlain 1:164). Champlain's statements leave no doubt that even by 1609, Algonquians were still acting as middlemen between the Huron and the French. In that year, the first Huron visited the French near the mouth of the Batiscan River, a few miles upstream from Quebec (Champlain 2:68). Several statements make it clear that this was the first direct contact between the Huron and the French. Champlain stated that he had never encountered these people before (Champlain 2:109), and when he fired his gun many of them expressed surprise ". . . especially those who had never heard or seen the like" (Champlain, Vol 2:70). More importantly the Huron did not bring much merchandise, nor were they particularly interested in trade (Champlain 2:71). Their purpose was to conclude an alliance with the French and help their Algonquian allies on a raid against the Mohawk (Champlain 2:68-70). The first meeting between Champlain and the Huron characteristically lasted several days and included speeches and gift-giving. It was exactly the kind of meeting one would expect the Huron to have conducted in concluding a treaty with another tribe.

Several other pieces of evidence lend support to the contention that the first direct contact between the Huron and the French was in 1609. Under Huron law rights of trade belonged to the group that had pioneered the new connection. This group was the *Arendaronnon*, who even in 1640 still considered themselves special allies of the French (JR 20:19). It was also among the *Arendaronnon* that Champlain stayed the winter of 1615-1616. An interesting point here is that it was Iroquet, an Algonquian chief, who introduced the Huron under Ochateguin to Champlain in 1609. Iroquet and his band were from the Ottawa valley and always wintered among the *Arendaronnon*. It seems therefore that Iroquet brought a group of *Arendaronnon* to Champlain in 1609 and that the *Arendaronnon* invited Champlain to visit Huronia (Champlain 2:105), a task which he could not accomplish until 1615. Because the *Arendaronnon* were the first to conclude a treaty and trade contacts with the French, they considered themselves special allies of the French and the rest of the Huron confederacy recognized the primacy of *Arendaronnon* rights to the Huron-French trade, a right the *Arendaronnon* later relinquished.

Inasmuch as trade was concerned, the first contact between Huron and French was disappointing (Champlain 2:71). Nor was the year 1610 much better. The highlight of that year, as far as the Indians were concerned, was another raid on the Iroquois. The Huron contingent arrived too late to participate in the raid and consisted of only eighty men (Champlain 2:138). As in the previous year, the Huron had been led to the rendezvous with the French by Iroquet and his Algonquians. Apparently most of the trading was done with the Montagnais (Champlain 3:125); the Huron only stayed three days and then departed (Champlain 3:138). Later Champlain (3:146) commented that the trade had been particularly disappointing that year.

The year 1611 is important because this was the first year that the Huron came to the St. Lawrence for reasons other than war. On the 13th of June a group of some 200 Huron and Algonquians, again let by Iroquet and the Huron Ochateguin, met at the Lachine Rapids with Champlain and the other traders. Several important points emerged from this meeting. First of all, the alliance made in the previous two years had to be reaffirmed by further gift-giving and lengthy speeches (Champlain 2:-189-191). After the gift exchanges were completed, Champlain had to listen to lengthy Huron and Algonquian complaints about the avariciousness of the French traders (Champlain 2:188-189, 193-194). Apparently this group of Indians was not used to bargaining and haggling, something that the Montagnais in the Tadoussac area had learned over many years of trading experience (Champlain 2:171). Another interesting point that emerged from this meeting was that the Montagnais, Algonquians and Iroquois all tried to prevent the Huron from coming to the St. Lawrence to meet with the French. The Montagnais and Algonquians had spread a story that the French had killed the Huron lad Savignon, who had been exchanged for Brulé the previous year (Champlain 2:187), while the Iroquois had leaked a story to the Huron that Champlain had made a pact with them and was waiting with 600 Iroquois near the Lachine Rapids to

234

kill any Huron and Algonquians that came to the St. Lawrence (Champlain 2:189-190). The latter ruse apparently worked, because the Huron claimed that for this reason some 400 traders had stayed home that year. The amount of trading that went on that year was ". . . very little . . ." a ". . . few articles . . ." (Champlain 2:192). The main point, as far as the Huron were concerned, was to cement the alliance made in the previous years. Trading seems to have been an afterthought, or rather an activity that seemed to be necessary to get French favour.

In 1612, while Champlain was in France, some 200 Huron and Algonquians had come to the Lachine Rapids to meet the French for another raid on the Iroquois (Champlain 2:217). Trading was light because the Indians had come prepared for war and were bitterly disappointed when the French traders would not help them. In 1613 the Huron resolved not to come to trade. In the previous year they had been ill-used by the traders who had also told them Champlain was dead, and that they would not help them in their wars (Lescarbot 3:29; Champlain 2:217-218, 254). Consequently, Champlain found only a few Algonquians at the Lachine rapids and very few furs (Champlain 2:252-254).

When trade did not materialize by the spring of 1613, Champlain realized that he had to change his tactics. Up to now, the French fur trade had relied solely on furs supplied by the Montagnais. Abenaki and the Algonquian bands along the shore of the St. Lawrence and the lower Ottawa. The Huron and Algonquians of the upper Ottawa had hardly entered the fur trade directly, and seemed to be more interested in going to war than engaging in trade. Champlain realized by 1613 that he had to visit these groups personally and use promises of help in war as a guise to induce them to come to trade. In the years 1613 and 1615 Champlain's trips up the Ottawa and to Huronia laid the basis for close Huron-French relations and the gradual expansion of the Huron trade network.

Champlain's trip up the Ottawa in 1613 is usually seen as an exploratory trip to gain information about the "northern sea" (Rich 1967:11-12). While this was certainly part of the reason why he ascended the Ottawa, also important was the promotion of trade. Failure for trade to materialize at the Lachine rapids in the spring of 1613:

> . . . made me resolve in carrying out my explorations, to make my way into their country in order to encourage those who stayed at home with an assurance of the good treatment they would receive and the quantity of fine wares that were at the Rapids, as well as of my desire to help them in their wars (Champlain 2:254).

On May 27th, 1613, Champlain proceeded up the Ottawa, well-supplied with presents, his ultimate aim being to contact all the Algonquian bands as far as the Nipissing. These plans were frustrated when Champlain found that the Allumette would not guide him past their territory (Champlain 2:283-297). Disappointed, Champlain tried to make the best of the situation by asking the Allumette to relate his wishes to the other bands. Specifically, the message he wanted to get across was that he wished to aid all the groups in war (Champlain 2:283-284); to make alliances with them (Champlain 2:286); and to ask them to come and trade at the Lachine rapids (Champlain 2:297). The Allumette, in turn, promised to spread the message to their neighbours and collect a large war party for the next year (Champlain 2:284, 297-298).

On the way back from the Allumette, Champlain ran into a number of lower Ottawa River Algonquian groups (mainly from the Petite Nation) ultimately totaling about eighty canoes ". . . with a great deal of merchandise . . ." (Champlain 2:298-299). After trading was completed, Champlain asked them to take two French youth's along ". . . in order to keep the Indians friendly, learn something of their country, and place them under the obligation of coming back to us" (Champlain 2:307). At no time were any Huron or upper Ottawa River Algonquians involved.

An interesting point that received confirmation from this voyage was the reality of longstanding Iroquois raids to the lower Ottawa, well before the organization of the first Huron fur brigades. The Algonquians told Champlain that the Iroquois were in the habit of raiding the lower Ottawa from Lake St. Louis to Allumette Island (Champlain 2:260, 266-268, 278-279). The threat of these raids may have been a partial deterrent to an earlier development of close trading contacts with the upper Ottawa River Algonquians, the Huron and the French. In later years the benefits accruing from trade had to be constantly weighed against potential losses at the hands of the Iroquois along the lower Ottawa and upper St. Lawrence. As early as 1615 the Huron asked the French to establish a post at the Lachine Rapids in order ". . . to give them safe passage by the river on account of their fear of their enemies . . ." (Champlain 3:172). Until Champlain's visit to the upper Ottawa Algonquians and Huron in 1615, these fears as well as other difficulties probably far outweighed any benefits they could see from trade.

In summarising the early contact period, several important points should be noted. This was essentially a period of frustration and disappointment to the French. Even though the Huron had been contacted by 1609, accompanied by peace treaties and aid in war, little trade resulted. The underlying reasons behind this slow development of Huron-French trade can be found in the conventions governing Indian trade and the inter tribal relations of the pre-contact period. Huron trade had been primarily oriented to the north and northwest of Huronia. The south-eastern route to the St. Lawrence was closed by the Iroquois, while the route via Lake Nipissing and the Ottawa River was across the territory of allied Algonquian bands. These Algonquians had acted as middlemen between the French and Huron for some time, and were reluctant to lose their position. For this reason, the Algonquians had nothing against Huron warriors coming to the St. Lawrence, but were reluctant to see any development of Huron-French trade. On their part, the Huron seem to have been fairly content with this situation. What Champlain interpreted as a reluctance to trade seems to have been partly a desire on the part of the Huron to preserve friendly relations with the Algonquians. It is also doubtful whether the Huron as a whole understood at that time what the implications of close trading relations with the French could mean. Champlain knew that in order to expand trade past the Algonquian bands he had to visit the Huron and intervening groups personally. He had to point out the advantages of trade to the Huron as a whole and find some means of negotiating a passage for them past the Algonquians along the Lake Nipissing Ottawa River route. In 1615 Champlain decided to visit the Huron with the view of placing Huron-French trade on a securer basis.

4. CHAMPLAIN'S TRIP TO THE HURON AND THE BEGINNING OF THE HURON FUR TRADE

In 1614 Champlain stayed in France, reorganizing his company and getting support for a group of Récollet priests to come to New France. As far as Huron-French trade is concerned, nothing much seemed to have happened. In June 1615 Champlain found a group of Huron and Algonquians at the Lachine Rapids ready for a raid on the Iroquois. Again it was pointed out to him that ". . . only with difficulty could they come and see us if we did not help them, because the Iroquois, their ancient foes, were continually along the route and prevented them from passing" (Champlain 3:31). It was the same old story; the Iroquois threat and the Huron preference for war over trade combined to assure a minimal supply of furs. Only a massive show of strength and friendship could overcome these hindrances to trade (Champlain 3:31-32). For this reason, Champlain decided to visit Huronia and organize the Huron on a mass raid against the Iroquois. The Huron were delighted and promised 2,500 warriors.

As far as Huron-French relations were concerned, Champlain's voyage in 1615 had a number of important consequences. For the first time, the bulk of the Huron population were contacted directly by a number of Frenchmen including Champlain, a priest (Joseph Le Caron) and fourteen others. These stayed among the Huron for ten months (August 1st, 1615 to May 20th, 1616) visiting various villages with assurances of friendship and, no doubt, promises of trade. The raid on the Onondaga, while a disappointment to Champlain, demonstrated to the Huron the reality of the French alliance. Their growing concern for continued French good-will was clearly demonstrated by their behaviour when on one occasion Champlain got lost on the retreat from the Onondaga. Champlain was told that, ". . . If you had not come back and we had been unable to find you, we should not have gone down to the French any more for fear lest they should have accused us of having put you to death" (Champlain 3:91). From then on Champlain was closely watched, the Huron fearing that French-Huron relations would be severed if they were somehow involved in his death. The arrival of a priest among the Huron had no immediate effect on the Huron, but it set a precedent for later years.

Besides visiting the Huron, Champlain also journeyed to the Petun with whom he "made friends" and ". . . a good number promised to come down to our settlement" (Champlain 3:95). On the western edge of the Petun territory he renewed his friendship with the Ottawa, who likewise promised to come to trade (Champlain 3:96-97). While visiting the Ottawa, Champlain met some Neutral, and regretted that he could not visit their country as well (Champlain 3:100-101). On his way back from the Petun Champlain stopped by some Nipissing, who were wintering on the borders of Huronia. These also promised to come to the St. Lawrence in the following summer (Champlain 3:104). It is therefore apparent that exploration and war were not the only motives that induced Champlain to visit Huronia. During this visit he personally contacted the Nipissing, Ottawa, Petun, Huron and some Neutral, as well as a number of Algonquian bands, notably the one led by Iroquet, asking all of these to come to trade at the Lachine Rapids (Champlain 3:113). Apparently the trip to these groups paid off, because a large number of men accompanied Champlain back to the Lachine Rapids on May 20th, 1616 (Champlain 3:168-169). Biggar went so far as to state, "The barter at the rapids this summer was unusually large, for all the tribes visited by Champlain during his winter among the Huron now came down to the St. Lawrence for the first time" (Biggar 1901:106). Whether the Petun, Neutral, or Ottawa came to trade is doubtful, but at least they had seen some Frenchmen and acquired first-hand knowledge of the kind of goods it was possible to obtain.

238

During his visit to the Huron Champlain sketched out the salient features of trade relations in the Eastern Great Lakes area. The Huron regularly traded corn, corn meal, wampum, and fishnets for furs with the Nipissing and other Algonquian bands (Champlain 3:53, 131). On both occasions where Champlain mentions this trade, he points out that the furs traded from the Algonquian bands were used by the Huron to make clothing and robes. The Huron did not have enough skins of their own for clothing and had to get more through trade from various Algonquian groups. At no time did Champlain state that these furs were gathered by the Huron in order to trade them to the French, an implication that has been read into Champlain's statements by Hunt (1940:54). The main trade item the Huron got from the Neutral and Petun was tobacco (Champlain 3:99; 6:248). There is no evidence that at this time any other products were involved. Even in later years, tobacco seems to have been a major trade item between these groups. Judging from passages in the *Jesuit Relations* the Huron grew some tobacco (JR 11:7) near their long-houses (JR 15:79). Tobacco was always a highly valued product among the Huron (JR 9:273; 10:301) and on many occasions the priests either gave it to them or used it to induce the Huron to attend church services (Sagard 1939:85; JR 13:141, 171; 24:151). The impression one gets is that the Huron did not grow enough tobacco to satisfy their own needs as well as the needs of some of the Algonquian groups they were trading tobacco to (JR 6:273). Before 1615, Petun and Neutral tobacco seems to have come mainly to the Huron and some of the Algonquian groups that were wintering in the area. What the Huron traded to the Petun and Neutral at this time is not known.

Among the Algonquian groups of this period the Ottawa were regarded by Champlain as great traders, covering some 400 to 500 leagues every summer (Champlain 3:97). Their connections with the Petun, Neutral and areas to the north-west were noted earlier. Champlain observed that they were semi-agricultural, a fact that probably allowed them to undertake such long trading voyages (Champlain 3:97). The Nipissing were undoubtedly the Huron's strongest trading partners. On several occasions Champlain noted their connections to groups north of Lake Nipissing (Champlain 3:41), and to the north and northwest into the upper and western Great Lakes (Champlain 3:105). Nipissing, Ottawa, and Huron connections to the east seem to have been slight; at least, up to 1615 the Huron were brought to the Lachine Rapids by lower Ottawa River Algonquians (Iroquet's band), and neither the Nipissing nor the Ottawa ever passed that far until much later.

The major trade routes in existence by 1615 can be identified by means of Champlain's maps and journals (Maps 3 and 4). The Ottawa River (River of the Algonquians) was evidently the trunk route for all the Algonquian bands living to the north and south of it (Map 24). Between Lac des Chats and Allumette Island, the Muskrat Lake chain to the South of the Ottawa was used to avoid the dangerous Calumet Rapids (Champlain 2:272; 6:242-243). Along the Ottawa, Champlain pointed out some of the tributaries that led to the various Algonquian bands. Of these tributaries the Rouge and Petite Nation Rivers led to the *Ouaouechkairini* (*Ouescharini* or Petite Nation) (Champlain 2:266; Map 4:point 57). The Gatineau led up to another Algonquian band, not specifically identified (Champlain 2:266). Apparently the Gatineau was sometimes used to get to the upper St. Maurice and thence to Trois Rivières, thus avoiding Iroquois raids on the lower Ottawa (Champlain 2:266-267). This seems to have been largely an Algonquian route. It is not mentioned anywhere else, nor does it appear on any maps. Apparently few Indians inhabited the areas upstream along the Rideau River. Champlain mentions the Rideau as a route used by Iroquois raiders (Champlain 2:268). An Algonquian band (the *Atontrataronon*) may have inhabited this area at one time. They are marked on Sanson's map of 1656 (Map 9) in the general area of the upper Rideau near the St. Lawrence, but appear to have been ejected from the area some time before 1643 by the Iroquois (JR 27:37). Along the Madawaska River Champlain noted an Algonquian band the *Mataouchkarini* (*Matou-oues-carini*) (Champlain 2:271), and along the Muskrat Lake route the *Kinounchepirini* (*Quenongebin*), whose chief may have been Nibachis whom Champlain visited in 1613 (Champlain 2:264, 275). On Allumette Island were the powerful *Kichespiirini* (Allumette) who proved to be so troublesome to later Huron trading voyages (Champlain 2:277-278). Sources to be discussed later show that it was the Allumette who were playing the role of middlemen between the French and the groups to the west until Huron trade was better developed. The Ottawa north of Allumette Island was apparently thinly inhabited (Champlain 3:37-38). Only the *Kotakoutouemi* (*Otagouttouemin*) are mentioned, a band whose main territory appears to have been in the upper Dumoine River area (JR 18:229). While in the upper Ottawa River area Champlain mentioned a river that was used to get to the "Northern Sea", Trois Rivières and the Saguenay (Champlain 3:38-39). Judging from his map of 1616 (Map 3), this river was the Dumoine. In this respect, the map of 1616 is considerably more accurate than the map of 1632 (Map 4); it leaves no doubt that the Dumoine River route was meant and not the upper Ottawa-Lake Timiscaming route as some have suspected (Cham-

240

plain 3:39, footnote one; Hunt 1940:60, Map). It is doubtful if the Huron used the Dumoine River route at this time; most of Champlain's information seems to have come from the Algonquians with whom he travelled.

The Nipissing occupied the shores and island of the lake of the same name, trading up the Sturgeon river (*Rivière d Estarjon;* Maps 3, 4 and 5; Champlain 3:41) to the *Timiscimi* and *Outimagami.* In this case Champlain noted that the Nipissing traded French goods for furs (Champlain 3:41). Nipissing connections to the north-west, at least as far as the east shore of Lake Superior, were mentioned earlier. Champlain's information for the shore of Lake Huron northwest of the French River, Sault Ste. Marie, and Lake Superior (Maps 3 and 4) evidently came from the Ottawa and Nipissing. In 1615, near the mouth of the French River, an Ottawa chief sketched a map of the area for Champlain, even pointing out the general area where he got his yearly supply of blueberries (Champlain 3:44). The location of the blueberry grounds, and, it seems, the map, were reproduced by Champlain for his map of 1632 (Map 4). Other information on the northern areas was obtained from the Nipissing (Champlain 3:104-105).

In examining the sources up to 1615, there is no evidence that the Huron had any trading connections beyond Lake Nipissing to the north, the Petun to the west and the Neutral to the south. By and large, the Nipissing seem to have carried the trade to the Huron and the Ottawa to the Petun. The Nipissing traded to the north and northwest of Lake Nipissing, sharing the north-western route with the Ottawa. To the east the Nipissing were in contract with the Allumette, and may have used the Dumoine River route. The central and lower Ottawa River area was controlled by the Allumette and Petite Nation, who seem to have been the major suppliers of furs to the French until 1616. The other Algonquian bands along the Ottawa were either unimportant in the early fur trade or were serviced by the Allumette and Petite Nation.

Judging from this trade pattern, only the Algonquian bands from the Nipissing eastwards seem to have been strongly affected by the French fur trade up to 1615. Although the Huron had received French trade goods in some quantities before 1615, there is no evidence that they participated directly in the collecting and trading of furs. Up until 1616 the French sources for furs were various Algonquian groups and of course the Montagnais.

241

5. THE DEVELOPMENT OF TRADE TO 1629.

a) Yearly Trading Activities: 1616-1629

That the summer of 1616 was a trading success involving some Huron has already been noted. Nothing is known of 1617, but in the summer of 1618 Champlain was back in New France. He met ". . . all the savages of my acquaintance and with whom in their own country I had become intimate . . ." at Trois Rivières (Champlain 3:208). Trading went on from July 7th to the 14th and was evidently successful. Complaints were made of Iroquois raids and, as usual, Champlain was asked to aid his allies in war (Champlain 3:209). Again, nothing is known of trading activities in 1619. In 1620 trade in the upper St. Lawrence area went on at the mouth of the Richelieu River, but Champlain does not recount how successful it was (Champlain 5:4, 9). In 1621 and 1622 trade was conducted at Trois Rivières (Champlain 5:31, 35, 82). In June, 1622, two Iroquois came to Trois Rivières in an attempt to arrange a peace (Champlain 5:74-80). Apparently the peace negotiations were successful; at any rate, in 1624 after a Montagnais had killed an Iroquois, peace was retained in spite of the difficulties arising out of intertribal murder (Champlain 5:130-131). In all, thirty-five Iroquois canoes came to the St. Lawrence in 1624 to trade and finalise the treaty (Biggar 1901:124). This treaty seemed to last from 1622 to 1627, and was a period of excellent trading. Hunt (1940:69-70) stated that the French were worried over a Huron-Iroquois treaty and sent Sagard, Nicolas Viel, Le Caron and eleven others to Huronia to prevent the treaty from being ratified. In the light of Champlain's and Sagard's writings, Hunt's supposition does not seem to be correct. No treaty between the Huron and Iroquois would have diverted the fur trade to the Dutch; on the contrary, the French stood to gain from the treaty, by diverting Iroquois trade to the St. Lawrence.

The year 1623 is important, not only because the information on trading is unusually complete, but also because it marked the re-introduction of missionaries to Huronia. From that date to 1629 some missionaries were always present among the Huron. The Huron-Algonquian fur brigade in 1623 consisted of about sixty canoes and some two hundred men (Champlain 5:100-101). Trading was done at the mouth of the Richelieu River. An interesting point is that the Huron complained bitterly that some Algonquian groups barred certain routes to them, levied heavy tolls and even robbed them (Champlain 5:103).

Two priests, Nicolas Viel and Joseph Le Caron, a lay brother Gabriel Sagard, and eleven other men returned with the Huron. Besides hoping to Christianise the Huron, the Récollet missionaries were also supposed to induce the Huron to come and trade (Champlain 5:108; Sagard 1939: 77-78). In return for their hospitality to the Récollets, the Huron expected the priests to persuade the traders to give better prices for their furs (Sagard 1939:244-245). Later the same was expected of the Jesuits by the Huron. The role that the Récollets had to play as intermediaries in the fur trade was not new. In addition to being an interpreter, it was a job Brulé had been paid to do, for some years (Champlain 5:132). Besides Brulé, other Frenchmen had been in Huronia between 1616 and 1623. How many Frenchmen were involved, and what years they went to Huronia, is not known. At least some were in Huronia in 1622 (Champlain 5: 100-101), probably staying at *Carhagouha* (Le Clercq 1881:205). The express function of these men was ". . . to keep them (Huron) steady in their friendship, and dispose them to come to us" (Champlain 5:101; JR 4:197). With the Récollets, Champlain put this relationship on a permanent basis.

Le Caron and Sagard returned to Quebec in 1624; Nicolas Viel stayed in Huronia only to be drowned in the Ottawa on his return in 1625. In 1624 at least forty-five Huron canoes arrived for trade (Champlain 5: 131-133), as well as the thirty-five Iroquois canoes mentioned earlier. In 1626 the Récollet Joseph La Roche de Daillon and the Jesuits Jean de Brébeuf and Anne de Noüe were sent to Huronia with a few Frenchmen ". . . to induce the savages to come down and trade" (Champlain 5:207) and to carry on the mission. Michel, one of the French interpreters, later accused the Jesuits of trying to "convert the beaver", rather than the Indians (Champlain 6:137); demonstrating that the development of trade contacts was an important function of the priests. The year 1627 was regarded as one of the best years for trading, but unfortunately marked the end of the Iroquois peace (Champlain 5:229-232). Between the years 1622 and 1627 there do not seem to have been any Iroquois raids on the Huron and Algonquian fur brigades. Sagard put this lack of Iroquois activity to the presence of the few Frenchmen who regularly travelled with Huron, implying that the Iroquois were frightened of them (Sagard 1939:261). In the light of previous and later Iroquois activity, this hardly seems a plausible reason for the cessation of the Iroquois raids. As a matter of fact, during this period the Iroquois were embroiled in a quarrel with the Dutch and Mahican, and were therefore trying to stay on friendly terms with the Huron, Algonquians and Montagnais (Champlain 5:214-219).

There are no records of trade being carried on in the upper St. Lawrence area during 1628. Instead, the English blockaded Quebec and captured French vessels bringing supplies (Champlain 5:275-296). By July, 1629, the French at Quebec were reduced to desperate straits. The previous fall they had even bought food from local Algonquian bands at the price of one good beaver skin for five eels (Champlain 5:298). When the missionaries returned from Huronia with twelve canoes on July 17th, the French tried to barter corn from the Indians, but with little success (Champlain 6:45-47). A few days later the Huron decided to return to Huronia ". . . with the little merchandise they had brought . . ." (Champlain 6:49). With the evacuation of Quebec in September, 1629, French-Huron trade relations ceased until the return of the French in June 1632 (JR 5:17).

b) The Logistics of Huron Trade and Huron Trade Contacts: 1616-1629

Sagard's account of 1623 to 1624 provides an unusually clear picture of the nature and extent of Huron trade in the early 1620's. During the winter the Huron women would prepare corn meal for the men to take along on their summer trading (Sagard 1939:101-102). Along the route, corn would be cached at a two days' travel distance apart (Sagard 1939:-60). While travelling, an attempt was made to catch fish by dragging a line behind the canoe. The usual meal, therefore, consisted of corn soup and fish, the Huron eating twice a day (Sagard 1939:61-62).

According to Sagard, Huron canoes were at a maximum eight to nine paces long (twenty to twenty-two feet), one to one-and-a-half paces wide (two-and-a-half to four feet) (Sagard 1939:100); and held a maximum of five to six men (Sagard 1939:56). Smaller canoes holding two or three men were especially built for difficult journeys on narrow rivers with many rapids and portages (Sagard 1939:246). These descriptions fit well with those of Champlain and the Jesuits, showing that the average Huron canoe changed very little in size between 1615 and 1650. Champlain put the average capacity at four to five men (Champlain 2:289-299; 5:100); Charles Lallemant in 1626 also put the capacity at four to five men (JR 4:205); in 1642 (JR 24:275) and 1648 (JR 32:97) it was still about four men to a canoe. Bressani put the capacity of a Huron canoe at three to four men but mentioned that some could hold eight or ten (JR 38:247). Besides its complement of men Bressani stated that the average canoe held about "2,000 livres burden" (JR 39:47). If Bressani was referring to beaver skins, it would mean that a canoe could hold four men plus 200 skins weighing perhaps one to two pounds each (JR 4:255; 28:235). Sagard put the capacity of a Huron canoe at a similar figure; one hogshead or cask which comprised about 200 pounds (Sagard 1939:100; JR 28: 235).

244

Under very good conditions, a Huron canoe could cover some 25 to 30 leagues in a day (60 to 90 miles) (Sagard 1939:101). The usual length of a trip between Huronia and Quebec was about three to four weeks, depending on the weather and point of destination or departure on the St. Lawrence (Champlain 3:36-46, 163-169; JR 8:89; 10:89; 15:161; 16:-231; 18:11, 17; 31:21). The usual time of arrival at the St. Lawrence between 1611 and 1629 was anywhere from mid-June to mid-July (Champlain 2:186; 3:31-32; 5:101-102, 129; 6:45). For various reasons to be discussed later, arrival times at the St. Lawrence grew later in the years during the 1630's and 1640's.

Throughout this period the Huron travelled to and from the St. Lawrence in small separate groups, travelled at different speeds, and departed and arrived at different times (Champlain 5:129-133; Sagard 1939:56, 63, 255). Apparently these small flotillas were organized on a village basis; at least, canoes from the same village travelled together. Thus, for example, Sagard travelled to Huronia with the Huron from *Tequenonquiaye* and departed with those from *Quieunonascaran,* while Brulé travelled with those from *Toanché* (Sagard 1939:247, 251). This mode of travel would account for Sagard's statement that each small flotilla put up the coat-of-arms of its particular village (or lineage?) at camping places along the way. The fact that trade was in the hands of individual lineages within each village, who had their own separate trade contacts, probably helped to splinter trading voyages into small separate groups.

Judging from Champlain's descriptions the Huron war parties travelled in large compact groups; at least, the ones that came to the St. Lawrence and the ones he travelled with. It was not until well into the 1640's that the character of Huron trading voyages began to change, and took on more the appearance and organization of a war party (JR 32:179).

Throughout the entire period between 1615 and 1629, the main route between Huronia and the St. Lawrence was the Georgian Bay-French River-Lake Nipissing-Ottawa River route. Both Champlain (3:38-39) and Sagard (1939:249, 253) refer to a route up the Dumoine River and thence to the Saguenay; but it is not clear whether the Huron were using this route to travel the entire distance to the Saguenay (Map 24). There is no evidence that any Huron ever traded in the Saguenay-Tadoussac area, or that Huron canoes ever approached Quebec from the east or the north. Since the Huron usually left Huronia sometime between mid-May and mid-June, (Jones 1908:404) there was simply not enough time for them to have travelled across central Quebec, through at least three band territories, and still have arrived at the usual trading places upstream from Quebec in mid June or July. What seems more likely is that the bulk of the Huron travelled the normal route to Quebec, stopping at various places along the way, notably among the Ottawa, Nipissing and Allumette (Champlain 3:39-42, 43-44; Sagard 1939:63, 66, 249-250, 255-258), to gather more furs or pay toll charges. Some Huron may have gone up the Dumoine River to trade with the *Kotakoutouemi* and *Attikamegue* before 1629, thus accounting for Sagard's statements that they were reluctant to show the French some of their fur sources north-east of the Ottawa (Sagard 1939:87). Once the Huron were among the *Kotakoutoumi* or *Attikamegue,* it would have been easier for them to return via the Dumoine and Ottawa than to go on to Lake St. John or pass down the St. Maurice. Since the Huron were at peace with the Iroquois from 1622 to 1627 there was really no reason why they would want to avoid the shorter and easier Ottawa route. Hunt (1940:57-62) tried to make a case for a northern Huron route, but did not handle his material chronologically. Going strictly by the available evidence, the case for a northern route before 1629 is decidedly weak. The arrival times on the upper St. Lawrence of the Huron fur brigades, the routes travelled by Champlain and Sagard, and the fact that every Huron fur brigade approached the French posts from the upper St. Lawrence seems fairly conclusive evidence that in the main only the Ottawa River route was used.

One of the most troublesome aspects of the entire trip to the St. Lawrence seems to have been the passage through Allumette territory (Champlain 5:103; Sagard 1939:255-258). As the Huron canoes came down the Ottawa, the Allumette would delay them until a good-sized fleet had assembled. They would then force the Huron to give up a goodly portion of their corn and barter some furs. Presumably those Huron who gave the best prices for Allumette furs were allowed transit first. At the same time, the Huron had to suffer insults and other indignities. Apparently the Huron got off more lightly when a priest accompanied them. Sagard relates that the Allumette feared reprisals from the French traders if the priests were attacked or insulted (Sagard 1939:257). During the 1620's at least, the Allumette seem to have prospered as a result of toll charges. Over the 1630's Allumette opposition to Huron trading voyages increased until the Allumette were reduced by smallpox between 1642 and 1644 (JR 24:267; 26:301-305) and virtually wiped out by the Oneida in 1646 (JR 28:225). These events will be examined in greater detail later in this chapter. It should also be pointed out that similar to the Allumette, the Montagnais at this time tried to prevent the Huron from travelling down the St. Lawrence to trade in their territory. Toll charges were also set in corn (Sagard 1939:268).

By the mid-1620's the Huron seem to have developed stronger trade contracts with the Neutral. Judging from Sagard's few remarks in 1623, Huron-Neutral contacts were not particularly highly regarded (Sagard 1939:151, 157). The major Neutral product seems to have been tobacco (Sagard 1939:158). Exotic skins also came from the Neutral country such as raccoon (*tiron*) and black squirrel skins (Sagard 1939:224; JR 17:165). Neither of these skins were traded to the French, but were made into robes for the Huron's own use. Ragueneau singled the black squirrel skin robes out as a Huron's most valued possession (JR 33:193). In return, the Huron traded French goods to the Neutral.

In 1626 the Neutral were visited by the Récollet Jospeh de la Roche Daillon, having been preceded earlier by Brulé and on various occassions by French traders (Sagard 1939:194). The purpose of Daillon's visit was to contract an alliance between the Neutral and the French, and to induce them to come to the St. Lawrence to trade (Le Clercq 1881:263-272). The Neutral seemed interested in going to trade with the French, but did not know how to get there. Although some Algonquians and Huron knew the southern Lake Ontario route to the St. Lawrence (a ten day's journey), they refused to show Daillon and the Neutral the way. The result of Daillon's efforts to get the Neutral interested in trade was an immediate Huron response in the form of rumors and innuendo well calculated to spread fear of the French among the Neutral. This propaganda war was so successful that Daillon was fortunate to get away with his life. It is, therefore, clear that by 1626 the Huron began to value Huron-Neutral trade to such an extent that they tried hard to prevent the formation of any ties between the Neutral and the French.

A trip to the Neutral country took some five days from the Petun (Le Clercq 1881:263-265; Sagard 1939:158), and five to six days from Huronia (JR 18:39; 20:95). The nearest Neutral villages could be reached in four to five days under good travel conditions (JR 21:189, 205-207). All travel to the Neutral was over narrow, difficult trails. There is no evidence that canoes were ever used. Consequently, all goods that were exchanged between the two groups had to be carried on the backs of the traders. Under these conditions, it is difficult to envisage any products being exchanged except high-value goods such as furs, tobacco, trade goods, and a few luxuries. There is no evidence that at this date or any other the Huron were trading corn from the Neutral (Hunt 1940:56-58). Hunt's thesis that the Huron monopolised the corn from the Neutral "farms" is without foundation. Indeed, it would be difficult to envisage a trade based on corn being carried on over some 100 miles without canoes or carts, but entirely on the backs of a few traders. If such a thing had occurred, surely someone would have observed it.

247

Even less is known about Huron dealings with the Petun during the 1620's. Like the Neutral, the Petun were visited by Frenchmen other than priests (Sagard 1939:194). Daillon was even guided to the Neutral by the Petun (Le Clercq 1881:263-264), showing that the Petun, unlike the Huron had no objections to French-Neutral contacts. The major Petun product seems still to have been tobacco (Champlain 6:248). Judging from Sagard (1939:85) this herb was always scarce among the Huron. Undoubtedly furs were also traded from the Petun for trade goods, because one never hears of any Petun going to trade in the St. Lawrence area. In the light of what happened in the late 1630's, the Huron probably discouraged direct Petun-French contact, although none of the pre-Jesuit writers refer to it.

Huron-Ottawa relations during the 1620's are rather nebulous. Sagard, like Champlain, pointed out that some of the northern bands, notably the *Nation des Bois* (Ojibwa), were dependent on the Ottawa for trade (Sagard 1939:64). Exactly which branch of the Ojibwa was meant is not clear. Possibly it was the *Saulteur* or some band at the eastern end of Lake Superior (Map 24). At any rate the Ottawa travelled to the northwest to trade for ". . . furs, pigments, wampum, and other rubbish" (Sagard 1939:67). Like Champlain, Sagard stated that some of their trips encompassed 400 to 500 leagues. When the Huron returned from the St. Lawrence, the Ottawa stationed themselves on Georgian Bay near the mouth of the French River to trade with the Huron (Sagard 1939:66). This followed a pattern similar to the one observed by Champlain eight years earlier (Champlain 3:43-44). In 1623, trading between the two groups took two days. There is no evidence that the Ottawa at any time during the 1620's went to the St. Lawrence to trade.

Unlike the Ottawa, the Nipissing seem to have travelled to the St. Lawrence to trade (Champlain 5:129). On several occasions when Champlain referred to Algonquians travelling with the Huron, he probably meant the Nipissing. Like Champlain, Sagard observed that the Nipissing wintered among the Huron (Sagard 1939:86). In the summer they traded with some groups at a four to six weeks' journey north of Lake Nipissing. These bands were in contact with ". . . a certain people who reach the place by sea, in great wooden boats or ships laden with different kinds of merchandise . . ." (Sagard 1939:86-87). In all probability, the groups the Nipissing traded with were in contact with British traders on Hudsons Bay. Later sources identify these northern groups as the Cree or *Kilistinon* Algonquians (JR 21:125). By the late 1640's and early 1650's some of these Cree became identified as the "*Kilistinon* of the Nipissing" (JR 44:249; Map 11).

On their way from the St. Lawrence, the Huron still stopped among the Nipissing to rest and trade (Sagard 1939:63). The same procedure was followed on the way to the St. Lawrence (Sagard 1939:248-249).

c) Summary and Discussion: 1616-1629

In spite of the meagre amount of information, some generalizations can be made about this period. With Champlain's visit to Huronia trade began to develop with groups in the interior, especially with the Huron and Nipissing. Both of these groups were in unique geographical positions to become middlemen to their neighbours. The Neutral and Petun would have had to cross Huron territory to get to the Nipissing-Ottawa route and then pass through Nipissing and Allumette territory, two bands with whom they had no relations. The Huron discouraged this from the beginning and neither the Petun or Neutral seem to have tried to break intertribal law by forcing their way.

The Nipissing in turn were in an excellent position to block all groups in the upper Great Lakes area from coming to the headwaters of the Ottawa. As far as we know, they never had to exercise their right to prevent passage. Huron canoes could easily pass through Nipissing territory because of the long-standing relations between the two. Both Huron and Nipissing, however, ran into constant trouble with the Allumette who exacted heavy tolls along the Ottawa, and the Montagnais who extracted dues once the Huron and Nipissing tried to go very far down the St. Lawrence. The Huron, therefore, acted as middlemen primarily to the Petun, Neutral and some of the Georgian Bay Ottawa, while the Nipissing traded to the north to the Cree and other Algonquian groups. Both Nipissing and Huron seemed to have traded together in the area of the upper Ottawa and Dumoine Rivers.

Throughout this period Champlain and the other traders felt it necessary to place Frenchmen among the Indian groups "to induce them to come and trade". It is hard to tell if Champlain's fears were justified. He obviously felt that if the French were not among the Huron and various Algonquian bands, these would stop coming to the St. Lawrence.

One factor that probably helped trade to get started, and one that is usually overlooked, is the Iroquois peace. From 1622 to 1627 there are no records of Iroquois hostilities along the trade routes. Prior to that time, these incursions were a constant source of complaint and a strong factor in the reluctance of the Huron to come to the St. Lawrence area except to wage war.

Throughout this period the major route was the Georgian Bay-French River-Lake Nipissing-Ottawa River route. Huron and Nipissing traders went up the tributaries of this trunk route to trade with various Algonquian bands. It is doubtful if large numbers of Huron ever attempted voyages of the kind described by Hunt. There is little evidence to suggest that Huron ever paddled from the head-waters of the Ottawa to the Saguenay River. At the time when Champlain and Sagard were writing, "the Saguenay" did not have the specific meaning that it has now; it was rather a vaguely-defined area, encompassing most of interior Quebec north of the St. Lawrence and east of the Ottawa. All Sagard and Champlain really said was that Huron and Nipissing were trading up the tributaries of the Ottawa into the interior.

Throughout the period, travel by canoe was in small groups, probably organized on a lineage and village basis. The size of canoes varied with the difficulty of the journey. The standard canoe running the trunk route was about twenty feet long and held up to five men with their baggage. Smaller canoes with two or three men were used to get up the difficult tributaries of the Ottawa.

The quantity of furs taken during this period is unknown. In 1623 Sagard observed that: "Such a quantity of them (beaver) is brought every year that I cannot think but that the end is in sight" (Sagard 1939:232). The number of beaver in storage at Quebec, when the English took the post in 1629, was between 3,000 and 4,000 pelts, and probably represented that year's trading (Champlain 6:141; Biggar 1901:162-163). If, as stated earlier, the average canoe held about 200 lbs. of beaver, twenty canoes could have brought this quantity to Quebec. As observed earlier, 1629 was a very bad year for trade. In 1626, Charles Lallemant wrote that the annual take of beaver in the St. Lawrence area was 12,000 to 15,000 skins. In one unusual year the merchants got as many as 22,000 skins (JR 4:207). It must be remembered that all the Indians trading with the French contributed to this total.

The number of Huron canoes that usually came to trade is known only for 1624, when about forty-five canoes attempted the trip (Champlain 5:131-133). In 1623 there had been sixty Huron and Algonquian canoes with some three hundred men (Champlain 5:100-101). In view of Bressani's and Sagard's statements that a Huron canoe could hold about two hundred pounds of skins, the Huron and Algonquians together probably accounted for about two-thirds of the annual take of the French merchants.

To the bulk of the Huron trading could not have been an important activity during the period 1615 to 1629. In all, probably never more than 200 men participated in the annual trading voyages. This number is very small out of a population estimated at 21,000. The importance of trade must be seen in terms of the goods that were brought to Huronia and the social and utilitarian value of these goods, rather than as an activity that employed the efforts of a major segment of the population.

6. TRADE AND POLITICS TO THE END OF 1641.

a) Yearly Trading Activities and Intertribal Relations: 1632-1641

In 1632, New France was ceded back to the French. The amount of trading that took place between the British and the French Indian allies is difficult to estimate. Brulé had been sent back to Huronia in 1629 and may have brought the Huron to trade with his new English allies in 1630 (Champlain 6:102).[1] At any rate, the year 1630 was successful for the British merchants. Champlain estimated that their total take from the former French possessions was 300,000 livres worth, or about 30,000 lbs. of skins (Champlain 6:183). In 1631 the trader de Caen went back to the St. Lawrence hoping to contact the Huron; however, trade was so bad that year, the British would not let him compete with them (Champlain 6:214, 216; Biggar 1901:157-158). Apparently the Huron were dissatisfied with the British in 1630 and simply did not come the following year (Le Clercq, 1881:311). Nicolet, the French interpreter and explorer who had been left behind during the British occupation may also have had a hand in persuading French Indian allies not to come to trade.

With the return of the French to the St. Lawrence Valley, Huron trade began to pick up again and continued roughly in the same manner as it had during the 1620's. Various factors complicate the picture during the 1630's, but during the early 1640's several events happened, notably increased Iroquois hostility, that make it practical to treat the 1640's in a separate section. As with the previous sections in this chapter, each year will be examined separately and then combined into a set of generalizations for the period.

Apart from the fact that about 50 Huron canoes arrived at Quebec in 1632, little is known about the Huron during this year (JR 5:71).

The description of events and attitudes in 1633 is unusually complete. Virtually every facet of Huron-French relations is brought to light, as well as Huron relations with other groups. The beginning of the trading season was marred by an Iroquois attack on a French bark and shallop in the

1. Brulé was probably killed by the Huron in 1631 or 1632. In 1633 the Jesuits got the first news of Brulé's death, and some Allumette warned the Huron not to go to Quebec, claiming that the French were seeking vengeance (JR 5:239).

upper St. Lawrence area, in which two Frenchmen were killed and scalped (JR 5:213-215). Apparently the Iroquois departed, because on the 22nd and 23rd of June twelve canoes led by Iroquet and twelve to fourteen canoes of Nipissing arrived for trading (JR 5:219). Towards the end of July the Huron arrived:

> Already a few canoes had arrived on different days, sometimes seven or eight, sometimes ten or twelve at a time; but at last, on the 28th of July; there arrived about one hundred and forty all at once, carrying easily five hundred Hurons – or 700 as some say – with their merchandise (JR 5:239).

Bressani, recounting these events at a later time, put the number of Huron canoes at 150, with 700 to 800 men (JR 39:51). Apparently more Huron would have come, if some had not been frightened away by the Allumette who claimed that the French wanted to avenge Brulé's death (JR 5:-239-241). Amid the trading, the usual councils were held between the Huron and the French in which presents were exchanged, friendships renewed and an agreement made to send some Jesuits to Huronia (JR 5:245-267). Champlain even proposed Huron-French intermarriage ". . . that we be one people" (JR 5:211). The Huron seemed delighted with events, and began arguing among themselves as to which village should have the honour of giving passage to a Jesuit (JR 5:259-263). Shortly before the Jesuits were to embark, a very interesting event occurred that throws considerable light on the role of the Allumette and Petite Nation as controllers of the Ottawa River route. A member of the Petite Nation had murdered a Frenchman and was being imprisoned by Champlain. When Champlain refused the usual payments for murder, the Allumette told the Huron not to give any Frenchmen passage across Petite Nation and Allumette territory. The Huron took these threats at their face value and told Champlain that they could not take the Jesuits. The reasons given by the Huron was that the Ottawa River was not under their control and that they had to abide by the wishes of the Allumette and Petite Nation if they were going to pass in security. The Huron did not want to be put into the position of endangering their access to the St. Lawrence (JR 6:7-17). The manner in which the Jesuits saw the matter is worth quoting in detail. They advanced two reasons why the Huron could or would not take them along:

> The first is found in the interests of the Island Savages (Allumette), the Algonquains, and the other tribes which are between Kebec and the Hurons. These people, in order to monopolize the profit of the

trade, prefer that the Hurons should not go down the river to trade their peltries with the French, desiring themselves to collect the merchandise of the neighbouring tribes and carry it to the French; that is why they do not like to see us go to the Hurons, thinking that we would urge them to descend the river, and that, the French being with them, it would not be easy to bar their passage. The second reason may be found in the fear of the Hurons, who see that the French will not accept presents as a compensation for the murder of one of their countrymen; they fear that their young men may do some reckless deed, for they would have to give up, alive or dead, any one who might have committed murder, or else break with the French (JR 6:19).

These very astute observations mirror experiences on the Ottawa in the 1620's. As Sagard had observed, the Huron got past the Allumette much easier when there were Frenchmen with them; and from the beginning the Allumette had opposed French-Huron trade contacts. With increased Huron and Nipissing activity among the upper Ottawa River Algonquians, the Allumette probably saw their position as middlemen eroding. If the French started travelling the Ottawa, even the lucrative tolls might disappear.

Only a few Huron canoes came to trade in 1634 (JR 7:213: 39:51). Brébeuf put the total at about eleven (JR 8:69). The reasons for this small number were as follows. During the autumn of 1633, smallpox made its first appearance among the Huron (JR 8:43, 71-73), and in the next spring they suffered heavy losses at the hands of the Iroquois (JR 8:69). In the early summer news of a new invading Iroquois army prompted most Huron to stay at home to defend their villages (JR 7:213). Furthermore, the villages that had participated in Brulé's murder were still afraid to go to the St. Lawrence; as a matter of fact, the other Huron villages prevented them from doing so, probably fearing that they could be drawn into a Huron-French blood feud if the French tried to arrest the murderers (JR 8:99). Fortunately, some Nipissing canoes had come to trade with whom some of the priests could travel to Huronia (JR 8:71). Again the Allumette objected to the passage of Frenchmen through their territory (JR 7:215; 8:71, 83); in fact, they told the priests that the same would be done to them as had been done to Brulé. In the end the priests were given passage by some Huron and Nipissing, but it was made clear by their hosts that they would have preferred Frenchmen with guns instead of priests (JR 7:217).

Sometime during the summer of 1634 the Huron made peace with the Seneca (JR 6:57; 7:125; 8:59, 115), and possibly also with the other Iroquois tribes (JR 8:117).

During the winter of 1634 to 1635 some Allumette came to Huronia spreading a story that Champlain did not want the Jesuits to live in Huronia anymore because of Brulé's death, and that he demanded four Huron heads as revenge (JR 8:103). The Jesuits managed to persuade the Huron that none of this was true, but claimed that the stories would have been successful in disrupting trade if they had not been there to refute them. Another attempt to sow discord between the French and Huron came in the spring of 1635 when some Montagnais arrived at Quebec with the story that the Huron had killed the Jesuits for spreading disease among them (JR 8:43).

To everyone's relief the first canoes arrived from Huronia on July 10th; exactly how many arrived, is not known (JR 8:45). On the 22nd of July Champlain held a council with the Huron, explaining to them that French goodwill depended on good treatment of the priests and adoption of Christianity. Adoption of Christianity would assure victory over the Iroquois, and the coming of many Frenchmen to Huronia would mean intermarriage. The Huron would be taught to make all the articles they were now trading from the French (JR 8; 49-51).

During that summer, rumours began to circulate that the Iroquois had attacked some canoes of the Petite Nation and had attempted to bribe the Montagnais into attacking the Huron (JR 8:59). The Jesuits saw these stories as an attempt by the New England traders to alienate the Huron from their Algonquian, Montagnais and French allies, and through the Iroquois-Huron peace, to divert the Huron fur trade to the south (JR 8:61). Other rumors spoke of an impending Iroquois attack on Huronia.

In the same year the Jesuits observed that the Huron country, and presumably adjacent areas, were out of beaver; the Huron had to go ". . . elsewhere to buy the skins . . ." (JR 8:57).

Towards the end of March, 1636, a group of Allumette arrived with presents among the Huron and the Algonquians and Nipissing who were wintering in Huronia, with the request to join them in a war against the Iroquois (JR 10:73-77). Apparently some Iroquois had raided the Allumette, killing a number of them. The Huron and their allies turned the request down, ". . . on account of the extortion practiced on them by the Island Savages (Allumette) in going down for trade" (JR 10:77). Other reasons that were given for turning down the Allumette were that men were needed for protection at home. The *Attignaouantan* refused outright to participate in the raid because the Allumette had slighted them by not

254

giving them presents. The Allumette, disappointed in their requests, warned both Huron and French that they would refuse to let them pass through their territory in the summer (JR 10:77). Next, the Allumette turned to the priests, trying to win them over with flattery, and pointing out that the Huron had killed Brulé and Nicolas Viel; and that the best thing would be if they returned to Quebec (JR 10:79).

After the Allumette left, a small group of *Amikoua* arrived from the mainland north of Manitoulin Island with the request that the French help them in a war against the Puan (JR 10:83). This is the only reference since the 1620's to Indian relations northwest of Huronia.

Huron raids against one of the Iroquois tribes in the spring of 1636 (JR 10:83); and subsequent fears of an Iroquois invasion delayed the trip to Quebec that year (JR 9:245; 13:7). Finally, on July 22nd, the first major contingent of eight to ten canoes left followed by others over the next week (JR 13:7-9). A few canoes seem to have left during late May, because the first Huron canoe arrived at Trois Rivières on July 15th (JR 9:245). Apparently it had been sent ahead to negotiate a passage with the Allumette (JR 9:247). On August the 15th another canoe arrived with the news that the Allumette were holding up the main Huron contingent (JR 9:271). Initially the Huron were unable to pass and thirteen canoes returned to Huronia (JR 9:271). The main body of Huron waited until the priests got to Allumette island, who eventually got them through after much haggling and gift-giving (JR 9:271-277). The upshot of the incident was that, no matter by how many the Huron outnumbered the Allumette, they observed the laws governing passage. Furthermore, the Huron saw that it was essential that some Frenchmen accompany them. The Jesuits interpreted this incident as further evidence that the Allumette ". . . would prefer that the Huron should not come to the French nor the French go to the Huron, so that they themselves may carry away all the trade" (JR 9:275).

On August the 19th the Huron finally arrived at Trois Rivières (JR 9:279). The contingent was made up of only a ". . . few canoes but they carried a great amount of merchandise" (JR 9:273-275). After trading was completed, the Huron were persuaded to leave twenty boys with the French to start a seminary. In return, the French promised to send more Frenchmen to Huronia (JR 9:283-293).

During this year the Iroquois peace seems to have been only between Huron and Seneca (JR 13:45). Both the Montagnais and Algonquians organized raids against the eastern Iroquois (JR 9:251-253). The Huron also engaged in some fighting (JR 9:225) but there were no reports of Iroquois warfare along the trade routes.

255

During the winter of 1637 to 1638 smallpox raged through the Huron villages. Since no one was able to find a specific cause for the disease, an amazing variety of theories circulated. Some Allumette, trying to sow discord between the French and Huron, claimed that the Huron were bewitched by Champlain's cloak and that the explorer who had died in 1635 wanted them to join him in the afterlife (JR 13:247). Other Algonquians said it was a deliberate act of the French (JR 12:85-87). Some Huron saw the diseases as French venegance for the death of Brulé (JR 12:87); others said Brulé's uncle was avenging him (JR 14:17); and still others said it was a curse from Brulé's sister (JR 14:53). At times, French trade goods were blamed as the carriers of the disease, and some Huron stopped using French kettles (JR 12:237; 15:21). Most often the Jesuits were accused of causing the diseases, and several councils were held to decide what to do with them (JR 13:215; 14:15-23; 15:37-51). At a council meeting in January 1637, one of the influential chiefs told the others that getting rid of the Jesuits would mean the ruin of the country, because French-Huron ties would be severed and trade would come to an end (JR 13:215-217). At a meeting in August a decision was made to defer all actions against the Jesuits until the Huron traders returned from Quebec (JR 15:47). Since the traders were well-satisfied with French conduct at the trading posts and could not see the French being deliberately responsible for the diseases, the matter was shelved (JR 15:55).

As usual, during the winter a number of Nipissing lived near the Huron villages (JR 13:191; 14:7). These departed, sadly decimated by smallpox, on April 19th when the waters of Georgian Bay became navigable (JR 14:37). During the winter the Ottawa also came to Huronia. Their purpose was to return 2,400 beads they had once stolen from Brulé thinking that this was what caused the diseases (JR 14:99-103). Apparently, the Jesuits had little prior knowledge of the Ottawa because they spoke of them as a "strange nation" with whom the French had no formal relations (JR 14:103). During this time some Jesuits visited the Petun (JR 14:87). In contrast to later years, no Huron opposition was recorded.

During the spring rumours circulated that the Iroquois were going to attack as soon as the Huron left for trading (JR 14:39). Due to these rumours embarkation was deferred until mid-June (JR 14:55, 109). Apparently the attack on Huronia did not materialize; instead, the Iroquois waited near the junction of the Ottawa and St. Lawrence River. On June 28th a group of Algonquians led by Iroquet managed to rout an Iroquois contingent on Lac St. Louis (JR 12:181); and in late July the first Huron canoes arrived at Trois Rivières (JR 12:193). In the meantime, however, the Iroquois had returned; and on August 6th they ambushed a group of

Huron just above Trois Rivières (JR 12:199). The Iroquois followed up their victory by coming right up to the French trading post (JR 12:-201-203). In total the Jesuits estimated that the Iroquois army was made up of some 500 men. Further Huron losses took place at various times during August (JR 12:97-99, 207-211). On August 27th four Huron canoes managed to make it through the Iroquois blockade (JR 12:227), followed by one more on August 29th (JR 12:235). The main Huron contingent of 150 men finally arrived on September 5th (JR 12:235-237). Most of the canoes were filled with sick people, and it is a wonder that trading was attempted at all (JR 12:231).

During the usual council meetings, presents were again exchanged and the Huron were assured that the French had not spread the diseases deliberately (JR 12:249-251). The Huron were again urged to return next year, bringing with them some families to settle at Trois Rivières and Quebec (JR 12:255-257). The Huron village at Quebec was seen in four main ways: to have a group of hostages nearby, and thus help to insure the safety of the Jesuits in Huronia; to insure that the Huron would come trading in succeeding years; to create a group of Christian Huron, who would hopefully help to convert others; and, lastly, it was hoped that the men in the Huron village would help defend the French against the Iroquois (JR 12:79-81).

On October 3rd the Huron fleet arrived back at Huronia, apparently well-satisfied with the trading they had done, and with the conduct of the French (JR 15:53-55). As usual, the Nipissing spent the winter of 1637 to 1638 in Huronia (JR 14:7).

In contrast to the previous years, 1638 and 1639 are poorly documented. During 1638 the Nipissing as well as the Huron were badly hit by the diseases (JR 15:135-137). In spite of the diseases, a Huron trading party managed to make it to Trois Rivières sometime in August (JR 14:267). At about the same time a Huron-Algonquian war party of some 300 men successfully battled the Oneida (JR 17:63-71) showing that by no means all Huron men were actively engaged in trade. On two occasions that year, the Allumette made their presence felt. When Jérôme Lalemant went to Huronia in August of that year he was seized by the Allumette and had to be ransomed from them by some Huron (JR 14:269-271). The other occasion came in early September when the returning Huron traders were again told not to take any more Frenchmen to Huronia (JR 15:151). During the fall of 1638 the Jesuits were repeatedly blamed for causing all the "current troubles" but nothing positive was done about it (JR 17:115-119). No major Iroquois incursions were noted that year. The Seneca, at least, seem to have been busy on their Neutral frontier. In

August 1638 some 600 *Wenrôh* evacuated the Niagara area and settled among the Huron (JR 17:25).

There is almost no specific data given for trading activities in 1639. Some Huron canoes must have begun arriving at Trois Rivières during July, because Father Chaumonot who travelled back with them to Huronia arrived there on September 10th (JR 18:11, 15). To the French, at least, trading was very successful that year. Not only did the Huron come down, but also 100 canoes of Allumette and those from the Petite Nation (JR 16:43, 125). Besides these two Algonquian bands Nipissing and *Attikamegue* also appeared for trading (JR 16:47, 71).

On the whole, Iroquois activity seems to have been light during 1639. Jérôme Lalemant did, however, mention that even though this activity only consisted of "a few broken heads," the Huron got consistently the worst of it (JR 19:81).

During the winter of 1639-1640 the Jesuits attempted to open a mission among the Petun. On their arrival they found almost universal hostility (JR 20:47). The Petun were, of course, afraid that the Jesuits had come to spread more disease amongst them. This fear was fanned by ". . . some Hurons, who went thither from time to time to effect some trades . . ." (JR 20:51). These Huron urged the Petun to drive the Jesuits out of their country.

The fact that the Huron spread sinister stories about the Jesuits to the Petun is usually interpreted as Huron protection of their commercial interests among the Petun (Hunt 1940:56). While this may be true, also important was the genuine fear the Petun had of smallpox. The stories that the Huron circulated among the Petun were no different from the stories that the Huron were circulating among themselves. The Jesuits arrived among the Petun after the disease had been rampant for a number of years. It probably did not take much to fan the natural fear that the Petun had of the Jesuits.

By the summer of 1640 the diseases had diminished, and the Petun began seeing the Jesuits in a more favourable light (JR 20:97). It was then that the Huron spread stories that could be construed as a protection of commercial interests. The Jesuits observed that the Petun did not travel to the French to trade; that the Huron did not permit them to trade with the French; and that the Huron spread stories among the Petun designed to breed distrust of the French (JR 21:177).

The principal Petun trading crop was still tobacco (JR 20:43). In return, the Huron probably exchanged French trade goods. There is not the slightest hint or suggestion that the Petun traded corn or, for that matter, anything else except tobacco. The supposition by Hunt (1940:56) that the

258

Huron used the Petun area as granary seems to be without foundation.

During the winter of 1639 to 1640 some Algonquians again wintered in Huronia (JR 20:39). The Jesuits continue to describe this as a regular yearly affair (JR 20:41).

During the summer of 1640 the Huron canoes left as usual for Quebec in small groups and at various times. The last group apparently left in early August (JR 20:77-85). In contrast to previous years, the Jesuits and Huron noted a sharp increase of raids on the Ottawa-St. Lawrence route during 1639 and especially 1640 (JR 17:223; 18:33). In the spring of 1640 the Iroquois even struck within sight of Trois Rivières (JR 18:187), as well as further upstream (JR 20:169). In the late summer these attacks were repeated near Trois Rivières, as well as Montreal Island, where the Iroquois captured several Frenchmen (JR 21:23). As a result of these raids fewer canoes seem to have passed through to the French posts, and the Jesuits began to express genuine concern that if this were kept up, their line to Quebec could be severed (JR 20:77). Another result of these raids was that some of the Algonquian groups were moving up the Ottawa and into the interior away from the St. Lawrence (JR 18:245). During this year the Allumette still bragged that they controlled the movements of the Huron, but their power seems to have been on the decline (JR 20:-155-159).

Although small Iroquois raids continued into Huronia during 1640, there is no mention of Huron retaliations (JR 20:79). Instead the Allumette, Petite Nation and other Algonquians organized a war party against the eastern Iroquois (JR 20:167). On the whole, the Iroquois seem to have come out somewhat better over the season's exchange of hostilities.

By 1640 a sizeable group of Indians had settled at Trois Rivières and Quebec. These were principally composed ot Algonquians, some Montagnais and Huron. It is these Indians who now started trading northwards into the interior. During the summer of 1640 some travelled down the St. Lawrence to trade up the Saguenay (JR 18:111), while others, principally Algonquians, headed up the St. Maurice river system as far as Lake St. John to trade with the *Papinachois* and from there to Lake Mistassini to tap the fur resources of the *Outagomois* (JR 18:115-117) (Map 24). The description of these trips shows that the Algonquians had pushed the fur trade to the northern margins of the boreal forest. This new pattern in the fur trade became stronger over the 1640's, and was one that the Huron who were settled at Trois Rivières and Quebec soon participated in.

In November 1640 Fathers Brébeuf and Chaumonot set out for the Neutral to attempt a new mission (JR 17:37-41; 21:187-237). The reaction of the Neutral to the Jesuits was similar to their reaction against Joseph Daillon fourteen years earlier and the reaction the Jesuits got from the Petun in 1639. Prior to the Jesuits' arrival among the Neutral the Huron had laid a groundwork of rumours, suspicion and ill-feeling. Huron opposition to this trip was so strong that it was only by pure chance that the Jesuits found someone who was willing to guide them (JR 21:-205). Realizing that there might be opposition from the Neutral to a group of priests, the Jesuits set out well-supplied with trade goods and two French domestics in order to pass into Neutral territory on the pretext of being traders (JR 21:205). Although they were greeted with suspicion the pretext of trade opened up several villages for them (JR 21:207). After they were among the Neutral for some time, the domestics were sent home and all pretext of trade was removed (JR 21:209). Immediately the situation changed. Neutral interest in the Jesuits flagged. The Huron, whose suspicion had been aroused as soon as the Jesuits made a pretext of trading, immediately redoubled their efforts to have the Jesuits ejected from the Neutral villages or killed (JR 21:209-223). In the end, the Jesuits were forced to leave, convinced that the Huron ". . . feared the removal of their trade . . ." (JR 21:205). Apparently Montmagny's[1] warnings to the Huron, not to engage in such calumnies against the Jesuits, had had little effect on their behavior when they felt their trading interests were threatened (JR 21:143; 22:310).

As usual, some Algonquians came to winter in Huronia. About 250 Nipissing camped a short distance from Ste. Marie (JR 21:143, 243) and fifteen cabins of *Atontrataronon* near St. Jean Baptiste (JR 21:247).

In February, 1641, the Iroquois held a council among themselves to decide whether they should approach the French with a proposal for peace (JR 21:29). According to Dutch sources the year 1640 marked the exhaustion of the Iroquois beaver supply (Hunt 1940:34, 74). It also marked the enforcement of Dutch legislation against the sale of firearms to the Iroquois (Hunt 1940:74, 165-169). Faced with these problems, an Iroquois delegation of some 350 well-armed men arrived at Trois Rivières in the early summer of 1641 (JR 21:37-39). At least another 150 Iroquois stationed themselves at various places along the St. Lawrence ready to intercept Algonquian and Huron canoes (JR 21:33, 41, 49). In their meeting with the French, the Iroquois stated that they were unhappy with the Dutch and distrusted the English (JR 21:33, 55). What they wanted to do was form an alliance with the French, but not the French Indian allies (JR 21:37-39). The main trade item the Iroquois wanted was guns (JR 21:53,

1. Montmagny was Champlain's successor.

260

61). This was, of course, not the kind of peace proposal the French could accept. Any peace would have had to include the Huron, Algonquians and Montagnais, as these would cease to trade with the French if they were excluded (JR 21:57). By mid-summer, the peace negotiations collapsed and the Iroquois fanned out to raid the Huron and Algonquian fur brigades. Immediately some Huron canoes were taken, while others turned back to warn the rest who were coming down the Ottawa (JR 21:65-67). During these skirmishes the French noted that at least 36 out of the 350 Iroquois had guns which they knew how to use very effectively (JR 21: 63-65, 119). By the late summer the Iroquois finally departed, allowing the Huron to get through (JR 21:75).

During the summer several Huron villages launched raids into the Iroquois country (JR 23:173). Their success is uncertain.

During the late summer, besides the Huron, a number of Algonquian bands also arrived for trade (JR 21:117). These included the *Kotakoutouemi, Iroquet, Allumette* and *Petite Nation* (JR 20:259). The *Attikamegue* came, as usual, to Trois Rivières to trade; but they departed almost immediately, due to their fear of the Iroquois (JR 20:271-273; 21:117). During the same summer some Huron from the French St. Lawrence settlements followed the example of the Algonquians, set the previous year, by trading into the interior to the *Ondoutawaka* on the upper Saguenay (JR 22:75).

Nipissing trade with the French had dropped off during the beginning of the 1640's. According to the Jesuits the reason for this was because they were no longer permitted passage along the lower Ottawa (JR 21:241). During this period, however, the Nipissing still held the routes to the northern and western bands (JR 21:185, 239). In the spring some Nipissing would depart up the northern rivers supplied with corn and trade goods which they would exchange for furs to the Cree (JR 21:123-125). They would trade there for ten days and then return to Lake Nipissing, where some gathered to go down to the French to trade while others exchanged their furs to the Huron (JR 21:239). At least in 1640, the Nipissing found Montagnais traders among the Cree (JR 21:123-125). In the autumn the Nipissing slowly made their way to Huronia, fishing along the way. They would dry the fish later and sell it to the Huron for corn (JR 21;239). The success of the Nipissing trading expeditions was summed up by the Jesuits, who considered them ". . . rich people who live in comfort" (JR 21:239).

Trade and inter-tribal relations in the years from 1632 to the end of 1641 were, in a sense, a continuation of the main themes of the 1620's. However, a few elements had been added that were to become dominant in the 1640's. Chief among those was the ascendancy of Iroquois power.

During the 1630's the Huron were hard hit by smallpox. These diseases created strained relations with the Jesuits but did not seem to affect Huron relations with the French traders. As a matter of fact, in spite of the frightful death toll, trading went on throughout all the years that the epidemic lasted. No doubt the reason why the Huron were able to carry on trading in spite of these difficulties was that, of the total male population, only a fraction was engaged in trade. Besides, the diseases hit the young and old harder than the adult men.

Huron trade with the Neutral and Petun went on as in the 1620's. At no time did either of these tribes come to the St. Lawrence and, in contrast to the years before 1626, Frenchmen were discouraged from attempting to form any strong contact with them. Throughout the period, furs and tobacco seem to have been the main Neutral and Petun trade items. In return they received French goods. There does not seem to be any evidence that corn was traded by either the Petun or the Neutral to the Huron.

Huron relations with the Algonquian bands were more complex than with the Neutral and Petun. Until the late 1630's, the Nipissing still travelled the route to the St. Lawrence. After that some still continued, but most seem to have given up the yearly voyages in favour of trading their furs to the Huron. Opposition from the bands along the Ottawa and, no doubt, the increasing Iroquois raids did not make the trip worthwhile. In contrast to the Huron, the Nipissing did not have Frenchmen to help them through the blockades set up by the Allumette. Nipissing control over the northern and western fur routes remained complete. Some Huron probably travelled with Nipissing and Ottawa traders as far as the eastern shores of Lake Superior, but on the whole these seem to have been Algonquian routes.

During the winter the Nipissing consistently came to Huronia. At this time they would lay in a supply of corn, which they traded from the Huron for fish, and perhaps furs. The corn was later re-traded to the northern groups by the Nipissing. It was this activity that prompted Brébeuf to write that Huronia was ". . . the granary of most of the Algonquins" (JR 8:115). In view of the number of Algonquians involved, this statement seems like a gross exaggeration. As pointed out earlier, it is difficult to know whether the Huron strove to create a corn surplus specifically for trading. In view of the occasional Huron famine and the number of Algonquians involved in the corn trade, one would be inclined to think that the Huron traded any surplus corn above their seed and subsistence needs, but did not produce large surpluses specifically for trade.

Until the beginning of the 1640's, the Allumette were a major power along the Ottawa. Every year, Huron canoes were delayed at Allumette Island, where they had to pay toll charges in corn and furs. During the 1620's and early 1630's some Huron were moderately successful in evading Allumette tolls by having Frenchmen travel with them. Due to trading ties with the French, the Allumette hesitated to force Frenchmen into paying toll charges. By 1638, however, the Allumette were even stopping the Jesuits.

The stiffening of Allumette behavior can be seen in several ways. Firstly, through inter-tribal law the Allumette had the right to stop anyone from passing through their territory, or make them pay toll charges. Secondly, the Allumette wanted to retain their position as middlemen between the French and those bands to the north and west. Because of their relations with the French, the Allumette could not stop the Huron coming down the Ottawa, but they could make it costly and unpleasant for them. The Huron, in turn, did not force their way across Allumette territory. Had they done so, the whole intricate trading system might have collapsed. It would have given the Petun and Neutral the excuse to force their way across Huron territory; and would certainly have caused a major rupture with a number of Algonquian bands such as the Petite Nation, with whom the Allumette had close relations.

The rules regarding rights of passage were universally accepted in Eastern North America and had a bearing on restricting the extent of the Huron trade network during this period. In the west, the Huron traded furs from the Neutral, Petun, Ottawa, and Nipissing, but did not seem to travel to the fur sources of these groups. More furs were picked up along the tributaries of the Ottawa. Passing down the St. Lawrence, the Huron traders got as far as Trois Rivières and sometimes Quebec. They were not allowed to pass further down the river because the Montagnais did not permit it (JR 8:41; 12:187-189). The Huron traded a little corn, some tobacco, nets and squirrel skins to the Montagnais for moose skins (JR 6:273; 309; 7:13), they aided each other in war, and neither trespassed on the others' trade routes. The routes followed by the Huron throughout this period as well as the organization and execution of trade seems to have been similar to the previous period.

Towards the end of this period some trends began to appear that were to become dominant themes in the 1640's. Algonquians and a few Huron settled at Trois Rivières and Quebec were beginning to pass up the rivers leading north from the St. Lawrence to tap the furs in what is now central Quebec. Several references show that they were working some of the same areas as the Montagnais. It is not clear why the Montagnais permitted this. The best explanation seems to be that, since these traders were Christian Algonquians settled with the French, the country was more open to them.

The major factors that bring this period to a close and usher in the 1640's are the activities of the Iroquois. Iroquois raids on Huronia and the lower Ottawa/upper St. Lawrence area had been sporadic throughout the 1630's. In the traditional annual raids on each other's territory the Huron seem to hold their own. Along the trade routes Huron losses were annoying, but not really serious, until 1640 and 1641. The growing intensity of Iroquois raids after 1640 can be ascribed to the decline of beaver in the Iroquois territories and perhaps to a political reorganization of the five Iroquois tribes. As events show later, the annual raids on the Huron fur brigades did not really bring in enough furs for Iroquois purposes. The Iroquois peace proposals of 1641 were the first of a number of half-hearted attempts by the Iroquois to gain access to French trade and the northern fur resources by peaceful means. Each rejection of peace was followed by an intensification of warfare and a major change in tactics. It is this pattern that highlights the 1640's.

7. THE INTERRELATIONS OF TRADE, PEACE AND WAR TO 1649.

a) Yearly Trading Activities and Inter-tribal Relations: 1642-1649

The year 1642 was marked by a series of Huron disasters, which began to crystallize into a pattern, leading ultimately to the collapse of the trade network and the complete society. This pattern consisted of two main elements: firstly, much more intensive and extensive raids into Huronia, carried out primarily by the Seneca, Cayuga, Oneida and Onondaga; secondly, almost constant year-round harassment along the Ottawa and St. Lawrence trade route by the Mohawk and some Oneida. The intensification of Iroquois activity can be explained by a change in Iroquois motives, and in the means and opportunity for carrying out warfare; and their success, by the inadequate response of the weakened and divided Huron, who never seemed to grasp these changes.

During the winter of 1641 to 1642 the Iroquois lauched a series of raids on Huron frontier villages, with the result that one village among the *Arendaronnon* was entirely destroyed (JR 23:105-107; 26:175). Harrassment of Huron villages by roving Iroquois troops continued throughout the summer (JR 26:179, 205). The successful destruction of an entire village, and the fact that warfare went on the entire summer, was a marked departure from the traditional yearly raids.

Along the Ottawa and St. Lawrence, Iroquois activities reached a new height. Their blockade was so complete that for the first time virtually no Huron canoes got through (JR 22:273, 277; 23:35, 267, 269; 24:273-293; 26:201). In addition to destroying or capturing the small fleets of Huron canoes, the Mohawk managed to capture Father Jogues, who was attempting to reach Huronia (JR 22:269).

A by-product of the Iroquois raids along the Ottawa and St. Lawrence was the withdrawal of the Algonquian bands into the northern interior (JR 22:93, 127, 249; 25:105-115). In the spring of 1642, Iroquet's Algonquians were partially destroyed (JR 22:269), and in the autumn of the same year the Allumette (JR 24:257). By the winter of 1642 to 1643, the Allumette were referred to as a "scattered tribe," "reduced to nothing," exterminated by "disease and decimated by war and famine"(JR 24:267; 26:303). So effective was the destruction of the Ottawa River Algonquians, that they never caused the Huron fur brigades any more problems.

Huron counterattacks during this year seem to have been ineffective (JR 22:305). Iroquois successes were explained in terms of two chief factors. The first of these was the possession of guns and, in particular, their effective use (JR 22:269, 279, 307). This observation was repeated almost every year until the demise of Huronia. Although the number of guns the Iroquois had was not large, they knew how to fire them from ambush in unified volleys. The disorganization caused by the discharge of the guns seems to have been highly effective, particularly in attacking the fur brigades. A second factor in the success of the Iroquois raids on the fur brigades was their change in tactics:

> In former years, the Iroquois came in rather large bands at certain times in the Summer, and afterward left the River free: but this present year, they have changed their plan, and have separated themselves into small bands of twenty, thirty, or a hundred at the most, along all the passages and places of the River; and when one band goes away, another succeeds it (JR 24:273).

In previous years the small Huron fleets had often waited on the upper Ottawa until the main body of the Iroquois war party had left the St.

Lawrence area. This was the main reason why the Huron sometimes arrived late in the summer at Trois Rivières. Now, however, the Iroquois were along the trade route from early spring until late autumn.

The motives for Iroquois warfare were also becoming increasingly clearer to the Jesuits. The Iroquois were, in fact, after the furs being carried in the Huron, Algonquian and Montagnais canoes (JR 24:271). The reasoning was that the Iroquois needed the furs in order to trade powder and guns from the Dutch (JR 24:271-273). The depletion of furs in the Iroquois country by 1640 was noted earlier. Judging from the coordinated way the Iroquois were carrying out their aims, it is likely that their political system had undergone changes late in the 1630's.

The only highlight of the year was the arrival of 13 canoes with some 60 *Attikamegue,* who came down the St. Maurice to Trois Rivières to trade and spend the winter (JR 23:309; 24:67). Their territory lay some three to four days journey up the St. Maurice (Map 24). The fact that the *Attikamegue* made the trip down the St. Maurice and the Huron were not able to make it to Trois Rivières in 1642, points out that the Huron were not using a northern route. It simply does not make any sense that the Huron would run the risk of being captured by the Iroquois on the Ottawa and St. Lawrence if another route was available to them, as Hunt supposes (Hunt 1940:60-62). The closing of the Ottawa-St. Lawrence route in 1642 and the fact that the Huron did not get through to Trois Rivières or any other St. Lawrence trading post, shows that a northern Huron route did not exist. References to events in the later 1640's seem to confirm this conclusion.

In the winter of 1642 to 1643 several Algonquian groups wintered in Huronia. Among these were some refugee Allumette, Nipissing and *Atontrataronon* (JR 26:301-307; 27:37, 55). In the spring a group of some 100 Neutral came to Huronia for a short visit (JR 27:21-27). According to the Jesuits the reason for this visit was to receive religious instruction and to ask the Fathers to open a mission among their villages. Apparently, the Jesuits had some Huron converts operating among the Neutral. It was these converts who ostensibly arranged the visit. Whether the Neutral were also seeking aid in their wars against the *Assistaeronon* or trying to make trade connections, is not known. As far as one can tell from the ethnohistoric sources, this was the only time a sizeable group of Neutral visited the Huron.

During the summer of 1643 the Huron suffered a number of severe defeats. Attempting to carry the war into Iroquois country, a major Huron war party was defeated with no survivors (JR 28:45). Similar disasters occurred on the route to Trois Rivières (JR 28:45). The net effect was that only a few Huron got through to carry on trade (JR 24:105). As far as the Jesuits were concerned, the Iroquois had ". . . closed all the passages and avenues of the River that leads to Kebec" (JR 27:63).

Although the Huron carrying the furs from Huronia and the western Great Lakes area had little success in penetrating to the St. Lawrence, the Huron settled at Sillery near Quebec, Tadoussac and Trois Rivières appear to have continued in their effort to tap the fur resources of the Montagnais. Two references show that some Huron were operating in the upper Saguenay-Lake St. John area (JR 24:155; 27:27). Apparently the Huron had a regular meeting place which they called *Maouatchibitonam* somewhere on the north shore of the Saguenay near Lake St. John, in the traditional territory of the *Cacouchaqui* (JR 24:155). Of the thirteen small Montagnais bands which came to this meeting-place, six are identifiable on the contemporary maps. These six all lived within the area drained by Lake St. John or in a rough arc of some 200 miles from the west of Lake St. John, through Lake Mistassini and Lake Manuan to the shore of the St. Lawrence (Map 24). There is no evidence that Huron were travelling from Huronia to these groups. Several references make it clear that the Christian Huron at Trois Rivières, Sillery (Quebec or St. Joseph) and Tadoussac were operating this trade (JR 24:103-155), together with Algonquians and Montagnais resident at the same French settlements. In 1647 we learn that the Huron from Huronia had a similar meeting place to the north of the upper Ottawa where they contacted a portion of the *Attikamegue* and other northern bands (JR 31:219). In both cases the Huron had a well-established meeting place to which the Algonquian and Montagnais groups travelled. The Huron themselves did not seem to have travelled beyond these meeting places into the areas occupied by these groups. As a matter of fact, it would have been highly impractical. The Montagnais and Algonquian groups with whom the Huron were trading consisted of small, highly nomadic bands. To contact them individually would have been too time-consuming. The successful operation of trade, therefore, depended on the establishment of a regular meeting place which was accessible to all the groups. The lack of a northern route from the meeting place in the upper Ottawa area to Trois Rivières and the Saguenay is further demonstrated by the Jesuits' discussion of their mail delivery to and from Huronia in the years when the lower Ottawa-upper St. Lawrence area was blocked by the Iroquois. Mail was brought by the Huron from Huronia to the meeting place north of the Ottawa, where it was taken by the *Attikamegue* to Trois Rivières. Mail from Trois Rivières was given to the *Attikamegue* and delivered to the Huron at the same meeting place (JR 31:219). There is no mention of the Huron travelling over this route.

The year 1644 was no better than the previous years from a Huron and French point of view. Apparently the Huron had tried to arrange some sort of peace in 1643, but these efforts did not materialize (JR 26:31). By April, the Iroquois had blockaded the St. Lawrence, leading to the capture of Father Bressani who was attempting to get to Huronia (JR 25:193). As in previous years, Iroquois war parties were scattered along the entire trade route above Trois Rivières (JR 26:35-37). Later in the summer several Huron fur brigades were captured, and raids were launched in the vicinity of the French posts from Montreal to the mouth of the Richelieu (JR 27:221-225; 28:45).

Only two major Huron groups seem to have passed the Iroquois blockade. The first of these groups brought Fathers Brébeuf, Gareau and Chabanal to Huronia, escorted by about twenty French soldiers (JR 26:71; 28:45-47). The next year the soldiers were to escort the Huron through the Iroquois blockade (JR 27:89; 28:47). The second group that managed to get through the Iroquois blockade was a Huron war party of some sixty men (JR 26:53). These linked up with a party of Algonquians and attacked a small force of Iroquois near the mouth of the Richelieu. In the skirmish three Iroquois were taken prisoners and taken to Trois Rivières for torture. The ensuing events were of paramount importance to trading activities in 1645 and 1646 (JR 26:59-71).

When Montmagny heard that the Huron had two prisoners and the Algonquians one, he decided to ransom the three men in the hope of getting them to arrange a peace treaty. The Algonquians readily accepted payment in return for their captive, but the Huron did not. As a matter of fact, the Huron made it clear that they were not traders, but warriors whose prestige and glory depended on bringing captives to Huronia, not trade goods (JR 26:63-67). The Huron went on to say that if these captives were to be used in order to treat for peace it was a matter for their chiefs to decide. Finally, it was decided that the Huron should make an attempt to arrange a peace treaty (JR 26:69-71). As will be shown later, these moves resulted in a peace with the Mohawk until the fall of 1646.

As in previous years, the *Attikamegue* came to Trois Riviéres to trade (JR 26:81). With them came a small group called the *Ouramanichek* whose location is not known, but who apparently had trade connections north of the *Attikamegue* (JR 26:91-93).

From a Huron trader's point of view, the years from 1641 to 1644 had brought nothing but a series of unmitigated disasters along the trunk route to the French. The amount of Huron fur that got through during these years must have been small. At any rate, Montmagny considered the .situation serious enough to send French soldiers to Huronia to escort the

268

fur brigades, and to ransom Iroquois prisoners in the hope of making a peace. His fears were, of course, entirely justified, because in May 1645 Jérôme Lalemant wrote from Huronia that the Huron were thinking " . . . of giving up the trade with the French, because they find that it costs them too dear, and they prefer to do without European goods rather than to expose themselves every year . . ." (JR 28:57). A strong effort had to be made by the Huron and French to assure safe passage on the Ottawa and St. Lawrence.

The year 1645 was dominated by two events; a partial peace with the Mohawk and the successful passage of a Huron fur brigade.

In the spring of 1645 some Algonquians successfully ambushed a small party of Mohawk on the Richelieu River and took two prisoners (JR 27:229-231). The prisoners were taken to Quebec, where Montmagny negotiated for their release into French custody. In a council with the Iroquois prisoners and the Algonquians, it was then decided to release the Mohawk captured the previous year, with instructions to contact his chiefs with a proposal of peace. The prisoner was released in mid-May, and on the 5th of July returned with two important Mohawk spokesmen for a preliminary council. With them came Guillaume Cousture, who had been captured with Father Jogues in 1642 (JR 27:245-247). The ensuing council was attended by Algonquians, Montagnais, *Attikamegue,* French, and Huron (JR 27:251-253). The main conclusions of the conference were that the Mohawk promised safe passage on the Ottawa-St. Lawrence trade route as well as safe conduct to anyone who wanted to visit them (JR 27:259). In return, they wanted an assurance that the Algonquians and Huron would quit their raids into Mohawk territory (JR 27:263-265). Over some objections by the Huron, Montmagny accepted the peace and told his Indian allies to do the same (JR 27:267-269). As a token of friendship Montmagny sent two French boys with the Mohawk when they returned to their villages on July 15th. A decision was made to reconvene the council in the fall, giving all tribes concerned adequate time to canvass their villages.

An interesting point that emerged during these negotiations was that the Mohawk kept urging the Huron in particular to accept the peace, " . . . and after taking the resolution to go to the Iroquois country, to pass by that of the Algonquians and that of the French" (JR 27:263). It appears, therefore, that the fur trade was of interest not only to the French and their allies, but also to the Mohawk. The fall negotiations make it clearer that the real reason that the two sides were willing to negotiate a peace was because they both hoped to divert the fur trade into their hands.

269

Between the preliminary peace talks in July and the grand council in the fall, there were no major incidents on the St. Lawrence. Not so in Huronia. Iroquois raids began in the early spring and lasted into the late summer (JR 29:249-255). The principal Iroquois tribes involved in these raids were the Seneca, Oneida and Onondaga. As a result of these raids the Huron fur brigades did not leave Huronia until August.

On September 10th sixty Huron canoes arrived at Trois Rivières accompanied by the twenty soldiers sent to protect them, Jérôme Lalemant, one of the two Mohawk prisoners from the previous year and a lot of furs (JR 27:277). This was the first time in ". . . five or six years . . ." that any effective trading took place between the Huron and the French (JR 29:-247). Shortly before the arrival of the Huron, the *Attikamegue,* some Montagnais, Allumette, Iroquet and other Algonquian bands had arrived at Trois Rivières for trade and to participate in the peace council (JR 27:279). On the 15th of September the Mohawk ambassadors arrived. The result of the council was a general peace between the Mohawk and the French Indian allies. Specifically, they promised not to raid each other's villages; nor would the Mohawk attack the annual trading voyages (JR 27:281-305). As usual people were exchanged, two Algonquians, one Huron and a Frenchman leaving with the Mohawk (JR 27:303). During the peace talks the Mohawk made an interesting point, namely that now since they, the Algonquians and Huron, are "one people", they could hunt in Algonquian territory (JR 27:289-291).

The trading activities that year netted approximately 30,000 pounds of furs, visible evidence that peace along the trade routes was absolutely essential for trade (JR 27:85). Of this quantity, the soldiers who had gone to Huronia accounted for 4,000 pounds (JR 27:85, 89). If the ratio of 200 pounds per canoe holds true, the sixty Huron canoes accounted for half of the furs taken by the French in 1645.

During the winter of 1645 to 1646 small incidences occurred that were at first blamed on the Mohawk (JR 27:93, 99-101). On closer inspection the Mohawk were exonerated (JR 28:277). At the same time the Algonquians were becoming more convinced that the Mohawk would attack them in the spring (JR 28:149). These suspicions seem to have been founded on the fact that the Mohawk originally did not want peace with the Algonquians, but were forced into it by Montmagny (JR 28:149-153, 315). Besides hostilities that went back for generations between the two groups, the Mohawk had also hunted all winter in Algonquian territory (JR 28:279-287). The peaceful opening of the Algonquian beaver lands seems to have been one of the main motives behind the Mohawk peace overtures and one that was, no doubt, resented by the Algonquians.

270

Towards the end of February 1646 the Mohawk felt it necessary to go to Trois Rivières to assure the French that they were not responsible for the winter's disturbances (JR 28:291). At the same time they warned the French and their allies that this peace did not include the Seneca, Oneida and Onondaga (JR 28:293; Vol. 29:147). Again the Mohawk made a special point to the effect that they would like to have unhindered access to the hunting territory of their new allies:

> . . . that the chase be everywhere free; that the landmarks and the boundaries of all those great countries be raised; and that each one should find himself everywhere in his own country (JR 28:299).

True to the warning of the Mohawk, the other Iroquois tribes continued to go to war. In the spring of 1646 a combined force of Onondaga and Oneida nearly captured a Huron village (JR 29:149). By July, however, Huronia seems to have been at peace.

In order to consolidate the Mohawk peace Father Jogues set out for the Mohawk country on May 16th, arriving there on June 4th (JR 29:49-51). While among the Mohawk, Jogues met a number of Onondaga, to whom he gave presents in the hope they would persuade their chiefs to join in the peace (JR 29:57). On June 16th the Mohawk persuaded Jogues and his party to leave because a force of "Iroquois from above" (beyond the Mohawk) had set off to intercept the Huron (JR 29:59). It is not entirely clear why the Mohawk were so anxious to get Jogues out of their country. The only recorded incidents along the trade route that summer concerns a small band of Oneida. At first these attacked some Allumette in mid August but were apparently routed by a group of Iroquet (JR 28:225) or Huron (JR 29:233). One Oneida was taken captive. The intention was to send him back to his chiefs in order to arrange a peace similar to that of the Mohawk.

On the 26th of August the first Huron canoe arrived at Trois Rivières, followed by eighty others with some 300 men in the beginning of September (JR 28:141, 231; 29:233). The results of the trade were considered even better than the previous year (JR 28:141). Apparently some Huron had to return with their beaver because not enough merchandise was available (JR 28:231). On the return journey, one Huron canoe decided to take the Lake Ontario route but was captured by a small band of Iroquois. During the fall 35 canoes of *Attikamegue*, accompanied by some canoes from a northern band who were in contact with groups still further north, arrived at Trois Rivières for trade (JR 29:109, 119-121). About the same time the Christian Indians at Trois Rivières decided to organize themselves into a separate band in order to carry out winter hunting and summer trading more effectively (JR 29:107).

On September 24th, Father Jogues accompanied by Jean La Lande set out for the Mohawk with two specific goals; first, to attempt a peace with the other four Iroquois tribes; and second, failing such a peace, to ask the Mohawk not to give the other Iroquois passage across their territory to the Huron trade routes (JR 29:61, 181-183). As soon as Jogues set foot in Mohawk territory, he was taken captive and on the 18th of October murdered along with La Lande (JR 30:219-221). According to Jérôme Lalemant the peace was broken because of the age-old rancours of inter-tribal warfare, because the Mohawk saw more profit and glory in war than in peace, and because anti-French Huron who were living among the Iroquois blamed Jogues' visit on a recent outbreak of disease and crop failure (JR 30:227-229). Immediately the Mohawk fanned out along the St. Lawrence, resuming the hostilities of the previous years. The first attacks in the St. Lawrence area occurred on the 17th of November, 1646, and continued through the entire next year (JR 30:161, 165, 173, 175, 193, 229-253). The Algonquians, Montagnais and Huron from the French settlements along the St. Lawrence of course retaliated (JR 30:167, 179–181, 187).

Rumours of an attack on Huronia and the knowledge of an Iroquois blockade of the trade routes kept the Huron from travelling to the French posts in 1647 (JR 30:195, 221; 32:29, 179; 33:69). The only news that got through from Huronia was *via* the *Attikamegue* (JR 30:189, 193, 221; 31:209–219). The references make it perfectly clear that Huron did not travel *via* any northern route, but simply passed mail to the *Attikamegue* who delivered it at Trois Rivières.[1]

Early in 1647 the Huron were contacted by the *Andaste* with an offer to join them in a mutual alliance against the Mohawk (JR 30:253; 33:73). On the 13th of April a Huron delegation travelled to the *Andaste,* returning on the 5th of October (JR 33:129–131). The agreement with the *Andaste* was that they should arrange a peace with at least the Onondaga, Oneida and Cayuga; and, if possible, also with the Seneca (JR 33:133). If the Mohawk refused the peace offers, the *Andaste* were to attack them.

1. Hunt (1940:61) even has Father Claude Pijart travelling over this route in 1647. What Hunt overlooked was that there were two Pijarts. Father Claude Pijart was among the Nipissing in 1647 (JR 30:109–125; Jones 1908:370). Father Pierre Pijart was at Trois Rivières on May 29th, 1647 (JR 30:177); from there he travelled to Montreal, arriving back at Trois Rivières in time to receive the mail from the *Attikamegue* and bring it to Quebec on August 6th, 1647 (JR 30:189).

At the same time as the *Andaste* were trying to arrange a peace, the Huron sent a delegation to the Onondaga to negotiate a peace that would hopefully include the Oneida and Cayuga as well (JR 33:71–73, 117–127). This delegation returned to Huronia on July 9th with instructions to parley. In the meantime the Onondaga, Seneca and Cayuga held back their army to await the outcome of the talks (JR 33:119). The Huron were divided on whether to negotiate for peace. The *Arendaronnon* were for it, hoping to exchange prisoners; the *Attignaouantan* were against it. In general, the frontier villages wanted peace, the others not (JR 33:119–121). In other words, the Huron confederacy was divided at a time when unity was absolutely essential. Only the tribes and villages who had suffered losses wanted a peace. On the Iroquois side the Onondaga, Cayuga and Oneida were ready to agree to the peace, the Mohawk and Seneca were bitterly opposed (JR 33:121–125). In the end, nothing came of it, because the Mohawk murdered the Huron ambassadors on their way for the final arrangements (JR 33:125–127).

No major attacks seem to have been launched against Huronia in 1647. The Onondaga, Oneida and Cayuga were awaiting the outcome of the peace negotiations; the Mohawk blockaded the St. Lawrence, and the Seneca were occupied in wiping out one of the Neutral tribes.[1]

During the winter of 1647 to 1648 the *Arendaronnon* abandoned their tribal area and retreated to the central and western Huron villages (JR 33:81). This was the beginning of the end for Huronia.

Early in the spring of 1648 the Huron fleet left for the St. Lawrence, arriving at Trois Rivières on July 22nd (JR 32:97, 179; 34:101). The organization of this particular fur brigade shows a definite change in Huron tactics. For the first time the Huron organized themselves into a single large group that travelled together. Significantly, the leadership of the group was not in the hands of the traders, but of five chiefs (JR 32:179). In all, some 250 Huron had come down to trade in 60 canoes (JR 32:97, 179, 185). On the way to the St. Lawrence the Huron had run into an Iroquois army which they defeated (JR 32:97, 179–185).

Prior to the Huron arrival the Mohawk had sent out several peace feelers to the French. On the 18th of May they parleyed at Montreal stating that they wanted peace with the French, but not with the Algonquians (JR 32:87, 143–149). The matter came to nothing. Apparently, all the Mohawk were interested in was to get some French prisoners (JR 32:-

1. The *Aondironnon* were a Neutral tribe on the northern frontier of the Neutral area. The Seneca attacked them because they had allowed the Huron to take a Seneca near one of their villages; characteristically, the other Neutral tribes did nothing to help the *Aondironnon*.

147–151). On the 20th of June the Mohawk made peace overtures at Trois Rivières (JR 32:153–157). Judging from the ensuing events, the Mohawk were only interested in exchanging prisoners and so, perhaps, lulling the French into a false sense of security (JR 32:153–171).

Trading that year was not quite as successful as in 1646 (JR 32:179), but in all brought in about 22,400 pounds of which one-sixth came from Tadoussac (JR 32:103). How much of this was brought by the Huron, is difficult to say. While the Huron were at Trois Rivières some forty canoes of *Attikamegue* also arrived JR 32:283), so that it is perhaps fair to say that the Huron as usual accounted for half of the furs received by the French in 1648.

On August 6th the Huron left Trois Rivières accompanied by 26 Frenchmen of whom eight were soldiers (JR 32:99). They arrived back in Huronia in the beginning of September, only to learn that in their absence the Iroquois armies had dispersed the population of St. Ignace I and entirely destroyed two other villages among them the large village of St. Joseph II (JR 33:85–89, 99, 167, 259–269; 34:87–101). The Jesuits put the blame on the fact that too many men were absent from the villages that summer. Some were off to trade, others had gone hunting and a large number had left Huronia on a raid to the Iroquois (JR 33:259; 34:87). A further factor seems to have been the reorganization of Iroquois warfare. Instead of small groups of men travelling to Huronia bent on terrorizing and gaining captives, the Iroquois were now moving in larger forces bent on destroying entire villages. Iroquois motives and methods of carrying out warfare had changed substantially during the 1640's.

The fact that 250 men had gone to trade in 1648 probably weakened Huronia to some extent. Why, then, did they go? The Huron themselves stated that they needed French trade goods, particularly hatchets (JR 32:-179). It is probable that by 1648 they had become to some degree dependent on French goods, particularly goods like hatchets, kettles and iron arrowheads; implements that were superior to their own. Two other factors may have played a role. One of these was the fact, noted earlier, that the bulk of the traders did not consider themselves warriors, and left that function to others. Another factor may have been a false sense of security into which the Huron were lulled by the lack of warlike activity and the peace proposals of 1647.

In 1649 only a few Huron attempted the voyage to the St. Lawrence. On July 20th some arrived with the news that Huronia had ceased to exist (JR 23:57). On August the 7th a group of 20 Huron arrived at Trois Rivières (JR 34:59), and on September 22nd Father Bressani with a group of Huron and soldiers (JR 34:59–61). Several groups departed for Huronia; one on June the 6th including 34 Frenchmen (JR34:53), and another August 12th including a number of soldiers (JR 34:59). Father Bressani tried to return to Huronia on September 28th, but his Huron would not go past Montreal JR 34:61). Apparently the trade route was relatively free of Iroquois in the summer of 1649.

Instead of blockading the trade route, the Iroquois had turned their attention on Huronia. As early as the 16th of March the Iroquois army hit the village of St. Ignace II, completely destroying it (JR 34:123). Apparently they had spent the winter near Huronia with an army estimated at 1,000 men. A few hours after St. Ignace II was taken, St. Louis was attacked and destroyed (JR 34:125). In the process Father Jean de Brébeuf and Gabriel Lalemant lost their lives. After a few skirmishes with a Huron force the Iroquois withdrew (JR 34:127–137).

After a joint decision between Huron and Jesuits, Ste. Marie I and the remaining Huron villages were burned and abandoned. Huronia ceased to exist.

b) Summary and Discussion: 1642–1649

On summarizing Huron trade between 1642 and 1649, only three years stand out during which trade was carried out successfully. The years 1645 and 1646 were successful because of the Mohawk peace, and 1648 because of the excellent organization of the Huron fur brigade and because the Iroquois armies were busy in Huronia. Virtually no Huron got through to the St. Lawrence between the years 1642 and 1644; and in 1647 they did not undertake the journey.

In their attempt to get at the Huron, the Iroquois divided the task, devoted themselves completely to it and were flexible enough to change tactics for maximum success. The Seneca, Onondaga, Cayuga, and, at times, the Oneida consistently raided Huronia. Few of them were ever reported on the St. Lawrence. In 1642 they began to change their tactics from traditional patterns of warfare, consisting of small raids along the Huron frontier, to massive, well-organized attacks bent on destroying entire villages. This new type of warfare became effective in the winter of 1647 to 1648 and continued through 1648, 1649 and 1650. The same tactics were later used to disperse the Petun, Neutral and Erie. The Mohawk and, at times, the Oneida were responsible for blockading the trade route to the French settlements. They too changed their tactics. Until 1642 some Huron had always managed to get through by waiting until the Mohawk army returned to their villages in the late summer. In 1642 the Mohawk split into smaller groups along the entire trade route, picking off the small Huron flotillas as they came down to trade. The object of the Mohawk was to get furs. Algonquian counterattacks, and the fact that the Mohawk were not getting enough furs through raiding, induced them to seek a peace with the French. Part of the peace agreement was that the Mohawk could hunt in Algonquian territory. The instability of such a peace, or any Indian peace for that matter, was demonstrated by the fact that a few murders could touch off immediate intertribal war.

Over the years Huron weaknesses became very obvious. They were politically divided, in the sense that the intertribal councils could not agree on common defence or peace proposals. They were socially divided between Christian and pagan, while before the 1640's the Huron had at least a common social and religious structure. They were debilitated by disease, and had lost at least half of their population. Particularly serious was the loss of many old men and women who were the traditional leaders of the society. Since there was no acceptable means by which young men could gain power, political factions developed which further hindered unified action.

In spite of the problems at home and the Mohawk blockade, the Huron traders actually seem to have expanded the Huron trade network in the 1640's. Three factors seem to have been responsible for this expansion. By the early 1640's the Nippissing stopped travelling to the St. Lawrence to trade. They retained their trade routes to the north and brought their furs to the Huron at Lake Nippissing and to Huronia, where they wintered throughout the 1640's. The importance of the winter trade in Huronia was pointed out by the Jesuits in 1649, namely now that the Huron were destroyed the Algonquians would no longer come south to trade (JR 34:203). By the early 1640's, therefore, the Huron effectively became collectors and carriers of Nipissing furs. Some Huron may have travelled with the Nipissing to the north, but by and large the northern and western routes seem to have been in the hands of various Algonquian bands. The *Achirigouan* and probably the Ottawa traded to the west (JR 30:113), the *Saulteur* into the Lake Superior area (JR 33:149), and the Nipissing to the north. The Huron, instead of travelling these routes, collected the furs and brought them to the St. Lawrence. There was really little point in the Huron travelling to Lakes Superior and Michigan. The routes were long and time-consuming; other groups controlled the territory; and, most importantly, other groups brought the furs to the Huron, thus saving them the trouble.

A second factor in the expansion of Huron trade during the 1640's was the collapse of the Allumette and Petite Nation. From the beginning of French-Huron contact to the early 1640's, these bands controlled the lower Ottawa. They forced the Huron to pay toll charges and controlled the trade up the tributaries of the Ottawa, except perhaps the Lake Timis-kaming-Dumoine River area. With the depopulation of the Ottawa valley, the Huron established regular meeting places with the bands of the north-ern interior. This zone of Huron influence seems to have extended into, but not completely encompassed, the territory of the *Attikamegue*. The *Attikamegue* seem to have controlled the trade immediately to the north of their territory as far as the routes leading north-west out of Lake St. John, which were in the hands of the Montagnais. During the early 1640's, therefore, the Huron became the middlemen for all the Indian groups west of about 76° longitude.

A third factor in the expansion of the Huron trade network was the growth of the Christian colony at Trois Rivières, Québec and Tadoussac. Here Christian Huron, Algonquians and Montagnais traded into the areas north of the St. Lawrence, particularly into the drainage basin of Lake St. John. It is not entirely clear whether the Montagnais, who originally held the trade up the Saguenay, shared in with the newcomers or whether they had declined so much in numbers through smallpox that they could no longer carry the trade themselves. In view of the smallpox epidemics that raged in the Tadoussac area, the latter seems more probable.

Throughout this period there does not seem to be any evidence for the northern system of Huron routes postulated by G. T. Hunt. Until 1648, the Huron travelled in small groups from Huronia picking up furs at predetermined meeting places along the shore of the Georgian Bay, Lake Nipissing and the northern tributaries of the Upper Ottawa. In exchange for the furs some corn, tobacco, fishnets and French trade goods were given. The Huron then passed down the Ottawa and the St. Lawrence to Trois Rivières. In 1648 the Huron organized themselves into one large fleet of canoes, but still used the same route. There is no record of Huron ever getting to the French posts by any other way than Ottawa and the St. Lawrence. It is because only this route existed that the Mohawk were able to seal Huronia so effectively from the French posts.

8. A SUMMARY AND INTERPRETATION
OF HURON TRADE

The description of Huron trade presented in this chapter differs in some ways from previous work, particularly that of G. T. Hunt (1940). In the light of a careful rereading of the documentary sources, Hunt seems to have overestimated the extent of Huron trade. Perhaps his greatest contri-bution lies in pointing out the fact that economic motives had entered Iroquois warfare, leading ultimately to the disintegration of Huronia.

Three basic differences between Huron trade as presented here, and Hunt's interpretation, are the relative speed with which the French-Huron trade developed, the extent of the Huron trade network, and the extent to which trade was an important Huron economic activity. The first two points are by necessity related and will be treated together.

It is reasoned here that prior to French-Huron contact, Huron trade relations were primarily with the Algonquian bands, in particular the Nipissing and Allumette. The principal products that were exchanged were Huron fishnets, corn and tobacco, for Algonquian skins, fish and perhaps meat. It was essentially an exchange between complementary economies. In the winter Algonquians would camp outside some of the Huron villages; the eastern Algonquian bands among the *Arendaronnon* and the northern Algonquian bands such as the Nipissing among the *Attignaouantan.* In the summer Huron travelled north to the Nipissing and perhaps as far as the east shore of Lake Superior.

Before the advent of French-Huron trade, Huron trade with other Iroquoian tribes seems to have been minimal. Some tobacco was perhaps traded from the Petun for items the Huron got from the Algonquians, but otherwise trade relations between such similar economies appear to have been slight.

Huron trade with the French began slowly. It was virtually non-existent until Champlain established personal contact with the Huron in 1615. Up to that time, and certainly prior to 1609, most of the French goods that arrived in Huronia came *via* various Algonquian bands, particularly those of the Ottawa valley. The existence of a series of middlemen between the Huron and the French, and subsequent Huron problems in opening a trade route to the St. Lawrence, demonstrates that intertribal trade regulations and regulations regarding passage through tribal territories predate French arrival. It also demonstrates that Huron trade penetration to the east was weak before French contact and that the routes that were to become the Huron trade network had really been Algonquian routes before 1615.

The development of Huron trade after 1615 was initially with the Petun and Neutral. Along the trunk route to the St. Lawrence, the Huron were barely tolerated until the Ottawa valley Algonquians were decimated by smallpox and the Iroquois armies. Until the early 1640's, therefore, the Huron were primarily collectors of furs from their own territory, the Petun, the Neutral, and a few bands along the shore of Georgian Bay such as the Ottawa. The Ottawa in turn brought furs to the Huron from the west and north-west. The Nipissing controlled the trade to the north, and until the early 1640's did their own trading on the St. Lawrence.

Similarly, until the Ottawa Valley Algonquians were dispersed in the early 1940's, they collected furs from tribes adjacent to the Ottawa and brought them to the French posts. Prior to the 1640's the Huron may have collected furs in the Lake Timiskaming and Dumoine River areas. Before the 1640's various Montagnais groups traded to the north-west from Tadoussac into the interior of Quebec. There is no evidence that the Huron ever penetrated very far into the north-eastern interior from the Ottawa. On every occasion the Ottawa-St. Lawrence route was used to get to the French posts.

After the height of the smallpox epidemics among the Nipissing, Montagnais, and Ottawa Valley Algonquians, followed by severe Iroquois raids into the Ottawa Valley, Huron trade began to open up. The Nipissing ceased travelling to the St. Lawrence, and the Ottawa Valley Algonquians were dispersed. The Huron now became the middlemen for all the groups west of about 76° longitude. The Huron role in this trade must be viewed as that of a middleman between the bands along the trunk route and the French. Without penetrating into any new territories the Huron could receive the furs from groups they would never even see. Bands such as the Ottawa, Nipissing, *Attikamegue* and others would bring the furs from groups still further away to regular meeting places with the Huron. The bulk of the Huron traders had no reason to travel any further than the regular meeting places, nor did they have the time. The Mohawk blockade of the lower Ottawa and upper St. Lawrence area demonstrates very clearly that the Huron did, in fact, have no routes through the interior of Quebec.

The Huron penetration of the Saguenay area and beyond seems to have been carried out by Christian Huron, or at least Huron and Algonquians settled at the French posts, after the smallpox epidemics had decimated the Montagnais of the Tadoussac area. There is no evidence that the old Montagnais trading areas were penetrated by Huron directly from Huronia.

The development of Huron trade, and its effective execution in spite of the epidemics, seems to be founded on two fundamental factors. These were the large population of Huronia and their agricultural economy, which provided food for the traders and allowed some to specialize in this occupation. Huron agriculture was largely operated by the women. Between the spring and fall fishing seasons the men could carry out other tasks, among which trading was one. This, of course, was not true for the Algonquians and Montagnais, who were largely hunters and gatherers. Among these bands the men were also the prime providers of sustenance, and the gathering and trading of furs was incidental to the provision of food. Of these two tasks (gathering and transporting of furs to the French), gathering of furs could be carried out as a regular part of the hunting and gathering routine. Travel to the fur posts was much more difficult especially after these groups had been hit by smallpox. With the decimation of groups that already had small populations, travel to the St. Lawrence became next to impossible.

The smallpox epidemics among the Huron, on the other hand, were not nearly as disruptive to trade as among the Algonquians. Even after the Huron population had been cut in half, there were still more than enough men to carry out effective trading. The fact is that normally fewer than 300 Huron carried out the entire trade between Huronia and the French posts. The largest number of Huron ever to travel to the St. Lawrence for trade was in 1633, just after the English occupation ended. In that year, 140 to 150 canoes with 500 to 700 men arrived for trade. The next highest figure was in 1646 when 300 men came in 80 canoes. In all the other years between 1615 and 1649, the usual figure was 60 canoes with perhaps 200 men, or less. Even after the epidemics, 300 men, out of a population of 9,000, is not a severe drain on the male population of a society whose subsistence economy during the trading months was operated by women.

Essentially, Huron trade was an efficient system, operated by a small segment of the population, bringing desired goods to the entire population and social recognition and prestige to the trader. The successful execution of trade depended on Huron abilities to organize the collectors of furs as well as protecting the primary route to the markets of the St. Lawrence. Although the Huron managed to put together an effective system for collecting furs, their ultimate failure lay in their inability to come to terms with the Iroquois tribes. The tragedy was that although the Huron had a sound subsistence economy and a flexible trading system, their political system was too slow to recognize the changing motives and powers of the Iroquois confederacy, and too inflexible to adjust effectively to meet this threat.

Chapter VIII

Summary and Conclusions

The stated purpose of this study is the reconstruction of the geography of Huronia during the first half of the 17th century. One of the basic approaches to such a problem is to define the spatial extent of the area to be studied in terms of the effective occupance of the culture group that inhabits it, and examine the spatial behaviour of that group and the nature of its interaction with the biophysical environment. All human beings interact with each other and the physical environment over terrestrial space; and, in so doing, they organize space into a reflection of their culture values. The ability of a group to interact with the biophysical environment, and the nature and extent of interaction, depend principally on group culture, because it is culture that shapes what men perceive in their surroundings. In reconstructing the geography of Huronia the Huron are therefore examined as the bearers of a culture interacting with the natural environment of the area they occupied to produce a landscape organized according to their perceived needs and wants.

The task of reconstructing the geography of Huronia is subdivided into six broad, interrelated, and basically geographical themes: the delimitation of the settled area; the physical characteristics of the settled area in as much as they relate to the Huron occupance; population estimates for the period; settlement patterns; the subsistence economy; and the interrelated phenomena of politics and trade. Where necessary, socio-political factors are introduced in order to interpret some of the geographical patterns.

In assessing the interrelationships between the six major themes, the basic point of departure is the area of effective occupance. It is the physical environment of this area and its surrounding waters that satisfied almost all the basic needs and wants of some 21,000 Huron. Huron settlement patterns were essentially a reflection of the distribution of perceived resources and social values. Social values influenced the size and morphology of the village, while limitations in Huron technology determined construction materials and site requirements. All of the latter were found in the physical environment of the settled area. The subsistence economy was in turn related to the biotic potential of the settled area, to Huron technology and social values, and to the needs of the Huron population. Huron technology set the limits to which the physical environment could be exploited; Huron social values influenced the organization of labour and field patterns; and the size of the Huron population, together with Huron technological capabilities, determined the extent and intensity of resource exploitation.

Huron trade presents a complex pattern of interrelationships between culture and environment. While the purpose and operation of trade were rooted in Huron social and political traditions which changed little over time, the articles being traded and the areas from which they were obtained changed soon after contact. Before contact, Huron trade was based on a variety of products obtained or manufactured in Huronia, but after contact the Huron trade network expanded and became based on fur resources from most of Ontario and parts of western Quebec. The social and political basis of trade remained rooted in patterns established before the contact period.

Although the culture of the Huron changed during the period under discussion, cultural change as such is not explored, except where it had a direct bearing on geographical phenomena such as changes in population size, politics and trade. As yet, there is little evidence to suggest that settlement patterns or the Huron subsistence economy were widely affected by cultural change; except, perhaps, when metal goods made the erection of villages and the carrying out of agricultural pursuits more efficient. This is not to deny the reality of cultural change in aspects of religion, family relations, social structure and the like. These changes become particularly evident in the last ten to twelve years of Huronia's existence, but to what degree they affected the geography of Huronia is as yet not known. Basically, therefore, this study is an attempt to reconstruct the geography of an area in the past by describing it in terms of the geographical behaviour of the people who occupied that area. The remainder of this chapter will be devoted to a brief re-examination of the major themes of the study, some of the approaches used in describing these themes, remaining problems, and suggestions for future research.

One of the most crucial steps in the geographical study of any society is the delimitation of the area that that society occupied, and an assessment of the natural resource potential of that area. This is particularly relevant for technologically unsophisticated societies such as the Huron. Except for some trade which the Huron carried on with their neighbours, they were almost completely dependent for everything, from sustenance to building materials, on the natural productive capacity of their territory. Even though they modified the landscape they occupied, the Huron had little control over it. They did not fertilize their fields, did not practice irrigation, and did not breed animals or fish. The Huron subsisted on the natural productivity of the soil, forest, fish, and, to a lesser extent, game resources of their area of occupance. One of the keys to an understanding of the human geography of Huronia is therefore the delimitation of the area of active occupance and a description of the physical geography of that area in terms of Huron abilities to utilize it.

In the case of this study, the criterion for delimiting the area of effective occupance is the distribution of settlements during the period of French contact. Both the distribution of village sites with trade goods and the location of Jesuit missions are used. Of these two criteria, the latter is obviously more useful. French trade goods entered Huronia some time before the period encompassed by this study and therefore indicate a larger area of occupance than that of the 17th century. In spite of the shortcomings of the early maps and locations given in the *Jesuit Relations,* the territory known as *le pays des Hurons* or Huronia can be delimited fairly accurately. No settlements occurred south of the large frontier villages of la Conception (*Ossossane*), St. Michel (*Scanonaenrat*), St. Joseph II (*Teanaustaye*) and St. Jean Baptiste (*Contarea*). The village of *Ekhiondastsaan* is sometimes placed south of the frontier as defined here. However *Ekhiondastsaan* appears to be a synonym for *Tiondatsae* (*La Chaudiere,* or Caldaria*), which according to three maps was well north of St. Michel. No contact sites or Huron Missions lay north of a line joining Matchedash Bay to the "Narrows" of Lake Couchiching. The territory thus defined encompassed some 340 square miles. It is from this territory and bordering waters that the Huron derived their food.

It is doubtful whether there are any means by which Huronia can be more accurately delimited than the methods employed here. More precise dating techniques and intense archaeological work on all contact sites might alter the proposed location of some of the Jesuit missions, but would not appreciably alter the territorial limits as defined here. The magnitude of the archaeological work involved would preclude such a study for many years. Whether actual mission villages could be more precisely identified, is also doubtful. A few, such as St. Joseph II and Ihonatiria may have had a Church, which should be archaeologically identifiable; others may show a French influence on house or palisade construction. A precise knowledge of temporal changes in French trade goods, and extensive testing of sites in the general area of a mission as indicated by the early maps, would be a logical beginning to solving the problem.

In describing the physical environment of Huronia, an effort is made to assess it in terms of conditions at the time of the Huron occupance. This is necessary in order to assess what resources the Huron had at their disposal. Using descriptions in the ethnohistoric sources, it is postulated that the climate was essentially similar to that of the present. The inland water table was somewhat higher and swamps more extensive, due to the fact that the Huron did not engage in drainage operations. The forest composition was similar to the present, although much more extensive. Since the Huron showed a high preference for well-drained sandy loams in the upland areas, these areas underwent repeated clearance. The landscape of the upland areas during the Huron occupance must have been a patchwork of corn fields, meadows and second generation deciduous forest. Heavy stands of mixed forest occupied the area of less desirable soils, and a thick tangle of cedar, hemlock, tamarak and alder occupied the poorly-drained lowlands.

The description of the physical geography of Huronia is derived by comparing the ethnohistoric descriptions to present conditions and those of the early part of the 19th century just prior to the European settlement. Of course, no exact reconstruction can be made. As far as climate is concerned, drought patterns, references to the length of seasons, seasonal activities and seasonal abundance of food resources, point to a climate essentially similar to that of the present. The staple food source, corn, with a maturing period of 90 to 120 days, was grown successfully; and this indicates a growing period, frost-free season, and rainfall régime that were, for all practical purposes, similar to the present.

Without extensive work on palaeosoils and pollen cores in Huronia, it is doubtful if our knowledge of the climate and vegetation of the period could be much improved. Preliminary results from pollen, soils and snail studies on the Robitaille site one mile west of Thunder Bay show a climate similar to that of today; but a larger element of coniferous vegetation is found in the forest composition. Many more sites will have to be studied, but the work conducted at the Robitaille site demonstrates clearly that such studies can provide excellent results (Heidenreich, *et al.,* 1971; Latta 1971).

From a Huron point of view, one of the great assets of the physical geography of their territory must have been the large and relatively contiguous tracts of well-drained sandy loams and loamy sands. Of the 139 village sites examined, 87 per cent occurred on these soil types. Together these two soil types comprise 66 per cent of Huronia, or some 224 square miles. Although from a modern point of view these are far from the best soils in Huronia, Huron perception of their soil resources was circumscribed by the limits of their technology. No other soils in Huronia are as easily cleared and worked with a digging stick or crude hoe, as the sandy loams and loamy sands. An understanding of these soils is crucial to an understanding of Huron agriculture.

In order to clarify later chapters on settlement patterns, economy, external relations, and trade, a short section has been included, outlining the Huron social structure, political organization, migration into Huronia and organization of Huronia into tribal areas. Together with the discussion on the delimitation of Huronia and its physical geography, this section is a part of the background on which the later chapters are based.

The essential feature of the Huron social system was kinship solidarity traced through the female line. Kinship operated at four major levels; the extended family, the lineage, the clan segment and the clan. The extended family formed the basic residence and economic unit, whose physical expression was the longhouse. Similarily, the lineage structure may have been reflected in the village morphology and sharing of work and produce. Since marriage had to be outside the lineage, the lineage structure and marriage rules helped to promote kinship ties between families in the same village and between villages. Similarly, clan segment and clan loyalties would cut across village and tribal boundaries, helping to promote social cohesion at the tribal and confederacy level.

Huron government operated at village, tribal and confederacy levels. Of these, village government was the most effective. Government at all levels was mainly by group consensus, although at the village level a highly-regarded and clever chief could exercise some physical force by accusing dissidents of witchcraft, and thereby placing them under the threat of execution. Village matters were debated by a council of men presided over by a chief. At the tribal and confederacy levels the village chiefs met with their advisors to discuss matters of mutual interest. All council decisions were derived by consensus, but were not necessarily binding on any individual, village or tribe. There was no police force or army to administer the decisions of the councils or chiefs. Rather than being a governing body, the councils sounded out and expressed opinions and attitudes. Majority opinion simply stated the position a majority of people would take on a particular issue.

At all levels of government, great scope was left for individual behaviour. However, in a society such as the Huron, whose smooth functioning depended on co-operation, individual action had to be carefully balanced against majority opinion. The weakness of the Huron concept of government was that it did not permit any person or council to make decisions that were binding on any group of people. This weakness was reflected in the social instability of large villages and Huron relations with other tribes. Ultimately, it proved to be a key factor in the disintegration of Huronia.

To a Huron the tribe was an important unit, in spite of its loose governing structure. Members of the same tribe shared a common past; some tribes had a distinct dialect; and, what was probably very important to the Huron, villages within each tribe were linked together by marriages, much more so than villages between tribes. The tribe was, therefore, a unit made up of a number of villages with a common past and socio-political ties. Its geographical expression was the tribal territory.

With few exceptions, the boundaries of each tribal territory fall along distinct physiographic boundaries. Since there are no maps of the tribal boundaries, these have had to be reconstructed from the known tribal affiliations of each village. Apart from the fact that the Huron tribes varied in population size and the size of their tribal territory, they had somewhat different migration histories. It is not known what other geographical differences existed between them. Intensive archaeological work on contemporary sites with different tribal affiliations would be the only way in which tribal differences could be determined. Such work is absolutely necessary before detailed problems of tribal migration are tackled. Similar work would be necessary to delineate the tribal territories with greater precision.

A knowledge of the size of tribal areas and their populations permits a more accurate assessment of the relationship between population size and available soil resources. A discussion of the five tribal areas permits one to derive and compare five separate estimates for population adjustment to the soil resource base, rather than basing such estimates on one area of occupance.

The precise population prior to the smallpox epidemics will probably never be known. Three independent approaches to the problem indicate that the early estimate of 30,000 Huron is too high. In this study a figure of 21,000 is adopted for the pre-epidemic population, and about 9,000 for the post-epidemic population. Barring the discovery of new documents, about the only way these figures could be improved is through intensive and extensive archaeological work. It would, in fact, be necessary to identify all Huron villages occupied during the contact period; date them as accurately as possible; and determine the size of the sites and number of longhouses within them. This is a staggering task, which would take a long time to complete.

A reliable estimate of population and its distribution is of obvious importance, because these are often related to subsistence patterns and resource use. One of the really gratifying aspects of the population estimates is the close relationship of tribal area to tribal population. This relationship was found to be even closer when tribal area was viewed in terms of preferred agricultural soils. Such a close relationship between population and soil resources lends credence to the population estimates, the fact that the Huron were highly dependent on agriculture, and the possibility that Huronia was approaching a maximum population for the size of the territory. It would be interesting to see if similar relationships existed among other Iroquoian groups. For the Petun and the five Iroquois tribes, such a study should be possible.

In selecting a site for their village, the Huron were guided primarily by water availability and soil resources. Other factors, such as proximity to navigable waterways, types of vegetation, and natural defences seem to have been of secondary importance. Only in the case of the larger, more important villages does a natural defensive position seem to have been deliberately chosen. In view of the difficulty of clearing large tracts of mature forest and the need for suitable building materials, it is more than likely that areas of immature forest growth were sought. This hypothesis could be tested by searching the area around the contact sites for earlier sites, dating them, and estimating the location and extent of their cornfields. Work done in the vicinity of a few villages shows that this hypothesis is likely to be true. In general, at least during the contact period, a preferred village location was beside a permanent spring, on a bluff overlooking a navigable waterway, with a large hinterland of arable soils under a young secondary forest succession.

While Huron village site selection may be explained through physical factors and a limiting technology, the size and morphology of the village seems to be largely determined by socio-political factors. The basic residence unit was the longhouse, which varied in length with the size of the extended family that occupied it. As such, the longhouse was the physical manifestation of social solidarity and economic security. The egalitarian nature of Huron society was reflected by the similarity of the longhouses within the village. The chief's house was usually somewhat larger than the rest, but this did not denote special status. The chief's house had to be larger because many of the village functions were held here.

On the basis of societies similar to the Huron, one can postulate that longhouses were grouped within the village according to lineages or clan segments. In view of the importance placed by the Huron on their kinship structure, such a morphological pattern seems logical. A morphological feature that definitely appears to have been present was an open village meeting place. Careful archaeological work on some of the larger villages in Huronia has to be done to test these hypotheses.

On the basis of a few known villages, a close relationship between village size and the number of longhouses was demonstrated. Since the number of longhouses may be used as a rough estimate of population, village size reflects population size. Among the Huron, village population densities were in the order of 180 to 220 people per acre. The average village size was about four acres, few exceeding six acres in size. In terms of population, this would mean that Huron villages rarely exceeded 1,000 to 1,200 people. The few very large villages appear to have been multiple villages, or to have had chiefs who demonstrated unusual governing ability. An explanation of village size must be sought through environmental and social factors. A strong factor keeping village populations to a level below 1,200 was the social complexity of village life and the lack of coercive institutions to cope with it. This observation is supported by the work of Naroll (1956). Huron agriculture and the extent of arable village hinterlands certainly could have supported larger villages in some locales. The existence of a few large and multiple villages in substantially the same environment as the smaller villages rules out the quality of the environment as a general factor placing limits on settlement size well above 1,200 people. Technological limitations and environmental potential may have become more dominant features in placing a maximum size on the largest villages in Huronia. Multiple villages were a perfect solution to the problems inherent in large single villages. Social strife was minimized through segregation, yet social interaction, when desired, could easily take place. A multiple village was easier to defend than a large single village; and, in times of stress, a multiple village had a larger pool of chiefs to draw on for leadership.

Functional differences between Huron villages were slight. What functional differences there were, rested on the fact that a few villages were regional strongholds and residences of tribal leaders. Since the Huron did not have a market-oriented economy, and all villages were able to engage in foreign trade, economic functions could not be used as a basis for differentiating villages.

The lack of strong functional differences between the villages is reflected by their almost random distributional pattern. Only the regional strongholds (*Ossossane, Scanonaenrat, Teanaustaye* and *Contarea*), with their complement of tribal leaders, had a distinctive location. All four villages were on the southern frontier of Huronia. The random location of the majority of the villages are a reflection of the self-sufficiency of each village, and of a random to uniform distribution of site requirements.

The extent to which Europeans influenced the construction of Huron villages is not clear. The documentary sources point to European modifica-

288

tion of the palisades at *Ossossane* and St. Ignace II, while Jury claims to have found a strong European influence on the palisade and houses at St. Louis. The usual Huron palisade followed the natural contours of the land and enclosed a village in a rough oval. Palisades varied in complexity, the largest being up to seven rows in thickness with galleries, complex gates and watchtowers. Until the late 1640's when Iroquois offensive tactics changed, the traditional Huron palisade was fairly effective. Against massive, well-organized surprise attacks they proved to be totally inadequate.

On the whole a Huron village could be constructed in a few months work, providing the work forces were organized and the village was located in an area where building materials were readily available. Since most of the construction material consisted of posts under ten inches in diameter, the task of village construction would have been rendered almost impossible in any area but that of a young growth of secondary forest. It is probable that such forest conditions were a strong requirement for a village site.

Communications between villages in Huronia, to the Petun and the Neutral was entirely by trails. The canoe appears to have been used only for fishing and long distance trade.

Huronia was covered by an extensive network of trails connecting all the villages. According to the Jesuits, these trails were narrow and poorly-marked. In the winter they were extremely difficult to negotiate. The amount of inter-village communication is hard to estimate. Except for social occasions and times of war it is difficult to envisage much travel between the villages. Huron villages were economically self-sufficient, so that inter-village activity was largely confined to the social activities of the fall and early winter.

The Huron subsistence economy revolved around agriculture, fishing, hunting and gathering. As was to be expected, these activities reflected the complex relationships between sociocultural factors such as a limiting technology and the dynamics of the biophysical environment. Because quantifiable data on the Huron economy is not available, an approach has to be devised that would allow one to make reasonable food production estimates. The approach chosen is to estimate the per cent each segment of the economy contributed to the general diet; the production techniques that were used to produce this food; and, finally, the amount of food that had to be produced to support 21,000 people.

The initial problem is to estimate the per cent each sector of the economy contributed to the general diet. From the ethnohistoric sources it is apparent that corn constituted at least 65 per cent of the Huron dietary intake, and that fish was eaten more than meat. Gathering contributed very little, except in times of famine. Because the reconstructed Huron diet is an estimate, it is open to some argument. At the moment, however, it is difficult to see how this estimate could be improved. The inescapable fact is that approximately 21,000 people lived in an area of 340 square miles. They could not have existed if they did not have a reasonably efficient agricultural system with a high intake of agricultural products. In testing the estimated diet for dietary deficiencies, it is apparent that no serious deficiencies were present. This conclusion is supported by skeletal evidence and the writings of the early travellers, none of whom reported dietary deficiencies among the Hurons or themselves.

From the dietary information, and the knowledge that about 21,000 people subsisted on that diet, an estimate may be made of the amount of food the economy had to produce in order to feed that many people. In terms of corn alone, some 189,000 bushels were needed annually. Since the Huron were so heavily dependent on agriculture, their agricultural system is examined in some detail.

Essentially, Huron agriculture followed a classical pattern of slash and burn cultivation. Family plots were cleared by cutting down all vegetation and burning it. Corn, beans, and squash were planted together in small mounds, spaced closely together. Manuring was not known and land ownership practices assured that there was no organized system of fallowing or field rotation. Land was used until it was exhausted, and then it reverted to common ownership.

At least two major corn varieties were grown, of which the hardier flint corns were the most common. Except for occasional summer droughts, the climate of Huronia was adequate for corn culture. Although the sandy soils utilized by the Huron are not the best for corn, additional nutrients were added to the soil by burning over the fields every spring and by planting beans in the same mounds as corn. With these agricultural practices, it is estimated that the Huron could cultivate a sandy soil for up to six years and a sandy loam for up to twelve years. During this period the Huron obtained an estimated average of 27 bushels of corn to the acre. This figure compares favourably with yields obtained by Europeans and American Indian groups in the last century, using agricultural techniques similar to the Huron.

The problem of village movement can only be approached through a study of environmental and cultural factors. The oft-cited causes of soil and firewood exhaustion resulting from an interplay of a limited technology on the physical environment certainly played a dominant role. However, these two factors by themselves do not account for village movement. Part of the answer seems to be that after eight to twelve years, the number of family plots increased to such an extent, over such a large area, that efficient working of the fields was no longer possible. The women who cultivated, weeded and protected the plots from animal pests could no longer do an adequate job, nor could they be effectively protected from enemy raids. A form of land inheritance coupled to a planned fallowing system might partially have overcome this problem, but this would have required a major readjustment of Huron cultural values. It is doubtful if manuring could ever have been introduced without domestic animals.

By necessity, Huron agriculture has to be reconstructed in the form of an elaborate hypothesis. The only way this hypothesis may be tested is to conduct experiments in Huron agriculture. This would, of course, be a long term project which would have to run for at least eight to twelve years. Such an experiment would be of enormous interest, not only because it would shed light on the nature of shifting agriculture in northern latitudes; but also because soil nutrient loss, erosion, plant succession, and the effects of repeated burning could be studied.

Of the other three aspects of the Huron subsistence economy, gathering was the least important. Gathered produce such as berries was considered a welcome additive to the ubiquitous corn gruel, and was a major source of Vitamin C. Only in times of famine were gathered foods, particularly acorns, important. In modifying their environment through continuous cycles of clearing and land abandonment, the Huron were creating an excellent habitat for a variety of fruits and herbs.

Although virtually every animal was eaten, the major sources of meat were deer, bear and dog. For the efforts expended in hunting, deer and bear brought the highest returns. The most effective means of hunting deer was in organized mass drives during the early spring, when the deer "yarded"; and in the late fall, when they congregated for rutting. Bear were caught in the same drives or hunted singly. Both animals, as well as some others, were considered to be more plentiful outside of Huronia. This was because Huronia was thickly settled and much hunted, and because there were good grazing areas to the south and east of Huronia.

Dogs appear to have been eaten primarily at feasts. These were the only domesticated animals, and therefore the only certain supply of meat that the Huron had. By and large, meat was considered a feast food because of its scarcity. The results of a successful hunt were shared and often precipitated some sort of festive occasion.

In providing a food supply, fishing had several distinct advantages over hunting. Pound for pound, fish were more plentiful, easier to catch and more predictable in their habits. Moreover, fish could be dried and stored.

There is no evidence that the Huron could preserve and store meat for any length of time. Fish was, therefore, a staple along with corn; and game was a seasonal supplement.

Fish were caught most commonly in nets and weirs; less commonly, on the line and by spearing. Archaeological and documentary evidence show that the entire "Narrows" between Lake Couchiching and Lake Simcoe was blocked off by weirs. Similar weirs probably existed at the mouths of creeks and streams flowing into Nottawasaga and Georgian Bay. It is difficult to think of more sophisticated fishing methods in these waters. For the type of fish caught, Huron nets and weirs were comparable to those used by commercial fishermen in the last century in the same area. According to the Ontario Department of Lands and Forests, the techniques used by the Hurons could have netted them anywhere up to 8,000 pounds of fish per day during the spawning runs at the "Narrows" alone.

A study of Huron trade and war is in some respects a departure from the other themes of this study, because it takes the discussion out of Huronia. Nevertheless a discussion of Huron trade is an essential aspect of the historical geography of Huronia. The relationships between trade and external politics permit one to outline the wider role of Huronia in the Great Lakes-St. Lawrence area. From space relations that were fairly limited in the area they covered, Huron trade and political relations expanded after French contact to encompass an enormous area. At the same time, factors were introduced that led to the destruction of Huronia as a geographical entity and a re-arrangement of the space relations within the Great Lakes-St. Lawrence area.

In most studies trade can be treated as an aspect of the economy. In the case of the Hurons this is not advisable, because trade was not primarily economically motivated. Unlike aspects of the subsistence economy, trade also changed rapidly over time and was closely related to external politics and inter-tribal relations. From a geographical point of view, the value in studying Huron trade lies in assessing the changing space relations between Huronia and its surrounding area, as well as the operations of a non-market-oriented trading system.

Existing documents allow one to reconstruct at least an outline of Huron external political relations and trade. Although a reasonable case can be made for the manner in which trade operated and the types of goods involved, Huron trade routes and the extent of involvement of other groups is less certain. Even less can be said about quantities of goods involved and the number of men who took part in the yearly trading operations. Since no new documents are available, existing documents are re-examined in order to determine if an alternate interpretation to that of

292

Hunt (1940) is possible. The results indicate that Hunt seriously overestimated the importance and extent of Huron trade at the beginning of the contact period. Huron-French trade evolved slowly over time, and Huron dominance in the Great Lakes-Ottawa River area was not really achieved until the early 1640's, when the Algonquian bands in the area between the Huron and the St. Lawrence were dispersed. In order to document this interpretation of Huron trade it is necessary to examine the events of the contact period, year by year.

Prior to direct European contact Huron trade relations were closest with the Algonquian bands to the north, particularly the Nipissing, and a few groups in the Ottawa Valley. With these bands the Huron exchanged corn, tobacco, fishnets, and other items, for fur (to make clothing), some fish, meat, and European trade goods that the Algonquians were acquiring from Indian and European traders along the St. Lawrence. Since most of these goods were perishable, it is impossible to estimate the magnitude of pre-contact trade. The fact that these groups had been trading for a long time before European contact has been proven archaeologically and can be seen by the elaborateness of the rules that regulated trade. Throughout this early period Huron traders went at least as far as Nipissing and the south-eastern shore of Lake Superior. As yet, there is no proof that they were in direct contact with any parts of the St. Lawrence.

Huron trade with the Petun and Neutral was slight, and was mainly confined to tobacco, chert, exotic skins, and perhaps wampum beads. References to recurring hostilities during the 16th and early 17th century show that these contacts were not particularly highly valued. The closer contact with the Algonquians is to be expected, in view of the fact that the Huron and Algonquians had complementary economies. The similarity between Huron, Petun and Neutral economies would have precluded extensive trade relations. This, of course, changed once the Huron acquired large quantities of European trade goods.

The motives behind Huron trade were not dictated by economic need, except in times of famine. Huron traders regarded their journeys as an adventure, and their gains as a means of achieving prestige and social status. Success in trade or war were ways of gaining recognition and therefore political influence. The goods acquired in trade were gained by barter, but were given away back in the village or used to prepare feasts and festivals. Part of the road to social recognition was generosity, and trade made generosity possible.

The laws governing trade were fairly elaborate. Political alliances had to be concluded before a Huron could trade with any member of another group. In this way, trade and individuals were protected by the assurance that inter-tribal war would result if a trader was harmed. The entire tribe therefore, protected the rights of an individual. Similarly, the tribe recognized the rights of an individual and his lineage to the route and trade contacts he had established. No one was allowed to trade on another person's route unless he had received permission. This system assured a multiplicity of trade contacts and lack of competition. An extremely important aspect of inter-group trade was the integrity of group territories. In order to trade with groups beyond the territory of one's nearest neighbour, permission had to be sought to cross that territory. If permission was refused, and the refusal ignored, war would result. Such a war would have been a very serious matter because of the widespread system of alliances that existed in Eastern Canada. It was this regulation which prevented early Huron trade contacts on the St. Lawrence, and which permitted the Ottawa Valley Algonquians and Montagnais to establish themselves as middlemen between the French and groups in the western and northern interior. In later times, French pressure and toll charges allowed Huron travel across the territory of the Ottawa Valley Algonquians. The Huron in turn exercised their rights by never permitting Petun and Neutral across Huron territory.

Huron-French trade developed slowly once a political alliance had been made, and the French had proven themselves reliable allies in war. Three other factors that contributed to this slow development was Algonquian reluctance to permit Huron traders to travel to the St. Lawrence; Huron fears of Iroquois raids on the lower Ottawa; and the fact that during the first years of direct contact Huron warriors, and not traders, were going to the St. Lawrence. Another contributing factor may have been that the *Arendaronnon* considered French trade their exclusive right until Champlain's visit to Huronia in 1615.

The development of trade after 1615 was initially with the Petun and Neutral. Along the trunk route to the St. Lawrence, the Petite Nation and Allumette did their own trading, and the Nipissing controlled the trade to the north. The Huron, therefore, became the collectors of furs and middlemen to the Petun, Neutral and a number of Algonquian bands along the Georgian Bay, among whom the Ottawa were the most important.

After the height of the smallpox epidemics among the Nipissing and Ottawa Valley Algonquians, followed by severe Iroquois raids into the Ottawa Valley, Huron trade began to open up. The Nipissing, as well as the Algonquian bands to the north and east of the Ottawa, now delivered their furs to the Huron. Regular meeting places were established and the

Huron got access to furs from the western Great Lakes to James Bay and the western interior of Quebec, without ever having to travel very far from their trunk route. Central and Eastern Quebec as well as Labrador were finally penetrated by Huron and Algonquian traders from the French St. Lawrence Valley posts after the power of the Montagnais had declined. Direct Huron penetration from Huronia to these areas is doubtful, not only because of a lack of evidence and the long and difficult routes involved, but also because there was no need for it.

The development of Huron trade and its effective execution in spite of smallpox and Iroquois raids was founded on two fundamental factors. These were the large population of Huronia and the Huron subsistence economy. The economy was important in three ways: it provided a small surplus of corn that could be traded; the division of labour permitted some men to be absent from Huronia during the summer to specialize in trade; and corn could be dried and taken along as food for the traders. Since only about 300 men participated in trade, the epidemics which reduced the total population from 21,000 to 9,000 would not have appreciably affected trading operations. It must also be remembered that this drop in population affected the old and young more than the middle-aged male population.

The above was decidedly not the case with the Algonquians. Among all the Algonquian bands, the men were an integral part of the subsistence economy. Furs could be gathered in the normal course of hunting, but their transport to the St. Lawrence would mean the absence of a large number of men out of a relatively small total population. This situation became crucial after the smallpox epidemics, when the men were needed at home more than ever.

The failure of Huron trade lay not so much in the mechanics of trade, which were very efficient, but the inter-group relations that were a part of trade. In spite of sporadic efforts on the part of some of the Iroquois tribes, as well as the French and their allies, to find a peaceful solution to inter-tribal war, nothing lasting ever came of it. Old feuds, jealousies, and the inability of tribal and confederacy councils to enforce a peace, made the continuation of conflict inevitable. Changing Iroquois motives for war and a reorganization of Iroquois tactics were recognized too late. In spite of a sound subsistence economy and an excellent trading system, the Huron political organization was too ineffectual to deal with the situation. As a result, the entire confederacy was destroyed.

The Huron subsistence system reflects an extensive knowledge of, and close adjustment to the natural environment: an adjustment shaped largely by the technological, sociological, and ideological aspects of Huron culture. Huron technology limited Huron agriculture to certain soil types, while Huron social organization and values determined field patterns and working of the fields. Together, these cultural factors exposed limitations in the natural environment that resulted in declining yields over time, fuel exhaustion, and village relocation. These limitations could have been avoided by a readjustment of social values and technology.

Huron technology applied to fishing and fish preservation was considerably more efficient than hunting. Due to limitations in the carrying capacity of the physical environment, it is difficult to see how yields of meat could have been very much improved. Preservation techniques could have assured a more even yearly meat supply, but this would have necessitated a change in technology and in cultural attitudes, which regarded meat primarily as a feast food. The lack of potential domesticates (except the turkey) precluded the invention of a mixed farm economy.

Huron technology severely limited the society in its use of building materials, and sociological factors determined the morphology of houses and villages. Until the introduction of the iron axe, the Huron had no means of coping with a mature forest. If large trees were chopped down, there was no method by which they could be utilized. Technological limitations in the use of building materials, coupled with their agricultural system, resulted in transitory villages which constantly had to be rebuilt. As in most societies, the layout of houses and villages was purely a reflection of social values, while the choice of the site reflected physical needs. Ultimately, the social system also played a dominant role in determining the size of settlements.

Like other shifting cultivators, the bulk of the Huron existed in a fairly circumscribed area. Most of the women never left Huronia. A few accompanied the men on hunting and fishing expeditions, perhaps as far as fifty miles from their village. Only a few men travelled any great distances. Before the French contact period, some men went as far as 300 miles from Huronia on trading and war expeditions. After contact, some men travelled perhaps twice the distance. Except for the traders and warriors, Huron contact with other people was limited to those who came to the Huron villages. With the exception of the *Andaste*, first-hand knowledge of other groups was confined to those that bordered Huronia. After contact, Huron intercourse with distant areas broadened extensively, especially to the north and north-east.

It is not within the scope of this study to draw extensive parallels between the Huron and other societies. Most of the generalities made about Huron technology and resource use are also applicable to other tribal societies of shifting cultivators, as are Huron social values and political concepts. Only a large comparative study could derive theoretical principles about societies such as the Huron, and outline those aspects of Huron culture that make the Huron unique.

Future work in Huronia must, by necessity, be interdisciplinary. No one discipline has the variety of approaches and techniques available to solve the multitude of problems connected with the reconstruction of an entire society.

Biologists and zoologists could make a major contribution through a study of animal and plant remains in the middens. This would aid our understanding of Huron diet, as well as the natural environment of the period. The midden material itself would be an interesting area of work for chemists and biologists. A study of the microbiology, organic matter, and inorganic elements of this material might provide some knowledge of the original material that went into the middens.

Palynological studies on bogs near some of the village sites could provide some information on the environment of the period when the site was occupied, as well as an insight into Indian landscape modification. Preliminary work in the Penetang Peninsula demonstrates that the Indian occupance shows up clearly by the presence of *Zea* pollen and rises in *Ambrosia, Plantago, Pteridium,* the *Graminae* and *Compositae*. The decline in arboreal species was slight, compared to the European sequence higher up in the pollen spectrum (Heidenreich, *et al.*, 1971).

Soils studies are a particularly promising approach to a variety of problems. Work presently carried out by the author demonstrates that villages and longhouses can be delimited on the basis of soil phosphorus, calcium, and magnesium analysis. The soils within a village usually have at least twice the phosphorus and calcium content of soils outside the village, while the centres of the longhouses and middens usually have at least three times their normal content. Due to the ash content of the fireplaces, an analysis of magnesium values allows one to pick out the centres of the longhouses. By running a series of tightly-spaced transects, the precise size of an average four-acre site, and the number and location of houses can be found in a few months of work. Previously, this would have taken several summers of extensive digging. Soils analysis is also of use in determining the amount of erosion caused by village activity and Indian agriculture. Since buried soils are often found under the depositional material caused by erosion, an analysis of these palaeosoils could provide information on past vegetation. Supporting information on past vegetation and climate can be gained from a comparative study of past and present snail populations, out of the midden material and buried soils.

The only way in which the problems relating to Huron agriculture can be solved is to duplicate the process. Corn similar to that of the Huron could be developed out of strains still to be found on present Indian reserves. A careful experiment would then have to be set up, whereby land was cleared, burned and cultivated similar to the practices employed by the Huron. Soil nutrient loss would have to be noted, as well as the effects of burning, erosion, and the interplanting of beans and squash. The most important observations would be those related to changes in yield over different soil types. After field abandonment, vegetation successions should be studied, as well as soil regeneration rates. Such a study could easily take twenty years or more to complete.

In tackling the overall problem of the geography of Huronia the first and most crucial step is a systematic site survey of the area. Such a survey should note in particular the precise location of the site, its size, site characteristics, the degree to which it has been disturbed and its date. Of these, the problem of dating is the most difficult and the one on which a great deal of research effort must be expended. For most of the sites in Huronia radio carbon dating is inadequate not only because the sites are too recent, but also because of the large plus or minus factors attached to radio carbon dates. The most logical step is to start with the contact sites, and to evolve a dating system based on the type and quantity of European trade goods present. At the same time, Huron artifact assemblages should be examined by means of attribute analysis and correlated with the chronology based on trade goods. Only by establishing a chronology based on European trade goods independently of Huron artifacts, can the problem of regional differences be examined. European trade goods will vary with time, but not over space, for the same time period. This is not necessarily the case with Indian artifacts. *Arendaronnon* pottery may, for example, be somewhat different from *Attignaouantan* pottery within the same time period; not only because they were two different tribes, but also because they were spatially separated. Once a chronology based on European goods has been established and correlated with Huron artifacts, and regional differences noted, the dating procedures based on Huron artifacts can be extended into the pre-contact period. Underlying the whole problem of establishing chronologies is the problem of site sampling. The author knows of no site where an effort had been made to obtain a statistically random sample of artifacts. Statistically random samples could be obtained by sampling a quantity of every midden, based on the number and total bulk of midden material on a site. While this method still has problems, it is better than simply obtaining a sample from a portion of one or two middens.

298

After site surveys and dating procedures have been completed, the next step should be a systematic excavation of sites starting with the latest contact sites. Because of the number of sites involved, a random sample must be taken. This sample should be representative of different parts of Huronia as well as site size differences. Once the characteristics of the latest sites are understood, earlier sites can be tackled and the whole problem of tribal migration and culture change examined.

The procedures outlined above should lead to a systematic reconstruction of the geography of Huronia. Due to the interdisciplinary nature of such work, it should not be an exclusive field for archaeologists. In general, Ontario archaeologists have regarded the ultimate aim of their work an attempt at reconstructing past social behaviour. Very little thought has been given to the relation of man to the natural environment, subsistence patterns, theoretical aspects of settlement and spatial relationships. All of these are aspects of human behaviour to which a geographer can make a contribution. No one discipline can possibly encompass the variety of approaches and techniques that are necessary to interpret the variety of material available. It is hoped that this study demonstrates that a geographical approach to the problem of reconstructing aspects of the past is a valid one and one which is capable of deriving significant questions and results. Reconstructing the geography of past periods always creates special problems, most of them arising out of a lack of adequate data. The approach used in this study has to be a compromise between the elements that constitute a geographical study and the available material. Throughout the study special problems are raised, and hypotheses formulated, that can be solved with future field work. However, before these special problems are tackled it is necessary to have an overall survey of the period and area. It is hoped that this study provides such a survey.

Appendix I

TRANSLATIONS OF HURON TRIBAL, VILLAGE
AND PLACE NAMES.

a. Huron Tribal Names and their Translations

The Huron seem to have called themselves collectively *8endat* (*Ouendat* or *Wendat*), rendered *Hoüandate* by Sagard (1866, 4:*nationes*). This appellation occurs only once in the *Relations* (JR 16:227), and most probably came into common usage after the destruction of the confederacy. The Huron referred to themselves primarily as members of a certain village or tribe rather than by the confederacy name.

Potier (1918:154) and Sagard (1866, 4:*nationes*) simply translate *8endat* or *Hoüandate* as "Huron." Jones (1908:419-420) attempted a translation of the name rendering it as "The One Language," "The One Land Apart," or "The One Island." The latter two translations are usually given as "The Islanders" or "Dwellers of the Peninsula." Jones' translation is based on the roots *a8enda* (language) (Potier 1918:452) and *ah8ênda* (island, or a piece of land separated or distinct) (Potier 1918:448). In view of the fact that a peninsula is *ondia*, (Potier 1918:455), the meaning "Dwellers of the Peninsula" seems unlikely. Similarly, it would have been illogical for the Huron to call themselves speakers of "The One Language," because theirs was only one of several Iroquoian dialects. As a matter of fact, there were even differences in the dialect spoken among the Huron tribes (JR 10:11). The contention that *8endat* means "a land apart or distinct" (*i.e.*, an island in either a physical or conceptual sense) finds some support through two lines of evidence. First, Huronia is almost an island, surrounded along 60 per cent of its perimeter by water and most of the remainder by vast swamps (Map 20). Secondly, on at least two occasions the Huron referred to themselves as islanders or occupying an island (JR 15:21; 33:237-239). The case for *8endat* meaning "Islanders" is admittedly tenuous, but at least plausible. This, however, does not end the question. The root *a8enda* used by Jones can also mean "a bundle of fish" or "a joint of meat," depending on where the accents are placed (Potier 1918:448). If Sagard's spelling is used (*Hoüandate*) the problem becomes greater. The prefix *Hou* can be rendered as *8*, the *h* being silent (Potier 1918:5) (*i.e.*, *8andate*). This looks similar to *8endat*, except that the root *andata* (*endata*) could mean "village" (Potier 1918:448). A translation of *8andata* or *8endata* as "the One Village" or "Villagers" is at least as plausible as "Islanders."

In 1639, Jérôme Lalemant listed four tribes as constituting the Huron confederacy. These were the *Attignaouantan* (1642) (JR 23:43), [Attigouautan (1615) (Champlain 3:46), Atignouaatitan (1615) (Champlain 3: 101), Attigouantan (1632) (Champlain 4: 238), Atingyahointan (1623) (Sagard 1939:91), Attignawantan (1639) (JR 16:227), Attignaouentan (1640) (JR 19:125), Atinniawentan (1643) (JR 26:214), Atinniaoenten (1649) (JR 34:131)]; the *Attingneenongnahac* (1640) (JR 19:183), [Atigagnongueha (1623) (Sagard 1939:91), Attiguenongha (1635) (JR 8:71), Atignenonghac (1636) (JR 10:235), Atignenongach (1637) (JR 13:125), Attigueenongnahac (1638) (JR 15:57), Attigneenongnahac (1639) (JR 16:227), Attinguenongnahac (1640) (JR 19:125), Attingueennonniahak (1640) (JR 20:259), Attingueenongnahak (1641) (JR 21:-169)]; the *Arendaronnon* (1643) (JR 27:29), [Henarhonon (1623) (Sagard 1939:91), Renarhonon (1636) (Sagard 1866, 4:nationes), Arendarhonon (1635) (JR 8:71), Arendoronnon (1636) (JR 10:235), Arendarrhonon (1637) (JR 13:37), Arendahronon (1638) (JR 15:51), Ahrendaronon (1640) (JR 19:125), Arendaronon (1640) (JR 20:19), Arendaeronon (1641) (JR 21:169), Arendaenhronon (1642) (JR 23:151), Arendaenronnon (1647) (JR 33:81), Arendae'ronnon (1651) (JR 36:141), Arendageronon (1657) (JR 43:41)]; and the *Tahontaenrat* (1643) (JR 26:293), [Tohontaenras (1637) (JR 13:55), Tohontaenrat (1639) (JR 16:227), Atahonta, enrat (1651) (JR 36:141)]. In 1637 a fifth tribe was mentioned, the *Ataronchronon* (1640) (JR 19:125), [Ataconchronon (1637) (JR 13:61)].

The *Attignaouantan* were consistently called the "Nation of the Bear" by the French because "they wear a bear on their coat of arms" (JR 34:131). The name is not too difficult to transliterate: *Ati* is a prefix for the third person plural; *annionen*, *agnionen* (Potier 1918:451) or *agnouoin* (Sagard 1866, 4:*animaux*) means "bear," while *annia8enten* or *agnia8enten* means "country of the bear" (Potier 1918:450). Properly the "bear tribe" should therefore be written as *Atianniaouenten* or *Atiagniaouenten*, *i.e.*, "They of the country of the bear").

The *Attingneenongnahac* present a real problem. A "Cord" tribe is listed by the Jesuits in 1656 along with the "Bear" and "Rock" (JR 43:191), and it has always been assumed that these were the *Attingneenongnahac*. However, "cord" means *arenda* (Potier 1918:452), *achira* (Potier 1918:446) or *chira* (Sagard 1866, 4:*habits*). None of these roots are recognizable in the tribal name. Perhaps "cord" was a mistranslation of *Arendaronnon* since the words for "rock" and "cord" are similar (*i.e.*, *ȧrenda*, rock; *arenda*, cord) (Potier 1918:452). At any rate the term "cord tribe" occurs only once in the ethnohistoric sources and cannot be positively identified with the *Atingneenongnahac*. Any translation of the name is somewhat speculative. A reasonable guess is that the name is made up of the roots *gagnenon* (Sagard 1866, 4:*animaux*), *annienon* or *agnienon* (Potier 1918:451) (dog) and *hihangya* (Sagard 1866 vol. 4:*abbayer*), *angiahak* or *anniahak* (Potier 1918:307) (barking) (i.e.: *Atiagniennoniahak*, the "They of the barking dogs"). Allowing for variations in pronunciation, these roots are recognizeable in Sagard's name for the tribe as well as that of the Jesuits.

The *Arendaronnon* were called the "Rock Nation" by the French (JR 43:191); *ạrenda* meaning "rock" (Potier 1918:452), and *ronnon* meaning "nation" or "people" (Potier 1918:66).

The *Tahontaenrat* have been called "The White Thorns" or "The White Canoes" by Jones (1908:178-79), and the "White-eared People" or "Deer People" by Hewitt (Hodge 1913:207). These translations are based on the following roots: *atahonta*, meaning "ear"(Potier 1918:445) and *aenrat* "to be white" (Potier 1918:247). The word for "thorns" or "brushwood" is *ahonta* (Potier 1918:447), for "canoes" it is *ahona* (Potier 1918:447), and for deer it is *sconoton* (Sagard 1866, 4:*animaux*) or *oskennonton* (Potier 1918:352) (roebuck). Of these, either *ahonta* or *atahonta* seem the most plausible. If *ahonta*; then *T* signifying "place" (Potier 1918:76), *ahonta* meaning "brushwood" or "thorns" and *aenrat*, "to be white" (*i.e.*, *Tahontaenrat*, the "place of the white thorns" etc.). If *Atahonta* is used, the translation becomes "The White Ears" or *Atahontaenrat* which is one of the alternate spellings of the name. The name "Deer People," while attractive, does not seem plausible in view of the Huron words for deer.

The *Ataronchronon* were translated by Jones as meaning "Nation beyond the intervening fen or mud-bottom-lake" (Jones 1908:314). The roots for the word are *atara* or *ata* (swamp, mud) (Potier 1918:453), *aron* (obstacle) (Potier 1918:348), *chi* (beyond) (Potier 1918:92), and *ronnon* (nation) (Potier 1918:66) (*i.e.*, "Nation beyond the intervening swamp").

b. Huron Village Names

Adiatae (Andiatae, Adiatac)
   "At the bridge" or "Bridgetown" (Jones 1908:150).

Angoutenc (Angwiens, Angouteus)
   "Beyond (beside) the rapids (torrent)" (Jones 1908:131).

Anonatea (Anenatea, Aneantea)
   1. "The Village of abundance" (Jones 1908:142).

2. "Guardian of the water."

2. *annon*: "signas garder quelque chose ou quelque personne, en avoir soin" (Potier:308), to guard something or some person, to take care of; *atea*: "eau, liqueur" (Potier:454), water. Meaning: "Guardian of the water".

Arendaonatia (Anendaonactia)
"The mouth (arch) at the flat rock" (Jones 1908:144).

Arent (Arentat, Arrente, Arenta)
"At (in) the mouth of the river" (Jones 1908:134).

Arethsi (Aretsi, Arhetsi)
1. "The straggling village" (Jones 1908:152).
2. "The long clearing" (Jones 1908:152).

Arontaen (Taruentutunum)
"The town where many trees lie felled" (Jones 1908:54).

Ataratiri
"The place supported by mud."
atara: "terre fange" (Potier:453), mud, mire, dirt;
   atiri: "appuyer" (Potier:191), to prop up, support, stay, consolidate.
Meaning: "Mud-supported" or "the place supported by mud."

Cahiagué
1. "The fish spearing place" (Jones 1908:195).
2. "The place on the lesser trail."
2. The meaning was derived by P. J. Robinson (Orillia Historical Society 1966:17), but he does not state his references. The root *ahia* does not seem to exist in that form in Huron.
3. "The place always divided (in two)."
3. *C*: never used without *h*, i.e.: *Ch*, used here as the hard K, pronounced *Kha* or *Xa* (Potier:I), "hic, haec, hoc, hi, hae, haec", here, this, in this place or spot; *ahia*: here not given in its complete form; could mean several things; if *aiaxon*: "to spear fish" (Potier:264); "to break or divide" (Potier:263); if *ahiati*: "to fear or tremble" (Potier:163); if *ahiaton*: "to write" (Potier:261); if *Kaia* or *Kaiaxe*: "to divide in two" (Potier:264); *cue*: probably *Koue*, written *k8e* meaning "something always going on," or simply "plurality" (Potier:766). The final meaning could be "the place always divided (in two)," or *Kaiak8e*. This fits the double village now thought to be Cahiagué.

Carhagouha (Carragouha)
1. "The great forest walled town" (Jones 1908:192).

303

2. "The great palisaded fortress" (Jones 1908:192).

Carmaron (Karenhassa, Karenhaysa, Ekarenhatasa)
   "The place of the little treetops" (Jones 1908:59).

Contarea (Kontarea, Contareia)
   "Where there is a little lake" (Jones 1908:74).

Ekhiondastsaan (Khiondaesahan, Ekhiondaltsaan)
   1. "The places (lands) which exude water" (Jones 1908:148).
   2. "The places where kettles are owned" or "The domain of the kettles".
   2. *Ekhi*: rendered by Jones (1908:48) as, "the place where" (Potier:2,
   26). This means the same as *Ti* (Potier:242). *Ti* and *Ekhi* are therefore
   interchangeable. *Ondasta*: no such word; the closest is *andatsa* meaning
   "chaudiere", kettle (Potier:499); *Ekhiondastsaan* could therefore read
   Tiandatsaan. *An*: place names do not have such an ending; if *an* means
   aen then, "possessivum personale", or, "avoir quelque chose à soi, en
   avoir, le domaine, la propriete, la posseder," to have something, to
   come to, to have, the domain, property, etc. (Potier:221). Possible
   meaning is "The place where kettles are owned", or, "The domain of
   the kettles."

Iahenhouton
   "The one skillful manager of many important affairs" (Jones 1908:-
   146).

Ihonatiria
   "The little village above the loaded canoe" (Jones 1908:187).

Kaotia (Kaontia)
   1. "Behold the village" (Jones 1908:196)
   2. "All the paraphernalia of the medicine man" (Jones 1908:197).

Koutarcanô
   "The place guarded by swamps."
   Kou: must be rendered as *K8* (Potier:5), denoting the infinitive of
   verbs admitting *te* dual or affirmative (Potier:28); *tar*: from *atara* "terre
   fange," swamp (Potier:453); *cano*: from *xa* and *annon*; the bar over the
   ô denotes omission of an *n* (Jones 1908:196); *xa*, "hic, haec, hoc," here,
   at this place, etc. (Potier:I); *annon*: "signas garder quelque chose ou
   quelque personne, en avoir soin" (Potier:308), to guard something, to
   take care of, etc.. Meaning: "Much swamp guards this place." Note: This
   is an excellent description of the site of Ste. Marie I.

Oenrio (Wenrio, Ouenrio)

1. "The great spruce plantation" (Jones 1908:140).
2. "The beautiful firs" (Jones 1908:140).

Onnentisati
1. "the village located in the mountain hollow" (Jones 1908:135).
2. "The village located in the evergreen glade" (Jones 1908:135).

Ossossane (Osasan, Ossosane, Ossossarie)
1. "Where the corn tops (tassels) droop into the water" (Jones 1908:-183).
2. "Where the corn tops wave" (Jones 1908:183).

Quieunonascaran (Khinonaskarant)
1. "Entrance to the thunder channel" (Jones 1908:189).
2. "The beginning of the trolling channel" (Jones 1908:190).

Scanonaenrat (Scanouenrat, Scanonaentat)
"The bone white cabin" (Jones 1908:179).

Taenhatentaron (Tahententaron)
1. "Where the dry poles lie in the way" (Jones 1908:196).
2. "Where the two dry poles lie in the way" (Jones 1908:196).

Taentoaton
"Where the shore disappears."
   Te: denotes place, *i.e.*, "the place where" (Potier:76); *aenton*: "etre à terre" (Potier:222), to be on land, ashore; *aton*: "se dissiper, s'effacer, se detruire," (Potier:194), to disappear. Meaning: "The place where the shore disappears," or, "The place where the land ends."

Teanaustaye (Teanaostaiae)
1. "The guardian of the beautiful spring" (Jones 1908:176).
2. "The beautifully shaped cliff" (Jones 1908:177).
3. "The beautifully coloured cliff" (Jones 1908:178).

Teandatetsia
"The long village."
   Te: denotes place, where (Potier:76); *andata*: village (Potier:448); *etsia:* "etre long" (Potier:385), to be long. Meaning: "Where there is a long village."

Teaontiae
"The only place at the two waters."
   Te: denotes duality if followed by the affirmative (Potier:76); *ea*: "liqueur, eau" (Potier:454), water; *ontia*: affirmative of *ontion*, "a specific

place, the very site of, the one place" (Potier:424). Meaning: "The only place at the two waters." Note: this village is located at the entrance of Wye River; it is therefore between two lakes (Map 13).

Tequenonquiaye (Quieuindohian, Tequeunonoikuaye)
Has not been deciphered.

Tiondatsae
"The place at the kettles."
Ti: denotes many things, including "the place where" (Potier:104; Jones 1908:118); *ondatsa*: from *andatsa*, "chaudiere" (Potier:449), kettle; *e*: contraction of *ae*, denoting plurality of numbers (Potier:242). Meaning: "The place at the kettles," or, "La Chaudiere," or, "*Ekhiondast-saan*."

Toanche (Otouacha, Troenchain)
1. "Opposite the sand-white point" (Jones 1908:194).
2. "The sand-white point" (Jones 1908:194).

Tondakea (Tundatra, Etondatra, Tondakhra)
1. "The land gives out" (Jones 1908:54).
2. "Lands end" (Jones 1908:54).
Note: *Tondakea* is identical in meaning to *Taentoaton*.

Touaguainchain
Has not been deciphered.

c. Huron Place Names

Anaouites (Anaotte, Anaoisey) (Cranberry Lake)
"There the swarms of canoes being continually paddled about" (Jones 1908:204).

Anatari (Thora Island)
"The dry firewood island" (Jones 1908:205).

Ascensionis (Hope Island)
"Ascension Island". Huron name not known.

Chantie
1. "The place where one goes fishing."
2. "The place where one goes upstream."
1. and 2. *Chantie* could be transposed to *Achandi*: "remonter un riviere," or, "monter un riviere" (Potier:211), to go upstream; or, *Achenti*: "aller à la peche en tel lieu" (Potier:211), to go fishing at a certain place; *e*: "ad, apud", in.

306

Chion Kiara (Khionchiara) (Area along the eastward flowing part of the Severn River)
"There in the distance where the great sun rises" (Jones 1908:208).

Contarea (Lake Couchiching and Midland Park Lake)
"The Little Lake" (Jones 1908:74).

Ekaenouton Manitoulin Island)
"Where many things are washed up (littering) the shore" (Jones 1908:-200).

Ethahonra (Pefferlaw Brook or Black River)
"The channel into the meadows."
Etha: *Eta* or *Eθa* (Potier:23), "champ, prairie," (Potier:454), meadow; *ahonra*: "l'esophage" (Potier:447), throat, channel. Meaning: "The channel into the meadows," or, "the meadow channel."

Ethaionte (Holland Marsh)
"The arrival place at the meadows."
Etha: meadow (Potier:454); *ion*: "arriver" (Potier:314), to arrive; *te*: denotes place (Potier:76). Meaning: "The meadow arrival piace," or, "the arrival place at the meadow."

Ethaouatius Pagus (Etha ati) (North shore of Lake Simcoe area at the Lake Couchiching Narrows and east of them)
"The deeply indented meadow lands" (Jones 1908:201).

Etiaantarisati (Kempenfeldt Bay)
"The coming and going place on the very deep bay of the lake."
Eti: "aller ou venir en tel lieu" (Potier:378), to go or come in such a place; *a*: signifies "grandeur ou grosseur" (Potier:161), great; *ontar*: from *ontara*, *ontare*, or *atontara*, "lac ou mer" (Potier:61, 455), lake; *isati*: "heurter quelque chose, donner contre la toucher, lui donner q'attainte; etre enfonce, avoir des enfoncemens, des coins, enfonces" (Potier:398), a deep hollow or bay (literally). Meaning: "The great deep bay of the lake where one comes and goes," or, "the coming and going place on the very deep bay on the lake."

Etondatrateus Pagus (Northwestern tip of the Penetang Peninsula)
"Edge of the water and beach" (Jones 1908:56).

Gahoendoe Insula (Ahoendoe, Gahandoe, Gahuendoe, Gahoedoe) (Christian Island, Charity or St. Joseph's Island).
"There is an island in the lake" (Jones 1908:172).

Haskaont (Georgina Island)

"The place where meat and fish are stored."

askont: "retir de la viande, du poisson" (Potier:353), storage place of meat and fish. Meaning: "The place where meat and fish are stored."

Isiaragui (Wye, Mud Lake)
"The sunbeams dancing on the water" (Jones 1908:198).

Ouentarionk (Oentaronk, Oentarenk, Oentaronius) (Lake Simcoe)
1. "The fish spearing lake" (Jones 1908:203).
2. "The beautiful big lake."
2. *Oentar*: from *ontare*, "lac ou mer" (Potier:455), lake; *io*: "etre beau, bon, grand" (Potier:396),beautiful, good, greatness, grandeur, sublime; *nk, onk*: present indicative (Potier:63). Meaning: "The beautiful big lake."

Ondioe (Snake Island)
1. "The point of land where one arrives by water."
1. *Ondia*: "pointe de terre" (Potier:455), point of land; *oe*: could be a contraction of *oen*, signifying arrival at the water (Potier:404). Meaning: "The point of land where one arrives by water."
2. "Where one arrives at the lake's edge."
2. *ondi*: "l'eau arriver jusqu'a tel endroit," or, "arriver au bord de l'eau d'un lac d'une riviere" (Potier:402), to arrive at the edge of the water, or, the water comes up to this place; *oe*: the *o* signifies water (Potier:401), the *e* answers the question where. (See explanation for *oe* endings (Jones 1908:172-173). Meaning: "Where one arrives at the waters' edge (lake)."

Ondiontannen (Ondichaouan) (Giants Tomb Island)
"The island in view of our point" (Jones 1908:29).

Skiondechiara (Khiondechiara, Schiondekiara) (Beausoleil Island)
"The land to appear floating afar" (Jones 1908:207).

Tandehouaronnon (Lafontaine or Randolph Hill)
1. "The place of the sand dwellers" (Jones 1908:137).
2. "The place of the beaver skin people" (Jones 1908:137).

Tannenraki (Mouth of the Beaverton River)
"The place where the sun rises," or, "East".

T: signifying place; *annen*: asking the question where (Potier:88); *raki*: from *arak8i*, "designat partem horizontis in qua reventur" (Potier:325), designates part of the horizon where the sun rises. Meaning: "The place where the sun rises," or, "East".

Postscript to the translation of place-names.
Since the author is not a linguist he makes no pretense at having translated all the names correctly. He feels, however, that some of Jones' translations are not correct, or lend themselves to alternate interpretations. A translation of these names is a challenging job, and hopefully a qualified Iroquoian linguist will take up the task.

Appendix II

THE PRIMARY SOURCE MATERIAL: A DISCUSSION

Introduction

The major primary source materials dealing with the Huron can be divided into four convenient categories: first-hand travellers' descriptions, of which the works of Champlain, Sagard and the Jesuits are the most important; secondary contemporary accounts compiled from published works and interviews, such as the works of Du Creux and Le Clercq; published and manuscript maps dealing with the period; and, archaeological monographs.

1. Contemporary Accounts and Maps

The major primary sources dealing with the Huron stem from the writings of the explorer, trader, and coloniser, Samuel de Champlain, the Récollet friar Gabriel Sagard, and the Jesuit priests who had laboured among the Huron.

Champlain wrote a number of books (Champlain 1603; 1613; 1619; 1632; reprinted (1622-1636), of which his 1619 volume (Champlain 1929), revised in 1632 (Champlain 1932), has his most extensive observations on the Huron. There are several excellent biographies of Champlain, of which those by Bishop (1948) and Trudel (Brown 1966) deserve special mention. Champlain was an accurate observer of geographical detail and most of the material aspects of Huron culture. His observations on social, political and religious aspects of the Huron must be approached with caution; not only because he worked through interpreters, but also because of his strong religious convictions and firm belief in French social and political institutions. Nevertheless, his view of the Huron and other groups is essentially sympathetic, accounting for the excellent rapport he established with them and his proposals for Huron-French intermarriage (JR 5:211).

Sagard lived in Huronia among the *Attignaouantan* from 1623-24. His sojourn resulted in two books, *Le Grand Voyage* (Sagard 1939), first published in 1632, and the *Histoire* (Sagard 1866) published in 1636. The latter also includes a Huron dictionary, or phrase-book. Together with

Champlain's observations, the writings of Sagard depict the Huron before major culture changes occurred as a result of European contact. The best biographical sketch of Sagard is by Eccles (Brown 1966) and Wrong (Sagard 1939). A treatment on the role of the Récollets in Canada can be found in Jouve (1916).

Of all the early writers on Huronia, Sagard was perhaps the most sympathetic and understanding of what he saw. Tooker (1964:6) for example, calls him a "participant observer," one who "perhaps resembled most closely the modern anthropologist." Because Sagard could speak some Huron, his descriptions are much more complete than those of Champlain; and, in contrast to the Jesuits, his writings are almost free of moralising and lengthy descriptions of religious conversions. As a follower of St. Francis, Sagard was also interested in nature, and it is in his writings that we get the earliest and most complete descriptions of the vegetation and fauna of Huronia.

The Jesuits began their missionary work in Huronia in 1626, but did not establish a permanent mission until 1634. From that date to 1650 yearly accounts were published of the Huron mission, first by Fathers Jean de Brébeuf (1635-36) and François Le Mercier (1637-38), then by Jérôme Lalemant (1639-44) and finally by Paul Ragueneau (1646-50). *The Jesuit Relations and Allied Documents* were translated into English, annotated and meticulously indexed under the editorship of R.G. Thwaites (1896-1901). In 1959 the 73 volumes were reprinted, but unfortunately no re-editing took place. The majority of the information on the Huron lies in volumes seven to 40. Excellent biographical sketches on the Jesuits can be found in Brown (1966).

A great deal has been written about the usefulness of the *Relations* for ethnohistoric research and there seems little point in repeating it here (Jones 1908; Hunt 1940; Tooker 1964; Trigger 1969). Unlike Champlain and Sagard, who tried to set down a fairly concise account of Huron life, the Jesuits, with few exceptions, made no such attempt. The purpose of the *Relations* was primarily to present a report of the progress of the Church among the Huron. Yet in spite of the fact that the purpose of the *Relations* was not a description of Indian cultures, they contain the most complete information on Huron religion, mythology, government and law. They are weak to poor on Huron warfare, subsistence activities, aspects pertaining to settlement and anything relating to the natural environment.

There are a number of other primary sources dealing with the Huron, but they are of minor importance compared to Champlain, Sagard and the *Relations*. The most important of these are by Pierre Boucher (1883;

311

1896), first published in 1664 and François Gendron (1868), whose little volume appeared in 1660. Boucher had been Governor of Trois Rivières and Gendron a doctor; both had lived in Huronia. In 1664 the official Jesuit summary of the *Relations* was published (Du Creux 1951-52), covering the period from 1625 to 1658. Although the author, Father François Du Creux, had never been to Canada, in abridging the *Relations* he included some interview material from Jesuits who had returned to France. Another early compilation is a history by the Récollet Father Chrestien Le Clercq (1881), first published in 1691. Le Clercq's work is interesting for a contrasting view of the work of the Jesuits in Canada, and because he had some letters by Father Joseph Le Caron at his disposal. Le Caron had travelled to Huronia in 1615-16 with Champlain and went again in 1623-24. Some of his writings have been preserved by Jouve (1915); most have been lost.

Works of minor interest that make some reference to the Huron prior to their dispersal are by Charlevoix (1923), Hennepin (1903), La Hontan (Thwaites 1905), Lafitau (1724), and Radisson (Scull 1885; Adams 1961). Besides the phrase book by Sagard, the two most extensive published sources for a study of the Huron language are the *Elementa Grammaticae Huronicae* written in 1745, and the *Radices Huronicae* written in 1751, both by Father Pierre Potier (1918).

Thus far, four large-scale maps relating to Huronia have come to light. These are: Du Creux's inset map *Corographia Regionis Huronum* (*hodie desertae*), engraved in 1660; a map probably drawn by Bressani, *Huronum Explicata Tabula*, engraved in 1657; and two anonymous manuscript maps, *Corographie du Pays des Hurons*, and the *Description du Pays des Hurons, 1631* with the date corrected to read 1651. The latter two may have been drawn by Jérôme Lalemant and Jean de Brébeuf, respectively. Of these maps the *Corographie* is the most accurate; Du Creux's map appears to have been based on it. These maps are invaluable for reconstructing the distribution of villages and missions in Huronia. These maps, as well as the large-scale maps, have been discussed in detail by Heidenreich (1966; 1968).

2. Archaeological Sources

Archaeological work in Huronia related to Ontario as a whole, has been discussed by Kidd (1952). The following discussion will focus on some of the major work in the area, but cannot possibly cover all the work that has been undertaken, particularly since much of it has not been published.

Serious archaeological work in Huronia began near the turn of century with the extensive site surveys of Hunter (1889; 1898; 1899; 1901; 1902; 1903; 1906) and to a lesser extent Hammond (1904). The results of these surveys produced some 400 localities for which some archaeological material was recorded. One unfortunate aspect of these surveys is that the sites became public knowledge, leading to widespread looting. A more positive result of Hunter's work was its inclusion in the editorial notes of the Thwaites edition of the *Jesuit Relations* and Jones' (1908) massive study on the identification of Jesuit missions in the area. Recently Ridley (1947; 1966-68) has put site-surveying in Huronia on a more scientific and systematic basis.

In the twenties and most of the thirties, archaeological work in the area was in abeyance. In the late thirties W. J. Wintemberg of the National Museum of Canada began work on a site believed to be St. Ignace, the village where the Jesuits Brébeuf and G. Lalemant were martyred. Unfortunately, Wintemberg died before his work was completed. He did, however, prove to his own satisfaction that the site he had dug was not St. Ignace (Canada, National Museum, MSS Files). Wintemberg's doubts notwithstanding, work at the site was taken up and completed by W. Jury (Fox 1941; Jury and Fox 1947), with the assurance that the site was indeed St. Ignace: an identification that is at best dubious.

Interest in historic sites continued with Kidd's (1953) work on the Ossossane ossuary, Jury's (1955) work at St. Louis and the beginning of work at *Cahiagué* (McIlwraith 1947; Harris 1949). The most ambitious undertaking, however, was the excavation of the central Jesuit mission of Ste. Marie I, begun by the Royal Ontario Museum under the direction of K. Kidd (1949) and continued by W. Jury (1965). In 1971 a reconstruction of the mission was completed under the auspices of the Ontario Government, directed by W. Jury. Although the reconstruction is somewhat problematical, largely because it has failed to take Kidd's work into account (Kidd 1949; Russell 1965), it contains an excellent museum and archives. Recently work began at Ste. Marie II on Christian Island, the results of which have not been published (Carruthers 1965).

Published and unpublished reports on other sites in Huronia includes work on precontact sites by Jury (1948), Ridley (1952), Channen and Clarke (1965) and Noble (1968 and 1971), and contact sites by Kidd (1950), Emerson and Russell (1965), Tyyska (1968), Tyyska (1969), Latta (1971a) and Fox (1971). Work on Huron ossuaries is fragmentary; some of it is reported by Hammond (1924), Harris (1949), Kidd (1953), Jerkic (1969). Palaeoecological work, including faunal analysis (Bleakney 1958; Latta 1969; Latta 1971b; Savage 1971), soils and pollen analysis

313

(Cruickshank and Heidenreich 1969; Heidenreich *et al.* 1969 and 1971) has recently begun in Huronia.

One of the major problems that has occupied Ontario archaeologists is the question of Huron origins and migrations. Archaeological work on the problem began with MacNeish (1952) and has been continued by Emerson (1954; 1959; 1961; 1968), Emerson and Popham (1952), Ridley (1952; 1954; 1958; 1963), Wright (1966) and Noble (1968; 1969). The most comprehensive statements on the topic, including an attempt to reconcile the views of Emerson and Ridley are those of Wright (1966), Noble (1968) and Trigger (1970).

3. Secondary Sources

Secondary works on Huronia, based largely on the ethnohistoric sources, are numerous. No native group in Canada has been written about so extensively, and it is not possible to examine all the literature within the scope of this discussion. Early works, examining primarily the role of the missionaries among the Huron are by Shea (1855), Parkman (1867), Rochemonteix (1906), Jones (1908) and Crouse (1924). Some of the problems posed by these authors have been more recently examined by Trigger (1960; 1965; 1968). The French-Huron fur trade and its consequences is another topic that has received considerable attention (Biggar 1901; Innis 1962; Hunt 1940; Trigger 1965; 1968), as have topics relating the position of the Huron with respect to other Iroquoian groups (Fenton 1940; 1951; Trigger 1962; 1970). Huron mythology has been recorded by Barbeau (1915), corn growing and food production by Waugh (1916) and aspects of the geography of Huronia by Heidenreich (1967; 1971). Huron residence patterns have been examined by Richards (1967), property and land concepts by Herman (1956) and Snyderman (1951), while Wallace (1958) and Trigger (1963) have examined some of the psychosocial behaviour of the Huron.

The most complete works on the Huron are by Kinietz (1940), Tooker (1964) and Trigger (1969). Of these, Tooker's is a careful paraphrasing of the ethnohistoric sources and as such an excellent source book; while Kinietz's and Trigger's are an anthropological analysis of the Huron.

The greatest strength for studies on the Huron lies in the rich body of ethnohistoric material; the greatest weakness is the extent of the archaeological record to date. The archaeological work cited here is not really representative of the work that has been done on the Huron. The problem is that much is in field note form, or in inaccessible, preliminary, manuscript reports. This is particularly true for the potentially significant work

314

done by W. Jury at the precontact Forget site, the only village that has been completely excavated; the precontact Fournier site; and the years of work at *Cahiagué*, both excavated by the University of Toronto. It is doubtful if knowledge of the Huron can be much further advanced without concerted, problem-oriented archaeological research, the publication of that research, and its incorporation into studies that make use of the ethnohistorical material.

BIBLIOGRAPHY

Aberle, S. B., Watkins, J. H. and E. H. Pitney. 1940. "The Vital History of San Juan Pueblo." *Human Biology*, Vol. 12, No. 2, 1940, pp. 141-187.

Abler, R., Adams, J.S. and P. Gould 1971. *Spatial Organization: The Geographers View of the World*. Englewood Cliffs: Prentice Hall.

Adams, A. T. 1961. *The Explorations of Pierre Esprit Radisson*. Minneapolis: Ross and Haines Inc.

Ahlgren, I. F. and C. E. Ahlgren. 1960. "Ecological Effects of Forest Fires." *The Botanical Review*, Vol. 26, No. 4, 1960, pp. 483-533.

Aller, W. F. 1954. "Aboriginal Food Utilization of Vegetation by the Indians of the Great Lakes Region as recorded in the Jesuit Relations." *Wisconsin Archaeologist*, Vol. 35, No. 5, 1954, pp. 59-73.

Anderson, E. and W. L. Brown 1952. "The History of the Common Maize Varieties of the United States Corn Belt." *Agricultural History*, Vol. 26, No. 1, 1952, pp. 2-8.

Barbeau, C. M. 1915. *Huron and Wyandot Mythology*. Canada, Dept. of Mines, Geological Survey, Memoir No. 80. Ottawa.

Beckwith, S. L. 1954. "Ecological Succession on Abandoned Farm Lands and its Relationship to Wildlife Management." *Ecological Monographs*, Vol. 24, No. 4, 1954, pp. 349-376.

Bell, W. D. 1953. "The MacMurchie Site: A Petun Site in Grey County Ontario." Typewritten, M. S., 1953, pp. 1-98.

Bibliotheque Nationale 1892. *Catalogue des Documents Geographiques*. Paris.

Bidwell, P. W. and J. I. Falconer 1925. *History of Agriculture in the Northern United States, 1620-1860*. Washington: Carnegie Institution, Public. No. 358, 1925.

316

Biggar, H. P. 1901. *The Early Trading Companies of New France: A contribution to the history of commerce and discovery in North America.* Toronto: University of Toronto Press. ✕

Biggar, H. P. (ed.) 1922-1936. *The Works of Samuel de Champlain.* 6 Vols. Toronto: The Champlain Society, 1922, 1925, 1929, 1932, 1933, 1936.

Birket-Smith, K. 1963. *Primitive Man and His Ways.* Ch. 6; "Powhatan and Pamlico." New York: Mentor, 1963, pp. 157-178.

Bishop, M. 1948. *Champlain: The Life of Fortitude.* New York: Alfred A. Knopf. (Toronto: McClelland and Steward, 1963).

Bleakney, S. 1958. "The Significance of Turtle Bones from Archaeological Sites in Southern Ontario, and Quebec." *The Canadian Field Naturalist,* Vol. 72, No. 1, 1958, pp. 1-5.

Bogert, L. J., Briggs, G. M. and D. H. Calloway 1966. *Nutrition and Physical Fitness.* Philadelphia: Saunders.

Boucher, P. 1883. *Canada in the Seventeenth Century (1664).* Translated by E. L. Montizambert. Montreal: George E. Debarats and Co.

Boucher, P. 1896. "Histoire Véritable et Naturelle des Moeurs et Productions du Pays de la Nouvelle France (1664)." Sulte, B. (ed.). *Royal Society of Canada, Proceedings and Transactions.* Series 2, Vol. 2, 1896, Section 1, pp. 99-168.

Boyle, D. 1889. "The Land of Souls." *Appendix to the Report of the Minister of Education, Ontario, Ann. Rept. of the Canadian Institute,* 1889, pp. 4-15.

Bressani, Fr. F. J. 1653. *Breve Relatione.* Macerata.

Broek, J. O. M. and J. W. Webb 1968. *A Geography of Mankind.* New York: McGraw-Hill.

Brown, G. W. (ed.) 1966. *Dictionary of Canadian Biography.* Vol. 1. 1000-1700. Toronto: University of Toronto Press.

Brown, W. L. and E. Anderson 1947. "The Northern Flint Corns." *Annals of the Missouri Botanical Gardens,* Vol. 34, No. 1, 1947, pp. 1-28.

Bryson, R. A. and W. M. Wendland 1967. "Tentative Climatic Patterns For Some Late Glacial and Post-Glacial Episodes in Central North America." In: *Life, Land and Water;* W. J. Mayer-Oakes (ed.); Winnipeg: University of Manitoba Press, 1967, pp. 271-298.

Büsching, A. F. 1787. *Erdbeschreibung.* Vol. 1, Hamburg: Ernst Bohn.

317

Canada Department of Agriculture, and the Ontario Agricultural College 1962. *Report No. 29, Soil Survey of Simcoe County*. Guelph.

Canada Department of Agriculture, and the Ontario Agricultural College 1964. *Soil Associations of Southern Ontario*. Guelph.

Canada, National Museum, Division of Archaeology. Manuscript Files, Ontario County Section.

Canada, National Museum, Division of Archaeology. Manuscript Files, Simcoe County Section.

Canada, National Museum, Division of Archaeology. Manuscript Files, Victoria County Section.

Carruthers, P. J. 1965. "Preliminary Excavations at the Supposed Site of Ste. Marie II." (Unpublished, typewritten, M. S.), Toronto: Ontario Archives.

Champlain, S. de. 1859. *Brief Discours Des Choses Plus Remarquables Que Samuel Champlain De Brouage A Reconneues Aux Indes Occidentalles*. London: The Hakluyt Society.

Champlain, S. de. 1603. *Des Sauvages ou, Voyage de Samuel Champlain, de Brouage, fait en la France nouvelle, l'an mil six cens trois*. Paris.

Champlain S. de 1613. *Les Voyages Du Sieur de Champlain*. Paris.

Champlain, S. de 1619. *Voyages et Descouvertures Faites en la Nouvelle France, depuis l'année 1615 jusque a la fin de l'année 1618*. Paris.

Champlain, S. de 1632. *Les Voyages de la Nouvelle France Occidentale, Dicte Canada*. Paris.

Champlain, S. de 1922-1936. *The Works of Samuel de Champlain*. 6 Vols. (H. P. Biggar, ed.), Toronto: The Champlain Society, 1922, 1925, 1929, 1932, 1933, 1936.

Chang, K. C. 1958. "Study of the Neolithic Social Grouping: Examples from the New World." *American Anthropologist*, Vol. 60, April 1958, pp. 298-334.

Chang, K. C. 1967. *Rethinking Archaeology*. New York: Random House

Chang, K. C. (ed.) 1968. *Settlement Archaeology*. Palo Alto: National Press.

Channen, E. R. and N. D. Clarke 1965. "The Copeland Site." *National Museum of Canada, Anthropology Papers, No. 8*, Ottawa. 1965, pp. 27.

Chapman, L. J. and D. M. Brown 1966. *The Climates of Canada for Agriculture*. Dept. of Forestry and Rural Development, ARDA, Canada Land Inventory, Report No. 3, Ottawa.

Chapman, L. J. and D. F. Putnam 1937. "The Soils of South Central Ontario." *Scientific Agriculture*, Vol. 18, No. 4, 1937, pp. 161-197.

Chapman, L. J. and D. F. Putnam 1951. *The Physiography of Southern Ontario.* (1st edition), Toronto: University of Toronto Press.

Chapman, L. J. and D. F. Putnam 1966. *The Physiography of Southern Ontario.* (2nd edition), Toronto: University of Toronto Press.

Clark, J. G. D. 1945. "Farmers and Forests in Neolithic Europe." *Antiquity,* Vol. 19, No. 74, 1945, pp. , 57-71.

Cleland, C. E. 1966. *The Prehistoric Animal Ecology and Ethnozoology of the Upper Great Lakes Region.* Anthropology Papers, No. 29, Museum of Anthropology. Ann Arbour.

Cook, F. 1887. *Journals of the Military Expedition of Major General John Sullivan Against the Six Nations Indians in 1779.* Auburn.

Cook, S. F. 1955. "The Epidemic of 1830-1833 in California and Oregon." *University of California Publications in American Archaeology and Ethnology*, Vol. 43, 1955, pp. 303-326.

Cowgill, U. M. 1962. "An Agricultural Study of the Southern Maya Lowlands." *American Anthropologist.* Vol. 64, 1962, pp. 273-286.

Crouse, N. M. 1924. *Contributions of the Canadian Jesuits to the Geographical* X *Knowledge of New France, 1632-1675.* Ithaca: Cornell Publications.

Cruickshank, J. C. and C. E. Heidenreich 1969. "Pedological Investigations at the Huron Indian Village of Cahiagué." *The Canadian Geographer*, Vol. 13, No. 1, 1969, pp. 34-46.

Delabarre, E. B. and H. H. Wilder 1920. "Indian Corn-Hills in Massachusetts." *American Anthropologist*, Vol. 22, No. 3, 1920, pp. 203-225.

Devitt, O. E. 1943. "The Birds of Simcoe County, Ontario." *Transactions of the Royal Canadian Institute*, Vol. 24, Part 2, 1943, pp. 241-314.

Devitt, O. E. 1944. "The Birds of Simcoe County, Ontario." *Transactions of the Royal Canadian Institute*, Vol. 25, Part 1, 1944, pp. 29-116.

Dionne, N. E. 1963. *Champlain.* Toronto: University of Toronto Press.

319

Dobyns, H. F. 1966. "Estimating Aboriginal American Population: An Appraisal ot Techniques with a New Hemispheric Estimate." *Current Anthropology*, Vol. 7, .No. 4, 1966, pp. 395-416. Χ

Driver, H. E. 1964. *Indians of North America*. Chicago: University of Chicago Press.

Du Creux, F. 1664. *Historiae Canadensis seu Novae Franciae*. Paris.

Du Creux, F. 1951-1952. *History of Canada or New France*. 2 Vols. (J. B. Conacher, ed.; P. J. Robinson, transl.), Toronto: The Champlain Society.

Duffy, J. 1951. "Smallpox and the Indians in the American Colonies." *Bulletin of the History of Medicine*, Vol. 25, No. 4, 1951, pp. 324-341.

Dumond, D. E. 1961. "Swidden Agriculture and the Rise of Maya Civilization." *Southwestern Journal of Anthropology*. Vol. 17, No. 4, 1961, pp. 301-316.

Duncan, O. D. 1957. "The Measurement of Population Distribution." *Population Studies*, Vol. 11, July, 1957, pp. 27-45. Χ

Emerson, J. N. 1954. The Archaeology of the Ontario Iroquois. Ph. D. Dissertation, University of Chicago.

Emerson, J. N. 1959. "A Rejoinder Upon the MacNeish-Emerson Theory." *Pennsylvania Archaeologist*, Vol. 29, No. 2, 1959, pp. 3-11.

Emerson, J. N. 1961a. "Problems of Huron Origins." *Anthropologica*, Vol. 3, No. 2, 1961, pp. 181-201.

Emerson, J. N. et al., 1961b. *Cahiagué, 1961*. Public Lecture Series, University of Toronto Archaeological Field School at The Cahiagué Village Site, Simcoe County, Ontario, June 15-Aug. 15, 1961, p. 140.

Emerson, J. N. 1966. "The Payne Site: An Iroquoian Manifestation in Prince Edward County, Ontario." *National Museum of Canada, Contributions to Anthropology, 1963-1964*, Bulletin No. 206, Ottawa: 1966, pp. 126-257.

Emerson, J. N. 1968. "Understanding Iroquois Pottery in Ontario: A Rethinking." *Ontario Archaeological Society*, Special Publication, March, 1968.

Emerson, J. N. and R. E. Popham 1952. "Comments Upon the Huron and Lalonde Occupations of Ontario." *American Antiquity*, Vol. 18, No. 2, 1952, pp. 162-163.

320

Emerson, J. N. and W. Russell 1965. "The Cahiagué Village Palisade." Unpublished Report for the Archaeological and Historic Sites Board. University of Toronto, 1965, p. 33.

Encyclopédie ou Dictionnaire Raisonné Des Sciences Des Arts des Métiers. Tom 3, Paris, 1753.

Fenton, W. N. 1951. "Locality as a Basic Factor in the Development of X Iroquois Social Structure." *Bureau of American Ethnology*, Bulletin No. 149, 1951, pp. 39-54.

Fenton, W. N. 1940. "Problems Arising From the Historic North-Eastern Position of the Iroquois." *Smithsonian Miscellaneous Collections*, Vol. 100, pp. 159-251.

Ferguson, W. 1954. "Vegetable Growing." *Canada Department of Agriculture*. Publication No. 816, March 1954.

Flannery, K. V. (*et al*) 1967. "Farming Systems and Political Growth in Ancient Oaxaca." *Science*, Vol. 158, No. 3800, 1967, pp. 445-454.

Fowells, H. A. and R. E. Stephenson 1934. "The Effect of Burning on Forest Soils." *Soil Science*, Vol. 38, No. 3, 1934, pp. 175-181.

Fox, S. 1941. "St. Ignace, Canadian Altar of Martyrdom." *Transactions of the Royal Society of Canada*, Vol. 35, Series 3, Sect. 2, 1941, pp. 69-79.

Fox, W. A. 1971. "The Maurice Village Site BeHa-2: Lithic Analysis". In: Hurley, W. and C.E. Heidenreich (eds.), Palaeoecology and Ontario Prehistory. *Department of Anthropology, University of Toronto, Research Report No. 2*, pp. 116-136.

Funk, R. E. 1967. "Garoga: A Late Prehistoric Iroquois Village in the Mohawk Valley." In: Tooker, E. (ed.): *Iroquois Culture, History and Prehistory*, Albany: 1967, pp. 81-84.

Gabel, C. 1967. *Analysis of Prehistoric Economic Patterns*. New York: Holt, X Rhinehart and Winston.

Garrad, C. 1965. "The Rediscovery of a forgotten Ossuary in the Township of Nottawasaga, Ontario." *Bulletin of the Arch. Society of Western Ontario*. Vol. 2, No. 1, 1965, pp. 9-11.

Garrad, C. 1966. "A Survey of Lamont Creek in the Township of Nottawasaga, Ontario." *Archaeological Society of Western Ontario*, Research Paper No. 2, June 1966, p. 14.

Garrad, C. 1968. "Ontario Archaeology and Radiocarbon Dating." *Ontario Archaeological Society, Arch-Notes*, No. 68-4, April 1968, pp. 9-10.

Gendron F. 1868. *Quelques particularitez du pays des Hurons en la Nouvelle France, remarquées par le Sieur Gendron, docteur en médecine qui a demeuré dans ce pays-là fort longtemps.* Albany: J.G. Shea.

Gleason, H. A. 1958. *The New Britton and Brown Illustrated Flora of the Northeastern United States and Adjacent Canada.* 3 Vols. Lancaster: New York Botanical Gardens.

Gregory, S. 1963. *Statistical Methods and the Geographer.* Toronto: Longmans.

Griffin, J. B. 1961. "Some Correlations of Climatic and Cultural Change in Eastern North American Prehistory." *Annals of the New York Academy of Sciences*, Vol. 95, Article 1, 1961, pp. 710-717.

Guyan, W. U. 1954. *Mensch und Urlandschaft der Schweiz.* Zürich: Büchergilde Gutenberg.

Haggett, P. 1965. *Locational Analysis in Human Geography.* London: Edward Arnold. Χ

Hammond, J. H. 1904. "North and South Orillia." *Appendix to the Report of the Minister of Education, Ontario. Annual Archaeological Report*, 1904, pp. 77-86.

Hammond, J. H. 1924. "Exploration of Ossuary Burial of the Huron Nation, Simcoe County". *Appendix to the Report of the Minister of Education, Ontario. Annual Archaeological Report*, 1924, pp. 95-102.

Harris, R. I. n. d. "Notes on the Paleopathology of the Skeletal remains of Huron Indians from the ossuary at Cahiagué opened in 1946." Report to Prof. T. F. McIlwraith, Dept. of Anthropology, University of Toronto, n. d..

Harris, R. I. 1949. "Osteological Evidence of Disease Amongst the Huron Indians." *University of Toronto Medical Journal*, Vol. 17, No. 2, 1949, pp. 71-75.

Harris, W. R. 1893. *History of the Early Missions in Western Canada.* Toronto: Hunter Rose.

Harrisse, H. 1872. *Notes pour servir A L'Histoire, A la Bibliographie et a la Cartographie de la Nouvelle-France et des Pays Adjacents, 1545-1700.* Paris.

322

Hayes, C. F. 1967. "The Longhouse at the Cornish Site." In: Tooker, E. (ed.): *Iroquois Culture, History and Prehistory*, Albany: 1967, pp. 91-97.

Heagerty, J. J. 1928. *Four Centuries of Medical History in Canada*, Vol. I. Toronto: MacMillan.

Heidenreich, C. E. 1963. "The Huron Occupance of Simcoe County, Ontario." *The Canadian Geographer*, Vol. 7, No. 3, 1963, pp. 131-144.

Heidenreich, C. E. 1966. "Maps Relating to the First Half of the 17th Century and their Use in Determining the Location of Jesuit Missions in Huronia." *The Cartographer*, Vol. 3, No. 2, 1966, pp. 103-126.

Heidenreich, C. E. 1968. "A New Location for Carhagouha, Récollet Mission in Huronia." *Ontario Archaeology*, Publication No. 10, 1968, pp. 39-46.

Heidenreich, C. E. 1971."The Natural Environment of Huronia and Huron Seasonal Activities". In: Schott, C. (ed.), *Beiträge Zur Kulturgeographie von Kanada*. Marburger Geographische Schriften, Heft 50, Marburg, 1971, pp. 103-116.

Heidenreich, C. E. (*et al.*) 1969. "Maurice and Robitaille Sites: Environmental Analysis". In: Hurley, W. and C. E. Heidenreich (eds.), Palaeoecology and Ontario Prehistory. *Department of Anthropology, University of Toronto, Research Report No. 1*, pp. 112-154.

Heidenreich, C. E. (*et al.* 1971. "Soil and Environmental Analysis at the Robitaille Site". In: Hurley, W. and C. E. Heidenreich (eds.), Palaeoecology and Ontario Prehistory. *Department of Anthropology, University of Toronto, Research Report No. 2*, pp. 179-237.

Hennepin, L. 1903. *A New Discovery of a Vast Country in America*. Thwaites, R. G. (ed.), 2 Vols., Chicago.

Herman, M. W. 1956. "The Social Aspects of Huron Property." *American Anthropologist*, Vol. 58, No. 6, 1956, pp. 1044-1058.

Hill, A. F. 1952. *Economic Botany*. New York: McGraw-Hill.

Hinsdale, W. B. 1928. "Indian Corn Culture in Michigan." *Michigan Academy of Science Arts and Letters*, Vol. 8. 1928, pp. 31-49.

Houghton, F. 1916. "The Characteristics of Iroquois Village Sites in Western New York." *American Anthropologist*, Vol. 18, 1916, pp. 508-520.

Howells, W. W. 1960. "Estimating Population Numbers through Archaeological and Skeletal Remains." In: Heizer, R. F. and S. F. Cook (eds.); *The Application of Quantitative Methods in Archaeology*. Viking Fund Public. in Anthropology No. 28, Chicago: Quadrangle, 1960, pp. 158-185.

Hubbs, C. L. and K. F. Lagler 1947. *Fishes of the Great Lakes Region*. Ann Arbor: University of Michigan Press.

Hunt, G. T. 1940. *The Wars of the Iroquois*. Madison: University of Wisconsin Press. (Reprinted 1960).

Hunter, A. F. 1889. "French Relics from the Village Sites of the Hurons." *Appendix to the Report of the Minister of Education, Ontario. Ann. Rept. of the Canadian Institute, 1889*, pp. 42-46.

Hunter, A. F. 1898. "Sites of Huron Villages in the Township of Tiny (Simcoe County)." *Appendix to the Rept. of the Minister of Education, Ontario. Ann. Arch. Rept.*, 1898, pp. 5-42.

Hunter, A. F. 1899. "Notes on Sites of Huron Villages in the Township of Tay." *Appendix to the Report of the Minister of Education, Ontario. Ann. Archaeological Report*, 1899, pp. 51-82.

Hunter, A. F. 1901. "Notes on Sites of Huron Villages in the Township of Medonte." *Appendix to the Rept. of the Minister of Education, Ontario. Am. Arch. Rept.*, 1901, pp. 56-100.

Hunter, A. F. 1902. "Notes on Sites of Huron Villages in the Township of Oro, Simcoe County, Ontario." *Appendix to the Rept. of the Minister of Education, Ontario. Ann. Arch. Rept.*, 1902, pp. 153-183.

Hunter, A. F. 1903. "Indian Village Sites in North and South Orillia Townships." *Appendix to the Rept. of the Minister of Education, Ontario. Ann. Arch. Rept.*, 1903, pp. 105-125.

Hunter, A. F. 1906. "Survey of Village Sites in the Townships of Flos and Vespra." *Appendix to the Rept. of the Minister of Education, Ontario. Ann. Arch. Rept.*, 1906, pp. 19-56.

Hunter, A. F. 1911. "Historic Sites of Tay." *Bulletin of the Simcoe Pioneer and Historical Society*. November, 1911, Barrie.

Hunter, A. F. 1948. *A History of Simcoe County*. Barrie: Historical Committee of Simcoe County.

Hurley, W. M. and C. E. Heidenreich (eds.) 1969. Palaeoecology and Ontario Prehistory. *Dept. of Anthropology, University of Toronto, Research Report No. 1*.

Hurley, W. M. and C. E. Heidenreich (eds.) 1971. Palaeoecology and Ontario Prehistory II. *Department of Anthropology, University of Toronto, Research Report No. 2.*

Ingham, K. W. and Z. Kunikowska-Koniuszy 1965. The Distribution, Character and Basic Properties of Cherts in Southwestern Ontario. *Dept. of Highways, Ontario, Report No.* RB106, December, 1965, p. 35.

Innis, H. A. 1930. *The Fur Trade in Canada.* Toronto: University of Toronto Press. (Reprinted 1962)

Iversen, J. 1956. "Forest Clearance in the Stone Age." *Scientific American,* Vol. 194, No. 3, 1956, pp. 36-41.

Jameson, J. F. (ed.) 1909. *Original Narratives of Early American History:* Ⅹ *Narratives of New Netherlands, 1609-1664.* New York: Barnes and Nobel.

Jerkic, S. 1969. "The Maurice Ossuary, BeHa-1". In: Hurley, W. and C. E. Heidenreich (eds.), Palaeoecology and Ontario Prehistory. *Department of Anthropology, University of Toronto, Research Report No. 1,* pp. 49-61.

Johnston, C. M. (ed.) 1964. *The Valley of the Six Nations.* Toronto: The Champlain Society.

Jones, Rev. A. E. 1902. "Identification of St. Ignace II and of Ekarenniondi." *Appendix to the Rept. of the Minister of Education, Ontario. Ann. Arch. Rept..,* 1902, pp. 92-136.

Jones, Rev. A. E. 1908. "8endake Ehen" or "Old Huronia." *Ontario Bureau of Archives, Fifth Report,* Toronto.

Jouve, O. M. 1915. *Les Franciscains et le Canada: L'établissement de la foi.* Québec.

JR See: Thwaites, R. G. (ed.). *The Jesuit Relations and Allied Documents.*

Jury, E. M. 1963. "Indian Village and Mission Sites of Huronia." *Canadian Geographical Journal,* Vol. 67, No. 3, 1963, pp. 94-103.

Jury, E. M. 1967. "Toanché." *Canadian Geographical Journal.* Vol. 74, No. 2, 1967, pp. 40-45.

Jury, W. 1948. "Flanagan Prehistoric Huron Village Site." *University of Western Ontario, Museum of Indian Archaeology,* Bulletin No. 6, 1948.

325

Jury, W. and S. Fox 1947. "St. Ignace, Canadian Altar of Martyrdom." *Transactions of the Royal Society of Canada*, Vol. 41, Series 3, Sect. 2, 1947, pp. 55-78.

Jury, W. and E. M. Jury 1955. "Saint Louis: Huron Indian Village and Jesuit Mission Site." *University of Western Ontario, Museum of Indian Archaeology*, Bulletin No. 10, 1955, pp. 1-76.

Jury, W. and E. M. Jury 1965. *Sainte Marie Among the Hurons*. Toronto: Oxford.

Kalm, P. 1935. "Pehr Kalm's Description of Maize." (Larsen, E. L., transl.), *Agricultural History*, Vol. 9, No. 2, 1935, pp. 98-117.

Kalm, P. 1964. *Travels in North America by Peter Kalm*. New York: Dover.

Kenyon, W. A. 1966. "Champlain's Fish-Weir." *Archaeological Newsletter, N. S., No. 8, Jan. 1966; Royal Ontario Museum, Toronto, mimeo.*

Kidd, K. E. 1949,a. *The Excavation of Ste. Marie* I. Toronto: University of Toronto Press.

Kidd, K. E. 1949,b. "The Identification of French Mission Sites in the Huron Country: A Study in Procedure." *Ontario History*, Vol. 41, No. 2, 1949, pp. 89-94.

Kidd, K. E. 1950. "Orr Lake Pottery." *Royal Canadian Institute, Transactions*, Vol. 28, Part 2, 1950, pp. 165-186.

Kidd, K. E. 1952. "Sixty Years of Ontario Archaeology". In: Griffin, J. B. (ed.), *Archeology of the Eastern United States*. Chicago: University of Chicago Press, pp. 71-97.

Kidd, K. E. 1953. "The Excavation and Identification of a Huron Ossuary." *American Antiquity*, Vol. 18, No. 4, 1953, pp. 359-379.

Kinietz, W. V. 1940. *The Indians of the Western Great Lakes*. Ann Arbour: University of Wisconsin Press.

Kivekäs, J. 1941. "Influence of shifting cultivation with burning upon some properties of the soil." *Soils and Fertilizers*, Vol. 4, 1941, p. 194.

Kohn, C. F. 1954. "Settlement Geography." In: James, P. E. and C. F. Jones (eds.): *American Geography: Inventory and Prospect*. Syracuse: Syracuse University Press, 1954, pp. 125-141.

Kroeber, A. L. 1934. "Native American Population." *American Anthropologist*, Vol. 36, No. 1, 1934, pp. 1-25.

Kroeber, A. L. 1939. "Cultural and Natural Areas of Native North America." *University of California Publications in American Archaeology and Ethnology*, Vol. 38, Berkeley, 1939.

Lafitau, J. F. 1724. *Moeurs des Sauvages Ameriquains*. Paris.

Laidlaw, G. E. 1899. "North Victoria County." *Appendix to the Report of the Minister of Education, Ontario. Ann. Arch. Rept.*, 1899, pp. 41-50.

Laidlaw, G. E. 1901. "Notes on North Victoria Village Sites." *Appendix to the Report of the Minister of Education, Ontario. Ann. Arch. Rept.*, 1901, pp. 100-108.

Laidlaw, G. E. 1903. "Victoria County." *Appendix to the Report of the Minister of Education, Ontario. Ann. Arch. Rept.*, 1903, pp. 101-102.

Laidlaw, G. E. 1912. "List of Village Sites in Victoria County." *Appendix to the Report of the Minister of Education, Ontario. Ann. Arch. Rept.*, 1912, pp. 62-69.

Laidlaw, G. E. 1917. "Indian Village Sites-Victoria County and Vicinity, Recorded since 1912." *Appendix to the Minister of Education, Ontario. Ann. Arch. Rept.*, 1917, pp. 1-15.

Lamb, H. H. 1963. "On the Nature of Certain Climatic Epochs which Differed from the Modern (1900-1939) Normal." In: *Changes of Climate*, Proceedings of the Rome Symposium organized by Unesco and the World Meteorological Organization. UNESCO: 1963, pp. 125-150.

Latta, M. A. 1969. "Archeomalacology in Southern Ontario". In: Hurley, W. and C. E. Heidenreich (eds.), Palaeoecology and Ontario Prehistory, *Department of Anthropology, University of Toronto, Research Report No. 1*, pp. 104-112.

Latta, M. A. 1971a. "Archaeology of the Penetang Peninsula". In: Hurley, W. and C. E. Heidenreich (eds.), Palaeoecology and Ontario Prehistory. *Department of Anthropology, University of Toronto, Research Report No. 2*, pp. 137-165.

Latta, M. A. 1971b. "Snails From Four Ontario Sites". In: Hurley, W. and C. E. Heidenreich (eds.), Palaeoecology and Ontario Prehistory. *Department of Anthropology, University of Toronto, Research Report No. 2*, pp. 95-115.

Lawrence, J., Gavillier, M. and J. Morris 1909. "Exploration of Petun Indian Village Sites." *Huron Institute Papers and Records*, Vol. 1, Collingwood: 1909, pp. 11-18.

Le Blant, R. and R. Baudry 1967. *Nouveaux Documents sur Champlain et son époque.* Vol. 1, 1560-1622. Ottawa: Public Archives of Canada, Public. No. 15.

LeClair, E. E. and H. K. Schneider 1968. *Economic Anthropology: Readings in Theory and Analysis.* New York: Holt, Rinehart and Winston.

Le Clercq, C. 1691. *Nouvelle Relation de la Gaspésie.* Paris.

Le Clercq, C. 1691. Premier Etablissement de la Foy dans la Nouvelle France. 2 Vols. Paris.

Le Clercq, C. 1881. *The First Establishment of the Faith in New France.* 2 Vols. (J. G. Shea, ed.), New York.

Lee, T. E. 1958. "The Parker Earthwork, Corunna, Ontario." *Pennsylvania Archaeologist*, Vol. 28, No. 1, 1958, pp. 3-30.

Lee, T. E. 1965. *Archaeological Investigations at Lake Abitibi, 1964.* Centre d'Etudes Nordiques Travaux Divers, No. 10, Université Laval, 1965, p. 55.

Lescarbot, M. 1911. *The History of New France.* Vol. 2. (Grant, W. L. and H. P. Biggar, eds.), Toronto: The Champlain Society.

Logier, E. B. S. 1937. *The Amphibians of Ontario.* Toronto: Royal Ontario Museum of Zoology Handbook. No. 3.

McKay, H. H. 1963. *Fishes of Ontario.* Toronto: Dept. of Lands and Forests.

MacLeod, W. C. 1928. *The American Indian Frontier.* New York: A. A. Knopf.

MacNeish, R. S. 1952. "Iroquois Pottery Types." *National Museum of Canada, Bulletin* No. 124, Ottawa; 1952, p. 166.

Marcel, G. 1885. *Cartographie de la Nouvelle France supplement à l'ouvrage de M. Harrisse.* Paris.

Martin, Fr. F. 1848. "La Destruction des Hurons." In: *Album Litéraire de la Minerve.* Montreal: Dec., 1848.

Martin, A. C., Zim, H. S. and A. L. Nelson 1951. *American Wildlife and Plants: A Guide to Wildlife Food Habits.* New York: Dover.

McIlwraith, T. F. 1947. "On the Location of Cahiagué." *Transactions of the Royal Society of Canada*, Vol. 41, Series 3, Sect. 2, 1947, pp. 99-102.

Mead, W. R. 1953. *Farming in Finland*. London: Athlone Press.

Mooney, J. 1928. "The Aboriginal Population of America North of Mexico." *Smithsonian Miscellaneous Collections*, Vol. 80, No. 7, 1928, pp. 1-40.

Morgan, L. H. 1962. *League of the Iroquois*. New York: Corinth Books.

Morgan, L. H. 1965. *Houses and House-Life of the American Aborigines*. Chicago: University of Chicago Press.

Murdock, G. P. 1949. *Social Structure*. New York: MacMillan.

Naroll, R. 1956. "A Preliminary Index of Social Development." *American Anthropologist*, Vol. 58, No. 4, 1956, pp. 687-715.

Naroll, R. 1962. "Floor Area and Settlement Population." *American Antiquity*, Vol. 27, No. 4, 1962, pp. 587-589.

Narr, K. J. 1956. "Early Food Producing Populations." In: Thomas, W. L. (ed.), *Man's Role in Changing the Face of the Earth*. Chicago: University of Chicago Press, 1956, pp. 134-151.

Noble, W. C. 1968. Iroquois Archaeology and the Development of Iroquois Social Organization, 1000-1650 A.D. Ph.D. Dissertation, University of Calgary.

Noble, W. C. 1969. "Some Social Implications of the Iroquois 'In Situ' Theory." *Ontario Archaeology*, No. 13, 1969, pp. 16-28.

Noble W. C. 1971. "The Sopher Celt: An Indicator of Early Protohistoric Trade in Huronia". *Ontario Archaeology*, No. 16, pp. 42-47.

O'Callaghan, E. B. (ed.) 1848. *Documents Relating to the Colonial History of the State of New York*. Vol. I, Albany: Weed Parsons.

Ontario Department of Agriculture n. d.*Ontario Soils: Physical, Chemical and Biological Properties and Principles of Soil Management*. Public. No. 492, Ontario Agric. College, Guelph.

Ontario Department of Agriculture n. d. -a. "Let's Look at Corn." *Ontario Dept. of Agriculture, Public. No. 13*, Toronto.

Ontario Department of Agriculture 1951-1960. *Agricultural Statistics*. Toronto.

Ontario Department of Agriculture 1952. *Ontario Soils, Their Use, Management and Improvement*. Bulletin No. 492, Toronto: Sept. 1952.

Ontario Department of Lands and Forests (MSS., Book #405). "Goesman, J.: Survey of Flos Township, Fall of 1821."

Ontario Department of Lands and Forests (MSS., Book #526). "Chewett, J. G.: Field Notes for the Township of Medonte, June 30, 1820."

Ontario Department of Lands and Forests (MSS., Book #560). "Chewett, J. G.: Field Notes for the Township of Oro, June 1, 1820."

Ontario Department of Lands and Forests (MSS., Book #572). "Wilmot, S.: Survey of the Penetanguishene Road, August, 1811."

Ontario Department of Lands and Forest (MSS., Book #578). "Wilmot, S.: Survey of the Penetanguishene Road, August 31, 1811."

Ontario Department of Lands and Forests (MSS., Book #573). "Chewett, J. G.: Field Notes for the Townships of North and South Orillia, Sept. 16, 1820."

Ontario Department of Lands and Forests (MSS., Book #652). "Chewett, J. G.: Field Notes for the Township of Tay, Sept. 16, 1820."

Ontario Department of Lands and Forests (MSS., Book #665). "Goesman, J.: Field Notes for a Survey of Tiny Township, Sept., 1822."

Ontario Department of Lands and Forests (MSS., Book #703). "Chewett, J. G.: Field Notes for the Township of Vespra, June 30, 1820."

Ontario Department of Lands and Forests (MSS., Book #753). "Wilmot, S.: Diary of a Survey of the Penetanguishene Road, March 31, 1808."

Ontario Legislature 1953. *Report of the Select Committee of the Ontario Legislature on Lake Levels of the Great Lakes*. Toronto.

Orillia Historical Society 1966. *Orillia Portraits*. Vol. 1, Barrie: 1966, p. 92.

Parker, A. C. 1910. "Iroquois Uses of Maize and other Food Plants." *New York State Museum Bulletin, No. 144*, November, 1910, pp. 5-119.

Parker, A. C. 1916. "The Origin of the Iroquois as Suggested by Their Archaeology" *American Anthropologist*, Vol. 18, 1916, pp. 479-507.

Parker, A. C. 1920. "The Iroquois Occupation of New York State." In: The Archaeological History of New York. *New York State Museum Bulletin, No's. 235-236*, July-August, 1920.

Parkman, F. 1867. *The Jesuits in North America*. Boston: Little, Brown. (Reprinted 1963).

Pendergast, J. F. 1962. "The Crystal Rock Site, an early Onondaga-Oneida site in Eastern Ontario." *Pennsylvania Archaeologist*, Vol. 32, No. 1, pp. 21-34.

Pendergast, J. F. 1963. "The Payne Site." *National Museum of Canada, Contributions to Anthropology*, 1961-1962, Bulletin No. 193, Ottawa: 1963, pp. 1-27.

Pendergast, J. F. 1966. "Three Prehistoric Iroquois Components in Eastern Ontario." *National Museum of Canada*, Bulletin No. 208.

Pendergast, J. F. 1969. "The MacDougald Site." *Ontario Archaeology*, No. 13, pp. 29-53.

Peterson, R. L. 1966. *The Mammals of Eastern Canada*. Toronto: Oxford University Press.

Piggott, S. 1965. *Ancient Europe.* Chicago: Aldine.

Popham, R. E. 1950. "Late Huron Occupations of Ontario: An Archaeological Survey of Innisfil Township." *Ontario History*, Vol. 42, No. 2, 1950, pp. 81-90.

Potier, P. 1745. "Elementa Grammaticae Huronicae." Photocopy publ. by: *Ontario Bureau of Archives, 15th Report*. Toronto: 1918-1919.

Putnam, D. F. and L. J. Chapman 1938. "The Climate of Southern Ontario." *Scientific Agriculture*, Vol. 18, No. 8, 1938, pp. 401-446.

Quimby, G. I. 1960. *Indian Life in the Upper Great Lakes*. Chicago: University of Chicago Press.

Quimby, G. I. 1966. *Indian Culture and European Trade Goods*. Madison: University of Wisconsin Press.

Richards, C. E. 1967. "Huron and Iroquois Residence Patterns 1600-1650." In: *Iroquois Culture, History and Prehistory*, Tooker, E. (ed.), The University of the State of N. Y., The State Education Department, N. Y. State Museum and Science Service. Albany: 1967, pp. 51-56.

Ridley, F. 1947. "In Search for Ossossane and its Environs." *Ontario Hist. Society, Papers and Records*, Vol. 39, 1947, pp. 7-14.

Ridley, F. 1952. "The Huron and Lalonde Occupations of Ontario." *American Antiquity*, Vol. 17, No. 3, 1952, pp. 197-210.

Ridley, F. 1952 b. "The Fallis Site." *American Antiquity*, Vol. 18, No. 1, 1952, pp. 7-14.

Ridley, F. 1954. "The Frank Bay Site, Lake Nipissing, Ontario." *American Antiquity*, Vol. 20, No. 1, 1954, pp. 40-50.

Ridley, F. 1958. "Did the Hurons Really Migrate North from the Toronto Area?" *Pennsylvania Archaeologist*, Vol. 28, 1958, pp. 143-144.

Ridley, F. 1961. "The Lake Superior Site at Michipicoten." *Pennsylvania Archaeologist*, Vol. 31, No. 3-4, 1961, pp. 131-147.

Ridley, F. 1963. "The Ontario Iroquoian Controversy." *Ontario History*, Vol. 55, No. 1, 1963, pp. 49-59.

Ridley, F. 1966. Report On Archaeological Sites in Huronia, 1966. Dept. of Public Records and Archives, Toronto. M.S.S. Files.

Ridley, F. 1967. Report On Archaeological Sites in Huronia, 1967. Dept. of Public Records and Archives, Toronto. M.S.S. Files.

Ridley, F. 1968. Report On Archaeological Sites in Huronia, 1968. Dept. of Public Records and Archives, Toronto. M.S.S. Files.

Ritchie, W. A. 1956. "Prehistoric Settlement Patterns in Northeastern North America." In: Willey, G. R. (ed.): *Prehistoric Settlement Patterns in the New World*. New York: Viking Fund Public., No. 23, pp. 72-80.

Ritchie, W. A. 1965. *The Archaeology of New York State*. New York: Natural History Press, Garden City.

Robinson, P. J. and J. B. Conacher (eds.) 1951-1952. *Du Creux: History of Canada or New France*. 2 Vols. Toronto: The Champlain Society.

Rochemonteix, C. de 1906. *Les Jésuites et la Nouvelle France au XVIIe siècle.* 3 Vols., Paris.

Rose, M. S. 1939. *The Foundations of Nutrition*. New York: MacMillan.

Rowe, J. S. 1959. *Forest Regions of Canada*. Canada Dept. of Northern Affairs and National Resources, Forestry Branch, Bulletin #123, Ottawa.

Russell, E. W. 1961. *Soil Conditions and Plant Growth*. New York: J. Wiley.

Russell, W. A. 1965. "A Mill at Sainte Marie I." *Ontario Archaeology*, Series B, No. 3, Public. No. 8, 1965, pp. 11-17.

Russell, W. A. 1967. "Report on the Fournier Site." *Ontario Archaeological Society, Arch-Notes*, No. 67-9, November, 1967, pp. 1-2.

Sagard, Fr. Gabriel. 1632. *Le Grand Voyage du Pays des Hurons*. Paris.

Sagard, F. Gabriel 1636. *Histoire du Canada et Voyages que les Freres Mineures Recollects y ont faicts pour la conversion des Infidels*. Paris.

Sagard, Fr. Gabriel 1866. *Histoire du Canada et Voyages que les Freres Mineures Recollets y ont faicts pour la conversion des Infidelles depuis l'an 1615, avec un dictionnaire de la langue huronne* (1636). Paris: Edwin Tross.

Sagard, Fr. Gabriel 1939. *The Long Journey to the Country of the Hurons*. (G. M. Wrong, ed.; H. H. Langton, transl.), Toronto: The Champlain Society.

Sahlins, M. D. 1968. *Tribesmen*. Englewood Cliffs: Prentice Hall.

Savage, H. 1971. "Faunal Analysis of the Robitaille (BeHa-3) and Maurice Sites (BeHa-2)". In: Hurley, W. and C. E. Heidenreich (eds.), Palaeoecology and Ontario Prehistory. *Department of Anthropology, University of Toronto, Research Report No. 2*, pp. 116-179.

Scott, W. B. 1954. *Freshwater Fishes of Eastern Canada*. Toronto: University of Toronto Press.

Scull, G. D. (ed.) 1885. *The Voyages of Peter Esprit Radisson, 1652-1684*. Boston: Prince Society.

Schott, C. 1936. *Landnahme und Kolonisation in Canada am Beispiel Südontarios*. Kiel: Schmidt und Klaunig.

Shaw, G. 1942. "Brother Sagard's Huronian Triangle." *Culture*, Vol. 3, 1942, pp. 17-30.

Shea, J. G. 1855. *History of the Catholic Missions among the Indians*. New York.

Shea, J. G. (ed.) 1881. *Le Clercq: First Establishment of the Faith in New France*. 2 Vols. New York: J. G. Shea.

Shelford, V. E. 1963. *The Ecology of North America*. Urbana: University of Illinois Press.

Smith, R. E. F. 1959. *The Origins of Farming in Russia*. Paris: Mouton and Co.

Snyder, L. I. 1951. *Ontario Birds*. Toronto: Clarke, Irwin and Co.

Snyderman, G. S. 1951. "Concepts of Land Ownership Among the Iroquois and their Neighbours." In: *Symposium on Local Diversity in Iroquois Culture*. Bureau of American Ethnology Bulletin No. 149, Washington, 1951, pp. 15-34.

Soper, J. H. 1949. *The Vascular Plants of Southern Ontario*. Dept. of Botany, University of Toronto, and the Federation of Ontario Naturalists, Toronto: March, 1949.

Spiegel, M. R. 1961. *Theory and Problems of Statistics*. New York: Schaum.

Sprague, F. G. and W. E. Larson 1966. "Corn Production." *United States Dept. of Agriculture*, Agricultural *Handbook No. 322*, Washington: November, 1966, p. 36.

Steensberg, A. 1957. "Some Recent Danish Experiments in Neolithic Agriculture." *Agricultural Historical Review*. Vol. 5, Pt. 2, 1952, pp. 66-73.

Sterba, G. 1963. *Freshwater Fishes of the World*. New York: Viking Press.

Steward, J. H. 1949. "The Native Population of South America." In: *Handbook of South American Indians*, Vol. 5, J. H. Steward (ed.), Bureau of American Ethnology, Bulletin No. 143, 1949.

Stockhouse, E. J. and M. W. Corl 1962. "Discovery of the Sheep Rock Shelter." *Pennsylvania Archaeologist*, Vol. 33, No. 1, 1962, pp. 1-13.

Stuiver, M. and H. E. Suess 1967. "On the Relationship Between Radiocarbon Dates and True Sample Ages." *Radiocarbon*, Vol. 8, 1966, pp. 534-540.

Taverner, P. A. 1919. "Birds of Eastern Canada." *Canada, Dept. of Mines, Geological Survey Memoir No. 104*, Ottawa, 1919.

Taylor, W. P. (ed.) 1956. *The Deer of North America*. Harrisburg and Washington: Stackpole Co. and Wildlife Management Institute.

Thompson, D. 1962. *David Thompson's Narrative, 1784-1812*. (R. Glover, ed.), The Champlain Society: Toronto.

Thompson, L. M. 1952. *Soils and Soil Fertility*. New York: McGraw-Hill.

Thomson, D. W. 1966 *Men and Meridians*. Vol. 1, Ottawa: The Queens Printer.

Thwaites, R. G. (ed.) (1899). *The Jesuit Relations and Allied Documents*. 73 Vols. Cleveland: Burrows.

Thwaites, R. G. (ed.) 1903. *Hennepin: A New Discovery of a Vast Country in America*. 2 Vols. (First edition, 1699). Chicago.

Thwaites, R. G. (ed.) 1905. *New Voyages to North America by the Baron Lahontan, Reprinted from the English edition of 1703*. 2 Vols. Chicago.

Thwaites, R. G. (ed.) 1959. *The Jesuit Relations and Allied Documents*. 73 Vols. New York: Pageant.

Tooker, E. 1964. *An Ethnography of the Huron Indians, 1615-1649*. Smithsonian Institution, Bureau of American Ethnology Bulletin No. 190, Washington.

Trelease, A. W. (ed.) 1960. *Indian Affairs in Colonial New York: The 17th Century*. Ithaca: Cornell University Press.

Trigger, B. G. 1960. "The Destruction of Huronia: A Study in Economic and Cultural Change, 1609-1650." *Transactions of the Royal Canadian Institute*, No. 68, Vol. 33, Oct., 1960, pp. 14-45.

Trigger, B. C. 1962. "The Historic Location of the Hurons." *Ontario History*, Vol. 54, No. 2, pp. 137-148.

Trigger, B. G. 1963 a. "Settlement as an Aspect of Iroquoian Adaptation at the Time of Contact." *American Anthropologist*, Vol. 65, 1963, pp. 86-101.

Trigger, B. G. 1963 b. "Order and Freedom in Huron Society". *Anthropologica*, Vol. 5, No. 2, 1963, pp. 151-169.

Trigger, B. G. 1966. "Comments on Dobyns: Estimating Aboriginal Population." *Current Anthropology*, Vol. 7, No. 4, 1966, pp. 439-440.

Trigger, B. C. 1967. "Foreword." In: *Tooker, E.: An Ethnography of the Huron Indians, 1615-1649*. Huronia Historical Development Council. Reprinted from the Smithsonian Institution, Bulletin No. 190. Midland: 1967.

Trigger, B. G. 1967 b. "Settlement Archaeology--Its Goals and Promise." *American Antiquity*, Vol. 32, No. 2, 1967, pp. 149-160.

Trigger, B. G. 1968. "The French Presence In Huronia: The Structure of Franco-Huron Relations in the First Half of the Seventeenth Century." *Canadian Historical Review*, Vol. 49, No. 2, 1968, pp. 107-141.

Trigger, B. G. 1969. *The Huron: Farmers of the North*. New York: Holt, Rinehart and Winston.

335

Trigger, B. G. 1970. "The Strategy of Iroquoian Prehistory". *Ontario Archaeology*, No. 14, pp. 3-48.

Tuck, J. A. 1967. "The Howlett Hill Site: An Early Iroquois Village in Central New York." In: Tooker, E. (ed.): *Iroquois Culture, History and Prehistory*. Albany: 1967, pp. 75-79.

Tyyska, A. E. 1968. "Settlement Patterns at Cahiagué." Report Submitted to The Archaeological and Historic Sites Board of the Province of Ontario. Typewritten M. S., 1968, p. 12.

Tyyska, A. E. 1969. "Archaeology of the Penetang Peninsula". In: Hurley, W. and C. E. Heidenreich (eds.), Palaeoecology and Ontario Prehistory. *Department of Anthropology, University of Toronto, Research Report No. 1*, pp. 61-88.

United States Department of Agriculture 1938. *Soils and Men: Yearbook of Agriculture 1938*. Washington.

Upper Canada, Board of Agriculture 1856. *Journal and Transactions of the Board of Agriculture of Upper Canada*. Vol. 1, Toronto.

Vogl, R. 1969. "One Hundred and Thirty Years of Plant Succession in a Southeastern Wisconsin Lowland." *Ecology*, Vol. 50, No. 2, 1969, pp. 248-255.

Vogt, E. Z. 1956. "An Appraisal of 'Prehistoric Settlement Patterns in the New World'." In: Willey, G. R. (ed.): *Prehistoric Settlement Patterns in the New World*. New York: Wenner-Gren Foundation, Viking Fund Public. No. 23, 1956: pp. 173-182.

Walkinshaw, L. H. 1949. *The Sandhill Cranes*. Bloomfield Hills: Cranbrook Institute of Science, Bulletin No. 29.

Watters, R. F. 1966. "The Shifting Cultivation Problem in the American Tropics." *Reunion Internacional Sobre Problemas de la Agricultura en los Tropicos Humedos de America Latina*. Lima: May 22, 1966, pp. 1-16.

Waugh, F. W. 1916. "Iroquois Food and Food Preparation." *Geological Survey of Canada*, Memoir No. 86, Anthropological Series No. 12, Ottawa, 1916.

White, M. E. 1967. "1965 Excavations at the Simmons Site: A Niagara Frontier Iroquois Village." In: Tooker, E. (ed.): *Iroquois Culture, History and Prehistory*, Albany, 1967, pp. 85-89.

Will, G. F. and G. E. Hyde 1917. *Corn Among the Indians of the Upper Missouri*. Lincoln: University of Nebraska Press.

Willey, G. R. and P. Phillips 1962. *Method and Theory in American Archaeology*. Chicago: University of Chicago Press, Phoenix Edition.

Williams, T. 1908. "Memories of a Pioneer." In: *Simcoe County Pioneer and Historical Society*. Vol. 2, 1908.

Wilson, E. D., Fisher, K. H. and M. E. Fuqua 1967. *Principles of Nutrition*. New York: J. Wiley.

Wintemberg, W. J. 1926. "Foreign Aboriginal Artifacts from post-European Iroquoian Sites in Ontario." *Royal Society of Canada, Transactions*. Vol. 20, Sect. 2, pp. 37-61.

Wintemberg, W. J. 1930. Unpublished Notes on file in the National Museum of Canada, Archaeology Division. Section on Nottawasaga Township; Notes on G. Rogers farm, lot 9, Concession 6. Examined by Wintemberg in 1930.

Wolf, E. R. 1966. *Peasants*. Englewood-Cliffs: Prentice Hall.

Wright, J. V. 1963. "An Archaeological Survey Along the North Shore of Lake Superior." *National Museum of Canada Anthropology Papers* No. 3, 1963, p. 9.

Wright, J. V. 1965. "A Regional Examination of Ojibwa Culture History." *Anthropologica, Vol. 7, No. 2, 1965, pp. 189-227.*

Wright, J. V. 1966. "The Ontario Iroquois Tradition." *National Museum of Canada, Bulletin No. 210*, Ottawa: 1966, p. 195.

Wrong, G. M. (ed.) 1939. *Sagard: The Long Journey to the Country of the Hurons*. Toronto: The Champlain Society.

Yarnell, R. A. 1964. *Aboriginal Relationships Between Culture and Plant Life in the Upper Great Lakes Region*. Museum of Anthropology Papers No. 23, Ann Arbour: University of Michigan.

Zirkle, C. 1969. "Plant Hybridization and Plant Breeding in Eighteenth-Century American Agriculture." *Agricultural History*, Vol. 43, No. 1, 1969, pp. 25-38.

MAPS AND FIGURES

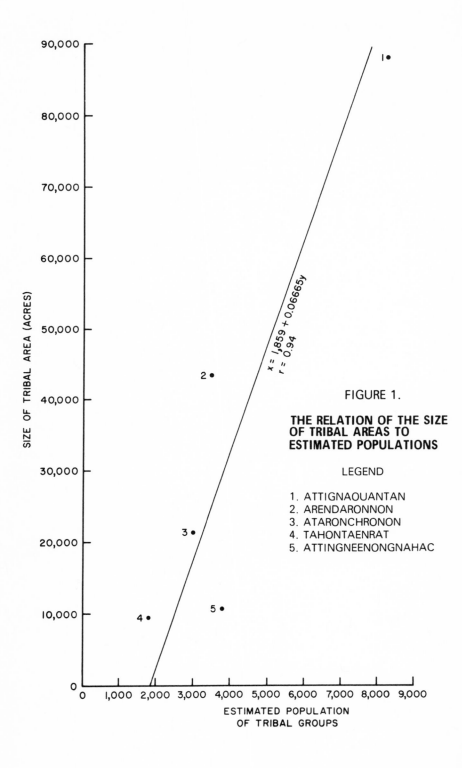

FIGURE 1.

THE RELATION OF THE SIZE OF TRIBAL AREAS TO ESTIMATED POPULATIONS

LEGEND

1. ATTIGNAOUANTAN
2. ARENDARONNON
3. ATARONCHRONON
4. TAHONTAENRAT
5. ATTINGNEENONGNAHAC

$x = 1,859 + 0.06665y$
$r = 0.94$

SIZE OF TRIBAL AREA (ACRES)

ESTIMATED POPULATION
OF TRIBAL GROUPS

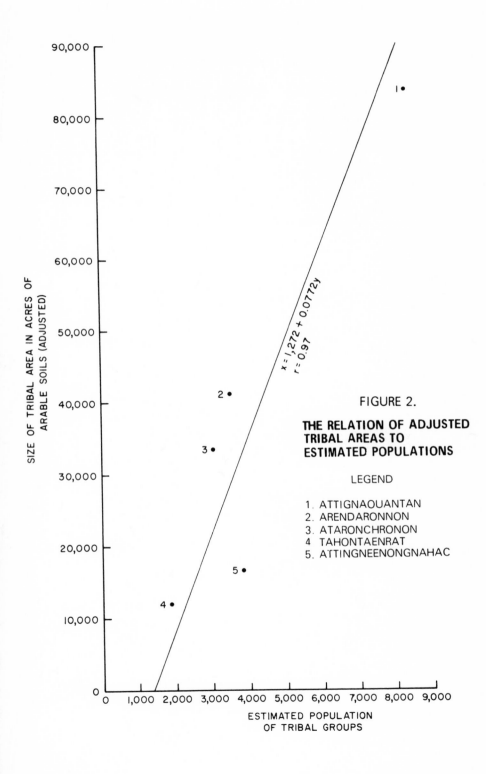

FIGURE 2.

THE RELATION OF ADJUSTED TRIBAL AREAS TO ESTIMATED POPULATIONS

LEGEND

1. ATTIGNAOUANTAN
2. ARENDARONNON
3. ATARONCHRONON
4 TAHONTAENRAT
5. ATTINGNEENONGNAHAC

$x = 1,272 + 0.0772y$
$r = 0.97$

SIZE OF TRIBAL AREA IN ACRES OF ARABLE SOILS (ADJUSTED)

ESTIMATED POPULATION OF TRIBAL GROUPS

FIGURE 3.

TWO LONGHOUSES FROM CONTEMPORARY DRAWINGS

Longhouse from Bressani's Map *Novae Franciae Accurata Delineatio.*

Longhouse from Champlain's *Voyages,* Vol.3, Plate VIII, p.163.

FIGURE 4.

RECONSTRUCTION OF A LONGHOUSE FROM DESCRIPTIONS

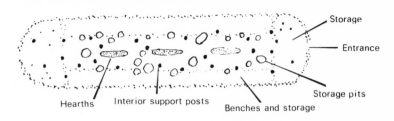

Storage

Entrance

Hearths   Interior support posts   Benches and storage   Storage pits

Idealized floor plan of a longhouse

0   10   20 feet

Reconstruction of longhouse from verbal descriptions and archaeology.

0   10   20 feet

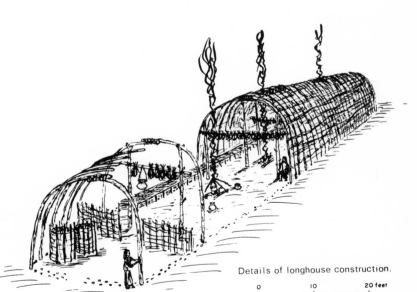

Details of longhouse construction.

0   10   20 feet

FIGURE 5.

SIZE OF HURON VILLAGES

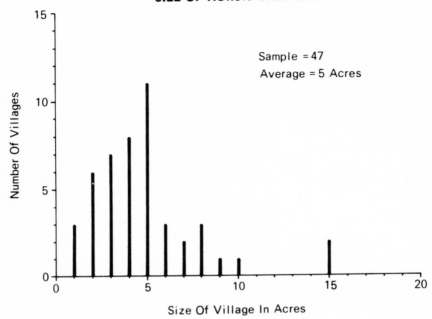

Sample = 47
Average = 5 Acres

Notice the sharp decline in the number of villages over 5 acres. With population densities estimated at 180 to 280 people per acre, it would seem that few villages exceeded 900 to 1,400 people. The upper limit in village size seems to be related to socio-political instability; as villages grew in population size so did the chances for devisive quarrels. It is theorized that due to a lack of coercive institutions and in order to avoid open conflicts, villages split or dissenting factions simply moved out thus keeping most villages below a certain (900-1,400) population level. Some villages did get much larger than the average. In the ethno-historic accounts these were regional strongholds and tribal centres. These had chiefs of unusual ability who often had limited coercive powers such as a strong body of followers and the power to accuse others of withcraft, which would put them outside the law for anyone to kill.

The sample of 47 village sites is probably under-represented in the number of sites less than three acres in size. Most of the small sites have not attracted enough attention to be surveyed and many have been obliterated by farm activities. It is interesting to note that some of the largest villages (both archeologically and ethnohistorically) were double *(Cahiagué,* St. Ignace and *Arethsi)* or triple villages *(Quieunonascaran).*

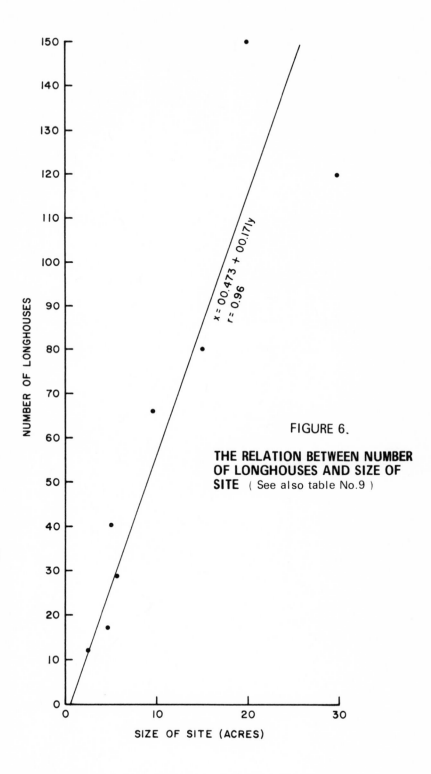

FIGURE 6.

THE RELATION BETWEEN NUMBER OF LONGHOUSES AND SIZE OF SITE (See also table No.9)

x = 00.473 + 00.171y
r = 0.96

NUMBER OF LONGHOUSES

SIZE OF SITE (ACRES)

FIGURE 7.
PALISADES FROM CONTEMPORARY DRAWINGS

5 – 8 FT.

Palisade of a temporary
League Iroquois encampment.
From Champlain's *Voyages*
Vol. 2, Plate V.

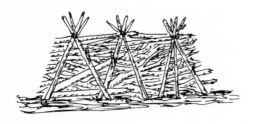

5 – 8 FT.

Palisade of a temporary
League Iroquois encampment.
From Champlain's *Voyages*
Vol. 2, Plate VI.

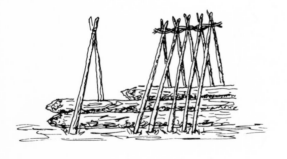

15 – 20 FT.

Palisade from Bressani's Map.
*Novae Franciae Accurata
Delineatio.*

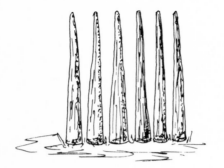

15 – 20 FT.

Palisade of *Hochelaga*
from Lescarbot's Map of
Nouvelle France.

FIGURE 8   THE MORPHOLOGY OF TWO HURON VILLAGES

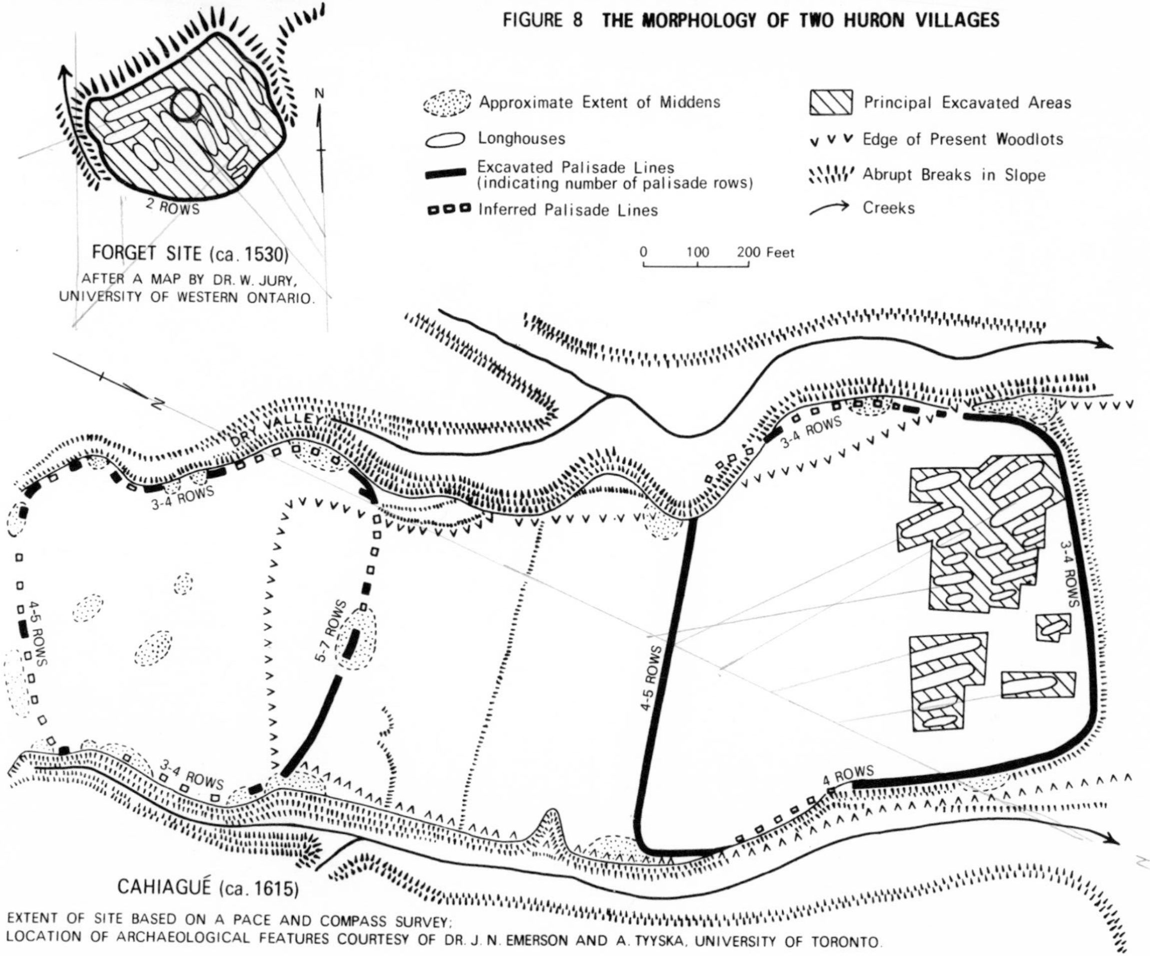

Approximate Extent of Middens

Longhouses

Excavated Palisade Lines
(indicating number of palisade rows)

Inferred Palisade Lines

Principal Excavated Areas

Edge of Present Woodlots

Abrupt Breaks in Slope

Creeks

0   100   200 Feet

FORGET SITE (ca. 1530)

AFTER A MAP BY DR. W. JURY,
UNIVERSITY OF WESTERN ONTARIO.

2 ROWS

N

3-4 ROWS

4 ROWS

4-5 ROWS

3-4 ROWS

5-7 ROWS

3-4 ROWS

3-4 ROWS

4-5 ROWS

DRY VALLEY

N

CAHIAGUÉ (ca. 1615)

EXTENT OF SITE BASED ON A PACE AND COMPASS SURVEY.
LOCATION OF ARCHAEOLOGICAL FEATURES COURTESY OF DR. J. N. EMERSON AND A. TYYSKA, UNIVERSITY OF TORONTO.

FIGURE 9.
RECONSTRUCTION OF CAHIAGUE PALISADE

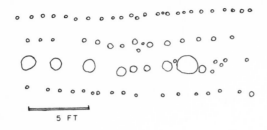

Post hole pattern at *Cahiague*,
south wall of northern component.
(From : Emerson and Russell,
1965 : Fig. V).

5 FT

Post hole pattern at *Cahiague*,
west wall of northern component.
(From : Emerson and Russell,
1965 : Fig. VIII).

5 FT.

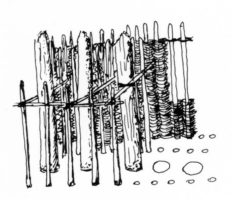

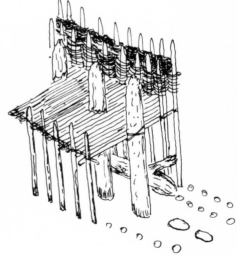

Possible reconstruction of a four rowed palisade at *Cahiague*.

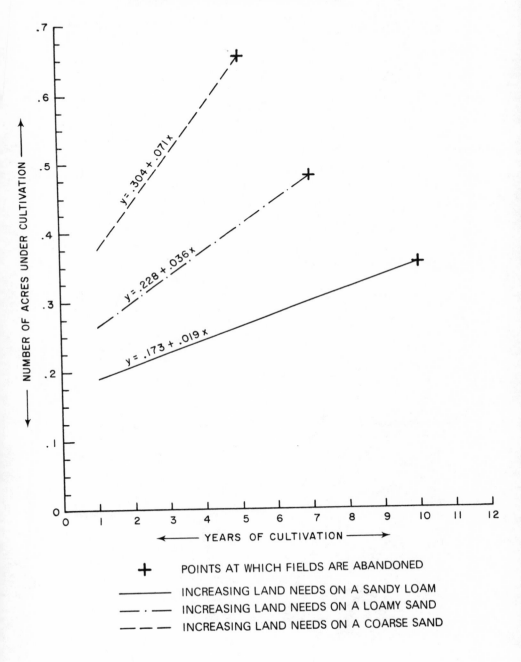

FIGURE 10.
INCREASING LAND NEEDS WITH DECLINING
YIELDS FOR ONE PERSON WITH A FIXED
NEED OF NINE BUSHELS PER YEAR

$y = .304 + .071x$

$y = .228 + .036x$

$y = .173 + .019x$

NUMBER OF ACRES UNDER CULTIVATION ⟶

⟵ YEARS OF CULTIVATION ⟶

✚   POINTS AT WHICH FIELDS ARE ABANDONED

——————   INCREASING LAND NEEDS ON A SANDY LOAM

——·——   INCREASING LAND NEEDS ON A LOAMY SAND

—— —— ——   INCREASING LAND NEEDS ON A COARSE SAND

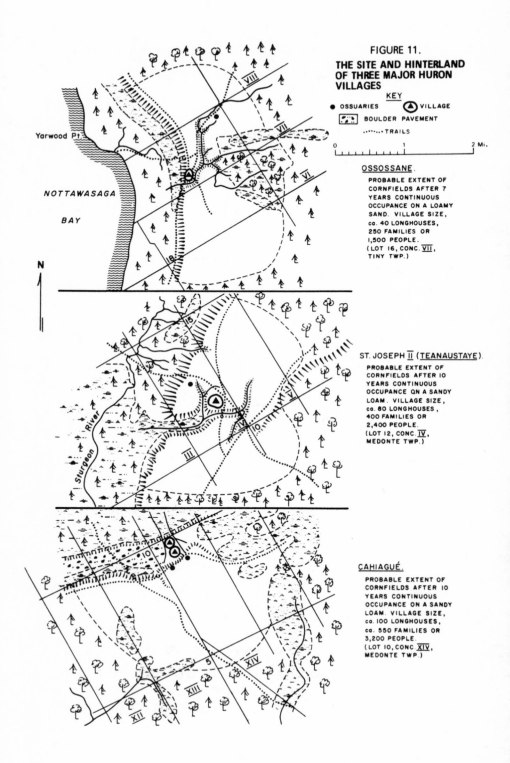

FIGURE 11.

THE SITE AND HINTERLAND OF THREE MAJOR HURON VILLAGES

KEY
● OSSUARIES ▲ VILLAGE
▦ BOULDER PAVEMENT
········ TRAILS

0   1   2 Mi.

Yarwood Pt.

NOTTAWASAGA BAY

N

<u>OSSOSSANE</u>.

PROBABLE EXTENT OF CORNFIELDS AFTER 7 YEARS CONTINUOUS OCCUPANCE ON A LOAMY SAND. VILLAGE SIZE, ca. 40 LONGHOUSES, 250 FAMILIES OR 1,500 PEOPLE. (LOT 16, CONC. VII, TINY TWP.)

ST. JOSEPH II (<u>TEANAUSTAYE</u>).

PROBABLE EXTENT OF CORNFIELDS AFTER 10 YEARS CONTINUOUS OCCUPANCE ON A SANDY LOAM. VILLAGE SIZE, ca. 80 LONGHOUSES, 400 FAMILIES OR 2,400 PEOPLE. (LOT 12, CONC. IV, MEDONTE TWP.)

Sturgeon River

<u>CAHIAGUÉ</u>.

PROBABLE EXTENT OF CORNFIELDS AFTER 10 YEARS CONTINUOUS OCCUPANCE ON A SANDY LOAM. VILLAGE SIZE, ca. 100 LONGHOUSES, ca. 550 FAMILIES OR 3,200 PEOPLE. (LOT 10, CONC. XIV, MEDONTE TWP.)

FIGURE 12.

THE SEASONAL CYCLE OF HURON ACTIVITIES AND NATURAL CYCLE OF HURONIA

A. SEASONAL CYCLE OF ACTIVITIES

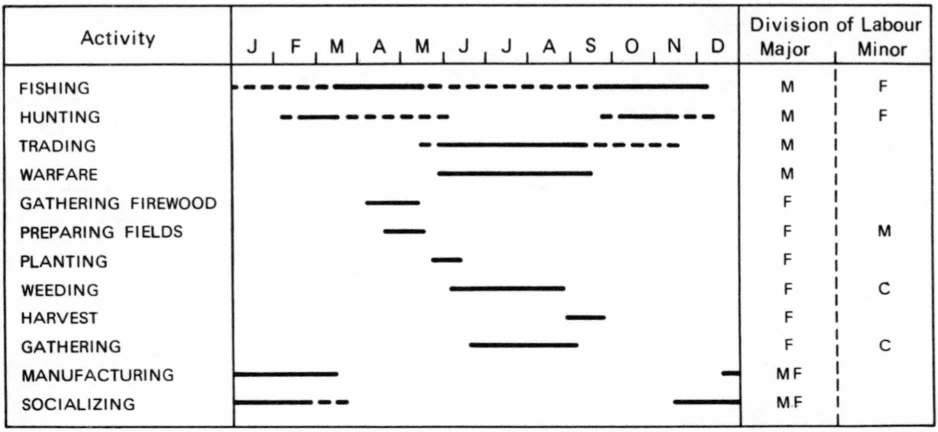

Activity	J F M A M J J A S O N D	Division of Labour Major	Minor
FISHING		M	F
HUNTING		M	F
TRADING		M	
WARFARE		M	
GATHERING FIREWOOD		F	
PREPARING FIELDS		F	M
PLANTING		F	
WEEDING		F	C
HARVEST		F	
GATHERING		F	C
MANUFACTURING		M F	
SOCIALIZING		M F	

```
━━━━━━━  Primary Period for Activity
- - - - -  Activity Also Carried On
M, F, C   Males, Females, Children
```

B. NATURAL CYCLE

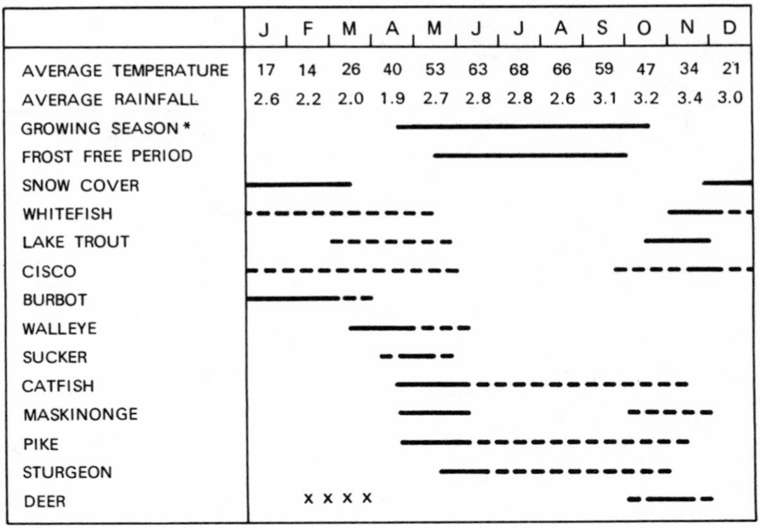

	J	F	M	A	M	J	J	A	S	O	N	D
AVERAGE TEMPERATURE	17	14	26	40	53	63	68	66	59	47	34	21
AVERAGE RAINFALL	2.6	2.2	2.0	1.9	2.7	2.8	2.8	2.6	3.1	3.2	3.4	3.0
GROWING SEASON *												
FROST FREE PERIOD												
SNOW COVER												
WHITEFISH												
LAKE TROUT												
CISCO												
BURBOT												
WALLEYE												
SUCKER												
CATFISH												
MASKINONGE												
PIKE												
STURGEON												
DEER		x x x x										

```
Fish: ━━━━━━  spawning runs          Deer: ━━━━━━  rutting season
      - - - - - frequent shallow waters      x x x x x  "yard" in deep snow conditions
                    * Daily Mean Temperature over 42° F.
```

FIGURE 13.
SPATIAL ASPECTS OF THE HURON SEASONAL CYCLE

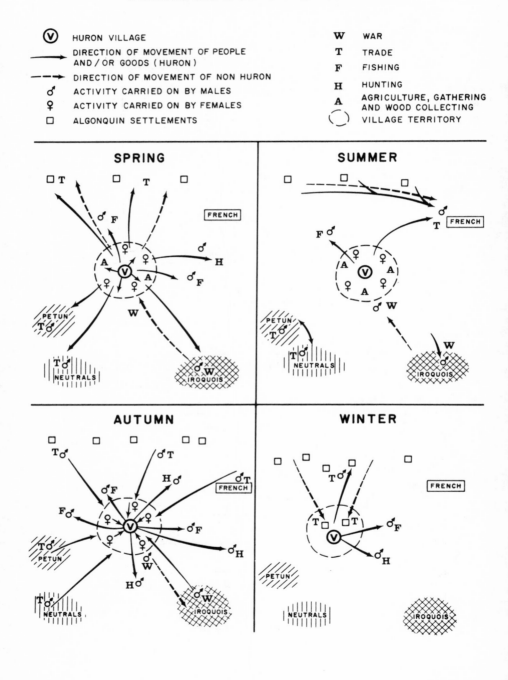

MAP 1. Ontario section from Champlain's *Carte Geographique de la Nouvelle France, 1612.* (Public Archives, Ottawa)

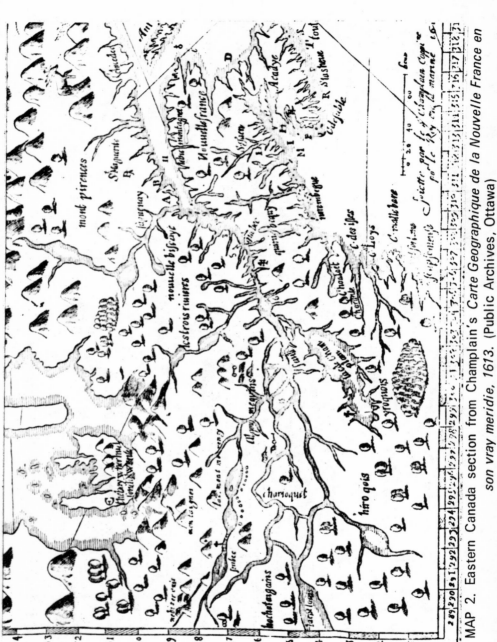

MAP 2. Eastern Canada section from Champlain's *Carte Geographique de la Nouvelle France en son vray meridie, 1613.* (Public Archives, Ottawa)

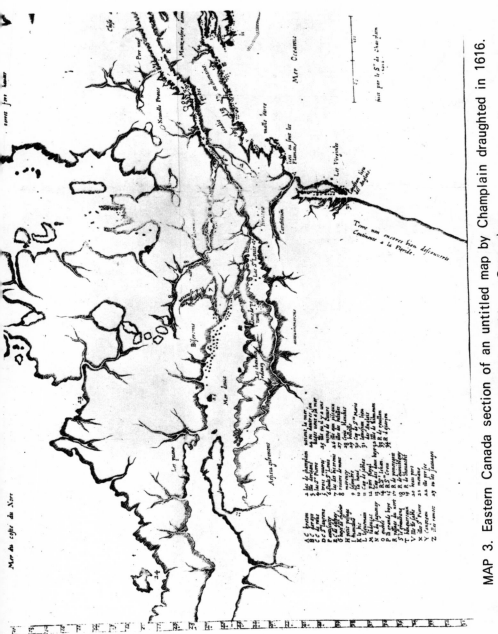

MAP 3. Eastern Canada section of an untitled map by Champlain draughted in 1616.
(Public Archives, Ottawa)

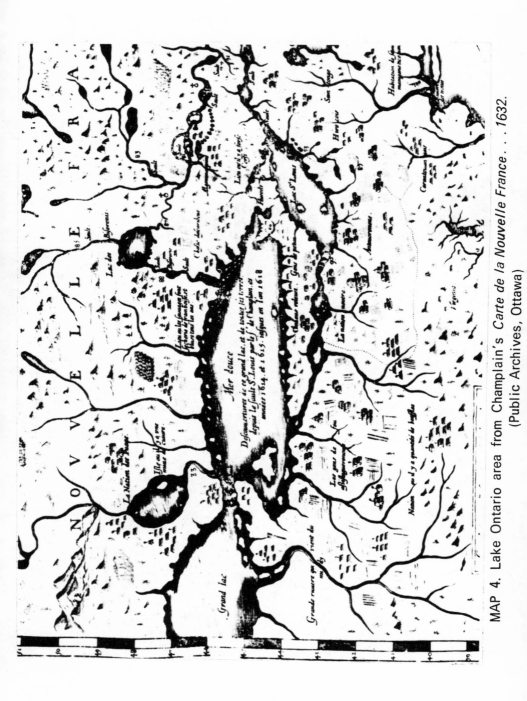

MAP 4. Lake Ontario area from Champlain's *Carte de la Nouvelle France. . . 1632.*
(Public Archives, Ottawa)

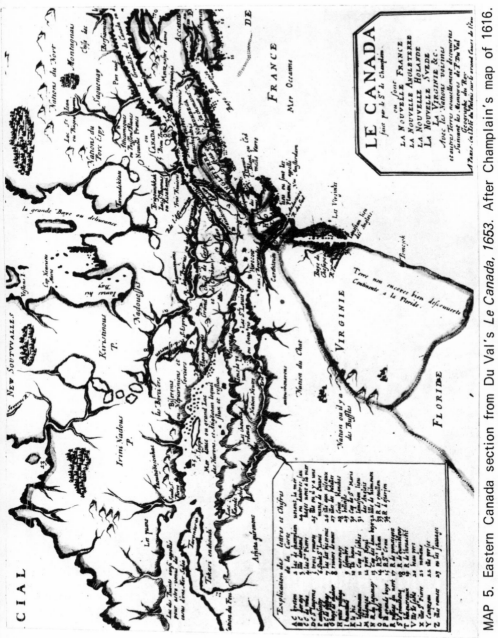

MAP 5. Eastern Canada section from Du Val's *Le Canada, 1653.* After Champlain's map of 1616. (Public Archives, Ottawa)

MAP 6. Eastern Canada section from Boisseau's *Nouvelle France*, 1643.
After Champlain's map of 1632. (Public Archives, Ottawa)

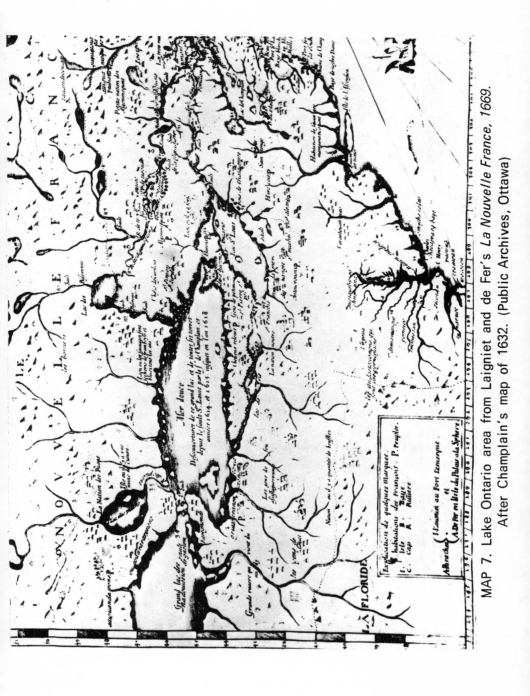

MAP 7. Lake Ontario area from Laigniet and de Fer's *La Nouvelle France, 1669.*
After Champlain's map of 1632. (Public Archives, Ottawa)

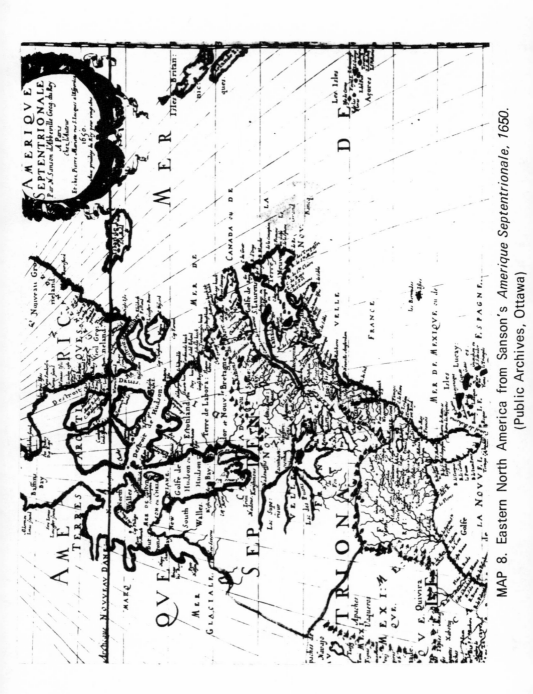

MAP 8. Eastern North America from Sanson's *Amerique Septentrionale, 1650.*
(Public Archives, Ottawa)

MAP 9. Great Lakes area from Sanson's *Le Canada ou Nouvelle France*, 1656.
(Public Archives, Ottawa)

MAP 10. Great Lakes area from Bressani's *Novae Franciae Accurata Delineatio, 1657.*
(Public Archives, Ottawa)

MAP 11.   Great Lakes area from Du Creux's *Tabula Novae Franciae, 1660*.
(Public Archives, Ottawa)

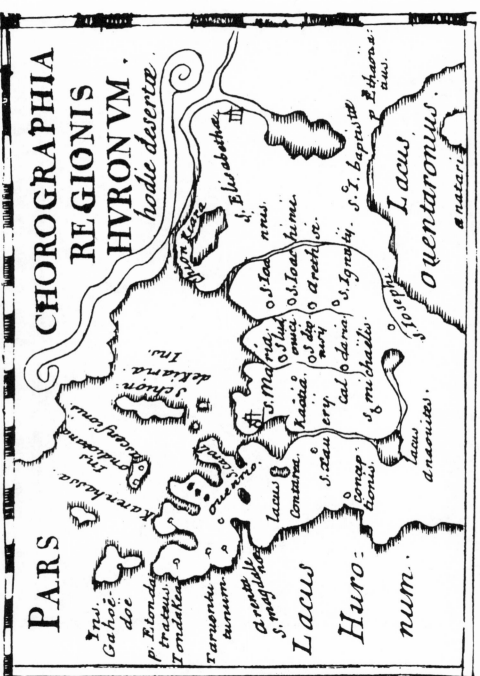

MAP 12. Du Creux's *Chorographia Regionis Huronum, 1660.* (Public Archives, Ottawa)

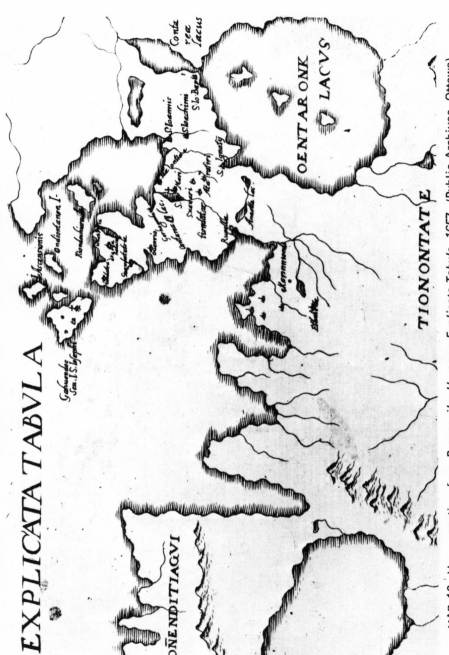

MAP 13. Huron section from Bressani's *Huronum Explicata Tabula, 1657.* (Public Archives, Ottawa)

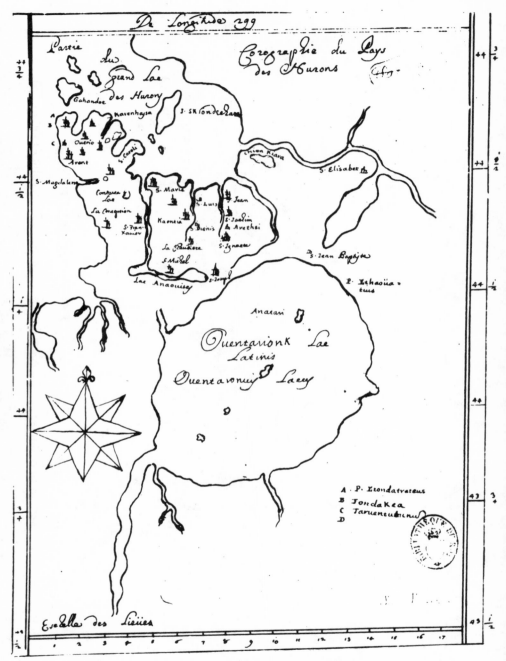

MAP 14. The *Corographie du Pays des Hurons.* Circa 1639-1648.
(Public Archives, Ottawa)

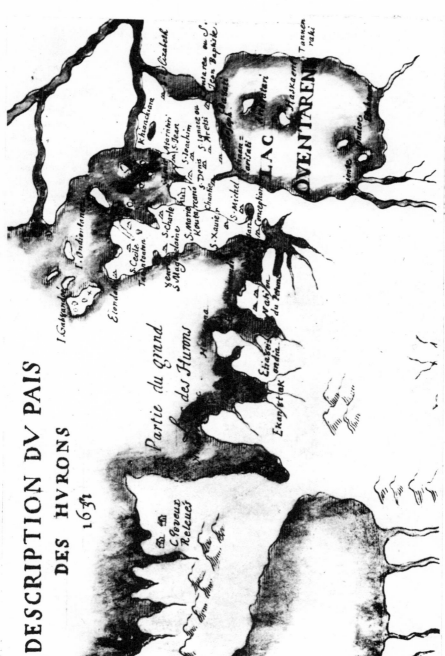

MAP 15. The *Description du Pais des Hurons*. Circa 1639-1651. (Public Archives, Ottawa)

MAP 16
COMPARISON OF THE "COROGRAPHIE DU PAYS DES HURONS" WITH A MODERN MAP OF HURONIA

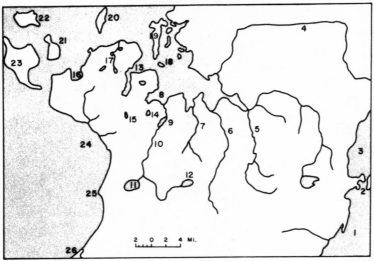

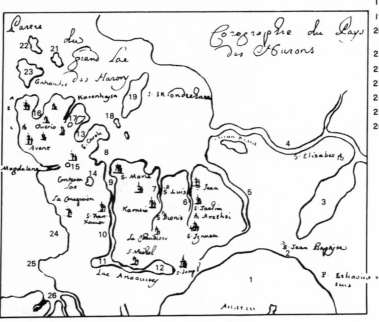

1. Lake Simcoe
2. The "Narrows"
3. Lake Couchiching
4. Severn River
5. Coldwater River
6. Sturgeon River
7. Hog River
8. Midland Bay
9. Wye (Mud) Lake
10. Wye River
11. Cranberry Lake
12. Orr Lake
13. Penetang Bay
14. Midland Park Lake
15. Lalligan Lake
16. Thunder Bay
17. Farlain, Second and Gignac Lakes
18. Present Island
19. Beausoleil Island
20. Giants Tomb Island
21. Beckwith Island
22. Hope Island
23. Christian Island
24. Nottawasaga Bay
25. Spratt Point
26. Nottawasaga River

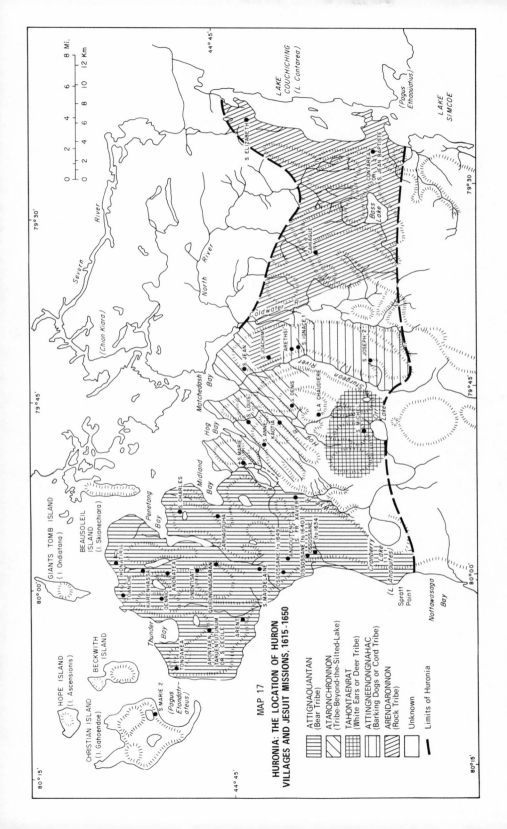

MAP 17

HURONIA: THE LOCATION OF HURON
VILLAGES AND JESUIT MISSIONS, 1615-1650

ATTIGNAOUANTAN
(Bear Tribe)

ATARONCHRONNON
(Tribe-Beyond-the-Silted-Lake)

TAHONTAENRAT
(White Ears or Deer Tribe)

ATTINGNEENONGNAHAC
(Barking Dogs or Cord Tribe)

ARENDARONNON
(Rock Tribe)

Unknown

Limits of Huronia

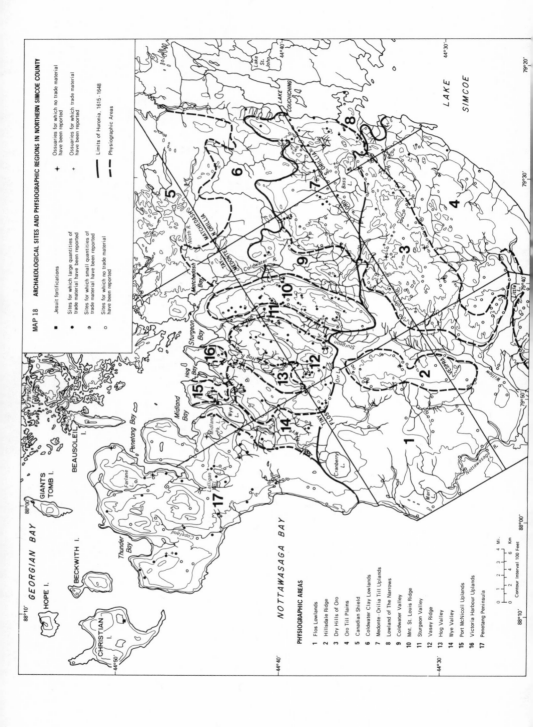

MAP 18   ARCHAEOLOGICAL SITES AND PHYSIOGRAPHIC REGIONS IN NORTHERN SIMCOE COUNTY

■ Jesuit fortifications

● Sites for which large quantities of
   trade material have been reported

◐ Sites for which small quantities of
   trade material have been reported

○ Sites for which no trade material
   have been reported

+ Ossuaries for which no trade material
  have been reported

+ Ossuaries for which trade material
  have been reported

━━ Limits of Huronia, 1615-1648

╌╌ Physiographic Areas

PHYSIOGRAPHIC AREAS

1 Flos Lowlands
2 Hillsdale Ridge
3 Dry Hills of Oro
4 Oro Till Plains
5 Canadian Shield
6 Coldwater Clay Lowlands
7 Medonte - Orillia Till Uplands
8 Lowland of The Narrows
9 Coldwater Valley
10 Mnt. St. Louis Ridge
11 Sturgeon Valley
12 Vasey Ridge
13 Hog Valley
14 Wye Valley
15 Port McNicoll Uplands
16 Victoria Harbour Uplands
17 Penetang Peninsula

0 1 2 3 4 Mi.
0 1 2 3 4 5 6 Km
Contour Interval 100 Feet

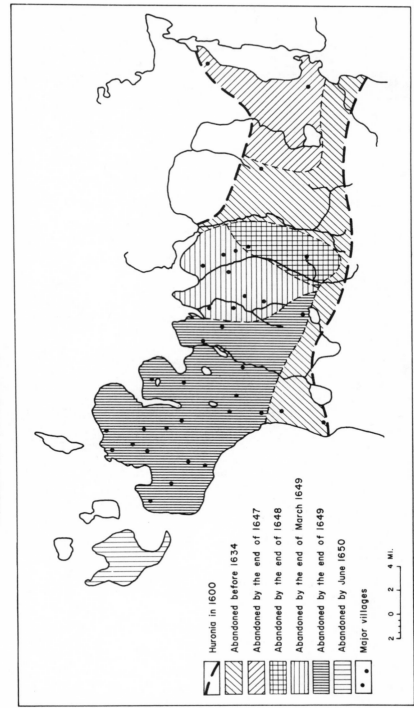

MAP 19

HURONIA: THE CHANGING AREA OF OCCUPANCE, 1600-1650

Huronia in 1600

Abandoned before 1634

Abandoned by the end of 1647

Abandoned by the end of 1648

Abandoned by the end of March 1649

Abandoned by the end of 1649

Abandoned by June 1650

Major villages

2   0   2   4 MI.

MAP 20   THE PRE-SETTLEMENT VEGETATION OF NORTHERN SIMCOE COUNTY

Fir (Abies balsamea)

Pine (Pinus strobus)

Hemlock (Tsuga canadensis)

Tamarack (Larix laricina)

Elm (Ulmus americana)

Birch (Betula papyrifera & B. lutea)

Oak (Quercus rubra)

Ash (Fraxinus sp.)

Maple Beech Basswood Assoc. (Acer saccharum, Fagus grandifolia, Tilia americana)

Maple Basswood Assoc. (Acer saccharum, Tilia americana)

Swamp: Usually contains Cedar (Thuya occidentalis) and some Alder (Alnus rugosa) along the margins

Rock Outcrops interspersed with swamp

Map compiled from Surveyors Notes in the Dept. of Lands and Forests, Ontario
—Penetang Rd. (1811)—Oro, Medonte, Tay, Vespra, N. & S. Orillia (1820)—
—Flos (1821)—Tiny (1822)—

GEORGIAN BAY

HOPE I.

GIANTS TOMB I.

BEAUSOLEIL I.

BECKWITH I.

CHRISTIAN I.

Thunder Bay

Penetang Bay

Midland Bay

Hog Bay

Sturgeon Bay

Matchedash Bay

Coldwater

Bass L.

Little

LAKE COUCHICHING

LAKE SIMCOE

Lake St. John

NOTTAWASAGA BAY

Wye L.

Midland Pt.

Cranberry L.

Mud L.

88°10'   88°00'   79°50'   79°40'   79°30'

44°50'   44°40'   44°30'

0 1 2 3 4 Mi.
0 1 2 3 4 5 6 Km

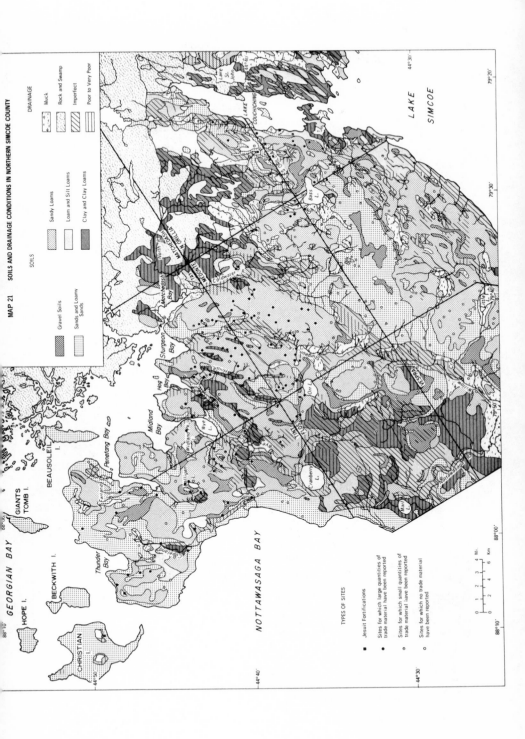

MAP 21   SOILS AND DRAINAGE CONDITIONS IN NORTHERN SIMCOE COUNTY

SOILS

Gravel Soils

Sands and Loamy Sands

Sandy Loams

Loam and Silt Loams

Clay and Clay Loams

DRAINAGE

Muck

Rock and Swamp

Imperfect

Poor to Very Poor

TYPES OF SITES

■ Jesuit Fortifications

● Sites for which large quantities of
   trade material have been reported

○ Sites for which small quantities of
   trade material have been reported

○ Sites for which no trade material
   have been reported

GEORGIAN BAY

HOPE I.

GIANTS TOMB I.

BEAUSOLEIL I.

BECKWITH I.

CHRISTIAN

Thunder Bay

Penetang Bay

Midland Bay

Hog Bay

Sturgeon Bay

Matchedash Bay

NOTTAWASAGA BAY

Coldwater

Orr L.

Cranberry L.

Marl L.

Bass L.

Lake St. John

Lake COUCHICHING

LAKE SIMCOE

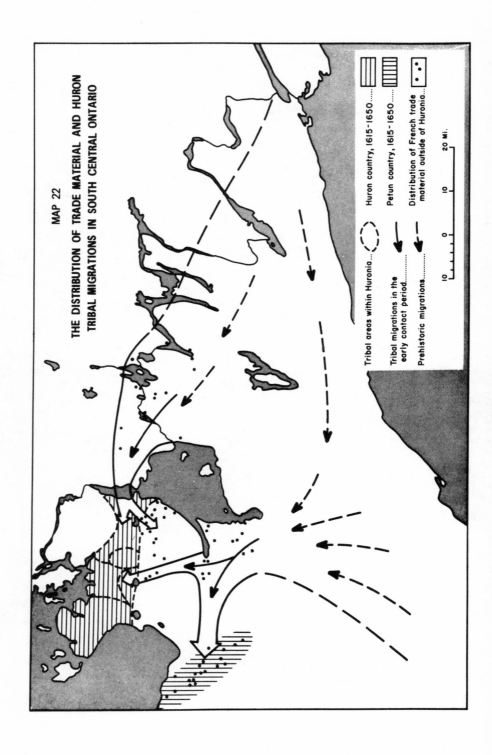

MAP 22

THE DISTRIBUTION OF TRADE MATERIAL AND HURON
TRIBAL MIGRATIONS IN SOUTH CENTRAL ONTARIO

Tribal areas within Huronia..........

Huron country, 1615-1650..........

Tribal migrations in the
early contact period..........

Petun country, 1615-1650..........

Prehistoric migrations..........

Distribution of French trade
material outside of Huronia....

10   5   0   10   20 MI.

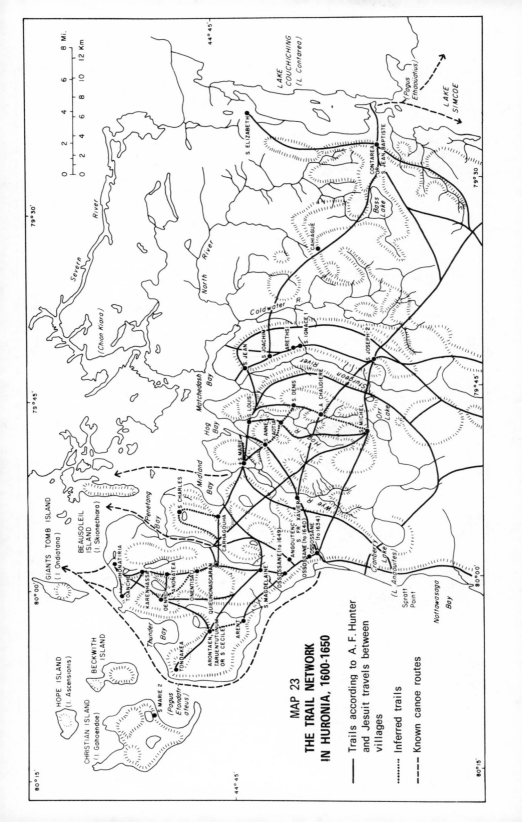

MAP 23
THE TRAIL NETWORK
IN HURONIA, 1600-1650

—— Trails according to A. F. Hunter
and Jesuit travels between
villages

········· Inferred trails

-- -- -- Known canoe routes

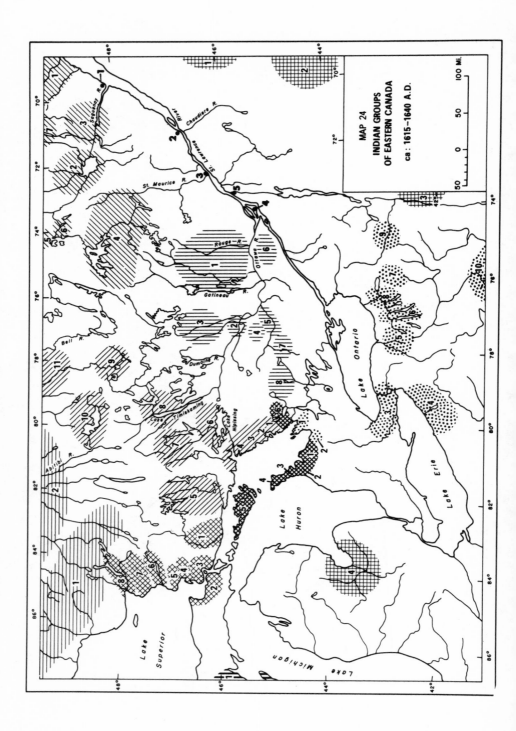

MAP 24
INDIAN GROUPS
OF EASTERN CANADA
ca: 1615–1640 A.D.

50   0   50   100 Mi.

The map was compiled from the Jesuit Relations and contemporary maps. The location of the Algonquian groups is approximate. Not all groups mentioned in the source material could be located. Only those groups were located when written and map sources were in agreement.

FRENCH TRADING PLACES

- 1. Tadoussac
- 2. Quebec
- 3. Trois Rivieres
- 4. Montreal-Lachine
- 5. Richelieu

IROQUOIAN GROUPS

1. Ouendat (Huron)
2. Khionontateronnon (Petun)
3. Attiouendaronnon (Neutral)
4. Eriehronnon (Erie)
5. Sonnontouan (Seneca)
6. Ouioenrhonnon (Cayuga)
7. Oneiochronnon (Oneida)
8. Onnontageronnon (Onondaga)
9. Agniehrononnon (Mohawk)
10. Andastaeronnon (Susquehannock)

SIOUAN GROUPS

1. Puans (Winnebago)

ALGONQUIAN GROUPS

A. *MONTAGNAIS GROUP*

1. Papinachois
2. Kakouchaki (Porcupine)
3. Chicoutimi
4. Attikameque (White Fish)
5. Nekubaniste
6. Chomonchouaniste
7. Outabitibec

B. *CREE GROUP*

1. O'pimittish Ininiwac (Gens de Terres)
2. Kilistinon (Various Cree Bands)

C. *OTHER ALGONQUIAN SPEAKERS*

1. Etechemin
2. Abenaki
3. Mahican
4. Assistaeronnon (Sauk, Fox, Maskouten)

D. *OJIBWA (CHIPPEWA) GROUP*

1. Mississague (Oumisagi)
2. Noquet (Nokes)
3. Pauoitigoueieuhak (Saulteurs)
4. Roquai
5. Mantoue
6. Outchibous (O'chibboy, Chippewa)
7. Marameg
8. Outoulibi

E. *OTTAWA (OUTAOUAC, CHEVEUX RELEVES) GROUP*

1. Ouachaskesouek (Nassauaketon)
2. Nigouaouichirinik (Negaouchiriniouek)
3. Outaouasinagouek (Sinago)
4. Kichkagoneiak (Kishkakon)
5. Ontaanak
6. Outaouakmigouek

F. *ALGONKIN GROUP*

1. Ouaouechkairini (Petite Nation)
2. Kichespiirini (Allumettes)
3. Kotakoutouemi
4. Kinounchepiirini
5. Mataouchkairini
6. Ononchataronnon (Iroquets, Atontrataronnon)
7. Ounchatarounounga
8. Sagnitaouigama

G. *NORTHERN ALGONKIN GROUP*

1. Sagahiganirini
2. Ouasouarini (Aousanik)
3. Outchougai (Atchougoue)
4. Atchiligouan (Achirigouan)
5. Amikoua (Beaver, Naiz-Percez, Amikouek)
6. Nipisirini (Nipissing, Sorcerers)
7. Outimagami (Timagami)
8. Timiscimi
9. Outourbi
10. Abitibi
11. Oumatachirini